Improvement of Communication with t

as an Issue in American Politics, 17

# Improvement of Communication with the Pacific Coast as an Issue in American Politics, 1783-1864

BY

ROBERT R. RUSSEL

*Professor of History*
*Western Michigan College*
*Kalamazoo, Michigan*

385
R

THE TORCH PRESS
CEDAR RAPIDS, IOWA
1948

COPYRIGHT 1948 BY
THE TORCH PRESS

PRINTED IN THE UNITED STATES OF AMERICA
BY THE TORCH PRESS, CEDAR RAPIDS, IOWA

# TABLE OF CONTENTS

## MAPS

# PREFACE

THE following pages represent an attempt to contribute to the history of the middle period of our national life. That history is gradually being rewritten. Sectionalism does not dominate the scene to the extent it formerly did; and slavery in the South and abolition in the North are no longer regarded as the sole explanation of Southern and Northern sectionalism. Various other matters, however, still fail to receive the attention in our general histories that they must if we are to have a balanced account and a satisfying interpretation. One of these relatively neglected matters is the improvement of means of communication between the older portions of the Union and the Pacific coast.

It is not contended for a moment that this volume cultivates a virgin historical field. There have been many scholarly monographs and articles on various subdivisions of the subject, for examples, on Asa Whitney's project for a railroad to the Pacific, the Pacific railway surveys, the overland mail, Anglo-American isthmian diplomacy, the Gadsden purchase, and the building of the Union Pacific Railroad. The story of the development of overland transportation facilities has been competently worked into general histories of the advance of the frontier. But, it is believed, no one has undertaken before to write upon the establishment of improved means of communication with the Pacific coast as a great national problem and a political issue before the American people related to and involved with other great problems and issues of the times.

The materials for this monograph have been secured mostly from original sources, as the citations will indicate. Innumerable facts and suggestions have been drawn also from secondary accounts; and an attempt, however inadequate, has been made to give credit for them in the footnotes. The authors are far too numerous to mention here, and to single out several for special mention would be invidious. To all of them I am deeply grateful. I have taken notes in many libraries, from Berkeley, California, to London, England, and have received unfailing courtesy and great assistance from the officers and staffs of all of them.

The initial impulse to write on the subject before us came when the late Professor Frank Heywood Hodder, of the University of Kansas, assigned it to me as the topic for a master's thesis, in 1914. Historiography was then to me one of the deeper mysteries, which I had scarcely been called upon to contemplate. I asked Professor Hodder, "How shall I start? Where shall I begin?" His reply was, "Just jump right into the middle and dig in all directions." That was the only instruction he ever gave me or, as far as I have ever heard, any of his pupils; but his contagious enthusiasm for historical research, his oft reiterated injunction in the classroom to "read the sources," and his rigid insistence on accuracy served his students better perhaps than a formal course in historiography would have done. The subject of this study was one of Professor Hodder's favorites, as members of the profession well know. His devotion to his teaching and the strict canons of authorship which he imposed upon himself prevented him from writing extensively upon it. I shall always regret that I could not complete this work in time to have the benefit of his deep knowledge and keen criticisms.

ROBERT R. RUSSEL

Kalamazoo, Michigan,
January, 1948.

CHAPTER I

# THE QUESTION RAISED, 1786-1848

IT was partly the hope of finding a shorter and cheaper route to Asia that inspired Columbus to sail westward on his fateful voyage. To him and numerous successors the New World was only partial compensation for failure to attain the original object. The search continued. After Magellan had demonstrated the southern Pacific's vast expanse the quest was only deflected to the north. Frobisher, Davis, Baffin, and Hudson sought the gorgeous East through the icy waters of the Arctic. Intrepid French explorers penetrated far up eastward-flowing American rivers hoping to find their headwaters interlocked with those of streams flowing into the China Sea. The famous Captain Thomas Cook, who had twice sailed around the world, explored the Northwest Coast, 1788, hoping to find the fabled "Strait of Anian" connecting Hudson Bay and Puget Sound.[1]

It was Captain Cook's voyage which first brought the problem of communication with the Pacific to the notice of statesmen of our Young Republic. Cook discovered that the Northwest Coast abounded in sea otter, whose furs were highly valued in the Canton market. Trading vessels of several nations, including the United States, were soon resorting thither. Cook had been accompanied by an American adventurer, John Ledyard. Ledyard tried to enlist various of his countrymen in schemes to develop the sea-otter trade. In Paris, 1786, he sought out the United States minister, Thomas Jefferson. Jefferson suggested that he cross Siberia, accompany a Russian trading expedition to Alaska, "fall down to the latitude of the Missouri, and penetrate to and through that to the United

[1] H. H. Bancroft, *History of the Northwest Coast*, I; K. Coman, *Econ. Beginnings of the Far West*, I, Pt. II, ch. i; Jos. Schafer, *History of the Pacific Northwest*, New Ed., chs. i, ii.

States." Ledyard undertook the adventure but was deflected to another enterprise.[2] Jefferson's interest persisted.

In 1793, while secretary of state in George Washington's cabinet, Jefferson sponsored an overland expedition to the Pacific to be led by a renowned French botanist, André Michaux. Jefferson acted, ostensibly at least, in behalf of the American Philosophical Society, of which he was a devoted member. He instructed Michaux to ascend the Missouri River by the branch which extends most directly toward the Pacific and select the best route thence to the sea. He suggested a river "called Oregon" as a possibility. The first of all objects, Jefferson wrote, was to "seek for and pursue that route which shall form the shortest and most convenient communication between the higher parts of the Missouri and the Pacific Ocean." [3] Michaux, unfortunately, became involved in the schemes of Citizen Genêt, who shortly arrived in the United States, and the proposed expedition was abandoned.

Meanwhile British subjects had continued to grapple with the great problem of transcontinental communication. In 1789 Alexander Mackenzie left Lake Athabasca, discovered the great river which bears his name, and descended it to the Arctic. In 1792-93, he again left Lake Athabasca, ascended the Peace River, crossed the Rockies, discovered the Fraser River, which he mistook for the Columbia, and eventually reached the sea.[4] Upon his return to England, he urged upon the British government the occupation of Oregon in the interests of a vast commercial scheme based upon the practicability of establishing a transcontinental route of communication from Hudson Bay by the Nelson River, Lake Winnipeg, the Saskatchewan, and the Columbia. "By opening this intercourse between the Atlantic and Pacific oceans," he wrote, "and forming regular establishments through the interior, and at both

[2] Paul L. Ford, ed., *Works of Thos. Jefferson*, V, 183, 343, 455; Bancroft, *op. cit.*, I, 349ff.; Schafer, *op. cit.*, 35-36; Thos. H. Benton, *Thirty Years' View*, I, 14.

[3] *Works of Thos. Jefferson*, VII, 208-12; Schafer, *op. cit.*, 36; Coman, *op. cit.*, I, 234.

[4] Mackenzie, *Voyages from Montreal through the Continent of N. A. to the Frozen and Pacific Oceans in 1789 and 1793* (London, 1802); *Cong. Debates*, 18 Cong., 2 Sess., 703; Schafer, *op. cit.*, 24-26.

extremes, as well as along the coasts and islands, the entire
command of the fur trade of North America might be obtained, from latitude forty-eight degrees north to the pole,
except that portion of it which the Russians have in the Pacific.
To this may be added the fishing in both seas and the markets
of the four quarters of the globe." [5] The American traders
would "instantly disappear before a well-regulated trade."
This vast project was not immediately undertaken, but later
the Hudson Bay Company, after having absorbed its great
rival, the North West Company, 1821, established its posts
along the line and transported quantities of furs over the
route.

On January 18, 1803, Thomas Jefferson, President of the
United States, sent a confidential message to Congress outlining a plan for an overland expedition to the Pacific. The
objects of the expedition as presented in the message, Jefferson's instructions to Captain Meriwether Lewis, and in letters
regarding it were (1) to give an impetus to the American fur
trade in the Missouri Valley region, where there was keen
competition with the British North West Company, (2) to
discover an overland route for the fur trade of Oregon and
other Pacific trade, and (3) to advance scientific knowledge.
Even the possibility of establishing a "route for the commerce
of Europe, Asia, and America" was suggested.[6] No doubt
there were political objects, also. In his instructions to Lewis,
the President wrote, "Should you reach the Pacific Ocean
inform yourself of the circumstances which may decide
whether the furs of those parts may not be collected as advantageously at the head of the Missouri (convenient as is
supposed to the waters of the Colorado and Oregon or Columbia) as at Nootka sound or any other point of that coast; and
that trade be consequently conducted through the Missouri
and U. S. more beneficially than by the circumnavigation now
practised." To the authorities of Louisiana, whose permis-

[5] Mackenzie, op. cit., 411; Benton, op. cit., I, 53-54.
[6] J. D. Richardson, ed., Messages and Papers of the Presidents, I, 352-54;
Works of Thos. Jefferson, IX, 421-34. Cf. R. B. Guinness, "The Purpose of the
Lewis and Clark Expedition," Miss. Val. Hist. Rev., XX (Je., 1933), 90-100.

sion must be secured, the expedition was at first represented as being solely in the interests of science. Before Lewis and Clark reached the Pacific, Jefferson advanced a claim to Oregon as a part of the Louisiana Purchase and upon other grounds.[7]

Lewis and Clark did not discover any practicable portage from the waters of the Missouri to those of the Columbia, nor did they demonstrate the feasibility of any considerable commerce across the continent.[8] However, John Jacob Astor's Pacific Fur Company, chartered in 1810, planned overland expeditions between the Great Lakes and its post, Astoria, at the mouth of the Columbia.[9] This design came to an inglorious end when the partners on the Pacific sold out in haste to the British North West Company during the War of 1812.

In 1818, while negotiations were being conducted with regard to Oregon between the United States and Great Britain, Thomas Hart Benton, then a practising attorney in St. Louis, wrote some essays on Oregon in which he proclaimed the Missouri-Columbia route to be "the great North American route to India" and prophesied the rise of the "Tyre of the Pacific" at its western terminus.[10] In several sessions of Congress, 1820 and following years, John Floyd, of Virginia, Benton, and others sought to secure the adoption of measures designed to insure acquisition of all of Oregon by the United States. There they expected a port to grow which would serve as a center for the fur trade, a base for our rapidly growing whaling fleet, a naval station to protect our new Pacific interests, and the entrepôt of a great trade with China which seemed to be developing. They believed that Oregon would be settled at no distant day, and contended that improved means of communication and the "federal principle" would enable new communities on the coast to become states in the Union. Specifically they envisaged steamboats — Fulton

---

[7] Thos. M. Marshall, *Hist. of the West. Boundary of the La. Purchase*, 13.

[8] Reuben G. Thwaites, ed., *Original Journals of the Lewis and Clark Expedition*, VII, 334-36.

[9] K. Coman, *op. cit.*, I, 307-09; Schafer, *op. cit.*, 67-78.

[10] In *House Reports*, 29 Cong., 1 Sess., No. 773 (*U. S. Docs.* Serial No. 491), App.; extracts in *Cong. Globe*, 29 Cong., 1 Sess., 920-21, and Benton, *Thirty Years' View*, I, 109-10.

had first driven the Clermont up the Hudson only in 1807 —
plying on the Missouri and the Columbia with turnpikes connecting the two. Opponents of the measures, and they were
in the majority, ridiculed the idea that overland communication
could be established with that distant shore or that settlements
on the Pacific could ever be one nation with those in the great
valley and on the Atlantic.[11] Soon across the path to the
Pacific in what are now Oklahoma, Kansas, and Nebraska
these Little Easterners established a "permanent" Indian
frontier. Thence tribes from east of the Mississippi were
removed and there were given lands "in perpetuity," in all
good faith. James Monroe, John C. Calhoun, John Quincy
Adams, Andrew Jackson, and most other great and wise of
the time espoused the policy.[12]

Without government aid, however, fearless American trappers and explorers penetrated the mountain barriers of the
West, explored their recesses, found their passes, and blazed
their trails.[13] Thus South Pass was discovered, probably by
men in the employ of General William H. Ashley, 1824, and
thus the Oregon Trail was made. The first wagon was taken
over this trail to Oregon in 1836, an augury of countless
wheeled vehicles to follow.

Meanwhile the first manifestations had been made of American interest in isthmian routes to the Pacific. The achievement of independence by the Spanish colonies in the New
World, and the successful construction of the Erie and other
canals, gave a stimulus to projects for establishing better
transportation facilities across the isthmus. In the fall of
1824, Señor Canaz, minister at Washington of the new Republic of Central America, published a topographical account
of the Nicaragua route.[14] A British firm and two American
firms soon sent agents to Central America to secure a contract

[11] *Ibid.*, I, 13, 50-54; *Annals of Cong.*, 17 Cong., 2 Sess., 413-22, 682; *Debates of Cong.*, 18 Cong., 2 Sess., 13-27, 36-41, 59, 687-95, 699-713; 20 Cong., 2 Sess., 192.
[12] Fred. L. Paxson, *Hist. of the Am. Frontier*, ch. xxxi.
[13] *Ibid.*, ch. xxxvii; K. Coman, *op. cit.*, I, Pt. II, ch. iii; W. J. Ghent, *The Road to Oregon*, ch. i; Schafer, *op. cit.*, 106-12.
[14] John B. McMaster, *Hist. of the People of the U. S.*, VII, 552-56; *H. Repts.*, 30 Cong., 2 Sess., II (546), No. 145, pp. 338ff.

for constructing a canal.[15] In February, 1825, Señor Canaz formally invited the United States government to send an agent to Central America to negotiate in regard to the right of way and the protection of the proposed canal. Secretary of State Clay moved warily and tardily.[16] However, in June, 1826, the United States charge d'affaires assisting, the Central American government granted a contract for building the canal to Aaron H. Palmer, of New York City, and associates under the name "The Central American and United States Atlantic and Pacific Canal Company." Palmer and his associates enlisted the aid of DeWitt Clinton, Edward Livingston, and other prominent men; but attempts to raise the requisite capital first in the United States and then in London failed, and the scheme came to naught.[17]

Anticipating that an isthmian canal would be one of the matters before the Panama Congress of 1826, Henry Clay instructed the United States representatives in regard to it. It would not be wise, he wrote, to make more than preliminary arrangements until fuller information could be secured. He then proceeded to lay down some general principles: The canal, if built, should be open to the ships of all nations; its construction should not be left to the separate and unassisted efforts of any one power but should be effected by common means and united exertions.[18] These principles, it is worthy of note, were incorporated by a successor in the famous Clayton-Bulwer Treaty a quarter of a century later. When, in 1831, General Verveer of the Netherlands secured a contract for a Dutch company to build a Nicaraguan canal and signed a treaty for its protection, Secretary of State Livingston expressed concern lest special privileges be granted to the Netherlands not accorded to the United States.[19]

In 1834 the Congress of New Granada authorized the Chief Executive to contract for the building of a carriage road or a railroad across the Isthmus of Panama. Thereupon a M.

---

[15] *Ibid.*, 390-93, 403.
[16] *Ibid.*, 216, 244-47.
[17] *Ibid.*, 216, 342-77.
[18] *Ibid.*, 330-31; *Cong. Debates*, 20 Cong., 1 Sess., App., 47.
[19] *H. Repts.*, 30 Cong., 2 Sess., II (546), No. 145, pp. 247-65.

de Vilvak appeared with a project for a railroad, and a Franco-English adventurer, Charles Baron de Thierry, sought and secured the exclusive privilege of deepening the Chagres and Grande rivers and cutting a canal between them.[20] Stirred by these developments, the United States Senate, on motion of John M. Clayton, adopted a resolution requesting President Jackson to consider the expediency of opening negotiations, particularly with the governments of Central America and New Granada, for the purpose of protecting such individuals or companies as might undertake the construction of a ship canal across the isthmus and for securing forever to all nations the free and equal right of navigating it [21]— another early statement of the principle of the Clayton-Bulwer treaty. In response Jackson sent a Colonel Charles Biddle to examine the proposed routes and to gather information. He was not authorized to negotiate.

Biddle proved to be unreliable. Contrary to instructions, he proceeded to Panama before going to Nicaragua. In Panama he easily persuaded himself that the Nicaragua route was impossible anyway. There, too, he learned that the people of Panama had lost faith in Baron de Thierry. He became convinced that a ship canal was chimerical but that a railroad could be built without extraordinary difficulty. Then he proceeded to Bogotá and, with the assistance of the United States consul McAfee and others, procured for himself and eighteen New Granadian citizens the exclusive privileges of navigating the Chagres River by steam and of building a railroad from the head of navigation on the river to the City of Panama. Upon learning of these activities, Secretary of State Forsyth reprimanded Biddle for disregarding his instructions and McAfee for abetting him. He instructed McAfee to inform the government of New Granada that, while the United States government did not disapprove Biddle's contract, it had no connection with it. Biddle died shortly, and thus another project fizzled out.[22]

[20] *Ibid.*, 280-94.
[21] *Ibid.*, 241.
[22] *Ibid.*, 240-43, 269-330.

In 1838 a memorial of certain citizens upon the subject of an isthmian canal was referred to the Committee on Roads and Canals of the United States House of Representatives. The committee recommended that the President be requested to open or continue negotiations regarding a canal.[23] President Van Buren thereupon sent a confidential agent, John L. Stevens, to Central America to investigate. Stevens actually performed the duties assigned and eventually reported that the Nicaragua route was practicable at an estimated cost of $25,000,000; but he believed the canal could not be built while Central American politics continued in the unsettled state in which he found them.[24]

These early isthmian projects were prompted not so much by existing commercial needs as by the promise of the future.

The late 1830's and early 1840's witnessed a rapid expansion of American interests in the Pacific. Our citizens began to settle in the Willamette and Sacramento valleys, and it came to be recognized that Oregon and California possessed great natural resources. Our whaling industry in the Pacific grew amazingly. Every year hundreds of vessels left Nantucket, New Bedford, or Martha's Vineyard on the long trip round the Horn. The whalers usually wintered in the Hawaiian Islands and returned with their valuable cargoes at the end of the second season. The islands served also as a station on the road to China. President John Tyler estimated that American vessels comprised five sixths of the craft which visited Hawaii for one purpose or another.[25] Our trade with China and other Oriental regions was growing. After the ancient English East India Company had lost, 1833, its monopoly of trade with China, as against other Britishers, the competition between American and British traders became keener. At the end of the First Opium War, 1842, Great Britain forced China to open four more ports, in addition to Canton, freely to British trade. China insisted upon extending the same privilege, if extend it she must, to all countries equally. President Tyler promptly sent Caleb Cushing to China to

[23] *Ibid.*, 230-38.
[24] *Ibid.*, 217.
[25] Richardson, *Messages*, IV, 211-12, 588.

get the proffered concession embodied in a treaty. His mission
was successful.[26] Meanwhile the stronger European powers
were seizing upon islands in the Pacific and points of vantage
on its coast. Great Britain, 1839, extended her sovereignty
over New Zealand. France seized upon Tahiti, 1842, and
looked hungrily upon Hawaii. Both England and France were
suspected of coveting California with its fine San Francisco
Bay. Imaginative people in the United States envisaged a
great struggle for the commercial supremacy of the Pacific
with Britain and the United States as the great protagonists.

Impelled by such developments and considerations as these,
the United States hastened to round out its possessions on the
Pacific. As early as 1835 Andrew Jackson had attempted to
purchase California.[27] Soon Lieutenant Charles Wilkes, U. S.
N., was sent to explore islands of the Pacific, San Francisco
Bay, the mouth of the Columbia, and Puget Sound.[28] Western
people became restive under the continued joint occupation of
Oregon, begun in 1818, which they professed to fear would
result in British ownership. In 1838 Senator Linn, of Missouri, began to introduce bills to provide for a line of military
posts on the way to Oregon and the extension of our laws over
the territory.[29] Daniel Webster, Tyler's first secretary of
state, seemed to be only mildly interested. However he renewed the offer to buy California;[30] and he wrote a message
which Tyler sent to Congress asserting the United States'
paramount interest in the Hawaiian Islands and warning other
countries not to interfere with existing political arrangements
there.[31] Webster's immediate successors renewed the Oregon

[26] Ibid., IV, 213-14, 263, 352, 358, 401, 550; J. B. McIntyre, ed., The Writings
and Speeches of Daniel Webster, National Ed., XII, 141, XVI, 392, 398, 401;
Niles' Weekly Register, LXV, 177, 236, 321, 332, LXVI, 17, 64, 363, LXVII, 36,
113, 128, 322; Benton, Thirty Years' View, II, ch. cxxii.

[27] House Exec. Docs., 24 Cong., 1 Sess. (291), No. 256; Cong. Globe, 29
Cong., 2 Sess., App., 127, 367; Marshall, Hist. of the West. Boundary of the
La. Purchase, ch. vi.

[28] Richardson, Messages, III, 502, 538, 618, IV, 160; Chas. Wilkes, Exploring
Expedition, 1838-42 (5 vols., Philadelphia, 1845); Schafer, Pac. Northwest,
175-77.

[29] Ibid., 130-32; Cong. Globe, 27 Cong., 3 Sess., 206; Geo. P. Garrison, Westward Extension, 1841-1850, p. 163.

[30] C. A. Duniway, Daniel Webster (in S. F. Bemis, ed., The Am. Secretaries
of State and Their Diplomacy, V), 19, 27, 57-60; Writings and Speeches of
Daniel Webster, XIV, 611, XVI, 395, XVIII, 153-56, 179-80.

[31] Ibid., XII, 137-38, 151-52, XIV, 432-35; Richardson, Messages, IV, 211-12.

negotiations but did not press them. The Democratic National Convention, 1844, noting the drift of public sentiment, demanded the "reoccupation of Oregon," along with the "reannexation of Texas." In pursuance thereof, James K. Polk quickly brought the Oregon controversy to a head and secured a settlement, with the present boundary, 1846. Meanwhile Polk took occasion to reassert the Monroe Doctrine, December 2, 1845, probably with special reference to California.[32] British and French agents in that remote province were kept under observation; and the friendship of the *rancheros* was cultivated. Shortly the War with Mexico, opportunely incurred, enabled the United States to seize California and intervening territory as "indemnity for the past and security for the future."

Multiplying interests in the Pacific stimulated consideration of the problem of improved means of transportation and communication. It is equally true that a growing conviction that the transportation problem was soluble gave a great impetus to projects of expansion.

In the public discussions which accompanied the settlement of the Oregon question and the acquisition of California, it was seriously considered whether, if these territories should be acquired and colonized, they could ever be bound closely enough to the rest of the country by ties of trade and intercourse to become integral and permanent parts of the Union.[33] Many people, especially in the East, professed to believe they could not be; the barriers interposed by the Great Plains and by lofty mountains and broad deserts seemed to them insuperable. Other people, while lacking confidence that the Pacific coast, if colonized by American people, would long remain a possession of the United States, nevertheless preferred to see there an independent republic nurtured by our care and, therefore, friendly to us rather than one fostered by Great Britain. Most of the advocates of expansion, however, had no misgivings. They were confident that the revolutionary develop-

---

[32] *Ibid.*, IV, 398.

[33] Benton, *op. cit.*, II, 430, 471ff.; *Cong. Globe*, 27 Cong., 3 Sess., 154, 198-200, 206, 227, 28 Cong., 1 Sess., App., 216-26, 307, 622, 29 Cong., 1 Sess., 149-52, 258-60, 475-78, 548, 582-83, 607, 913-21.

ments in transportation and travel which they were witnessing together with the "federal principle," which permitted a great degree of local self-government, could keep such distant regions in the Union. Some of them even professed to expect that much of our commerce with Asia would flow across the continent. Said John C. Calhoun, "What has taken place in China will in a few years be followed in Japan, and all the eastern portions of that continent. Their ports, like the Chinese, will be opened, and the whole of that large portion of Asia, containing nearly half of the population and wealth of the globe, will be thrown upon the commerce of the world, and be placed within the pales of European and American intercourse and civilization. A vast market will be created, and a mighty impulse will be given to commerce. No small portion of the share that will fall to us . . . is destined to pass through the ports of the Oregon Territory to the valley of the Mississippi, instead of taking the circuitous and long voyage round Cape Horn, or the still longer round the Cape of Good Hope." [34]

Thomas H. Benton and others were still, in 1844, placing reliance on steamboats and turnpikes. Others expected newer devices, the railroad, the locomotive, and the telegraph, to provide the solution. In fact, as soon as the practicability of the locomotive had been demonstrated, men of imagination envisioned railroad tracks stretching away to the Pacific. It is immaterial who made the very first suggestion or when or where he made it. But in December, 1844, Asa Whitney, a New York merchant, presented the first definite, well-considered plan for building a railroad to the Pacific.

Whitney would have the road start at Milwaukee, cross the Mississippi at Prairie du Chien, the Missouri at the Big Bend (site of Sioux City), and the Rockies at South Pass, and terminate at the mouth of the Columbia. The means for building the stupendous work were to be supplied by the public lands which lay along the route. Whitney proposed that Congress sell him a strip of land sixty miles wide along the proposed route for its entire length at 16 cents an acre. He, in

[34] *Ibid.*, 27 Cong., 3 Sess., 227.

turn, would sell the lands, under proper safeguards to insure performance, as the road should progress and apply the proceeds to the construction thereof. He at first estimated that it would require twenty-five years to complete his railroad, but, as he warmed to the subject, he cut his estimate to fifteen. When completed the railroad would be the property of the United States government or, if public ownership should be deemed unwise, of Whitney, his heirs, and assigns. In the latter case the rates should be established by law. Since no capital stock would be sold nor bonds floated and since the road would be exempted from taxation, the rates, Whitney said, could be kept very low.[35]

The publication of Whitney's plan prompted Stephen A. Douglas, then a young representative in Congress, to consider the subject. In an open letter to Whitney, dated October 15, 1845, he criticized Whitney's scheme and presented a rival.[36] He would have the railroad run from *Chicago* via Rock Island, Council Bluffs, and South Pass — this was the only pass in the Rockies then widely known. As to the best route west of South Pass, he was uncertain, but was inclined to choose San Francisco Bay for a terminus "if that country could be annexed in time." — This six months before the outbreak of the War with Mexico— He criticized Whitney's plan for financing the road, principally on the ground that Whitney was trying to have the railroad "precede, not follow, the tide of emigration and the settlement of the country." Douglas would establish a territory of Oregon and another of Nebraska, "with land enough on both sides the Platte for a good state," survey the lands, and open them to settlement. Then he would grant alternate sections of land for several

[35] The material on Whitney's plan is voluminous. Whitney assembled much of it in a pamphlet of 110 pages entitled *A Project for a Railroad to the Pacific, . . . with Reports of Committees of Congress, Resolutions of State Legislatures, etc., with Other Facts Relating Thereto* (N. Y., 1849). The plan was the subject of reports by no less than eight congressional committees, the more noteworthy of which are referred to below, notes, 44-46, 49. See also N. H. Loomis, "Asa Whitney: Father of the Pacific Railroads," *Miss. Val. Hist. Assn., Proceedings*, VI (1912-13), 166-75, and M. L. Brown, "Asa Whitney and His Pacific Railroad Publicity Campaign," *Miss. Val. Hist. Rev.*, XX (Sept., 1933), 209-224.

[36] Pamphlet; also in Chicago [Weekly] *Democrat*, Nov. 11, 1845.

miles on each side the proposed route to the states and territories through which it might run to be used in building their respective sections of the railroad. He would encourage settlement west of the Missouri by granting free homesteads to settlers. To the essential features of this early plan Stephen A. Douglas clung to the end of his days.

In the Southwestern Convention, held at Memphis, November, 1845, still another route for a Pacific railroad was suggested, but no plan for financing it. The convention was seeking to create interest in a chain of railroads from the Atlantic seaboard to the Mississippi at Memphis. More than one delegate looked forward to its extension to the Pacific. John C. Calhoun, who presided, conservatively prophesied that the construction of a Pacific railroad would be undertaken within a generation. Col. James Gadsden, who later, 1853, negotiated the Gadsden purchase largely to get the best southern route, reporting for a committee, mentioned two possible routes from Memphis to the coast, one terminating at Mazatlan, the other at San Francisco.[37] This also before the Mexican War had begun.

Another early plan which elicited considerable discussion was that of George Wilkes, editor of the New York *Police Gazette*. He proposed, also in 1845, that the federal government build the railroad as a great national work. He strongly objected to Whitney's plan on the grounds that it lent itself to speculation and land monopoly on a large scale and gave no guarantee of early completion. He believed the government could build the road in five years; and he thought Independence, Missouri, was the most eligible initial point.[38]

After the Mexican War was begun there came frequent suggestions, not all from Southerners, that territory be acquired or at least a right of way which would permit a railroad to be constructed to the Pacific by a southern route.[39] One

[37] *Journal of the Proceedings of the Southwestern Convention . . . Memphis . . . 1845*, pp. 9, 29-41; *DeBow's Rev.*, I, 22, III, 328.
[38] George Wilkes, *The History of Oregon, Geographical and Political* (N. Y., 1845), 47-62; *Project of a National Railroad from the Atlantic to the Pacific Ocean* (pamphlet); *H. Repts.*, 29 Cong., 1 Sess., No. 773 (491), 37ff.
[39] *DeBow's Rev.*, III, 148, 475-95; *Am. R. R. Jour.* XIX, 761.

would make the right of way to Mazatlan, away down on the Tropic of Cancer, a *sine qua non*. Calhoun suggested a route via El Paso and the Gila Valley to San Diego. Secretary of State Buchanan was informed of the possibilities. He instructed Trist, the commissioner to negotiate peace with Mexico, in regard to a railroad route through the Gila Valley.[40] Trist secured the incorporation in the treaty of a provision that, in case it should be found practicable to construct a road, canal, or railroad along the Gila, which was designated as a part of the boundary, within a marine league of either bank, the two governments would make an agreement regarding it, "in order that it may serve equally for the use and advantage of both countries." Trist also offered $15,000,000 for the right of transit across the Isthmus of Tehuantepec; but the offer was refused and not pressed.[41] Meanwhile the initial moves had been taken to secure the right of transit at Panama and Nicaragua.[42]

Asa Whitney, Douglas, Wilkes, and other early proponents of a Pacific railroad advanced a variety of arguments in support of their measure. Before the Oregon treaty was made, they represented it as a means of acquiring the Oregon country; after the event, as necessary to hold that possession. It would people the wilderness and help control and civilize the Indians of the Plains. It would facilitate the establishment of a naval station on the Pacific and a base for our whaling and merchant fleets in that ocean. But greatest advantage of all, it would provide a short route to Asia. Whitney had been in China, and his imagination had been stirred. He told how in all ages the country which had controlled the commerce of "the Indies" had enjoyed the commercial supremacy of the world and had waxed rich and mighty. Ever since the time of Prince Henry the Navigator men had sought a short route to the Indies. But in these latter days the problem which had defied them so long was being solved by new agents, iron and

---

[40] July 13, 19, 1847; *Sen. Docs.*, 30 Cong., 1 Sess, VII (509), No. 52, pp. 91, 93.

[41] *Ibid.*, 82; Richardson, *Messages*, IV, 538, V, 16.

[42] See below, pp. 54, 62.

steam. The United States was about to wrest the scepter of commerce from proud Britannia. The settlement of the Pacific coast of America and the development of commerce with Asia would carry the light of Western civilization to the teeming millions of the Orient. Whitney made intricate calculations of comparative distances, sailing times, prospective freight and passenger rates, insurance costs, and climatic effects upon cargoes of the Cape-of-Good-Hope, Cape-Horn, Panama, and trans-American routes from New York, Liverpool, and Le Havre to Canton and Calcutta and invariably found that the trans-American route would have the advantage over all others. Other enthusiasts adopted Whitney's method and accepted his conclusions. Said Wilkes: "The riches of the most unlimited market in the world would be thrown open to our enterprise, and, obeying the new impulse thus imparted to it, our commerce would increase till every ocean billow between us and the China seas would twinkle with a sail. By the superior facilities conferred upon us by our position and control of the route, we should become the common carrier of the world for India trade." [43]

Of the various plans and projects for establishing means of communication with the Pacific, Asa Whitney's easily held the center of the stage down to about the time of the California gold rush. Whitney's second memorial was presented to Congress in February, 1846. It drew an enthusiastically favorable report from a Senate committee headed by Sidney Breese, of Illinois.[44] A House committee, Smith, of Connecticut, chairman, thought the scheme "too gigantic and, at least for the present, entirely impracticable." The committee preferred the plan then being sponsored by Senator Benton of improving the navigation of the Missouri and Columbia and constructing a turnpike between them.[45]

Whitney then took his cause to the people. He toured the country addressing mass meetings, chambers of commerce, conventions, and state legislatures. He wrote pamphlets and

[43] The Hist. of Oregon, Geographical and Political, 53.
[44] Sen. Docs., 29 Cong., 1 Sess., IX (478), No. 466.
[45] H. Repts., 29 Cong., 1 Sess., IV (491), No. 773; Cong. Globe, 29 Cong., 1 Sess., 915ff. (Benton).

articles for periodicals. Whitney was a man of charming
manners and contagious enthusiasm, and he marshalled his
arguments most skilfully. He convinced many that a railroad
built by a more southerly route and on another plan would
not divert Asiatic trade from the all-sea routes. Perhaps the
strongest point in favor of his plan was that, since it would
be built from the proceeds of land sales without the issue of
stocks and bonds, his railroad would be under no necessity of
earning dividends and, consequently, the rates would be comparatively very low. He persuaded many, also, that on no
route farther south were the public lands sufficiently fertile
and well enough wooded and watered to invite settlement and
thus pay for the construction of a railroad.

Eventually eighteen state legislatures endorsed Whitney's
plan, not to mention innumerable mass meetings and chambers
of commerce.[46] Among the legislatures was that of Illinois,
despite the rival plan of a favorite son, Stephen A. Douglas.
Several Southern legislatures were also among the number,
and some of them adopted their resolutions after the Mexican
War had begun and the acquisition of California was virtually
assured. Perhaps a majority of the newspaper press fell in
line. The most influential railroad magazine, the *American
Railroad Journal*, held out against Whitney for a couple of
years and then, moved by manifestations of approval, announced its grudging support.[47] At one time *DeBow's Review*,
which was published in New Orleans and was strongly devoted
to Southern interests, became convinced that further opposition was useless and announced its preference for Whitney's
scheme over no railroad at all.[48] In the first session of the 30th
Congress, 1848, select committees in both houses reported in
favor of a Whitney bill.[49] The House committee believed "it
to be the almost unanimous desire of the people that the plan
be adopted." However, the bill was not passed. The spell of
the Whitney plan was soon to be broken.

[46] Most of these resolutions are in *H. Repts.*, 31 Cong., 1 Sess., I (583), No.
140, and in A. Whitney, *A Project for a Railroad to the Pacific* . . . , 89-107.
[47] Jan. 1, 1848 (XXI).
[48] IX, 601.
[49] *H. Repts.*, 30 Cong., 1 Sess., No. 733 (526).

# CHAPTER II

# THE ISSUE DEFINED

THE progress of events during the first few years following the settlement of the Oregon question, the outbreak of the Mexican War, and the conquest of California supplied new and powerful reasons for establishing better means of communication with the Pacific coast, indeed made it almost a matter of national convenience and necessity.

In January, 1848, gold was discovered in the Sacramento Valley. Then ensued a rush to California from all quarters of the globe which upset all previous calculations of the probable growth of population on the Pacific coast. California is estimated to have had a white population of about 14,000 when the United States gained title to it.[1] The census of 1850 found 92,597 persons there, before most of the immigrants of that year had arrived. The rush continued through the year. Immigration was not so great in 1851, but it rose again in 1852 and continued high in 1853.[2] The great movement of these early years, exaggerated at the time, led to exaggerated estimates of the probable growth of population in California.

People went to California in these early years by several means and routes. Thousands took ship around Cape Horn, a comparatively safe but long, tedious, and expensive journey. Other thousands went by ship or steamer to the Isthmus of Panama, crossed by river boats and pack mules or on foot to the City of Panama, and thence went up the coast by steamship or sailing vessel. The passage of the isthmus involved great risks to life and health. A considerably lesser number crossed by the Nicaragua route, which was more difficult but somewhat less unhealthy. Other thousands made the long, difficult journey overland by wagon train, the principal route

---

[1] Jos. Schafer, *The Pacific Slope and Alaska*, 278.
[2] J. B. McMaster, *Hist. of the People of the U. S.*, VIII, 56-66; Edw. Channing, *Hist. of the U. S.*, VI, 43.

being from Independence, Missouri, via the Platte Valley, South Pass, and Great Salt Lake. The overland journey involved comparatively little hazard of life and health if proper preparations had been made, but during the gold rush, starvation, thirst, and fatigue took impressive toll of human lives.[3]

For several years following the discovery of gold, while mining and prospecting were the all-absorbing occupations, the people of California imported immense quantities of building materials, mining machinery, merchandise, and even foodstuffs from the older portions of the Union and elsewhere. Notwithstanding warnings that these great importations could not continue, that California must soon begin to provide a large share of its own needs, most people were led to hold too high expectations of the extent of commerce between the Pacific coast and the rest of the country in the more immediate future.[4]

The government was obliged to establish postal service between the new settlements and the older-settled regions. And, with so many settlers only recently separated from families and friends in the East, the mails were great in volume.

It could, therefore, now be contended that a Pacific railroad or an isthmian railroad or canal was required to accommodate this great volume of trade, travel, and mail.

The new developments in California and Oregon also greatly strengthened the political reasons for desiring improved means of communication with the Pacific. In case of war the new and unexpectedly valuable possessions must be defended against attack. The government was also now obligated to protect the people of California, Oregon, New Mexico, and Utah and the emigrants who followed the trails across the plains against the Indians. By the Treaty of Guadalupe Hidalgo the United States had undertaken to prevent Indian incursions across the border into Mexico. Means were required to transport troops for these several purposes rapidly

[3] McMaster gives a detailed and graphic account of this early migration. *Op. cit.*, VII, ch. lxxxv, VIII, 56-59.

[4] A keen analysis of California's prospects was made by Thomas Butler King, whom President Taylor sent out as his personal representative. King, *Report on California* (Wash., 1850).

and cheaply and the necessary military supplies as well as naval supplies for squadrons in the Pacific. It was contended that it would be all but impossible, and most uneconomical, to keep sufficient troops and war material on the Pacific coast in time of peace to defend it if war should occur, and, without better means of communication, it would be impossible to send troops and supplies in time of war with sufficient dispatch and in necessary numbers and quantities.[5] This was a time when schemes of national expansion found ready favor: A railroad near the Mexican border might hasten the absorption of the northern tier of Mexican states;[6] one near Canada might help to draw her into our orbit.[7] The control of transit routes across the Isthmus might in the fullness of time bring the regions traversed under the Stars and Stripes.

Advocates of a transcontinental railroad or highway, as distinguished from isthmian projects, made much of the point that, in case of war with a stronger naval power, the isthmian routes might be closed against our commerce, mails, and troops. Furthermore isthmian facilities would be of no assistance in controlling the Indians of the interior or in policing the Mexican border.

With the prospect of a great commerce and much travel between the rising communities on the Pacific coast and the peoples of the Atlantic seacoast and the Mississippi Valley and the prospect of much transportation on government account, it began to appear more likely that a railroad or other improved means of communication would prove self-supporting than it had when Asa Whitney first announced his plan. Many conservative people who had doubted both the commercial advantages and financial soundness of such a project when little more than enthusiastic forecasts of China trade had been offered them were now convinced both of its commercial expediency and financial success. The more sanguine became

[5] Good arguments for the railroad as a military necessity are in Secretary of War Jefferson Davis's annual report to President Pierce, Dec. 3, 1855, and his letter to Rep. J. M. Sandidge, Jan. 29, 1856. Dunbar Rowland, ed., *Jefferson Davis, Constitutionalist*, II, 565-70, 588-90.

[6] *DeBow's Rev.*, XXI, 469-90; *Cong. Globe*, 33 Cong., 1 Sess., 882.

[7] *Ibid.*, 35 Cong., 1 Sess., App., 430.

extravagant in their claims. *DeBow's Review* stated the case
rather moderately:[8]

> If we can suppose a population on the route of this com-
> munication and in constant use of it of four millions only,
> and that it will reach the number in twenty years would not
> seem improbable, considering the riches of California and
> the past progress of our western country, and the impetus
> the road itself would give, that population alone could
> support the road, with its travel and trade, judging from
> the number of miles of railroad we at present require.
>
> Thus, then, if not one dollar of eastern trade is realized
> by our Pacific railroad, if begun now it is capable, in less
> than one generation of being as profitable as other Amer-
> ican roads!
>
> Demonstrate if it can be done, that we get the trade of
> India, or even make it *highly probable*, and what motives
> are there superinduced to gratify national avarice or
> ambition.

The early proponents of a Pacific railroad and to only a less
extent the sponsors of isthmian projects had found it necessary
to gloss over the engineering aspects of their great work.
There was little assurance when the first proposals were advanced that any route existed whereby a transcontinental railroad or an isthmian canal could be built and operated at a cost
not absolutely prohibitive. As geographic knowledge of the
Far West and the isthmian region grew, with the Oregon
migration, the Mexican War, and the gold rush, the conviction
spread that the construction of such a work would be found to
be a practicable feat of engineering.

As the provision of improved means of communication with
the Pacific coast came within the realm of probability for the
immediate future, an intense rivalry sprang up among the considerable cities and towns near the Mississippi frontier, such
as Chicago, St. Joseph, St. Louis, and Memphis, for the possession of the eastern terminus of the first and, probably for
many years, the only railroad to the Pacific; while the people
of cities and towns on the Gulf, especially, and the Atlantic
were inclined to lend their support to that isthmian project

[8] VII, 36.

which seemed best calculated to promote the interests of their particular locality. A city or town so located that it could not itself aspire to become an immediate terminus threw its support to that one of the rivals with which it might have closest commercial connections, for example, Cincinnati supported the claims of St. Louis.

The liveliest expectations were entertained of the advantages a city would reap from trade with the Pacific. Even people of cities which could never hope to be termini came to have glowing expectations of the nourishing qualities of the stream of Pacific commerce and travel even after it should have been divided and subdivided. For example, Richard Yates, representing Morgan County in the Illinois legislature, after having shown to his satisfaction that Quincy was the logical starting point for a railroad to the Pacific, remarked that members present might live to see cars "passing through Quincy, Jacksonville, and Springfield, bearing to our doors the commerce of India and China, and of the Islands of the sea, and opening to us the commerce of the world. And as for Quincy, this being the terminus on the great Father of Waters, it would make her a mighty city, — a city which would rival Carthage in her pride of power, — the great commercial emporium of the Mississippi Valley, into whose commission houses would pour the commerce of the world." [9] Said a citizen of New Orleans: ". . . we shall have all the commerce and travel of the Northern Atlantic States, and all the commerce and travel of Europe that is destined for the Pacific Ocean, for India and China, passing through our city; portions of their products will be left for sale here, or exchanged for our own, or those of the great West, and the thousand products of our artistical and manufacturing skill. Is not every state in the West and South interested in securing such a mart as New Orleans will then be for their productions? It will then be the market of the world." [10] And in Savannah, Georgia, which apparently could by no manner of means hope to profit greatly by communication with the Pacific, a citizen

[9] Springfield *Ill. Daily Jour.*, Nov. 3, 1849.
[10] *Am. R. R. Jour.*, XXV, 502.

wrote: "The subject of connecting the cities of Savannah, Mobile, and New Orleans by a railroad, has already been much agitated in the South. This will, undoubtedly, be soon undertaken; and, together with the New Orleans and Opelousas road, now under contract, would form the eastern half of the great connection between the Atlantic and Pacific. If the El Paso route is the one adopted by the government, Savannah would become the great Atlantic Depot, and San Diego the Pacific." [11] In 1850, Dr. William A. Smith, President of Randolph-Macon College, wrote in a public letter: "The road to Clarksville should be the commencement of one in due course of time to Memphis, Tenn., to connect with the prospective Government road through the territories to San Francisco, in California. The use of steam from thence to China must result in the introduction of imports from China (tea in particular) into this country. These must find a shipping port on the Atlantic coast. What point offers the advantages of the port of Norfolk? None; emphatically none. . . . To talk, then, of allowing that vast portion of this trade that would reach Memphis from San Francisco seeking the Atlantic coast to wind around by way of Lynchburg and down to Richmond and Petersburg and thence to sea, when it can be brought in a straight line, varying only three-fourths of a degree from San Francisco to Norfolk, is idle in the extreme." [12]

During the late 1840's and the early 1850's the main outlines of the railroad system of the settled portions of the United States were rapidly taking form either in the shape of roads built or building or in well-defined projects for which charters had been or were about to be secured. People had grasped already something of the future possibilities of railroads as "the rivers of these latter days"; and cities were contending in "mighty rivalry" for these arteries of commerce with future greatness as the prize of victory and stagnation and decay the penalty for defeat. Each was seeking to make itself the center of as many radiating railroads as possible.

[11] DeBow's Rev., XV, 641.
[12] William S. Forrest, Sketches of Norfolk, 248.

Most state legislatures sought to guide and direct the location of the railroads of their respective states in such a way as to develop commercial centers within their own borders, preventing any of their area from becoming tributary to cities of neighboring states while attracting the trade of areas in other states to their own cities. Railroad companies strove to locate their lines where they could best secure the traffic of prosperous or promising areas, attract feeders, and become "links" in "chains" of roads which might become great trunk lines. If, now, a city or town somewhere near the Mississippi-Valley frontier could secure its selection as the initial point of a railroad to the Pacific, it would at once become a focal point for railroads from farther east and thus its commercial future would be assured. Likewise if a railroad company, having a road or a project pointing westwardly anywhere near a possible starting point for a railroad to the Pacific, could manage to make it a part of, or a continuation of, or at least a branch of, a great railroad to the Pacific, the company could feel measurably sure of success. The possibility that a railroad might occupy such a favorable position was used to win the favor of investors and the public. It would seem, even, that the locations of several roads projected in the Mississippi Valley during this period were determined very largely by the possibility of making them links in, or continuations of, a Pacific railway.

A convention at Holly Springs, Mississippi, 1849, declared that the Mississippi and Alabama Railroad would "finally, and at no distant day, become the most important Rail Road in the world, by its extension [from Memphis] to the Pacific and its use for the transportation of the vast commerce between Asia and Europe." [13] Said the agent of the New Orleans, Opelousas, and Great Western: "The hundreds of millions of gold produced by California; the rapid development of our possessions in Oregon; the great increase in the whale trade in the North Pacific; an increased trade with Mexico and South America; the absolute certainty of finally crushing the Chinese walls and overthrowing Japanese non-

[13] *Memphis* [Tri-weekly] *Appeal*, Oct. 25, 1849.

intercourse; and the opening of commercial relations with 700,000,000 people who inhabit Asia, and the millions of the islands of the Pacific; . . . will furnish to this road and its St. Louis branch a transportation and business unknown to the annals of railroad prosperity on this globe." [14]

The shipping interests of the Atlantic seaboard could see no virtue in a transcontinental railroad. To the extent, however, that they thought trade with Asia might be diverted thereby from the Cape of Good Hope route or trade with the Pacific coast of the Americas encouraged, they looked with favor upon isthmian projects.

The question of establishing better means of communication with the Pacific came early to have sectional aspects also. The people of the South were becoming keenly aware of what they chose to call "Southern decline." The section was not keeping abreast of the North in various lines of economic development. The South remained almost exclusively agricultural. She was becoming more and more dependent upon the East and Europe for manufactures. Her extensive commerce was mostly carried in Northern ships. Most of the foreign goods consumed in the South were imported through Eastern seaports. Southern cities did not keep pace with Northern cities. This condition of backwardness and dependence was galling to the pride of patriotic Southerners. It seemed to them evidence that the South was not prospering and that the fruits of Southern labor were being drained off to build up other sections of the Union. Furthermore, the North, in consequence of its superior industrial and commercial development, was outgrowing the South in population; and this meant greater weight in the councils of the nation. The maintenance of something like a balance of political power seemed to Southern leaders to be necessary to protect the South's peculiar institution from attacks from hostile elements in the North. In the South, therefore, there was much analyzing of the causes of "Southern decline" and much searching for remedies.[15] The construction

[14] *Am. R. R. Jour.*, XXV, 517.
[15] Robert R. Russel, *Econ. Aspects of So. Sectionalism, 1840-1861* (Univ. of Ill. *Studies in the Soc. Sci.*, XI).

of a railroad to the Pacific along a southern route was one of
the most widely considered measures designed to effect the
regeneration of the section.

The Southern Commercial Convention, which met annually
or oftener, 1852-59, was the principal forum for discussing
the South's position and its improvement. In at least three of
the sessions, a Pacific railroad received more consideration
than any other proposed remedy. Said the New Orleans
*Delta,* commenting somewhat sarcastically on the deep interest shown in a Pacific railway by the Southern Commercial
Convention meeting in Memphis, 1853: "This was the Aaron's
rod that swallowed up all others. This was the great panacea,
which is to release the South from its bondage to the North,
which is to pour untold wealth into our lap; which is to build
up cities, steamships, manufactories, educate our children, and
draw into our control what Mr. Bell calls 'the untold wealth
of the gorgeous East'." [16]

In the North there was not so strong a disposition to look
upon a Pacific connection as a means of *sectional* economic
aggrandizement.

There was a sectional aspect of the question, however,
which the leaders of neither section overlooked. If, say, the
first railroad to the Pacific and probably the only one the
nation would build for a generation should follow a southern
route, southern territories would in all probability be settled
earlier than more northern ones and would earlier become
states. They would in all probability be settled largely by
Southern people and would be slaveholding. Upon arriving at
statehood they would send senators and representatives to
Washington who would help to defeat measures hostile to
slavery. California, itself, although it came into the Union as
a "free" state, 1850, was at no time before 1860 so irretriev-
ably "free" that close connection by rail might not have
bound it politically to the South. If, on the contrary, the first
railroad to the Pacific should follow a northern or central
route, the more northern territories would first develop into

[16] As quoted in the *Richmond Enquirer,* Je. 24, 1853.

states; and they would be settled principally by people from the free states or Europe, would be nonslaveholding, and would contribute to majorities in Congress hostile to slavery. If an isthmian railroad or canal should be built or a transcontinental railroad near the Mexican border, it might result in the annexation of territory which would probably become slaveholding.

As early as 1849 a distinguished Southerner wrote: ". . . the accursed question of slavery is already mixing itself up with the road, and the free States, who are removed from it, will not go for it if it is to go through slave territory." [17] The editor of the *Arkansas State Gazette and Democrat* understood the political implications: ". . . when the road is finally completed to the Pacific, . . . the State of California, and the States which will intervene between that and Texas, being so intimately identified with us, in their commercial relations, will, as a matter of course, from interest as well as sympathy, join with our division of the country, as a common community, contending for common rights." [18] The Southern Commercial Convention, at New Orleans, January, 1855, resolved that the construction of a railroad to the Pacific by a southern route was "indispensable to their [the Southern States'] welfare and prosperity, and even to their continued existence as equal and independent members of the confederacy." [19]

To the people on the Pacific coast satisfactory means of communication and transportation between their rapidly growing community and the rest of the Union were matters of urgent and vital importance. There the establishment of such facilities became the public policy of paramount interest and the highest object of statesmanship. People on the Pacific early learned to use all the arguments in behalf of a railroad and other projects, including mild threats of disunion in case they were not provided. After September, 1850, California had two senators and two representatives in Congress. They

[17] *DeBow's Rev.*, VII, 37. Stephen A. Douglas adverted to this sectional aspect of the question in a speech in Chicago. *Chicago Daily Jour.*, Oct. 12, 1849.
[18] Apr. 1, 1853.
[19] *DeBow's Rev.*, XVIII, 520.

proved to be the most zealous advocates of government action in behalf of better means of communication. At home their services were largely estimated by their degree of success in advancing that one cause.

It was understood, of course, from the outset that no private corporation could be formed to build a transcontinental railroad or even an isthmian work on an ambitious scale without outside aid. There would be little profitable business until such a work should be completed from end to end, and no private corporation would or could wait that long to begin the payment of dividends upon such an enormous investment.

Cities and other municipal corporations, in their corporate capacities, often contributed aid to railroad companies and other transportation agencies; but, of course, no one of the cities contending for the terminus of a Pacific railroad could contribute any considerable portion of the cost of so gigantic a work. States might do more. They could charter railroad or canal companies; and they could grant subsidies or lend their credit in aid thereof. The policy of state aid to "internal improvements" had been considerably discredited during the panic of 1837 and the depression which ensued; but so insistent was the demand for such improvements that a number of states resumed the policy. This was true especially in the South and Southwest, where private capital came forward slowly.[20] As soon as a transcontinental railroad came within the realm of possibility, it was recognized that, other things being equal (and they never were), the frontier state of the Mississippi Valley which first succeeded in pushing a railroad through to its western border would stand the best chance of having its road continued to the Pacific. In this competition Texas had an advantage no other state possessed in that she owned the unsettled lands within her borders and might make grants of land in aid of railroads. However, in every frontier state, effective state action in behalf of first links in a Pacific

[20] There are summary accounts of state aid to railroads in F. A. Cleveland and F. W. Powell, *Railway Promotion and Capitalization in the U. S.*, chs. xii, xiii; J. A. Million, *State Aid to Railroads in Missouri*, ch. vi; and Robt. E. Riegel, *Story of the Western Railroads*, ch. iii.

railroad was made difficult by internal divisions. Each had more than one town which aspired to be the terminus and more than one railroad company which desired to be the recipient of favor.

But however effective state aid might prove to be, as long as the Great Plains and the mountain region should remain largely unoccupied, no transcontinental railroad could be built without extensive federal aid. The federal government must grant the right of way across the public lands, survey the lands and open them to white settlement, remove the Indians, afford protection to the work as it should progress, and probably charter a company to build the portions which might lie within the territories; and, all who wanted a railroad at all agreed, it must at least give substantial gifts of money or lands to help construct the sections running through the vast unsettled spaces. Many people believed the federal government itself should construct the railroad as a great national public work. As for an isthmian canal or railroad, the federal government must at least secure the right of way for United States travelers, commerce, mails, troops, and government stores from the government or governments having jurisdiction over the route. And, because of the instability of governments in the isthmian region and their frequent failures to provide security for lives and property, the United States government must guarantee the safety and neutrality of the transit.

There were great obstacles in the way of getting effective federal action in behalf of improved means of communication with the Pacific besides the obvious one of uniting the friends of such a policy in behalf of one particular project. The matter could never be handled alone on its individual merits; it was deeply involved with many other issues of the time.

Proposals of federal aid for a Pacific connection always raised the old question of "internal improvements." This was one of the issues over which the two major parties of the time, the Whigs and Democrats, had originally divided. Democrats had been inclined to take the view that congressional appropriations, whether of money or public land, in aid of internal

improvements were unconstitutional. This was especially true
of the Southern wing of the party; for Southerners felt they
must insist upon a strict construction of the constitution in
order not to establish any precedents of liberal construction
which anti-slavery majorities might some day seize upon. Furthermore it was a cardinal principle of the Calhoun wing of
the Democratic party that the federal government must be
economically administered. Most of the taxes were collected
in the South, so ran the argument; most of the disbursements
were made in the North. This unequal fiscal operation of the
government, going on year after year, was building up one
section at the expense of the other.[21] Some Democrats believed the federal government could constitutionally aid internal improvements in the territories but not in the states.
Democrats from the Northwest, especially, occasionally broke
away from the traditional party position altogether and voted
for liberal aid. The Whigs had been inclined to take the position that federal appropriations in aid of internal improvements were constitutional and should be made in liberal
amounts. Whigs, naturally, were not inclined to help frame
Pacific railroad bills in such a way as to overcome the scruples
of Democrats.

Another related question over which there were similar
party divisions was the power of Congress to incorporate companies for building transportation facilities. Whigs upheld the
power. Some Democrats denied it altogether. Others believed Congress could incorporate such companies to operate
in the territories but not in the states, at least not without the
consent of the states concerned.

Bills relating to railroads were likely to involve the tariff
question also, especially if federal aid were proposed. Strong
friends of railroads, especially if Democratic, would demand
that railroad iron be admitted duty free. Strong friends of the
iron industry, especially if Whig, as they were likely to be,
would insist on maintaining the tariff or, even, upon the use
of iron of American production only.

[21] R. R. Russel, *op. cit.*, ch. iii.

The Pacific railroad question also became inextricably involved with that of public lands, a question which evoked as
much discussion in that day as any other one except slavery.
In every Western state and territory except Kentucky, Tennessee, and Texas, where it had never owned the lands, and
Ohio and Indiana, where they had been almost entirely disposed of, the federal government owned vast quantities of
lands. As already noted, the earliest plans for building a railroad to the Pacific proposed to finance it by means of public
lands, and, whenever thereafter transcontinental railroad bills
came up in Congress, it was certain to be proposed that a
portion of the public lands or the proceeds from the sale thereof be granted in aid. But such a proposal involved the whole
issue of the proper disposition of the public lands with all its
intricate cross currents and inherited viewpoints. Only the
briefest analysis of the public lands question can be given here,
but so much is essential to an understanding of some of the
struggles over Pacific railway bills.[22]

The people in the newer states and territories in which the
public lands lay advocated a liberal land policy. They wanted
the lands ceded to the states in which they lay, or given to
settlers, or, at least, sold at very low prices. Such a policy
would encourage settlement and promote the development of
the resources of the West. Many influential people back East,
on the other hand, opposed a liberal land policy. It would,
they believed, tend to drain off the population of the older
states, lower real estate values, and, by reducing the surplus
in the labor market, raise the wages of mill operatives, farm
hands, etc. The wage earners in the older states favored a
liberal policy for the very reason for which employers often
opposed it. Small farmers and younger sons who might want
to move West likewise favored it. These latter classes in the
East espoused especially the policy of granting the lands in
small lots to actual settlers for homesteads.

People in regions where the public lands lay believed they

[22] *Cf.* Geo. M. Stephenson, *The Pol. Hist. of the Public Lands from 1840 to
1862*; F. L. Paxson, *Hist. of the Am. Frontier*, chs. xlii, xlv, l; J. B. Sanborn,
*Congressional Grants of Land in Aid of Railways* (Univ. of Wisc. *Bulletin*, V).

should receive special benefits from these lands. They had the feeling that since they had conquered the wilderness, opened the trails and roads, and thus made the lands valuable the lands belonged to them. In the older states, however, where there were no public lands, people looked upon them as a great national fund to be used for the benefit of the whole nation. Eastern Whigs and Democrats, to be sure, differed as to the proper disposition of this common fund. Most of the Whigs supported the policy, originally sponsored by Henry Clay, of distributing the proceeds of lands sales or even the lands themselves among the several states in proportion to population to be used in aid of internal improvements, education, or other things to which the states might choose to apply them. Most Eastern Democrats believed the lands should be sold and the proceeds be put in the treasury and used to pay the debts of the United States and meet other legitimate expenses. They denied that Congress had the power to make gifts of public property or public revenues to states or individuals.

Strong anti-slavery people usually favored gifts of lands to settlers because they believed such gifts would act as a sort of emigrant aid society peopling the territories with small farmers and laborers from North, South, and Europe who would make free states of them. When the Republican party was organized, 1854, it championed free-homestead legislation for this same reason. Southern upholders of slavery opposed the free-homestead policy because they feared it would have the very effect the anti-slavery people hoped it would have.

Some time before the Pacific railway question came upon the stage, someone had conceived the alternate-sections principle or plan for granting public lands in aid of railroads and canals. This plan was cleverly devised to permit those congressmen who had constitutional scruples against voting for appropriations for internal improvements to satisfy their consciences and vote in aid of the much desired improvements at the same time. According to the plan Congress should grant to the state or territory in which the improvements lay every other section of land for a specified number of miles (six in

the early grants) on each side of the designated route on the
condition that the state or territory in turn grant it in aid of
the railroad or canal.  The federal government would reserve
the other checkered set of alternate sections in the strip along
the line and sell them for not less than double the minimum
price for such lands elsewhere, that is for not less than $2.50
per acre.  It was contended that by this plan, Congress would
not in fact be making appropriations for internal improvements at all but only acting as a prudent landlord might act.
By giving away half the lands in a given strip and getting a
railroad built through it, the government would be able to
sell the remaining half for as much as the whole would have
brought without the railroad and, because the railroad would
hasten settlement, would get its money sooner.

The first large grant in aid of railroads on the alternate-
sections principle was made to the states of Illinois, Alabama,
and Mississippi in 1850 in behalf of the Illinois Central and
Mobile and Ohio railroads.[23]  Thereafter the number of requests for such grants grew amazingly.  And it was only natural that such an alternate-sections grant should be frequently
proposed as a means of financing a railroad to the Pacific.

Land grants to railroads on the alternate-sections plan won
general approval in the West.  They offered one way of getting the lands settled rapidly and the country developed, and
these were the great objectives.  There was some murmuring
among Westerners to be sure because of the increase in prices
involved; but the opposition centered principally in the older
states.  Those who feared that Western development would
injure their interests opposed of course.  Although John C.
Calhoun had approved the principle, the strictest sect of constitutional interpretation was unreconciled.  Whigs occasionally tried to obstruct land grant bills with the object of forcing
acceptance of a general distribution measure.  Much of the
opposition came from advocates of homestead legislation.
Westerners could favor both homestead and land grant bills
without inconsistency, since both would hasten Western devel-

[23] W. K. Akerman, *Hist. Sketch of the Ill. Cent. R. R.*

opment. Eastern advocates of a homestead law, however, had other objects; they wanted the law as a measure of social reform.

After about 1848 land grant bills on the alternate-sections plan passed the United States Senate with ease and regularity, for in the Senate the equal representation of the states gave the newer states of the West influence out of proportion to their population. In the House of Representatives, where the more populous landless states had a majority, the opposition was usually strong enough to defeat the bills.

*CHAPTER III*

## THE LINES ARE DRAWN FOR THE PACIFIC
## RAILWAY STRUGGLE

THE beginning of the year 1849 saw a number of cities and towns near the Mississippi-Valley frontier well entered in the competition to be designated as the initial point of the Pacific railway. From north to south they were Milwaukee, Chicago, Quincy, St. Joseph, St. Louis, Memphis, and Vicksburg. Each had its merits, and none hid its light under a bushel.

Milwaukee enjoyed the advantage of having been designated as the terminus by Asa Whitney, whose plan had won such widespread popular support. The city's location on the west shore of Lake Michigan over a hundred miles above its southern tip precluded it from becoming a point of convergence for chains of railroads from the East. This, however, did not seem such a great disadvantage then, for railroads had hardly begun to demonstrate superiority over waterways. By the Lakes, the St. Lawrence, and the Erie Canal, Milwaukee had water communication with the Atlantic seaboard, except when the route was closed by ice, and a great area in the interior as well. Milwaukee people hoped also that some benefit might accrue from projects for two railways across Michigan from Grand Haven, opposite Milwaukee, to Detroit and Port Huron respectively, whence they would connect with roads in Canada that, in turn, when completed, would connect at Buffalo and Montreal with New York and New England railways.[1] Milwaukee suffered the serious handicap

---

[1] The statements in the next few pages regarding connecting railroads and railroad projects are based on a wide variety of sources, especially the *Am. R. R. Jour.; DeBow's Rev.; West. Jour. and Civilian; Niles' Register; Hunt's Merchants Mag.*; H. V. Poor, *Hist. of the Railroads and Canals of the U. S.* (1860); and *Poor's Manual of the Railroads of the U. S.* (1868—, annual). Helpful secondary accounts are C. E. MaGill *et al*, *Hist. of Transportation in the U. S. before 1860*; J. L. Ringwalt, *Development of Transportation*

of being a small city in a newly-admitted state which had little weight in Congress.

Chicago in 1849 was a town of only 30,000 souls but was already marked for greatness. Her waterways were even better than those of Milwaukee, for the Illinois-Michigan Canal, opened but the year before, afforded connection with the Illinois River and, through it, with the whole Mississippi system. In addition Eastern railroad interests had already designated the aspiring young city as a point of convergence. Both New York and Boston had rail connections with Albany and thence, by a chain of roads soon to be consolidated into the New York Central, with Buffalo. The New York and Erie was being built rapidly through southern York State toward Dunkirk on Lake Erie near Buffalo. A chain of short roads along the lake shore promised soon to connect Buffalo and Dunkirk with Toledo, while another chain in Canada would connect Buffalo and Detroit. From Toledo the Michigan Southern and Northern Indiana was being built toward Chicago, while from Detroit the Michigan Central was being pushed westward across the state. A project was maturing for a road to connect the lake-shore chain at Cleveland with the Pennsylvania at Pittsburgh. There were already two advanced projects for railroads from Chicago to the Mississippi River, the Chicago and Rock Island and the Chicago and Galena Union.

Quincy aspired to be the Mississippi River terminus of a "great central" chain of railroads, some of them still only on paper, from Philadelphia via Pittsburgh, Columbus, Indianapolis, and Springfield. The Illinois Legislature was doing what it could to make Quincy a city through its power to grant and to refuse to grant charters for railroad companies.[2] Only

---

Systems in the U. S.; F. L. Paxson, Railroads in the Old Northwest before the Civil War; U. B. Phillips, A Hist. of Transportation in the Eastern Cotton Belt to 1860; R. S. Cotterill, "Southern Railroads, 1850-1860," Miss. Val. Hist. Rev., X (Mar., 1924), 396-405; R. E. Riegel, The Story of the Western Railroads.

[2] Chicago Daily Jour., Oct. 27, Nov. 9, 12, 1849; Springfield Ill. Daily Jour., Nov. 3, 10, 1849; Daily Mo. Republican, Oct. 17, 1849; DeBow's Rev., VII, 403, 571.

eighteen miles south of Quincy but on the Missouri side of the
Mississippi was the little city of Hannibal. Directly across
the state on the Missouri River was St. Joseph, one of the
"jumping-off" places for emigrants bound for Oregon or
California via the Oregon Trail. February 16, 1847, the
Missouri Legislature chartered the Hannibal and St. Joseph
Railroad Company. People interested in this project hoped
it would attract eastern connections and were especially hope-
ful of deflecting the great central chain just mentioned. As
early as 1846 people in St. Joseph nominated their little town
as a candidate for the terminus of the Pacific railroad.[3]

St. Louis was, next to New Orleans, the largest city on the
Mississippi River. It was the center of an immense steamboat traffic, then at its height, on the Mississippi, Missouri,
Illinois, Ohio, Cumberland, Tennessee, and other rivers. It
was, therefore, a logical point of convergence for railroad
chains being hurried forward from the east. The promoters
of the Ohio and Mississippi Railroad from Cincinnati had refused to accept an Illinois charter designating Alton, twenty
miles up the river, as its western terminus, and citizens of St.
Louis were confident that Illinois must soon abandon her
"unenlightened" policy.[4] The Ohio and Mississippi was to be
the western link in a chain of which the Baltimore and Ohio
was the eastern and the Cincinnati and Marietta was to be
the middle. There was also a promising Virginia project,
although destined to be long deferred, for a railroad from
Richmond to the Ohio, whence, it was expected, rail connection
would be had with Cincinnati. St. Louis people also hoped
for railway connections with the Philadelphia-Pittsburgh-
Columbus-Indianapolis chain by means of a projected road
from Terre Haute. They were also watchful of a Tennessee
project, the Nashville, Chattanooga, and Charleston, which
would extend Charleston and Savannah roads in their direction. On March 12, 1849, the Missouri Legislature chartered
the suggestively styled Pacific Railroad Company to build
from St. Louis to the mouth of the Kansas River, the present

---

[3] St. Joseph *Gazette*, Je. 26, Jul. 10, 31, 1846.
[4] *DeBow's Rev.*, VIII, 364, 571.

Kansas City. St. Louis could truly be regarded as centrally located, and that was a great point in her favor when it was expected that only one railroad to the Pacific could be built.

Memphis was in 1849 and remained for several years thereafter the most formidable of the Southern rivals for the eastern terminus. Two great Southern chains of railroads promised to converge there, one from Charleston and Savannah, the other from Richmond and Norfolk. Savannah already had lines to Atlanta, the "Gate City." The State of Georgia was building (completed in 1850) the Western Atlantic between Atlanta and Chattanooga. The Memphis and Chattanooga (soon to be rechristened the Memphis and Charleston) was under construction. Richmond, Norfolk, and other Virginia ports had or soon would have connections with the Piedmont town of Lynchburg. The Virginia and Tennessee had been projected, and was soon built, to connect Lynchburg and Knoxville, Tennessee. The East Tennessee, Virginia, and Georgia would continue the chain to a junction with the Western Atlantic near Chattanooga, whence connection would be had with Memphis over the Memphis and Charleston. Another railroad project of the day (also shortly constructed) was the Memphis and Ohio, which was to join Memphis and Nashville and, it was hoped, eventually give Memphis connections with Louisville, Cincinnati, and, thence, with Baltimore, Philadelphia, and other Eastern cities. Thus, it could be urged, if a southern route should be chosen for a Pacific railroad, Memphis was the only Southern point upon which the railroads of the Ohio Valley and the Middle Atlantic seaboard could conveniently converge.

Vicksburg was the Mississippi River terminus of a projected and partially built (completed in 1861) chain of railroads from Charleston and Savannah via Macon, Georgia, Montgomery, Alabama, and Meridian and Jackson, Mississippi. Vicksburg, therefore, might expect some support from the cotton belt for her pretensions.

New Orleans was not a contender at this early date. In fact she had encouraged no railway connections whatever but still relied confidently on the great river which had made her the largest city in the Valley. Citizens of New Orleans early became interested in the project for a railroad across the Isthmus of Tehuantepec.[5] If this route should be chosen, no other Gulf or Atlantic seaport would be more strategically located to capture the Pacific trade.

Galveston and Matagorda Bay were urged as possible termini by patriotic residents of the vicinage. They had no powerful connections, of course. They were somewhat closer to California than their more prominent rivals and much closer to Mazatlan; and, if the construction of a railroad to the Pacific should be undertaken by the federal government primarily for military and political reasons, the mantle might well fall upon one of them.

In presenting the claims of various towns for consideration for the eastern terminus of a transcontinental railroad, their champions were not oblivious of the fact that the choice must depend largely upon what route or routes might be found most practicable for the construction and operation of a railroad across the lofty mountain ranges and mighty deserts which intervened between the Great Plains and the Pacific and also upon the choice of the terminus upon the Pacific coast. Railroad engineering was in its infancy. The Great West had been but little explored. There was no assurance when the first proposals for a Pacific railroad were advanced that any route existed whereon a railroad could be built and operated at a cost not absolutely prohibitive. One route might be found which possessed so many advantages over all others as to make its selection inevitable; or a number of eminently practicable routes might be discovered. It is not surprising, therefore, that once the idea of a transcontinental railway had fairly gripped the imagination of the American people, the study of the geography of the region to be traversed was taken up with great zeal.

Interested persons, and they were legion, pounced with avidity upon the various geographical items germane to the

5 See below, ch. vi.

subject as they came in. Accounts of western exploration and travel published before a Pacific railroad had been thought of were eagerly examined.[6] The fragmentary accounts of emigrants, travelers, trappers, and guides as well as the more formal ones of official and unofficial explorers were grist for the mill. One cannot but admire the dexterity with which various persons wove items of information culled from many diverse sources into detailed descriptions of "the most practicable, cheapest, and most advantageous" route. And one is sometimes amazed at the assurance and show of erudition with which politicians, lawyers, business men, and even preachers[7] demonstrated the superiority of their several favorite routes over all others. It is a remarkable fact that, before instrumental surveys had been made or even thorough reconnaissances by trained engineers, well-informed people had in mind as probably practicable routes the approximate locations of nearly all the transcontinental railroads of today.

When Asa Whitney first proposed his plan he undoubtedly had only slight knowledge of the topography of the region to be traversed. Much of his route followed the emigrant trail to Oregon. In the summer of 1845, he made a hurried reconnoitering expedition to the Missouri and beyond and then down the river some distance.[8] He thereby convinced himself of the impossibility of bridging the Mississippi and Missouri lower down than Prairie du Chien and Sioux City. The same

[6] Especially popular and useful were: Nicholas Biddle, *Lewis and Clark Expedition* (1814); Zebulon M. Pike, *Journal* (1806); Edwin H. James, compiler, *Account of an Expedition to the Rocky Mountains Performed in the Years 1819, 1820 . . . under the Command of Maj. S. H. Long* (1823); Alexander von Humboldt, *Political Essay on the Kingdom of New Spain* (4 vols., London, 1814); Charles Wilkes, *Exploring Expedition, 1838-42* (1845); Thos. Nuttall, *Travels into the Arkansas Territory, 1819-20* (1821); Washington Irving, *The Rocky Mountains: or Scenes, Incidents, and Adventures in the Far West; Digested from the Journal of Capt. L. E. Bonneville* (1837); Josiah Gregg, *Commerce of the Prairies, or the Journal of a Santa Fe Trader, 1831-39* (1844); and Geo. W. Kendall, *Narrative of an Expedition across the Great Southwestern Prairies from Texas to Santa Fe* (1844 and later). There was a partial list of such works in John Loughborough's *Pacific Telegraph and Railway* (1849), 75-78. Lt. J. K. Warren summarized the findings of all earlier surveys in 1859, in *Pacific Railway Surveys*, XI, No. 1.

[7] For examples: Rev. W. Adams, of Chicago, *Chicago Daily Jour.*, Sept. 11, 12, 1849; Rev. Calvin Colton, *A Lecture on the Railroad to the Pacific, Aug. 12, 1850, at the Smithsonian Institute.* . . .

[8] *Memorial of A. Whitney . . .* (1846), 3-5.

year John C. Frémont's report of his first two expeditions was published, the first scientific description of much the greater part of the route.[9] Frémont's report was not very favorable. By 1849, Whitney had decided, by some process which he did not make clear, perhaps by a more intensive study of Biddle's *Lewis and Clark Expedition*, that he could save 300 miles and the difficult descent of the Snake River by crossing the Missouri higher up at the mouth of the White River, following that stream to near its source, thence going somehow across the headwaters of the Yellowstone and Missouri to the Salmon River and down it to the Columbia. This amended route lay across the Black Hills and other extremely difficult country and would have been all but impossible. But Whitney and his supporters never spent much time discussing details of engineering. They claimed their route was the shortest, ran through the most extensive areas of cultivable land, and had the most timber and water on it. Only on this route, they said, would the sale of the public lands build the road.[10]

When Stephen A. Douglas, 1845, proposed his route from Chicago to San Francisco Bay he probably knew of the possibility of bridging the Mississippi at Rock Island and the Missouri at Council Bluffs. He knew something also of the Platte Valley and South Pass; for the Oregon Trail ran that way. Of the country beyond the point where the route must diverge from the Oregon Trail, he could not have known very much. A few pioneers and fur traders had traversed the region. Frémont supplied about the earliest scientific information in his report published in 1845. On his second expedition, 1843-44, he had followed the Oregon Trail to the mouth of the Columbia, with a side trip from Fort Hall to Salt Lake, explored the eastern base of the Cascades and the Sierra Nevada from the Dalles on the Columbia to Carson, crossed the Sierra by Truckee Pass in winter, and descended the South Fork of the American River to Sacramento. On his third

[9] *Sen. Docs.*, 28 Cong., 2 Sess., XI (461), No. 174, and in numerous commercial editions.

[10] Asa Whitney, *Project for a Railroad to the Pacific*, chs. iii, iv; letters in *Am. R. R. Jour.*, XXI, 773, 787, 805; *H. Repts.*, 30 Cong., 1 Sess., No. 733 (526).

expedition, in 1845, he went around the southern end of Great
Salt Lake, down the Valley of the Humboldt, and over the
Sierra Nevada by Truckee Pass, as before.[11] Information of
mountain passes and other features trickled in from travelers
and emigrants. Early in 1849, John Loughborough, St. Louis
lawyer, who had made the most exhaustive study of the subject to that time, could describe the route in great detail to
the Sierra Nevada and assert that there were three practicable
passes over those mountains of which Truckee Pass (now used
by the Southern Pacific) was the preferable one.[12] Advocates
of this route claimed that South Pass (which no railroad has
ever used) was the only practicable pass in the Rockies between Lewis and Clark's crossing at about the 47th parallel
and the southern boundary of the United States.

In the first suggestions of a southern route, no intervening
physical features between the Mississippi and the Pacific were
named.[13] The necessities of the Mexican War soon took a
number of trained observers into New Mexico whose reports
and accounts furnished reliable information. Especially valuable was the report of Major W. H. Emory of the Topographical Engineers, who accompanied General Phil Kearney
on his march from Fort Leavenworth to California by way of
Santa Fe and the valleys of the Rio Grande and Gila, 1846.[14]
A Colonel Cooke found a route (thereafter known as Cooke's
wagon route) south of the Gila for Kearney's wagon train.[15]
A Dr. Wislezenius, who accompanied the Doniphan expedition
from Santa Fe into Chihuahua, 1847, took barometric readings
for altitudes. Before the end of 1848, people of Tennessee
and Arkansas were describing a route from Memphis to the

[11] No formal report of this expedition was made, but a careful map accompanied by a *Geographical Memoir* was submitted and the Senate ordered
20,000 copies printed. See A. Nevins, *Fremont, the West's Greatest Adventurer*,
II, 392 (1928).
[12] *The Pacific Telegraph and Railway, an Examination of All the Projects
for the Construction of these Works* . . . (1849); also in *West. Jour. and
Civilian*, I, 644-50, II, 9-28, 105-21, 148-61, 288-98, 386-436.
[13] Letter of M. F. Maury to J. C. Calhoun, Mar. 29, 1848, *Am. R. R. Jour.*,
XXI, 457-58.
[14] *Sen. Exec. Docs.*, 30 Cong., 1 Sess., No. 41 (508); also commercially published, 1848.
[15] *Ibid.*

Arkansas River, up that stream and the Canadian branch thereof, over to Santa Fe, down the Rio Grande to El Paso, thence to and down the Gila and across the Colorado and southern California to San Diego.[16] The section from Fort Smith, Arkansas, to Santa Fe was not capably explored until Captain R. B. Marcy went over it in the summer of 1849.[17]

This zigzag route through Santa Fe and El Paso had hardly been proposed before Sam Houston suggested that the road could run from Galveston to El Paso.[18] Colonel J. J. Abert, Chief of the Topographical Engineers, suggested a continuation of the Gila route through San Antonio and Nacogdoches, Texas.[19] In the summer of 1849 Lieutenant W. H. C. Whiting explored a new route from San Antonio to El Paso.[20] The Pacific Railroad Convention in Memphis, October 1849, expressed a preference for a route from Memphis which entered northeastern Texas between the 32d and 33d parallels and crossed the state to El Paso.[21] Advocates of the route to El Paso via Santa Fe now dropped it for the route across Texas. Thereafter the terms "Gila route," "El Paso route," and "32d-parallel route" implied the crossing of Texas from east to west. The great advantages of this route were represented by its advocates to be a salubrious climate, making it possible to operate a railroad the year round without obstruction, an exceptionally low pass in the Rockies (not yet precisely located), the shortest length, low cost of construction, a terminus on the Mississippi below the mouth of most of its great navigable branches, and easy connections with the Gulf.[22]

In the Memphis Convention, a Dr. Lea proposed a route from Memphis to Santa Fe by way of the Canadian as already described, thence westward through the Navajo country, across the Colorado at about the 35th parallel, through the Sierra

[16] *Memphis* (Tri-weekly) *Appeal*, Jan. 20, 1849; *DeBow's Rev.*, VII, 12.
[17] *Sen. Exec. Docs.*, 31 Cong., 1 Sess., XIV (562), No. 64; also commercially published, 1852.
[18] *DeBow's Rev.*, VIII, 1ff.; J. Loughborough, *op. cit.*, 11.
[19] *H. Repts.*, 30 Cong., 2 Sess., II (546), No. 145, App.
[20] *Sen. Exec. Docs.*, 31 Cong., 1 Sess., XIV (562), No. 64.
[21] See below, p. 50f.
[22] *DeBow's Rev.*, VII, 1-31; *Mississippi and Pacific Railroad, Circular Address to the People of the U. S.* (in behalf of the Memphis Convention).

Nevada by Tehachapi Pass, and through the Tulare and San Joaquin valleys to San Francisco.[23] Colonel Abert and Lieutenant Peck had explored north and west of Santa Fe and Lieutenant Colonel Galpin had gone west from Santa Fe across the Sierra Madre in 1847.[24] Frémont and his men had explored the San Joaquin and Tulare valleys and Tehachapi and other passes on his second and third expeditions. The details of the route were filled in slowly. By 1851 and 1852 it had its champions and was commonly spoken of as the "35th-degree" or "Albuquerque" route.[25] Shortly Congressman J. S. Phelps, of Springfield, Missouri, became its most ardent champion. He, however, would have the road start at St. Louis and run down through Springfield to the Canadian.

Most people in St. Louis and central and northern Missouri looked with favor upon the South Pass route. St. Joseph and Independence, the Missouri points of departure, could be readily connected with the Platte Valley by following the emigrant trails. But in 1848 Senator Benton began to champion a route from Independence up the Kansas River, over to the great bend of the Arkansas, up that stream and through the Rockies at a pass, "Cochatope," near the 38th parallel, thence across what are now southern Utah and Nevada, over the Sierra Nevada by Walker's or Tejon Pass (near the 37th parallel), and down the San Joaquin Valley to San Francisco. This route from the eastern base of the Rockies westward had been explored by Frémont alone, and he, like his father-in-law, became its ardent advocate.[26] On his return from his second expedition, 1844, he had skirted the eastern edge of the Great Basin from south to north, had crossed the Wasatch and Uinta Mountains, and had then gone through the Rockies to the Arkansas River and down that stream to the Santa Fe Trail. On his fourth expedition, 1848, which was probably largely financed by persons interested in finding a railroad

[23] *Memphis Appeal*, Nov. 20, 1849.
[24] Loughborough, *op. cit.*, 15-16.
[25] *Am. R. R. Jour.*, XXIV, 359; *Cong. Globe*, 32 Cong., 2 Sess., 320-21.
[26] *Daily Mo. Republican*, Oct. 31, 1849; *Proceedings of the Convention in Favor of a Railroad to the Pacific Ocean . . . in Philadelphia . . . 1850*, pp. 28-36; *Am. R. R. Jour.*, XXV, 492.

route in that latitude, he attempted a winter crossing at the head of the Arkansas, lost his way, suffered a great disaster to his party, and had to abandon the attempt and follow the Gila route instead.[27] Subsequently, 1853-54, he did make a winter crossing of the Rockies by Cochatope, but he did not find a pass in the Sierra Nevada in the same latitude. Benton, Frémont, and their following asserted that theirs was the most direct route to San Francisco, crossed fewer rivers than any other, and was well wooded and watered. The terrain was obviously difficult; but if the route was practicable at all, St. Louis was the obvious terminus.

In 1852 some people in Wisconsin began to discuss a route just below the Canadian border from the head of Lake Superior to Puget Sound.[28] It was first described in detail, with modifications, in a book by Edwin F. Johnson, civil engineer, published in 1853.[29] Johnson had it run from Chicago via St. Paul, pass around the northern bend of the Missouri River, and cross the Rockies by Lewis' or some other pass to Clark's River. So little had the western portions of this route been explored that Johnson had to get most of his information from Lewis and Clark's *Journals*. The great advantages claimed for the route were its easy connection with the most western point of the greatest body of inland waterways in the world, the presence of more arable land than on any other route, its termination on the best harbor on the Pacific, and its saving in distance on the way to Asia.

Controversy over the comparative merits of these various routes waxed warm. Advocates of the Gila route attacked the South Pass route on the grounds that no practicable pass had been found in the Sierra Nevada, that snows would interfere with the operation of a railroad, and that the cost would be prohibitive. Friends of other routes quoted all the authorities, especially Frémont himself, to prove there was no practicable pass in the Rockies at the head of the Arkansas on Benton's route. The champions of all the more northern

[27] A. Nevins, *Frémont*, II, ch. xxiv.
[28] *Am. R. R. Jour.*, XXV, 492 (letter of Rep. Jas. D. Doty).
[29] *Railroad to the Pacific, Northern Route; Its General Character, Relative Merits. . . .*

routes trained their guns on the Gila route.  It lay, they said, in a parched and barren desert, with a climate very deleterious to articles of commerce.  In Texas east of El Paso lay the terrible Llano Estacado, or Staked Plain, where no water cound be found for man, beast, or "iron horse."  The Whitney route and the 49th degree route, when it was developed, were attacked as too far north to meet the commercial needs of any but the northern tier of states.  They also would be blocked by snow and ice.  Proponents of the northern and southern routes portrayed as a great obstacle to the construction of a railroad on a central route that the lands west of Arkansas, Missouri, and Iowa had been set aside for Indians and the title guaranteed to them in perpetuity by solemn treaties.

It was well understood everywhere, of course, that the selection of a route for a Pacific railroad would be greatly influenced by the choice of a Pacific terminus.  After the gold rush San Francisco grew amazingly and soon became fixed in the public mind as the future metropolis of the Pacific.  Friends of the three central routes made the most of this.  Champions of the Gila route asserted that San Diego had a salubrious climate and commodious harbor and would be made a great city by the road.  Furthermore the road could be extended to San Francisco and the length would still be less than by any other route, they said.  Asa Whitney and the champions of the 49th degree route contended that the remarkable growth of California and San Francisco was due merely to the gold rush and would prove but a flash in the pan.  The future of the Pacific coast lay with Oregon because of its great agricultural resources.  At any rate the great object of a Pacific railroad was to carry the Asia trade in comparison with which the California trade would be but a trifle.  More southern routes than theirs would not have sufficient advantage in time and distance over the water routes to deflect the Asiatic commerce from them.  California could be taken care of by a branch.

It was not enough to have the most eligible route.  Proponents of that route must also present a practical plan for building the railroad thereon.

In the short session of the 30th Congress, December, 1848-March, 1849, it was the Whitney route and plan against the field. A select committee of the Senate tried to have a Whitney bill taken up for consideration.[30] Borland, of Arkansas, thought surveys should be made first. Houston, of Texas, had a plan and a route. Benton announced his long-promised plan for a "Central National Highway." It should run from St. Louis to California with a branch to Oregon, be built by the government, financed by the proceeds of public lands sales, and leased to private corporations for operation.[31] A House select committee, dominated by Eastern members, reported adversely to a Whitney bill in particular and a Pacific railroad in general.[32] The committee preferred an isthmian canal. Congress merely appropriated $50,000 for further western explorations.

After Congress adjourned, private persons tried their hands at framing a plan more acceptable than Whitney's and better adapted to their respective favorite routes. The New York Chamber of Commerce offered a modified form of Whitney's plan.[33] H. V. Poor, editor of the *American Railroad Journal,* proposed that the route be selected and the road be built by a board consisting of one member from each state, chosen by the respective legislatures, the board to be constituted a body corporate. The road should be financed from the proceeds of the public land sales and other moneys supplied by the federal government.[34] John Loughborough, of Missouri, proposed a plan;[35] so also did Albert Pike, poet, soldier, and politician, of Arkansas.[36] Both of these gentlemen will be heard from again. Mr. P. P. F. De Grand, Boston railroad man, had ideas. He proposed a joint-stock company with a capital of $100,000,000, of which $2,000,000 should be subscribed by private persons and the remainder loaned by the federal government at 6%. The government should also grant in aid a

---

[30] *Cong. Globe,* 30 Cong., 2 Sess., 381.
[31] *Ibid.,* 473.
[32] *H. Repts.,* 30 Cong., 2 Sess., II (546), No. 145.
[33] *Hunt's Merchants' Mag.,* XXI, 415-22; *Am. R. R. Jour.,* XXII, 519.
[34] *Ibid.,* XXII, 614, 647, XXIII, 228.
[35] Loughborough, *op. cit.,* 20-46.
[36] *Am. R. R. Jour.,* XXII, 806; *Memphis* (Tri-weekly) *Appeal,* Nov. 27, 1849.

strip of land ten miles wide and the length of the road. The government would own one half the stock and appoint one half the directors and would hold a mortgage on the road as security for its loan. By this plan, with men working day and night in three shifts, De Grand believed the road could be built in five years. This came to be spoken of as the "Boston Plan" and appealed to "capitalists." [37]

In the summer of 1849, public spirited citizens of St. Louis and of Memphis, desirous of putting the claims of their respective cities before the public and hoping to crystallize public sentiment upon some particular plan of construction, called national Pacific railroad conventions to meet in October.[38] Both conventions aroused great interest. Over a thousand "delegates" appeared at St. Louis. Although the majority came from Missouri and Illinois, fourteen states were represented, including Louisiana, Virginia, Pennsylvania, and New York. About four hundred delegates assembled at Memphis from fifteen states.

Before the St. Louis convention met, a meeting was held in Chicago to determine the policy of the large delegation from the Windy City.[39] Senator Douglas, now a resident of Chicago, dominated the meeting. He reiterated his objections to Whitney's route and plan. He asked the meeting to give him its moral support in violating the instructions in behalf of Whitney's scheme that the Legislature had given him in 1847; and he promised to use his influence to get the obnoxious instructions repealed by a forthcoming special session of the Legislature. (They were repealed.) He criticized Colonel Benton's plan also, principally on the ground that it designated the route in advance of surveys. He offered a series of resolutions designed to guide the delegation. Those resolutions declared that the route should be fixed by Congress only after surveys should have been made but expressed the belief that

[37] *Proceedings of the Friends of a Rail-road to San Francisco at Their Meeting ... in Boston, April 19, 1849; West. Journal and Civilian*, III, 1-12, 193-201.
[38] *Proceedings of the National Railroad Convention* [St. Louis], 9-11; *Mississippi and Pacific Rail Road: Circular Address to the People of the U. S.* (pamphlet in behalf of the Memphis Convention).
[39] Springfield *Ill. Daily Jour.*, Oct. 24, 1849; *Chicago Daily Jour.*, Oct. 5, 12, Nov. 8; St. Louis *Daily Mo. Republican*, Oct. 12.

the route from Council Bluffs by way of South Pass would be found to possess more advantages than any other. Since the proposed route began west of the Missouri and lay entirely within the territories, no question could arise of the constitutional power of the federal government to construct a road within a state. Congress should encourage the building of branches from the Missouri River to Chicago, St. Louis, and either Cairo or Memphis by grants of public lands to the states through which they would run. This, it may be remarked, was one of the earliest suggestions for combining rival interests. The meeting unanimously adopted Douglas's resolutions. When the Chicago delegates met with down-state delegates, the latter objected to the resolutions on routes as cunningly devised to commit the state in favor of a Chicago terminus. The caucus accordingly tabled all resolutions relating to routes and adopted the others.[40] The Iowa delegation, however, adopted the Douglas resolutions *in toto*.

The Missouri delegation was unable to agree in caucus on any line of action.[41] The Democratic party in the state was divided into warring factions, one led by Benton. Benton was engaged in a desperate fight for reëlection to the United States Senate. His opponents charged that his plan for a "central national highway" was got up only to further his candidacy and were disposed to oppose it because it might do so.[42] The first day of the convention Benton managed to make a two-hour speech in advocacy of his route. A Judge Birch, of the vicinity of St. Joseph, offered and defended a resolution that the railroad should follow the South Pass route with a starting point on the Missouri "at about the 40th parallel." (St. Joseph is about fifteen miles south of the parallel.) He believed, he said, the resolution represented the sense of the majority of the Missouri delegation. Thereupon, Governor King, a partisan of Benton, addressed the convention from the gallery. The Legislature, he said, had almost unanimously chartered the Pacific Railroad of Missouri with the under-

40 *Chicago Daily Jour.*, Oct. 22, 1849.
41 St. Louis *Daily Mo. Republican*, Oct. 16, 1849.
42 *Ibid.*, July 12, 19, Sept. 10, 13, 15, 1849; *Am. R. R. Journal*, XXII, 711.

standing that St. Louis was to be the terminus, and no one had dreamed of the 40th parallel. Furthermore the Legislature had endorsed Benton's route and tendered its thanks to him.[43]

Douglas replied to Benton in a mass meeting held the evening of the second day. He had been made permanent chairman of the convention and could not well speak there. Congressman Bowlin, of Missouri, replied to Douglas and flayed the Illinois Legislature for refusing to charter railroads in Illinois having St. Louis as their destination. Douglas defended the Legislature and charged St. Louis with trying to turn a national convention to her own exclusive benefit. Later he accused the Missouri delegation of having had him made permanent chairman in order to muzzle him.

On the third day a row broke out over the constitutional power of the federal government to build a railroad within a state. Those who believed the federal government possessed such power wanted to ask the government to build the road from a point on the Mississippi, and that, to most of them, meant St. Louis. Those who believed the federal government did not possess such power and those who would avoid controversy on the point wished to ask the federal government to build the road in the territories, and, for most delegates, that meant the railroad must start at Council Bluffs or, possibly, St. Joseph. Congressman Smith, of Indiana, having made a strong speech in support of the first view and of the claims of St. Louis, Douglas resigned the chair and replied. The connection between the constitution of the United States and the terminus of a Pacific railroad was a subtle one indeed: If the federal government could extend money aid only in the territories, it could give only a land grant in aid within states. The public lands were about taken up along the route of the proposed Pacific Railroad of Missouri, and, therefore, a land grant on the alternate-sections principle would not help much; but a land grant for a road from Council Bluffs to Rock Island,

[43] Proceedings in *ibid.*, XXII, 663-64, 690-93, 720-23; *Proceedings of the National Railroad Convention*; St. Louis *Daily Mo. Republican*, Oct. 16-19, 1849; *Chicago Daily Jour.*, Oct. 18-26; *West. Jour. and Civilian*, III, 70-75, 140; J. Loughborough, *op. cit.*, iii-xii. *Cf.* R. S. Cotterill, "The National Railroad Convention in St. Louis, 1849," *Mo. Hist. Rev.*, XII, 203-15.

on the contrary, or even from St. Joseph to Hannibal would be quite helpful.

Eventually the convention accepted a compromise, drafted by John Loughborough. The resolutions declared it to be the duty of Congress to "provide for" (not necessarily to construct) a grand trunk railway from the "Mississippi Valley" with branches to Memphis, St. Louis, and Chicago. They asserted the constitutional power of Congress to build the railroad in the territories but passed no judgment on its power with regard to internal improvements within states. They recommended that Congress construct or authorize the construction of a line of telegraph along the route. As a preliminary measure they recommended the establishment of a line of military posts along the route and the encouragement of settlement thereon by sales or grants of lands on liberal terms. No way of financing the railroad was suggested.

After appointing a committee to represent the convention at Memphis the following week and another to present the resolutions to Congress, the St. Louis convention adjourned to meet at Philadelphia the following April — Philadelphia was friendly to a St. Louis terminus.

The Memphis convention was not so stormy as the St. Louis gathering.[44] Party politics could not be kept out entirely. Some of the delegates, as might be expected in such stirring times, showed strong sectional bias; but Asa Whitney was given a respectful hearing. Isthmian projects had strong champions, notably the distinguished Lieutenant M. F. Maury, director of the Naval Observatory at Washington, the chairman of the convention. While Maury approved of a Pacific railroad, he believed an isthmian canal would be worth "ten railroads" in a commercial way. The Louisiana delegation came up with instructions to approve the Gila route for a railroad, whatever the eastern terminus, and, especially, to get

[44] Proceedings in *Minutes and Proceedings of the Memphis Convention, Assembled Oct. 23, 1849;* Memphis (Tri-weekly) *Appeal,* Oct. 25, 27, 30; St. Louis *Daily Mo. Republican,* Oct. 30, Nov. 2; *Am. R. R. Jour.,* XXII, 709-11; J. Loughborough, *op. cit.,* xii-xv. Cf. R. S. Cotterill, "The Memphis Railroad Convention, 1849." *Tenn. Hist. Mag.,* IV, 83-94.

a resolution in favor of the project for a railroad across the Isthmus of Tehuantepec.

The delegation sent down by the St. Louis convention made a strong effort to secure concurrence in the resolutions adopted there. If the Memphis convention would concur, said John Loughborough, who acted as spokesman, nothing would be left for Congress but "to execute the national will." The general resolutions adopted bore some resemblance to those of St. Louis. They declared it to be the duty of Congress to "provide" for a railroad from the "Mississippi" to the Pacific. Surveys should first be made by competent engineers; and then that route should be chosen which was "easiest of access, best calculated to subserve the purposes of national defense, most convenient to the people of, and as far as practicable, central to, the United States, and upon which a railroad can be constructed on the cheapest and best terms." The public lands were a proper fund for financing the road. Congress should grant lands to the states in aid of branches to the Lakes, to the Gulf, and to points on the Mississippi where the best connection could be had with lines of improvement leading to the East. But, in spite of strenuous efforts to defeat it, a supplementary resolution was adopted recommending the Gila route to the "particular attention" of the federal government with a terminus on the Mississippi between the mouth of the Ohio and the mouth of the Red River. Another special resolution recommended as a preliminary measure the establishment of a line of military posts along the southern boundary and the encouragement of settlements about the posts by liberal grants of land to settlers. Still another special resolution approved isthmian projects as of great advantage to the country until the railroad should be built. No preference was stated among the isthmian routes. The convention further showed its unwillingness to play into the hands of St. Louis by refusing to adjourn to Philadelphia.

It will have been noted that the Memphis convention showed less reluctance than the one at St. Louis to request the federal government to construct internal improvements within a state. The reason is simple: the railroad could not well be built by the 32d-degree route, it was believed, unless federal aid could be secured for the long section across Texas.

In spite of the demonstrations made at St. Louis and Memphis in behalf of other routes and plans, the committee on roads and canals in both the House and Senate in the ensuing session of Congress reported in favor of the Whitney scheme.[45] The gist of the reports was that no other plan met the question of means. The conventions, said the House Report, "have pointed out *no means* of executing their respective plans, except by a dependence on the national treasury; and, the committee think, that if those conventions had been brought to the question of means they would have been confounded." Congress took no further action, except to appropriate another $50,000 to continue explorations. This was the session of the great sectional quarrel over slavery which culminated in the Compromise of 1850, and Congress had little time for other matters.

At the National Railroad Convention which met in Philadelphia in April, 1850, an attempt to secure an endorsement of the Whitney plan failed. The convention considered also De Grand's plan, Benton's, H. V. Poor's, the Rhode Island plan, and the St. Louis Convention plan. Counsels were divided. Eventually resolutions were adopted similar to those of St. Louis. The majority of the delegates clearly favored a route from St. Louis by way of South Pass.[46]

The spell of the Whitney project, it was now evident, had at last been broken. Whitney had been unfortunate in selecting a route too far north and topographically impracticable. Natural and logical though the selection had been at the time he made it, the progress of events had designated another terminus on the Pacific and raised up too many rivals better located for eastern railroad connections. Whitney's scheme would have put more power into the hands of one man than

[45] *H. Repts.*, 31 Cong., 1 Sess., I (583), No. 140; *Sen. Repts.*, 31 Cong., 1 Sess., I (565), No. 194.
[46] *Proceedings of the Convention in Favor of a National Railroad to the Pacific Ocean . . . in Philadelphia, April 1st, 2nd, and 3rd, 1850; Am. R. R. Jour.*, XXIII, 228-31.

the American people had been willing to entrust, at least since the days of Nicholas Biddle. Furthermore, Whitney's plan did not promise that early completion of the railroad which public opinion was coming to demand — it promised an earlier completion than the public got, in fact. Opponents in fighting Whitney's plan often ridiculed his method for financing the road and impeached his motives. Looking back now, Asa Whitney's purposes appear to have been thoroughly honorable and public spirited and his vision statesmanlike. In view of the rapidity with which the Trans-Missouri West was settled, it is highly probable that a road could have been built by his method. Whether it could have earned the cost of its operation and upkeep had it been constructed is highly problematical.

The executive branch of the federal government under Taylor and Fillmore showed little interest in the Pacific railroad project as compared with its great concern for isthmian transits. The small appropriations made in 1849 and 1850 for surveys of transcontinental routes were only partially expended, and the sums so expended were devoted to scattered and rather futile explorations.[47]

[47] *Cong. Globe*, 31 Cong., 2 Sess., App., 9 (Report of the Secretary of War).

# CHAPTER IV

## THE PANAMA RAILROAD

ISTHMIAN projects, as might be expected, took tangible form earlier than transcontinental railway schemes. They did not call for such huge amounts of private capital and promised earlier returns upon investments. They did not seem to require great expenditures by the government but rather diplomatic assistance. The latter was readily given; in fact it could not well be refused considering the great political and economic stakes involved. More or less fortuitous circumstances made the Panama Railroad the first eminently successful project.

December 12, 1846, while the Mexican War was in progress, Benjamin A. Bidlack, United States chargé d'affaires at Bogota, signed a treaty with New Granada that secured to the government and citizens of the United States the uninterrupted transit of the Isthmus of Panama by any wagon road, railroad, or canal which might be constructed upon the same terms that the government and citizens of New Granada should enjoy. In return for these privileges the United States was to guarantee the "perfect neutrality" of the isthmus and the "rights of sovereignty and property" of New Granada over the said territory. Bidlack, it seems, acted without specific instructions. The initiative came from the government of New Granada, which had become suspicious of the intentions of Great Britain and France, particularly the former, in the isthmian region.[1]

Because of the departure from established policy which the guarantee of neutrality and sovereignty would involve, Presi-

[1] Art. XXXV. Text in Wm. M. Malloy, Comp., *Treaties, Conventions, International Acts, Protocols and Agreements between the United States of America and Other Powers, 1776-1901*, I, 302-14. See S. F. Bemis, *A Diplomatic Hist. of the U. S.*, 244-46; J. B. Lockey, "A Neglected Aspect of Isthmian Diplomacy," *Am. Hist. Rev.*, XLI (Jan., 1936), 295-305.

dent Polk accepted Bidlack's treaty reluctantly. In submitting
it to the Senate, February, 1847, he argued that such a departure was justified by the urgent importance of communication with the Pacific and the virtual indispensability of such a
guarantee to the construction and operation of a railroad or
canal in the isthmian region. The object of the treaty, he said,
was commercial, not political. It was not exclusive; for it
secured to all nations the free and equal passage of the isthmus. Any other nation might make a similar guarantee if it
should choose to do so.[2] The Senate postponed consideration
until the next session, a protracted debate on the guarantee
having threatened.[3] In the next session, however, it ratified
the treaty by a large majority, June 8, 1848. The Senate was
no doubt influenced in its action by British activities near the
Nicaragua route and Trist's failure to get the right of transit
across the Isthmus of Tehuantepec at the conclusion of the
Mexican War.[4]

In accordance with President Polk's statement that the
treaty was not exclusive, Secretary of State Buchanan requested Crampton, the British minister, to ascertain the views
of Lord Palmerston in regard to an accession by Great Britain
and France or other commercial power to the guarantee of
the isthmus.[5] Palmerston made no reply. Buchanan's successor, Clayton, formally requested the British government
to make a treaty with New Granada similar to the American.[6]
The British did not heed this request; but by a clause in the
Clayton-Bulwer treaty, signed April 19, 1850, that government agreed to extend its protection jointly with the United
States to any practicable communication across the Isthmus of
Panama or the Isthmus of Tehuantepec as well as to the proposed Nicaraguan canal.[7]

Meanwhile, upon recommendations by the Secretary of the

[2] Richardson, *Messages*, IV, 511.
[3] John Bassett Moore, ed., *The Works of James Buchanan*, VII, 252-54.
[4] See below p. 62; above, p. 14.
[5] *Cong. Globe*, 32 Cong., 2 Sess., App., 252.
[6] Lawrence to Palmerston, Dec. 14, 1849, *Parliamentary Papers*, 1856, LX,
No. 13; Crampton to Clayton, Feb. 20, 1853, *John M. Clayton Papers* (Lib. of
Cong.).
[7] Below, p. 72.

Treasury and the Postmaster General, Congress, by act of
March 3, 1847, had authorized the Secretary of the Navy to
enter into contracts for the transportation of the mails by
steamships from New York and New Orleans to Chagres and
from Panama to Oregon. The contracts were duly let and a
supplementary contract was made for the transportation of
mails across the isthmus.[8] Steamships were put on the routes
just in time to reap a rich harvest from the gold rush to California. The contract for carrying the mails on the Pacific side
was assigned to William H. Aspinwall and associates, who
organized the Pacific Mail Steamship Company.

At the time of the gold rush, people and merchandise were
conveyed across the Isthmus of Panama in native bungos on
the Chagres River for a part of the way and upon pack mules
over execrable roads for the remainder. Aspinwall and his
associates at once saw the importance of improving the facilities. After consultation with officials in Washington, they
sent one of their number with a skilled engineer, the winter
of 1847-48, to make a preliminary examination.[9] Their report
convinced the associates that only a railroad would meet the
requirements. The government of New Granada had already, 1847, awarded a contract for building a wagon road
or a railroad across the Isthmus to a French "Panama Company." This company, however, failed to post the required
guarantee of good faith and forfeited its contract. Thereupon Aspinwall, Stephens, and Chauncey stepped in and secured it, with modifications, December 21, 1848.

The contract granted was most liberal. The contractors
were given eight years to build the road. After its completion
they were to have the exclusive privilege for 49 years of
operating a transit by railroad, turnpike, or canal. They received the right of way and a large grant of land and were
permitted to select their own route. They might fix their own

[8] Repts. of the Sec'y of the Treas. and the P. M. Gen., *Cong. Globe*, 29 Cong.,
2 Sess., App., 12, 22; rept. of the Sec'y of the Navy, *ibid.*, 30 Cong., 1 Sess.,
App., 25; rept. of the P. M. Gen., *ibid.*, 30 Cong., 2 Sess., App., 27; rept. of
the Sec'y of the Navy, *ibid.*, 31 Cong., 1 Sess., App., 13.
[9] F. N. Otis, *Illustrated Hist. of the Panama R. R.* . . . , 17; *H. Repts.*, 30
Cong., 2 Sess., I (545), No. 26, p. 22.

tolls, provided they be uniform and no preference be given to the citizens of one nation over those of another. The ports at the terminals were to be free ports. New Granada was to receive 3% of all dividends and retained the right to purchase the work after twenty years.[10]

In June, 1848, months before the contract with New Granada was signed, books of the Panama Railroad Company had been opened in New York City and the stock promptly subscribed.[11] The Legislature of New York granted a charter, authorizing a capital stock of $1,000,000 with the privilege of increasing it to $5,000,000. A large party of engineers under Colonel George W. Hughes of the United States Topographical Engineers was sent down early in 1849 to locate the railroad. In due course the engineers submitted a quite favorable report.[12] Meanwhile Aspinwall and his associates, encouraged by the ratification of the transit treaty with New Granada and numerous other signs of public interest in communication with the Pacific, memorialized Congress to encourage the prompt construction of the road by a twenty-years contract for transporting government officials, troops, munitions, and army and navy supplies. They did not ask for a contract for carrying the mails as they felt certain of getting that anyway.

Aspinwall's memorial drew a favorable report from the House Committee on Naval Affairs.[13] The report described the advantages which a Panama railroad would give the United States in its struggle with Great Britain for the commerce of the Pacific, the great traffic which would spring up with California, and spoke disparagingly of a rival project on the Isthmus of Tehuantepec. The argument was advanced that, in making the proposed contract with the Panama Company, the government would have an opportunity to impose limitations upon the rates which the company might establish. The bill that was introduced in accordance with the report

---

[10] *Ibid.*, 26ff.; *Panama Railroad Co. Capital $1,000,000* (Prospectus, 1849), 29-51.
[11] *Am. R. R. Jour.*, XXII, 408.
[12] *Panama Railroad Co. . . .* , 6-9.
[13] *H. Repts.*, 30 Cong., 2 Sess., I (545), No. 26.

provided for restrictions on charges which the company was unwilling to accept.[14] A Senate bill on the same subject, brought in by Benton, chairman of the Committee on Military Affairs, authorized the Secretary of the Navy to make the proposed contract for twenty years with compensation of $300,000 per annum, the contractors to begin their railroad within one year from June 1, 1849, and complete it within three years.[15]

The debates on the Senate bill gave an illuminating forecast of future alignments of individuals and even sections on propositions for aiding various projects for communication with the Pacific.[16] Douglas, of Illinois, Dayton, of New Jersey, and Cameron, of Pennsylvania, supported the bill almost without qualification. John M. Clayton, of Delaware, and Daniel Webster preferred the Tehuantepec route but considered it unavailable in view of the attitude of Mexico and, therefore, supported the bill as aiding the only railroad in immediate prospect. Benton regarded a Panama railroad as necessary temporarily until a transcontinental railroad could be provided. He wished no arrangements "which are to keep me out of my own country one moment beyond the time we are able to finish our road." Niles, of Connecticut, a champion of the Asa Whitney scheme, Underwood, of Kentucky, and Jefferson Davis, opposed aiding the Panama railroad at all as likely to postpone a railroad on American soil. Said Davis: "If that people [on the Pacific coast] are to be bound permanently to the Union, if it is to be made their interest in all time to come to remain a portion of the United States, then I say it is necessary that a ready and accessible means of communication must be continuous; towns, villages, and hamlets, must extend along the communication, from the seat of the General Government until we stand upon the shores of the Pacific. This must be our ulterior object, and all other measures in reference to the subject must be considered as temporary expedients

[14] *Panama Railroad Co. . . .* , 3.
[15] *Cong. Globe*, 30 Cong., 2 Sess., 40.
[16] *Ibid.*, 49-52, 59-60, 398-402, 411-15, 457-63, 626.

only." [17] Several senators were opposed to aiding a monopoly. One or two thought the United States government itself should construct the railroad. Strict constructionists denied the constitutionality of the proposed subsidy. Other senators said, truthfully, that the railroad would be constructed even if the government should give no aid.

The most determined opposition to the Panama bill came from a small group of senators who had become interested in the as-yet-immatured Tehuantepec project. Foote, of Mississippi, Downs, of Louisiana, and Wescott, of Florida, were the most talkative of the group. The pertinacity of this group defeated the bill in the short session, and it was never revived. The company decided, apparently, that it would be better to bargain with the government after the road should have been constructed, "when its services are found to be indispensable." [18]

The company let the contract for building the railroad to two competent engineers, J. C. Trautwine and Geo. M. Totten, who had had experience in a tropical region, having constructed a canal in New Granada. They established headquarters on the isthmus in January, 1850. The company and the public had high hopes of early completion of the road. However, the difficulties encountered were enormous, and the sanguine expectations could not be realized. The original plan provided for starting at the head of boat navigation on the Chagres, some twenty miles from the sea, and building thence to the Pacific before undertaking the Atlantic section. By this plan it was hoped soon to have a combined river and railroad transit which would earn dividends transporting California argonauts. The plan proved impracticable, for materials could not be brought up the shallow Chagres. The road then had to be started in a mosquito-infested swamp in an island in Navy Bay, the Atlantic terminus. It was difficult to collect and hold a labor force. The natives were indolent. Irishmen and others brought from the United States or Europe suc-

[17] *Ibid.*, 414.
[18] *Panama Railroad Co.* . . . , 4.

cumbed to fever or malaria in the unaccustomed tropical climate or deserted and joined the California gold seekers. The clearing of the dense vegetation had hardly begun before the rainy season came on to increase the difficulties. The contractors asked to be and were released from their contract. The company then undertook to build the road itself, retaining Trautwine and Totten as engineers. Soon Trautwine came home ill. By May, 1851, the company had expended its $1,000,000, with apparently little to show for it, had increased its capital by $1,500,000, and was in the market for a loan of $900,000. There had been a great loss of life. People back home heard rumors of bad management.[19]

Unabated efforts eventually brought results. A town christened Aspinwall was built on piles at the Atlantic end. The labor problem was solved by providing better housing and by bringing in men from Jamaica and the other West Indies, who stood the climate better. When seven miles of the road had been opened, to Galinas, in March, 1852, people crossing the isthmus began to use it. On July 23 the road was opened for twenty-three miles. An experienced English correspondent who covered this section shortly after wrote that the "difficulties and impossibilities" which had been overcome exceeded any he had seen anywhere else in the world. The entire road thus far had been built through swampy land on piles, and then earth had been dumped in to form the embankment.[20] Again in the summer of 1852 the company resorted to contractors. The contractors assembled a labor force of 7,000, largely Chinese and Hindu coolies. They succumbed to the climate as rapidly as Irishmen. The contractors failed, and again the company had to undertake construction itself. The road was pushed slowly forward. On January 28, 1855, a locomotive was run from sea to sea, forty-six miles. Much of the road was still of a temporary character, however, and it required about two years and $2,000,000 more to put it into proper shape.

[19] Account based on *ibid.*; Otis, *op. cit.*; *Am. R. R. Jour.*, XXIV, 27, 376, 817; London *Times*, Nov. 8, 1849, Oct. 19, 1852, Feb. 7, 1855.
[20] *Ibid.*, Oct. 19, 1852.

When complete the Panama Railroad had cost about $7,000,000, about 50% more than the original estimates. It was well equipped with rolling stock. It had a machine shop and a car repair shop at Aspinwall. It had wharves and piers at the terminals with most up-to-date machinery for transferring freight.[21]

For years the Panama route had almost a monopoly of transporting Pacific coast mails, California bullion, and the emigrants and travelers who chose not to take the overland routes. The great bulk of the freight business of the railroad, however, came not from the California trade as had been expected but from South American and Central American trade. In 1860 only one fifteenth of the freight business was from California trade. During the five years ending December, 1859, the railroad carried 196,000 passengers, $300,-000,000 worth of bullion, and 100,000 bags of mail. In its early years there was one train a day for six days a week. In 1861 four steamship lines connected with it on the Pacific side and five steamship lines and three sailing vessel lines on the Atlantic side, while numerous tramp vessels visited its terminal ports. The Panama Railroad Company began paying dividends as early as 1852. For several years after completion it regularly paid 12%. Its stock was constantly above par and almost unpurchasable.[22] It and its powerful ally, the Pacific Mail Steamship Company, were often charged with monopoly and extortion. They certainly lobbied in Washington against legislation designed to raise up rivals.

[21] *Ibid.*, May 10, 1852, Feb. 7, Sept. 28, Oct. 6, 9, 1855; Otis, *op. cit.*; *Am. R. R. Jour.*, XXV, 136, 345, 770, XXVI, 378, 602, 621, 805, XXVIII, 36-37, 546-47.
[22] Otis, *op. cit.*; *Am. R. R. Jour.*, XXVIII, 426, XXXII, 123.

## CHAPTER V

## THE ATLANTIC AND PACIFIC SHIP CANAL

SHORTLY after the Panama railroad project was put before the public, a more ambitious project for building a ship canal by the Nicaragua route was advanced by a group of New York business men. The United States government gave this new project almost unstinted diplomatic support and thereby became involved in a well-nigh interminable controversy with Great Britain, especially, whose consequences have affected the interests of this country down to now.[1] But the canal was not built.

The British government grasped the commercial and political importance of the Nicaragua route even earlier than our own. When the canal project came within the realm of practical accomplishment, Britain promptly seized the eastern terminus and held it so that no canal could be constructed without her consent and co-operation.

For many decades the British had exercised a sort of protectorate over the Mosquitos, a mongrel tribe of Indians and Negroes with a few whites interspersed, who lived along the east coast of Central America somewhat to the north of the Nicaragua route. The tribe numbered perhaps one thousand. The protectorate was of doubtful legality. For many years it had been in abeyance but had been revived about 1840. In 1841 the British Superintendent of Belize took the "King" of the Mosquitos down to the little town of San Juan del Norte

[1] The diplomatic aspects of this subject have been treated at length in Mary W. Williams, *Anglo-American Isthmian Diplomacy, 1815-1915*, chs. i-v; Ira D. Travis, *The Hist. of the Clayton-Bulwer Treaty*; and Lindley M. Keasbey, *The Nicaragua Canal and the Monroe Doctrine*. They are more briefly but more satisfactorily discussed in McMaster, *Hist. of the People of the U. S.*, VII, ch. lxxxiv; R. B. Mowat, *The Diplomatic Relations of Great Britain and the U. S.*, ch. xiii; and M. W. Williams, *John Middleton Clayton* (in S. F. Bemis, ed., *Am. Secs. of State*, VI), ch. iv. They are discussed here for the sake of completeness and because it is desired to give a somewhat different interpretation and emphasis. The objection to nearly all accounts is that they all but omit the canal project, the occasion and the cause for the diplomacy.

or San Juan de Nicaragua at the mouth of the San Juan River, along which the canal route lay, and laid claim to it on his behalf. San Juan del Norte was the principal seaport of the little Republic of Nicaragua. The Mosquito claim was not at once made good, but in February 1848 — about the time the Mexican War had been brought to a successful conclusion — British troops seized San Juan and compelled Nicaragua to sign a treaty, March 9, agreeing not to disturb the Mosquitos in their possession of the port. The place was rechristened Greytown. The British consul became for all practical purposes the government of Greytown; and one or more British war vessels were kept in the vicinity almost constantly. The Mosquito claim was soon extended to the Colorado River, which bifurcated from the San Juan some distance above Greytown and entered the Caribbean many miles to the South.

The British seizure of San Juan de Nicaragua together with the information that the governor of the Mexican state of Yucatan had offered to transfer the "dominion and sovereignty of the peninsula" to Spain or Great Britain — a position from which the Isthmus of Tehuantepec could be dominated — caused considerable concern in informed circles in the United States. President Polk sent to the Senate his famous Yucatan Message reaffirming the Monroe Doctrine.[2] Senator Foote, of Mississippi, suggested seizure of both Yucatan and Cuba. "With Cuba and Yucatan we will have complete control over the Gulf of Mexico. . . , we will have it in our power to establish at once a direct communication between the Pacific and Atlantic Oceans; we will be able to secure to ourselves the rich monopoly of the East India trade; we will be safe in every direction from foreign assailment."[3] George Bancroft, minister to England wrote home: "Now as we are gaining greatness in the Pacific . . . she [Great Britain] has seized the key to the passage to the Pacific by the lake of Nicaragua, . . . The subject is important, because the route to the Pacific which that town commands is here esteemed the best of all."[4]

[2] Richardson, *Messages*, IV, 581-82.
[3] *Cong. Globe*, 30 Cong., 1 Sess., App., 602.
[4] H. *Exec. Docs.*, 31 Cong., 1 Sess., X (579), No. 75, p. 223.

Nicaragua repeatedly appealed to the United States government for support in her quarrel with England. The Polk Administration moved cautiously; it confined its action to sending Elijah Hise as chargé d'affaires to Guatemala to investigate and report.

Meanwhile speculators, believing the time opportune, hastened to Nicaragua seeking a contract for building the proposed canal. In February, 1849, a Mr. Wheelwright made propositions on behalf of a British company.[5] In March, a Mr. Brown representing certain citizens of New York actually signed a detailed contract, which, however, never became effective.[6] The British vice-consul in Nicaragua wrote Lord Palmerston, the British foreign secretary, in April recommending negotiations for "a protectorate and transit favorable to British interests," desiring, he said, to obtain for his country "so desirable a spot in the commercial world." [7] June 21, Chargé Hise, although without instructions, signed a treaty with Nicaragua by which Nicaragua granted to the United States or a company chartered thereby the exclusive right to build and operate a canal or road across Nicaragua from the Caribbean to the Pacific.[8]

The Hise Treaty certainly did not reflect caution. It gave the United States the right equally with Nicaragua to fortify and occupy the territories of Nicaragua to the extent necessary for the defense of the canal and the preservation of the neutrality of Nicaragua. Vessels of countries at war with the United States were excluded from the canal. The governments of the United States and Nicaragua and no others might send troops across Nicaragua without tolls or charges. The United States was to protect and defend Nicaragua in the possession and sovereignty of all territory "that may be rightfully under

[5] Ibid., 234; E. G. Squier, Nicaragua; Its People, Scenery, Monuments, etc., 1st ed. (1852), II, 261.
[6] Ibid., II, 262; H. Exec. Docs., 31 Cong., 1 Sess., X (579), No. 75, pp. 141-44.
[7] E. G. Squier, op. cit., II, 264.
[8] Text in H. Exec. Docs., 31 Cong., 1 Sess., X (579), No. 75, pp. 110-117; Hise's account of the negotiations, ibid., 104-09; the treaty and Hise's correspondence in Carnegie Endow. for Internat. Peace, Wm. R. Manning, ed., Dip. Corres. of the U. S., Inter-American Affairs, 1831-1860, VIII, Central Am., 1831-1850.

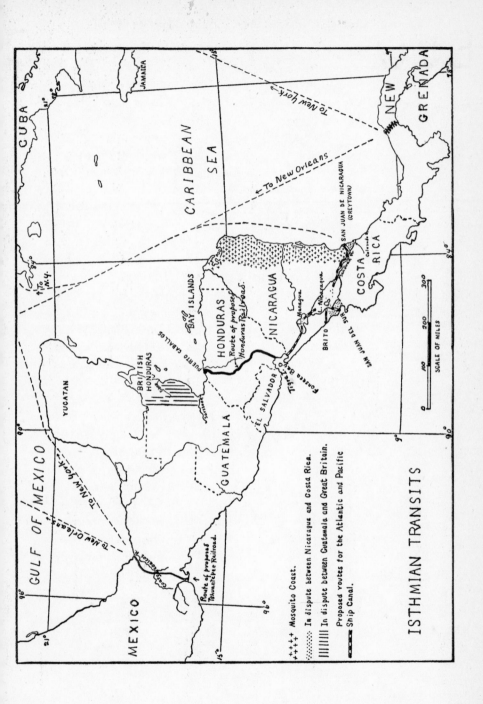

ISTHMIAN TRANSITS

+ + + +   Mosquito Coast.
. . . .   In dispute between Nicaragua and Costa Rica.
||||||||  In dispute between Guatemala and Great Britain.
━━━━━━    Proposed routes for the Atlantic and Pacific Ship Canal.

her jurisdiction and within the just and true limits and boundaries of the said State," that is to say, presumably, of San Juan, or Greytown, then in possession of Great Britain.

Before the Hise Treaty was received in Washington, Polk had been succeeded by Taylor, and Secretary of State Clayton had sent E. George Squier to succeed Hise and had formulated his isthmian policy. His policy was that foreshadowed by Henry Clay when secretary of state and by Clayton himself in his Senate resolution of 1835.[9] The policy was clearly stated in Squier's instructions, dated May 1, 1849.[10]

Squier, who was a civil engineer and had been selected for that reason, was to determine the practicability of a canal and the most advantageous route. The State Department was disposed to extend its aid to a responsible private company — it had been approached by interested persons — desirous of securing a contract with Nicaragua for building the canal to any extent compatible with prudence. The British possession of Greytown was clearly illegal; but, in view thereof, it was not expedient to guarantee to Nicaragua the territory through which the canal might pass. The United States wished no monopoly of the transit route and would submit to none. A monopoly would cause us more bloody wars than Gibraltar had caused Great Britain and Spain. Squier might make a treaty with Nicaragua stipulating that both the United States and Nicaragua would protect and defend the canal. Without such a guarantee capitalists would not embark upon the enterprise. Clayton desired that American citizens obtain the contract but was willing that they invite the assistance of foreign capitalists.

Upon his arrival in Nicaragua, Squier found a Mr. Joseph L. White, the agent of Cornelius Vanderbilt, seeking a contract for building the canal. Upon Squier's assurance that his government was favorable, a contract was signed and ratified, September 23, 1849. Squier himself drafted two articles, one making the contract inalienable by the company, the other requiring equality of treatment for the citizens and governments of all nations which might join in guaranteeing the neutrality

[9] See above, p. 7.
[10] H. Exec. Docs., 31 Cong., 1 Sess., X (579), No. 75, pp. 118-30.

of the canal.[11] The contract gave Vanderbilt and associates, styled "The American Atlantic and Pacific Ship Canal Company," the exclusive privilege for a period of eighty-five years of building and operating a ship canal by way of Lake Nicaragua and the San Juan River. The majority of the stock of the company must always be held by citizens of the United States. Surveys must be begun within a year and the canal completed within twelve years. Nicaragua was to receive $10,000 down and $10,000 each year until the canal should have been completed and thereafter a portion of the net profits. Pending the completion of the canal the company was given the exclusive privilege of operating a temporary transit by carriage road or railroad and river and lake boats. Nicaragua was to receive 10% of the net profits of the temporary transit. If a canal should be found impracticable, the company must provide a railroad or a combined water, railroad, and carriage line across the isthums within the period of twelve years.[12]

On September 3, 1849, Squier signed a treaty with the Nicaraguan government for the protection of the said American Atlantic and Pacific Ship Canal Company. Nicaragua granted the government and citizens of the United States free transit across the country without tolls, charges, or duties on merchandise. Both countries pledged themselves to protect and defend the company and the canal. The United States recognized "the rights of sovereignty and property which Nicaragua possesses in and over" the route — this seemed to guarantee to Nicaragua the title to Greytown — and guaranteed "positively and efficaciously" the entire neutrality of the same so long as the canal should remain under the control of United States citizens and the United States should enjoy the privileges mentioned above. Any other country might have the rights and privileges guaranteed to the United States if it would join in guaranteeing the defense and neutrality of the canal.[13]

On July 30, 1849, the British consul in New York had caused notice to be inserted in a newspaper that the navigation

[11] E. G. Squier, op. cit., II, 268; London Times, Oct. 30, 1849.
[12] Text in H. Exec. Docs., 31 Cong., 1 Sess., X (579), No. 75, pp. 173-80.
[13] Text in Parliamentary Papers, 1856, LX, 72-89.

of the San Juan River from a point about thirty miles below Lake Nicaragua to the sea belonged to the Mosquito protectorate.[14] Chatfield, the British consul general in Central America, taking advantage of certain claims against Honduras, threatened to seize Tigre Island in Fonseca Bay, intending thereby, no doubt, to get a position commanding the western terminus of the proposed canal, as Greytown commanded the eastern. Squier had come to the conclusion that the best route for the canal ran from Lake Nicaragua via Lake Managua to a terminus on Fonseca Bay.[15] So he hurriedly made a treaty with Honduras, ratified by the latter October 9, 1849, whereby that country provisionally ceded Tigre Island to the United States to prevent it from falling into the hands of "foreign and unfriendly powers." Squier notified Chatfield of his action, but the latter, claiming that he had spoken first, seized Tigre Island and refused to evacuate it.[16]

Complicating the problem still further, the little republic of Costa Rica had advanced a claim to the land bordering the San Juan River on the south and to the province of Guanacaste, lying between Lake Nicaragua and the Pacific. There was strong probability that the best route for the canal lay south of the San Juan for a considerable distance and a remote possibility that the best western terminus would be found in Guanacaste. Therefore either the boundary dispute must be settled in Nicaragua's favor or the canal company and the United States must come to a satisfactory agreement with Costa Rica. That little republic was strongly under the influence of Great Britain and relied upon her support.

Meanwhile, Secretary of State Clayton had become convinced that the Nicaragua canal was practicable, that an isthmian canal would be highly advantageous to the United States, and that there was no other practicable isthmian route.[17] He, therefore, resolutely set about the unpleasant task of coming

[14] N. Y. *Herald*, Sept. 25; Rives to Clayton, Sept. 21, 25, 1849, *Sen. Exec. Docs.*, 32 Cong., 2 Sess., III (660), No. 27, pp. 15-16, 18.

[15] E. G. Squier, *op. cit.*, 242-44; Squier to Clayton, Aug. 20, 1849, *H. Exec. Docs.*, 31 Cong., 1 Sess., X (579), No. 75, p. 157.

[16] *Parl. Papers*, 1856, LX, Nos. 14, 17.

[17] Clayton to A. A. Lawrence, U. S. Minister to Great Britain, Oct. 20, 1849, *Sen. Exec. Docs.*, 32 Cong., 2 Sess., III (660), No. 27, pp. 31-33.

to an agreement with Great Britain. He stated at the outset that the United States desired no special advantages. He requested the British government to restore Greytown and lands along the San Juan River to Nicaragua in order to bring the whole route under one jurisdiction and, thus, render the Nicaragua contract with the Vanderbilt Company sufficient. He asked the British government to then make a treaty with Nicaragua agreeing to protect and defend the canal and guaranteeing its neutrality. He asked for assurances that the British government would not establish a protectorate over Costa Rica and would not support Costa Rica's pretensions in her boundary dispute with Nicaragua but would use her good offices to facilitate a settlement.[18] On the side he tried to win over Costa Rica from her subservience to Britain.[19] As a guarantee of the good faith of the United States, he offered to enter into a treaty with Great Britain binding both nations "never to colonize, annex, settle, or fortify any part of the ancient territory of Guatemala, embracing Nicaragua, Costa Rica, and Honduras, and, indeed the whole Mosquito coast." He threatened that, in case the British government rejected these overtures, the President would submit the Hise treaty to the Senate — the Squier treaty not having arrived at the time. He was confident the Senate would ratify under such circumstances and the Executive would have the full support of the people in executing the treaty. Upon Lawrence, Minister to London, Clayton urged haste. "If we must have a collision with Great Britain about this matter, the sooner we understand it the better for us." If, however, Great Britain would meet the American proposition in the spirit in which it was made, the two nations would "engage in the accomplishment of an object which may redound more to the true glory of each of them than the most successful war on which either could engage." [20]

[18] There were numerous letters and documents, but all of Clayton's terms were stated in his instructions to Lawrence, Oct. 20, 1849, in *ibid.*, 24-34, and in a conversation with Crampton, British chargé d'affaires, reported to Palmerston, Oct. 1, in *Parl. Papers*, 1856, LX, No. 2.

[19] Abstracts of two letters written in Dec., 1849, and communicated to Clayton, Feb. 27, 1850, in *J. M. Clayton Papers* (Library of Congress).

[20] Letter of Oct. 20, 1849, cited in n. 18.

Lord Palmerston, the British foreign secretary, received Clayton's proposals in a friendly manner.[21] He disclaimed any desire to frustrate the building of a canal. Great Britain had no intention, he said, of occupying territory in Central America. The British government had refused a proffered protectorate over Costa Rica, Palmerston said, not quite truthfully, and had made no arrangements with her in regard to a transit route.[22] In reply to Lawrence's protest, Palmerston disavowed Counsul General Chatfield's seizure of Tigre Island.[23] In return, Clayton promised that the United States would not take it.[24] Crampton, the British chargé at Washington, demurred to entering into support of an American company. Clayton persuaded him to accept the company if it would offer one half its stock to British capitalists. The directors of the company readily agreed to this, knowing they could not raise all the capital in the United States anyway.[25] But on one essential point the British government was obdurate: It refused to abandon its claim, on behalf of the Mosquitos, to Greytown and land along the San Juan; and it insisted that Squier's treaty by which the United States recognized Nicaragua's title to the entire canal route should not be submitted to the Senate.[26] British honor, it was explained, would not permit abandonment of the Mosquito claim unless ample satisfaction and guarantees of security could first be secured for the Mosquitos.

Over the point of the Mosquito protectorate there were most intricate negotiations.[27] A draft treaty agreed upon February 3, 1850, between Clayton and Sir Henry Bulwer, the new British minister, contained the formula that neither power

[21] Rives to Clayton, Sept. 25, 1849, Palmerston to Lawrence, Nov. 13, *Sen. Exec. Docs.*, 32 Cong., 2 Sess., III (660), No. 27, pp. 18-23, 46-47.
[22] Lawrence to Clayton, Nov. 9, *ibid.*, 43-45. Palmerston later repeated the disclaimer. Letter to Bulwer, Mar. 31, 1850, *Parl. Papers*, 1856, LX, No. 28. His Lordship was not entirely ingenuous. Consul Chatfield had signed a treaty with Costa Rica and the British government had approved it. Bulwer finally showed it to Webster, Oct. 8, 1850, but claimed it was only an ordinary commercial treaty. Bulwer to Palmerston, Oct. 10, *Parl. Papers*, 1856, LX, No. 62.
[23] Feb. 13, *ibid.*, No. 18.
[24] *Ibid.*, Nos. 14, 26.
[25] *Ibid.*, Nos. 2, 3, 10; Jos. L. White to Clayton, Jan. 16, 1850, *Clayton Papers*.
[26] Bulwer to Clayton, Feb. 14, Apr. 19, 1850, *ibid.*
[27] They are described almost day by day in M. W. Williams, *Anglo-American Isthmian Diplomacy*, ch. iii.

would "occupy or fortify, or colonize, or assume or exercise any dominion over Nicaragua, Costa Rica, the Mosquito Coast, or any part of Central America." [28]  Clayton told Bulwer that he understood the word "occupy" to mean "take or keep possession." [29]  Clayton thought this formula accomplished all that was necessary, reducing the protectorate to a "shadow." But members of the Cabinet, to which the draft treaty was now submitted, insisted that the treaty plainly say that Great Britain abandon the protectorate in every way.[30] Bulwer, on his part, objected to Clayton's definition of "occupy" and continued to dissuade him from sending the Squier Treaty to the Senate.[31]  But when Clayton heard from Lawrence that Lord Palmerston refused to bind England not to seize territory in payment of debts, President Taylor submitted the Squier Treaty, March 19.[32]  In an effort to quiet the fears of Taylor's Cabinet, Bulwer secured from Lord Palmerston a statement that Great Britain would not make use of its protectorate over the Mosquitos for the purpose of occupying, fortifying, or colonizing their territory or of assuming or exercising dominion over the same.[33]  Clayton secured from Bulwer assurance that the American Atlantic and Pacific Ship Canal Company would receive British protection under the proposed treaty although, upon Bulwer's insistence, it was not specifically mentioned in the draft.[34]

Clayton now agreed to sign the treaty as drafted if Bulwer would accept with it a statement prepared in the Cabinet to the effect that the United States did not recognize the Mosquito protectorate and had signed a treaty with Nicaragua recognizing her title to the canal route.[35]  Bulwer refused and threatened that no British capital would be forthcoming for the

[28] Parl. Papers, 1856, LX, 38-40.
[29] Letter of Feb. 11, 1850, Clayton Papers; Cong. Globe, 34 Cong., 1 Sess., 1419, extracts from letters.
[30] Clayton to Bulwer, Feb. 15, Clayton to Lawrence, Feb. 15 (draft), Apr. 22, Clayton Papers; Bulwer to Palmerston, Feb. 18, Parl. Papers, 1856, LX, No. 21.
[31] Clayton to Lawrence, Feb., 1850 (day not given), Clayton Papers.
[32] Parl. Papers, 1856, LX, No. 32; Richardson, Messages, V, 33.
[33] Parl. Papers, 1856, LX, Nos. 21, 24; Clayton to Lawrence, Mar. 31, and to Bulwer, Apr. 6, Clayton Papers.
[34] Clayton to Bulwer, Apr. 3, and reply, Apr. 4, ibid.
[35] Clayton to Bulwer, Apr. 6, 8, ibid.

canal if the United States should recognize Nicaragua's title to Greytown. He was willing to receive a statement that the United States did not recognize the Mosquito claim and to agree to the incorporation in the Nicaragua Treaty of a clause pledging the United States to use its good offices to secure a satisfactory settlement with Great Britain.[36] After further discussion and after consulting influential senators, Clayton finally agreed to withdraw the Cabinet note; and Bulwer, on his part, agreed to incorporate Palmerston's assurance with regard to the Mosquito protectorate in the treaty itself.[37] The treaty was signed April 19, 1850. Clayton promised Bulwer that, if their treaty should be ratified, the Squier Treaty would be amended to conform.[38]

Clayton knew of course that he was not obtaining the abandonment of the Mosquito protectorate, but he believed he had pared it down to the point where Britain could not use a single ship or a single gun in support of it.[39] He believed also that by mediating between Great Britain and Nicaragua he could secure the abandonment of the protectorate altogether. He had hopes also of getting France to join in the guarantee and to help get rid of the protectorate.[40] On this point he may have been too sanguine. It is hard to escape the conclusion that Great Britain clung to its protectorate in order to continue control over the canal project.

Except for the ambiguous clause with regard to the Mosquito protectorate, the Clayton-Bulwer Treaty seemed well designed to effect the objects intended.[41] Neither the United States nor Great Britain was ever to obtain or maintain for itself any exclusive control over the proposed ship canal. Both parties undertook to protect the canal company from the commencement of the canal to its completion from "unjust deten-

[36] Bulwer to Clayton, Apr. 7, 8, 9, *ibid.*
[37] Bulwer to Palmerston, Apr. 28, *Sen. Exec. Docs.*, 47 Cong., 1 Sess., III (1991), No. 194, pp. 85-87.
[38] Clayton to Bulwer, Apr. 21, 23, Bulwer to Clayton, Apr. 21, 1850, *Clayton Papers.*
[39] Clayton to Lawrence, Apr. 22, 1850, *ibid.*; E. G. Squier, *Nicaragua*, II, 275-76; *Cong. Globe*, 32 Cong., 2 Sess., App., 256.
[40] Clayton to Rives, Jan. 7, 26, 1850, Rives to Clayton, Feb. 21, *Clayton Papers.*
[41] Text in Wm. M. Malloy, compiler, *Treaties, Conventions, International Acts*, etc., I, 659 ff.

tion, confiscation, seizure," or violence. They were to use their influence with "any state, states, or governments, possessing or claiming to possess any jurisdiction or right over" the route to induce them to facilitate the construction of the canal. They were to attempt to secure the establishment of a free port at each end of the canal. They undertook to protect the canal, when it should have been completed, from interruption, seizure, or unjust confiscation and to guarantee its neutrality. They engaged to invite other friendly nations to enter into similar stipulations with them. The American Atlantic and Pacific Ship Canal Company was given one year from the ratification of the treaty in which to give evidence of its ability to build the canal. If the company failed to give such evidence, the two countries would be prepared to afford their protection to any other company prepared to execute the work. Finally, it was agreed, the general principles of the treaty should be extended to any other practicable communication, whether by canal or railway, across the isthmus and particularly to the proposed projects by the way of Tehuantepec and Panama.

The Clayton-Bulwer Treaty was considered by the United States Senate in secret session. The debates have never been published, and but few intimations of their character leaked out to the press. There were many references to them, however, during a controversy in the Senate three years later in which Clayton himself (then back in the Senate) participated.[42] From these references it may be inferred that, in the Senate in 1850, there was opposition to the renunciation of future acquisition of territory in Central America and reluctance to entering into co-operation with Great Britain. This was offset by the desire to get the canal and to take advantage of Great Britain's promise to restrict her pretensions in Central America. Some of the senators seem to have voted for the treaty under the mistaken notion that Great Britain had agreed to abandon her Mosquito protectorate; and, if it had not been for this misunderstanding, the treaty probably would not have

[42] *Cong. Globe*, 32 Cong., 2 Sess., 237-38, 247-53, 265-72, 414-18, App., 274-80, 284-90.

been ratified.[43] There was much speculation as to whether or not, if the treaty should be rejected, Great Britain and other European powers could be bluffed into letting the United States have exclusive control of the canal; the consensus of opinion was that they could not. Senator Douglas was the most bitter opponent of ratification; but, in a three hours' conference with Clayton and Chairman King of the Foreign Relations Committee, he would not give it as his opinion that Congress would support the Administration in an application of the Monroe Doctrine. The eleven senators who voted against ratification were all Democratic partisans and with two exceptions came from states which would have no direct commercial interest in a canal.

Immediately the Clayton-Bulwer Treaty had been signed, Clayton again pressed the British government to come to an agreement with Nicaragua over Greytown and the Mosquitos. He had proposed that Greytown and vicinity be accorded to Nicaragua and that Nicaragua assign a definite reservation to the Mosquitos. As to the Nicaragua-Costa Rica boundary dispute, he proposed arbitration or mediation by the British and American governments acting jointly.[44] Palmerston countered with the proposal to give Greytown to Costa Rica. This would have put the two termini of the canal under different jurisdictions.[45] His proposal casts further doubt upon his lordship's sincerity in professing to desire to facilitate the building of the canal. Bulwer, on the contrary, was favorable to Clayton's suggestions.[46] So was the London *Times*.[47] At this stage of the negotiations Clayton was unfortunately superseded by Daniel Webster.

Webster continued the negotiations along the lines laid down by Clayton but in a dilatory manner. He made the blunder of not seeking ratification of the Squier Treaty with

[43] *Ibid.*, 237, 266; *Works of James Buchanan*, VIII, 381-82.
[44] *Sen. Exec. Docs.*, 32 Cong., 2 Sess., III (660), No. 27, pp. 54-60, 70-72; *Parl. Papers*, 1856, LX, No. 40.
[45] Palmerston to Bulwer, Mar. 25, Oct. 28, 1850, *ibid.*, Nos. 40, 63.
[46] Bulwer to Palmerston, July 1, *ibid.*, No. 47.
[47] May 27, Je. 13, 1850.

Nicaragua.[48] He had little regard for the sensibilities of the officials of Latin American republics.[49] He failed to bring Great Britain and Nicaragua to an agreement over the Mosquitos or to get Nicaragua and Costa Rica to settle their boundary dispute. In August, 1851, a revolution broke out in Nicaragua, there were rival governments, and it was almost impossible to conduct negotiations with the troublesome little state.[50]

Meanwhile Commodore Vanderbilt and his associates had not been inactive. In the summer of 1850 they sent steamers to the San Juan to establish a temporary means of crossing the isthmus. They also sent competent engineers to make surveys for the canal. Vanderbilt himself and White went to London to enlist the aid of English capital in accordance with the gentlemen's agreement between Clayton and Bulwer. Certain London bankers agreed to offer one half the stock to the public when it should have been demonstrated to the satisfaction of government engineers that the canal was practicable and likely to return reasonable profits.[51] In the summer of 1851, Joseph L. White, back in Nicaragua, sought to obtain a supplementary contract separating the temporary transit privileges from the canal project and authorizing the canal company to form a subsidiary company with the same stockholders to organize and operate the temporary communication. The Nicaraguan government feared this move implied a design to abandon the canal and refused. When the revolution, already referred to, broke out, however, and there were two rival governments, White, by promises of aid and claims of having great influence with the governments of the United States and Great Britain, prevailed on one of them to grant the coveted contract, August 19. The new company was styled "The Accessory Transit Company." The other government naturally

---

[48] *Cong. Globe*, 32 Cong., 2, 3, Sess., App., 256; Webster to Kerr, Je. 6, 1851, *Sen. Exec. Docs.*, 34 Cong., 1, 2 Sess., X (819), No. 25, p. 47.

[49] Squier to Clayton, Sept. 2, 1850, *Clayton Papers*.

[50] H. H. Bancroft, *Hist. of Central America*, III, 256; *Parl. Papers*, 1856, LX, No. 83.

[51] London *Times*, Oct. 15, 16, 1850; J. L. White *et al* to Baring Bros. *et al*, July 21, 1852, *Clayton Papers*.

denied the validity of the grant.[52] This action of the company
should have enlightened our State Department as to the character of the aggregation to whom it was giving its diplomatic
support. But Webster, believing that cirumstances would
brook no delay, approved the new contract and instructed
Chargé d'Affaires Kerr to support it.[53]

The temporary transit was opened with dispatch, in fact
before the end of the year 1851. Two small steamboats, the
*Clayton* and the *Bulwer*, were sent to ply on the lower course of
the San Juan River. A light railway was constructed about the
rapids. A light steamer and later a larger one were sent to
operate on Lake Nicaragua. Vanderbilt himself went down
to superintend running the larger steamboat through the
rapids. Passengers were at first transported from the west
shore of the lake to the Pacific at San Juan del Sur on mules
over a bridle path; but in 1854 a macadamized road was completed and comfortable carriages were provided. In 1851
Vanderbilt put two steamships on the Atlantic between New
York and Greytown and three on the Pacific side between San
Juan del Sur and San Francisco. The following year he added
two ships at each end. In spite of six transhipments the Nicaragua route between New York and San Francisco was often
about two days shorter than that by Panama. This item together with the shorter sea voyages required and the Nicaragua scenery made the route popular. At the height of its prosperity the Accessory Transit Company transported about
2,000 Americans across the isthmus each month, most of them
bound for California and the gold fields. Competition between
the two routes reduced the fare from New York to California
from $600 to $300.[54]

The American Atlantic and Pacific Ship Canal Company
was not entitled to the guarantees of the Clayton-Bulwer Trea-

[52] E. G. Squier, *Nicaragua*, II, 279-80; *Sen. Exec. Docs.*, 47 Cong., 1 Sess.,
III (1991), No. 194, pp. 88-90 (charter); *Sen. Exec. Docs.*, 34 Cong., 1 and 2
Sess., X (819), No. 25, p. 94.
[53] Nov. 20, 1851, *ibid.*, 55-56.
[54] *Harper's Weekly*, III, 146; Squier, *Nicaragua*, II, 278-79; Wm. O. Scroggs,
*Filibusters and Financiers* (1916), 78-80; Bedford Pim, R. N., *The Gate to the
Pacific* (London, 1863), 226-27; *Am. R. R. Jour.*, XXVIII, 741, XXX, 331-32.

ty until it should have begun actual construction. The Accessory Transit Company was not entitled to the guarantees at all. The State Department continued to give diplomatic support to both. The British Foreign Office was for the time friendly, in the spirit of the treaty, but British officials out in Central America were unreconciled and threw such petty obstacles in the way of the companies as they could. The companies on their part were exasperating to say the least.

The officials of Greytown, dominated by the British consul, Green, at first undertook to collect duties. The canal company refused to pay. Lord Palmerston prevented further friction on this point by instructing Consul Green not to interfere with the company's vessels and to make Greytown a free port.[55] Several months later the town council resolved on certain taxes and dues to meet "unavoidable expenses" collectible from all vessels except English mail steamers. American vessels refused to pay. On one occasion, after the usual refusal to pay, H. M.'s Brig, the *Express*, Captain Fead in command, fired shots across the bow of Vanderbilt's *Prometheus*, the "Commodore" being on board at the time. Vanderbilt paid, but appealed to Secretary of State Webster. Webster had a war vessel sent to Greytown and called upon the British government for a disavowal of Captain Fead's act. Lord Granville, who had succeeded Palmerston as foreign secretary, gave it and instructed Consul Green that Her Majesty's ships were not at Greytown to enforce fiscal regulations but only to guard against aggressive attempts to deprive the Mosquito government of possession.[56] Soon another incident occurred. The company had built its depot and warehouse not in Greytown but across the bay on a sandbar known as Punta Arenas, hoping probably to force the denizens of Greyton to move across and buy company real estate. The town council, Consul Green the chairman, countered by notifying the company that its ships must land their passengers and cargoes on the beach at Greytown and must vacate Punta Arenas as it was needed for "quarantine purposes." Commander Parker, of the United States ship, the

55 *Parl. Papers*, 1856, LX, Nos. 48, 61, 85, 87.
56 *Ibid.*, Nos. 84-88, 93-103.

*Saranac,* intervened and gave notice to Captain Fead that the United States did not recognize the right of Great Britain to exercise police power over American vessels or property outside British waters.[57]

Such irritating little incidents hastened negotiations at Washington.[58] Crampton, the British minister, Bulwer having retired, was friendly. Webster's concern was almost entirely for the two American companies and very little for justice for the two little Central American countries involved.[59] The immediate result of the negotiations was the "Webster-Crampton Basis of Agreement," signed April 30, 1852.[60] Its provisions were to be embodied in treaties among the United States, Great Britain, Nicaragua, and Costa Rica. The Costa Rican minister, Molina, refused to sign it at the last moment, and Marcoleta, the Nicaraguan representative was not invited to sign because it was believed he was not authorized by his government to do so.

According to the Webster-Crampton Basis, Greytown and vicinity were to go to Nicaragua. The Mosquito Indians were to receive a generous reservation and a small indemnity from Nicaragua. The San Juan River was to be the boundary between Nicaragua and Costa Rica except that the delta between the stream and its Colorado branch should also go to the former. The Province of Guanacaste, west of Lake Nicaragua, was to be given to Costa Rica. Inasmuch as the surveys, now complete, had shown that the canal would occupy the bed of the San Juan or the north bank and the western terminus would be well to the north of Guanacaste, these boundary provisions virtually assured that the canal, if built, would be entirely under Nicaraguan jurisdiction. But it was stipulated that, in case it were found that any portion of the canal route lay on the Costa Rican side, Costa Rica should afford every

[57] *Ibid.,* Nos. 101, 107, 108, 110-112, 126, 127.
[58] Earl Granville to Crampton, Jan. 23, Feb. 20, 1852, in *ibid.,* Nos. 104, 107.
[59] See, e.gs., Webster to Crampton, Jan. 18, 1852, *Writings and Speeches of Daniel Webster,* XVI, 636; Marcoleta to Clayton, Jan. 23, 1856, *Clayton Papers; Cong. Globe,* 34 Cong., 1 Sess., App., 139.
[60] Text in *Sen. Exec. Docs.,* 34 Cong., 1 and 2 Sess., X (819), No. 25, pp. 73-77. The negotiations may be followed in *ibid.,* 3-73, and in *Parl. Papers,* 1856, LX, Nos. 51-121, *passim.*

necessary facility for the construction of the canal. Costa
Rica was denied the right of navigating the San Juan or Lake
Nicaragua by steam during the life of the contracts of the companies. Both Nicaragua and Costa Rica were to be bound not
to do anything to obstruct the free operation of the canal or
the temporary transit. Greytown was to be a free port. The
canal company was to be given another year in which to complete its arrangements and win the protection of the Clayton-
Bulwer Treaty. That protection was to be extended forthwith
to the Accessory Transit Company. Finally the Basis contained a threat: If the proposals proved unacceptable to
Nicaragua or Costa Rica, the British and United States governments would immediately agree between themselves upon
such measures as they should deem advisable to carry into
effect the terms of the Clayton-Bulwer Treaty and accomplish
the design of an interoceanic communication.

The Webster-Crampton Basis having been agreed upon,
the British and United States agents in Central America were
charged with the task of securing the adhesion of the two little
republics. Immediately Lord Malmesbury, the British foreign
secretary, having learned that the people of Greytown were
unfriendly to Nicaragua, regretted the cession of the port to
Nicaragua and sought to get more favorable arrangements
for it. He complacently anticipated Nicaragua's refusal to
accept the disposition made of her by the two large powers,[61]
in which case Britain and the United States would be free to
make still other arrangements.

As Malmesbury expected, Costa Rica, Great Britain's pro-
tégé, accepted the terms and Nicaragua refused. Almost no
feature of the Webster-Crampton agreement was acceptable
to Nicaragua. The boundary settlement she considered unfair,
as it probably was. She did not want to indemnify the Mosquitos. Not the least unsatisfactory were the provisions relating to the canal company and its subsidiary. The companies
had become exceedingly unpopular in Nicaragua. They were
charged with having acted in a highhanded manner and with

[61] Malmesbury to Crampton, Je. 18, July 16, Crampton to Malmesbury, July
4, 1852, ibid., Nos. 125, 128, 129.

having evaded many of their obligations. Specifically, they were charged with smuggling, with having seized upon their sections of land without having consulted the government, and with having seized an old castle, one of the historic monuments of the country, and used its materials for building purposes.[62] Nicaragua also properly complained of the failure of the United States government to ratify the Squier Treaty — and presumably to restore Greytown to its rightful owner; the Squier Treaty had been practically a condition of the grant of the contract to the canal company by Nicaragua.[63]

Nicaragua's rejection of the Webster-Crampton Basis created the contingency in which the United States and Great Britain were to proceed to arrange matters without further regard to the wishes of the little state. However, before the ability and will of the two powers to co-operate further along this line could be tested, the canal project had received its death blow in another manner.

The survey for the canal had been carefully made under the direction of Colonel O. W. Childs, who had recently been in charge of the successful enlargement of the Erie Canal. His report, submitted early in 1852, gave detailed specifications for a canal which would accommodate vessels of a draught of not more than 17 feet and a length not over 250 feet. The cost was estimated at not more than $31,539,319. The cost of a canal of greater dimensions, the report stated, would be disproportionately greater. Childs contended that a 17-foot canal would be large enough to meet the needs of commerce, for there were few steamers with greater draught and sailing vessels of greater burden than the steamers could be so designed as to enable them to use the canal. It would perhaps be fair to read between the lines that he thought the cost of a 20-foot canal would be prohibitive. Brito Harbor was designated as the Pacific terminus.[64]

[62] *Sen. Exec. Docs.*, 34 Cong., 1 and 2 Sess., X (819), No. 25, pp. 79, 93-95, 99-106, 110-114, 120-29.
[63] *Ibid.*, 93-95, 101-103, 110-14; Clayton to Bulwer, Apr. 8, 1850, *Clayton Papers*; Squier, *Nicaragua*, II, 274.
[64] O. W. Childs and J. D. Fay, *Report of the Survey and Estimates of the Cost of Constructing the Inter-Oceanic Ship Canal . . . in the State of Nicaragua*, etc., *passim*.

At the request of the canal company, President Fillmore designated two distinguished army engineers to examine the report. They found its conclusions sound.[65] It was then sent to England and, in accordance with the previous agreement, submitted to two engineers designated by the British government. They not only examined the report but also submitted some of the detailed estimates to English contractors and subjected Colonel Childs to a thorough cross examination. The British engineers concluded that the canal was practicable, the survey accurate, and the estimates adequate. They thought, however, that Brito Harbor, the western terminus "unworthy of this great ship navigation" and to make the canal 20 feet deep instead of 17 and the locks 300 feet long instead of 250 "would be rendering the navigation more efficient for the general purposes of trade, by steam and sailing vessels.[66]

The plans and specifications were now laid before the London banking firms which in 1850 had agreed to offer one half the canal company stock to the British public provided the canal were found to be practicable and seemed likely to earn reasonable profits. After careful investigation the bankers refused to participate in the project or to recommend it to the public. They considered, so it was given out, the proposed dimensions too small to meet the demands of commerce. More than one third of the tonnage used in the Oriental trade could not pass through a 17-foot canal. The distance from London to Calcutta and Singapore would be 1000 miles shorter by the Cape of Good Hope route. With so much trade excluded the canal could not earn dividends.[67] The publication of the bankers' verdict caused great disappointment in America, but the public seems to have accepted it as having been made in good faith.

The London bankers' verdict may have been made in good faith; we can never be sure. The canal company made no

[65] *Ibid.*, 152-53.
[66] *Ship Canal between the Atlantic and Pacific Oceans: Report of British Engineers* (N. Y., 1852) ; London *Times*, Feb. 10, 11, 1853.
[67] Copies of the correspondence between the company and the bankers are in *Clayton Papers* under dates of July 17, 21, 31 and Aug. 6, 20, 1852. *Cf.* Squiers, *Nicaragua*, Rev. Ed., 662-63.

particular protest. Four years later Cornelius Vanderbilt wrote Secretary of State Marcy, "A ship canal of the requisite depth was found impracticable." [68] Certain it is that little if any of the shipping which then went via the Cape of Good Hope would have been deflected to a tolls canal in Nicaragua. On the other hand, there are grounds for strong suspicion that the real reasons for the adverse decision of the bankers were other than those made public. In a speech in the United States Senate, 1856, Ex-Secretary of State Clayton asserted: "The agents of the American Transit Company assure me that the British capitalists declined to aid them in cutting the canal, after advising with Lord Malmesbury, then in the British Foreign Office . . . on the ostensible ground that the profits of the canal would not reimburse them for the expense, but really on the ground that the work would inure chiefly to the benefit of the United States, and make us masters of the commerce of the world." [69] Clayton was defending his treaty. In 1850 Bulwer had warned Clayton that the company could not get "any English capital whatever" if the United States should recognize Nicaragua's title to Greytown; the British government could control the bankers.[70] E. G. Squier thought at the time that British policy "will not be directed to the construction of the works, but to its obstruction; not to the promotion of general commercial interests, but to the prevention of American supremacy in the Pacific." [71] Certainly the canal would have been of far greater advantage to the United States both commercially and politically than to Great Britain. The history of British isthmian diplomacy lends itself as easily to the interpretation that it was animated by a desire to frustrate the construction of the canal altogether as to the view that it was prompted by a proper desire to safeguard British interests in such a work. It is reasonably certain that about a decade later the British government sought to discourage the construction of a Suez canal because of the belief that it would

[68] *Sen. Exec. Docs.*, 34 Cong., 1 Sess., XIII (822), No. 68, p. 82.
[69] *Cong. Globe*, 34 Cong., 1 Sess., App., 441. See also White to Clayton, Apr. 6, 1856, *Clayton Papers*; N. Y. *Herald*, Apr. 5; London *Times*, Mar. 20.
[70] Bulwer to Clayton, Apr. 9, 1850, *Clayton Papers.*
[71] Squiers, *Nicaragua*, 1st ed., II, 302.

benefit the commerce of other nations at the expense of Great Britain's.[72]

After the announcement of the adverse decision of the English capitalists, the canal company requested the Nicaraguan government to modify the contract to permit the construction of a canal of even smaller dimensions than those contemplated in the Childs report. Nicaragua, of course, refused.[73] The company showed no further interest, and no other parties came forward to offer to construct the canal. But Lord John Russell, now British foreign secretary, having heard of the company's effort to get the contract modified, instructed Crampton to inform the United States Secretary of State that Great Britain could not undertake to guarantee a canal which failed to answer to the essential designation of ship canal as contemplated by the Clayton-Bulwer Treaty. Crampton was to show the Secretary how earnest Great Britain had been in desiring the speedy construction of a great interoceanic canal and "how deeply we should regret to see so splendid a conception dwindle down to the narrow compass of an ordinary transit route for mere coasting vessels, which, to distant nations, would be almost destitute of value." [74]

Some doubt is cast upon Lord John's earnestness by a proposal he made about the same time, contrary to the Webster-Crampton agreement of April 30, 1852, to make Greytown either unqualifiedly independent with an engagement to defend the Mosquito Indians or qualifiedly independent owing allegiance and support to the Mosquitos and assisted by British naval vessels.[75] Upon Lord Russell's proposal, Secretary of State Edward Everett dryly remarked, in a report which President Fillmore communicated to Congress: ". . . in all the negotiations carried on by this government, the only object has been to secure, as far as possible, the passage of the canal through one and the same civilized State, in order to preclude

[72] Howard Robinson, *Development of the British Empire*, Rev. and Enlarged ed., 338; Justin McCarthy, *A Hist. of Our Own Times*, IV, 354.
[73] *Sen. Exec. Docs.*, 34 Cong., 1 and 2 Sess., X (819), No. 25, p. 127; N. Y. *Herald*, Je. 11, 1856; *Parl. Papers*, 1856, LX, Nos. 137, 149.
[74] Jan. 13, 1853, *ibid.*, No. 139.
[75] Jan. 19, *ibid.*, Nos. 141, 142.

the evils too likely to arise from its passing through more than one jurisdiction." [76]

Further light was thrown upon British intentions regarding Central America and isthmian transits by the Bay Islands incident.

Ever since the seventeenth century there had been an English settlement in Belize, or British Honduras, and the British government had exercised some sort of jurisdiction over it. There had always been boundary disputes between the English settlements and their neighbors, latterly with the Republic of Guatemala. The British government had supported the settlers and, of late, had shown a disposition to make Belize into a full-fledged colony. The so-called Bay Islands, Ruatan, Bonacca, and several smaller ones, lay in the Gulf of Honduras over one hundred miles from the coast of Belize and considerably closer to the Republic of Honduras. Some British subjects had settled there comparatively recently, and the British government had developed a claim that the islands were "dependencies" of Belize. The Republic of Honduras stoutly claimed them also.[77]

At the time of exchange of ratification of the Clayton-Bulwer Treaty, Lord Palmerston had sought to guard against the possibility that the United States would construe the mutual pledge not to "occupy, or fortify, or colonize, or assume or exercise any dominion over Nicaragua, Costa Rica, the Mosquito Coast, or any part of Central America" as surrendering or weakening British claims to Belize and the Bay Islands. He, therefore, instructed Bulwer to hand Clayton the declaration that "Her Majesty's Government do not understand the engagements of that Convention as applying to Her Majesty's settlement at Honduras, or to its dependencies." Clayton, after some hesitation, accepted this declaration on condition that Bulwer accept from him a counter declaration, in which, while admitting that the mutual pledge did not apply to British Honduras "nor the small islands which may be known as its dependencies," he carefully avoided recognizing that the so-

[76] Sen. Exec. Docs., 32 Cong., 2 Sess., VII (665), No. 44.
[77] Mary W. Williams, Anglo-American Isthmian Diplomacy, chs. i, ii.

called Bay Islands were dependencies of British Honduras, or recognizing the boundaries claimed for British Honduras, or, for that matter, even admitting the rightfulness of Britain's title to Belize itself.[78]

Now, on July 20, 1852, while Webster and Crampton were trying to give effect to their "Basis," a royal proclamation erected Ruatan, Bonacca, and four smaller islands in the Gulf of Honduras into the "Colony of the Bay Islands." The ostensible object was to afford protection to the British settlers and to give them better government.[79] There may have been another object. Ruatan had a harbor good enough to serve as a naval base. It might, therefore, be used to command the northern terminus of a projected railroad across the Republic of Honduras and the Atlantic terminus of any railroad which might be built across Guatemala. The action of the British government was certainly in violation of the spirit if not the letter of the Clayton-Bulwer Treaty.

The results of four years of discussion, diplomacy, and finance were not very imposing — a moribund canal company; a group of speculators operating a passenger service across Nicaragua unprotected by a single specific treaty and out of favor in the country in which it operated; the knowledge that a ship canal was practicable but might not be profitable; the Clayton-Bulwer Treaty embodying wise and noble principles applicable only in a future contingency; and Great Britain still in a position to control or interrupt any transit across that portion of the isthmus, if she should choose to do so.

It may occur to some that the United States might still have secured the canal by insuring profits on the investment or by advancing a large part of the capital. Daniel Webster did, in fact, write to A. A. Lawrence in London, May, 1852, that the United States and Great Britain having jointly agreed to protect the company ought to put up the money. If England were not disposed to help, America would do it alone and the

---

[78] *Clayton Papers*, letters dated May 16, 21, 1856; *Sen. Exec. Docs.*, 32 Cong., 2 Sess., III (660), No. 12, pp. 2-4; *Sen. Exec. Docs.*, 47 Cong., 1 Sess., III (1991), No. 194, p. 187; *Cong. Globe*, 32 Cong., 2 Sess., 237, 250; *ibid.*, 33 Cong., 1 Sess., App., 96; *Parl. Papers*, 1856, LX, Nos. 42, 49.
[79] Williams, *op. cit.*, 139.

government would be disposed to aid to the full extent of its constitutional power.[80] But, what with opposition of champions of other routes to the Pacific, both transcontinental and isthmian, and the opposition of the strict constructionists and of those whose watchword was economy, such a proposal would have received short shrift in Congress. Furthermore, England's consent and diplomatic co-operation would have had to be secured.

The Taylor Administration and Clayton in particular have been criticized times without number for not boldly asserting the Monroe Doctrine, ejecting the British from Greytown, and securing the construction of a canal exclusively under American protection and control. The answer is that such an achievement would have required a war, and a successful one, at a cost far greater than the worth of the canal. It would appear in the light of future events that the Clayton-Bulwer Treaty had as well not have been made. In the 1850's, however, as the second ranking (not the first) maritime and commercial nation of the world, it was the proper policy of the United States to attempt to extend the principle of the internationalization of the great waterways of the world.

[80] *Writings and Speeches of Daniel Webster*, XIV, 481.

*CHAPTER VI*

## THE TEHUANTEPEC RAILROAD
## PROJECT, TO 1853

ANOTHER isthmian project which raised high hopes for a time in certain quarters was that of a railroad across the Isthmus of Tehuantepec.[1] Topographically the route was as favorable for a railroad as either of the others. The distance to California via Tehuantepec was less than by either Nicaragua or Panama. That a railroad was not built there under United States auspices was the fault of historical circumstances.

As we have seen, United States citizens began to evince an interest in the Tehuantepec route during the Mexican War, and Secretary of State Buchanan instructed Trist to offer the Mexican government a tidy sum for the right of transit. That government refused the offer on the alleged ground that it had already granted the transit privileges to a private citizen of the Mexican Republic who had in turn conveyed them to citizens of Great Britain.[2] This reply was not ingenuous, to say the least. Trist did not press the offer.

On March 1, 1842, Santa Anna, then dictator of Mexico, had granted to one Don Jose de Garay, a citizen of the republic, the exclusive right for sixty years to establish and operate a communication by railroad, canal, or natural waterways across the isthmus. Garay was to receive in fee simple all the unoccupied lands along the route for ten leagues on each side. Travelers and merchandise in transit were to be free from government taxes and tolls for a period of fifty years. Foreigners might acquire real estate and follow their trades and callings within a distance of fifty leagues of the route. In re-

---

[1] The diplomatic aspects of the first Tehuantepec project are discussed at length in P. N. Garber, *The Gadsden Treaty*, and J. Fred Rippy, *The United States and Mexico*, 47-67. They are discussed here for the sake of completeness and because, it is believed, they should be interpreted somewhat differently.

[2] See above, p. 14.

turn for these extensive privileges, the Mexican government was to receive one fourth of the net profits of the improvement and the full ownership at the expiration of the sixty years.

Whether Garay had any intention other than to sell his valuable franchise to the highest bidder does not appear. He did not establish any means of communication, but he sought diligently to keep his grant alive. He secured a reaffirmation of the grant from President Bravo in February, 1843. In December, 1843, he secured, this time from Santa Anna, an extension of time for beginning the work from July, 1844, to July, 1845. Not having commenced the work by the latter date, he sought another extension of time from the Congress of Mexico and, apparently, was on the point of getting it when Congress was dissolved by a new dictator, General Salas. From Salas, Garay managed to get a decree, dated November 5, 1846, extending the time for commencement to November 5, 1848, and granting still further privileges. Before the latter date, he did something which, it was later alleged, the Mexican government recognized as a beginning of the work.[3]

In 1847, Garay made certain contracts with Messrs. Manning and Mackintosh, British citizens, looking to the transfer of his contract to them. It was the Garay grant and this contemplated transfer which the Mexican government gave as an excuse for refusing Trist's offer. Garay's grant was not formally transferred to Manning and Mackintosh until September 28, 1848, long after Trist's offer was refused. What Manning and Mackintosh's original intentions may have been, the record does not show. At any rate they promptly sold the concession, February 5, 1849, to Peter A. Hargous, a shrewd New York merchant with connections in Mexico.[4] According to the rumor of the day, Hargous paid only $25,000 for the grant.[5] Certainly an American citizen secured for a

[3] On the Garay grant see Sen. Exec. Docs., 32 Cong., 1 Sess., X (621), No. 97, especially Letcher to Ramirez, Apr. 2, 1852; a long memoir by Judah P. Benjamin in Am. R. R. Jour., XXIV, 535; and documents in J. J. Williams, The Isthmus of Tehuantepec: Being the Results of a Survey for a Railroad. . . , App., 261-77.

[4] Sen. Exec. Docs., 32 Cong., 1 Sess., X (621), No. 97, pp. 163-74.

[5] Pierce Butler, Judah P. Benjamin, 124.

small sum a franchise for which his government had offered
$15,000,000.

Immediately after making his purchase, Hargous petitioned
Congress to examine the project of a railroad across Tehuantepec before deciding whether or not to lend support to the
Panama venture; and even at this early stage there was sufficient interest in his scheme to assist materially in defeating a
bill in the Senate for aid to the Panama Railroad Company.[6]
Hargous also appealed to the State Department for diplomatic
support, being mistrustful, no doubt, of the intentions of
the Mexican government. He had probably heard that the
Mexican government had notified Garay that his grant had
expired.[7]

Secretary of State Clayton quickly decided to support
Hargous. On April 30, 1849, he wrote Clifford, minister to
Mexico, that the United States government would regard any
infringement of the grant with "just dissatisfaction." When
Clifford made inquiry, the Mexican Minister of Foreign Affairs
was non-committal with regard to the grant, but tried to persuade him that the United States would have no just cause of
complaint in case the grant should be revoked. He inquired
whether or not the United States government would be willing to make a treaty with Mexico similar to the treaty with
New Granada.[8] In response to this, Clayton, in September,
instructed Letcher, who had succeeded Clifford, to make a
treaty affording protection to the construction and operation
of the proposed communication but not guaranteeing the sovereignty of Mexico over the Isthmus of Tehuantepec nor the
neutrality thereof. The United States would disavow designs
on the territory, he said. The guarantee made to New Granada Clayton described as a "conspicuous exception to our usual
cautious and wise policy." However, no foreign government
or corporation should ever be allowed to purchase the facilities
of transit.[9] Later on in the negotiations, after the Clayton-

[6] See above, pp. 57-59.
[7] Cong. Globe, 32 Cong., 2 Sess., App., 162; Sen Exec. Docs., 32 Cong., 1 Sess.,
X (621), No. 97, p. 80.
[8] Ibid., 5-10.
[9] Ibid., 10-14.

Bulwer Treaty had been signed, Clayton instructed Letcher to secure an article securing the same privileges at the isthmus for all nations which would make agreements with the United States or Mexico to protect the railroad.[10]

On June 22, 1850, Letcher signed a treaty with the Mexican commissioner, Pedraza. It was in substantial accord with Clayton's instructions. But the United States might assist in protecting the communication only upon the request of Mexico. The contracting parties were to use their best efforts to preserve the neutrality of the isthmus, even in case of war between them, and the full sovereignty of Mexico over the isthmus was recognized. The holders of the concession must give their consent to the treaty within four months, and until such consent should be given the instrument was not to be submitted for ratification. The treaty did not specifically recognize Hargous as holder of the concession. The United States government understood it to recognize him and the Mexican government, it later appeared, had mental reservations.[11]

Meanwhile Hargous had succeeded in interesting New Orleans parties in his grant. In May, 1850, a committee of citizens undertook to organize a company within two years to take over the concession. Hargous was to have one third of the capital stock of $9,000,000 and was to be paid $500,000 to cover advances he promised to make to meet the cost of surveys, land sales, etc. Until a charter could be secured (when the Legislature of Louisiana should meet), the Garay-Hargous grant was transferred by deed of trust to five prominent citizens of New Orleans.[12] Meanwhile a "Permanent Committee," headed by Judah P. Benjamin and unofficially styled "The Tehuantepec Railroad Company of New Orleans," undertook to act with Hargous in getting the project started. Subscriptions for stock were taken with some success, and the sale of Tehuantepec lands was begun.[13] The New Orleans press gave favorable publicity.

[10] Ibid., 17-18.
[11] Ibid., 20-23.
[12] Ibid., 175-77; DeBow's Rev., X, 94-96; Am. R. R. Jour., XXIII, 705.
[13] Ibid., XXIII, 689, 757, XXIV, 90, 295, 372, 451, XXV, 236; Butler, op. cit., 120-33.

In December, 1850, the "company" dispatched a party to make a new survey. The United States government permitted an army officer to act as chief engineer. The government of Mexico authorized the survey without specifically recognizing the company and instructed the governor of Oaxaca to afford the party every facility.[14] The surveyors reported a very favorable route. They estimated the cost of a railroad fully equipped at $7,847,896.17.[15] They recommended that, pending the construction of a railroad, a temporary transit be opened by means of light draught steamboats on the Coatacoalcos River on the Atlantic side and a short river on the Pacific side with a portage between by means of mules and horses. The company at one time expected to have this temporary transit opened by the early part of 1851.[16]

While these activities were going on, strong opposition was developing in Mexico to the Garay-Hargous grant and to the treaty which was designed to protect it. After the Mexican War the Mexican people were naturally antagonistic to any venture on Mexican soil sponsored by the United States. The grant was looked upon as an improvident bestowal of Mexico's natural resources, as indeed it was, and this impression was strengthened by bold statements made by the Tehuantepec Company as to the value of the lands it was to have. The colonization feature was especially odious. It was feared Tehuantepec would become another Texas. Rash statements in Southern newspapers lent color. The Hargous grant was opposed also by parties interested in a rival project for a railroad from Vera Cruz to Acapulco. There may also have been a hope in official circles that, if the grant could be annulled, the United States would renew its offer of $15,000,000 for the right of transit.[17]

When the Letcher-Pedraza convention, signed June 22, 1850, reached Washington, Clayton had been succeeded as

---

14 *Sen. Exec. Docs.*, 32 Cong., 1 Sess., X (621), No. 97, pp. 14-17.
15 J. J. Williams, *The Isthmus of Tehuantepec*. . . ; *Am. R. R. Jour.*, XXV, 236, 241.
16 *Ibid.*, XXIV, 372; J. J. Williams, *op. cit.*, 73 ff.
17 Letters and documents in *Sen. Exec. Docs.*, 32 Cong., 1 Sess., X (621), No. 97, especially Letcher to Webster, Oct. 22, 1850, Jan. 17, 1851, and Smith to Webster, Feb. 16, 1851 (pp. 36-38, 41-43).

secretary of state by Daniel Webster. Webster requested Hargous to give his assent to the treaty, as provided therein. Hargous refused, on the ground that his grant was not sufficiently protected, and asked Webster for assurance that, whether the treaty should be ratified or not, his property would be protected from "unjust confiscation and violence on the part of the Mexican Government." Webster gave the assurance of protection insofar as the "executive government of the United States can constitutionally and lawfully extend it." [18] He then attempted to secure amendments to the treaty to meet Hargous's objections. He demanded that the Garay grant be specifically named, that the United States have the right to send troops to protect the transit even though Mexico might not request assistance, and that the United States have equal right with Mexico in regulating tolls. He threatened that, if the Mexican government failed to comply with these demands, the United States would protect the grantee anyway and might withhold money still due Mexico under the Treaty of Guadaloupe Hidalgo.[19]

Letcher made strenuous efforts to get Webster's proposed amendments to the treaty accepted but, as he anticipated, to no avail. He was informed that they infringed the sovereignty, honor, dignity, and pride of Mexico and if the government accepted them it would be overthrown. Finally, with Webster's consent, Letcher signed with Pedraza, January 25, 1851, another convention which was almost identical with the former one.[20] Hargous now accepted it, and it was promptly ratified by the United States Senate.[21] The Mexican government procrastinated. The Executive submitted an opinion to the Congress that the Garay grant was invalid.[22] The Mexican minister to the United States tried to get Webster to admit that under the treaty Mexico alone had the right to pass upon the validity of the grant. Webster, however, insisted that "the

[18] *Ibid.*, 24-26, 28.
[19] *Ibid.*, 29-35.
[20] *Ibid.*, 47-50; Letcher to Crittenden, Sept. 15, 1850, in *J. J. Crittenden Papers* (Library of Congress).
[21] *Sen. Exec. Docs.*, 32 Cong., 1 Sess., X (621), No. 97, p. 43.
[22] *Ibid.*, 54-58.

very object of the treaty . . . is to secure rights derived from Mexico by a public act, amounting to a pledge, which she cannot but fulfil." [23] A number of American newspapers, however, expressed the opinion that the Garay grant was invalid or that Mexico alone had the right to pass upon its validity.[24] Some of these expressions may have been inspired by persons interested in the Panama, Nicaragua, or transcontinental projects. Others no doubt were prompted by a sincere belief in the justice of Mexico's position. Encouraged by these evidences of division in the United States, the Mexican Congress annulled the Garay grant, May 22, 1851, and the Executive ordered the survey discontinued and expelled the surveyors.[25]

Webster refused to regard the acts of the Mexican government as final. He protested against the expulsion of the surveyors and continued to demand the ratification of the treaty.[26] The New Orleans Company raised a great outcry, and there was rash talk of seizing the isthmus and building the railroad anyway.[27] Having received information that a proposition was being considered in Mexico to offer the right of building a Tehuantepec railroad to the British government, Webster seized the occasion to announce that the United States "could not see with indifference that isthmus, or any part of it, pass under the sway of any European State; or that the railroad or canal should be controlled by the government of such State." [28] The Mexican Minister of Relations offered to make a satisfactory treaty if protection to the Garay grant could be omitted, and he intimated that, in such case, Mexico would indemnify Hargous and the "company" for losses sustained.[29] Webster rejected these advances and instructed Letcher to insist upon the submission of the treaty.[30] President Fillmore was pre-

[23] *Ibid.*, 54-58, 60-66.
[24] *Am. R. R. Jour.*, XXIV, 517.
[25] *Ibid.*, XXIV, 451, 517; *Sen. Exec. Docs.*, 32 Cong., 1 Sess., X (621), No. 97, pp. 46, 50-52, 75-79, 80-85, 88.
[26] *Ibid.*, 85-88, 93-95, 100-103.
[27] *Ibid.*, 89, 90, 92, 100-103, 107-09; *Sen. Repts.*, 32 Cong., 1 Sess., II (631), No. 355, p. 10; *Am. R. R. Jour.*, XXIV, 517, 535; *DeBow's Rev.*, XIII, 45 ff.
[28] Webster to Letcher, Dec. 22, 1851, *Sen. Exec. Docs.*, 32 Cong., 1 Sess., X (621), No. 97, p. 110.
[29] *Ibid.*, 105-07, 155-56, 159-63.
[30] *Ibid.*, 127.

vailed upon to write to President Arista advising ratification.[31] Certain private citizens of the United States, however, probably interested in rival projects wrote to officials in Mexico urging rejection — to the great anger and disgust of Webster and Letcher.[32] Finally the treaty was submitted to the Mexican Congress and, as might have been anticipated, was rejected by an almost unanimous vote.[33]

Hargous and the New Orleans Company refused to accept defeat. Of the State Department they demanded either specific enforcement of the terms of the Garay grant or the collection of adequate damages. Webster, however, rather tamely intimated to the new Mexican minister at Washington his willingness to resume negotiations — good evidence that he had theretofore been bluffing — ; he said, though, that the United States "cannot be indifferent" to the claims of the Garay assignees.[34] The Senate requested the President to submit the Tehuantepec correspondence; this he did. The Committee on Foreign Relations reported resolutions recommending the suspension of further negotiations and, if Mexico failed to reconsider her position in a reasonable time, the adoption of such measures as would "preserve the honor of the country and the rights of its citizens." [35] In debate several senators were very severe in their denunciation of the course of Mexico. But Seward, of New York, and Hale, of New Hampshire, spoke against the resolutions. They denied that the United States was obligated in law or morals to protect the assignees of the Garay grant or that the Tehuantepec crossing was of such vital necessity to the nation as to justify the use of forceful measures. Both condemned Webster's methods.[36] The resolutions were not pressed to a vote.

The Mexican government, meantime, had offered a new contract to the highest bidder with terms less liberal than those of

[31] *Ibid.*, 157-59.
[32] *Ibid.*, 104-07, 110.
[33] *Ibid.*, 144; Garber, *Gadsden Treaty*, 53.
[34] *Sen. Exec. Docs.*, 32 Cong., 1 Sess., X (621), No. 97, p. 151.
[35] *Sen. Repts.*, 32 Cong., 2 Sess., II (631), No. 355; *Cong. Globe*, 32 Cong., 2 Sess., 458.
[36] Debate in *ibid.*, App., 134-47, 160-70.

the old grant.[37] Webster advised Hargous to bid.[38] Hargous did so, through an agent. However, after a scramble among speculators the contract was awarded, February 5, 1853, to Colonel A. G. Sloo, of New Orleans. Soon a "new" company, as distinguished from the "old" company was organized in Louisiana to take advantage of the new grant.[39] The new company displayed little energy. The old company refused to give up the ghost. By this time Daniel Webster was in his grave. In March, 1853, Conkling, a Fillmore appointee who had succeeded Letcher in Mexico City, negotiated a treaty affording protection for the Sloo grant and leaving the Garay grantees out in the cold.[40] Conkling acted without instructions. Franklin Pierce did not see fit to submit this Whig treaty to the Senate. Thus far and no farther four years of diplomacy and speculation had brought us.[41]

[37] Larrainzer to Webster, July 10, 1852, *Sen. Exec. Docs.*, 32 Cong., 1 Sess., X (621), No. 97, p. 152. See also *DeBow's Rev.*, XIV, 407.
[38] *Writings and Speeches of Daniel Webster*, XVI, 659.
[39] *DeBow's Rev.*, XIV, 407; Garber, *Gadsden Treaty*, 58, 59.
[40] Richardson, *Messages*, V, 233; *Sen. Exec. Jour.*, IX, 265, 276.
[41] For later Tehuantepec projects and diplomacy, see below, chapters ix, xv.

*CHAPTER VII*

## A CONGRESSIONAL EPISODE, 1853

CONGRESS first grappled in earnest with the Pacific railroad issue in the short session of the Thirty Second Congress, 1853. The short sharp struggle which then occurred illuminated practically all the ramifications and complications of the question.

In the long session of the Thirty Second Congress, Senator Rusk, of Texas, chairman of the Committee on Post Offices and Post Roads, had reported a bill providing for not one but *two* Pacific railroads. One was to be built by Asa Whitney upon his well-known plan. The other was to be built by persons named in the bill upon a similar plan and was to run from a point on the Mississippi not north of Memphis to San Diego, San Francisco, or other suitable point on the Pacific.[1]

Three weeks later, Stephen A. Douglas reported a bill from the Committee on Territories for the protection of the emigrant route to California, the construction of a telegraph line, and the establishment of an overland mail. The President was to be authorized to raise three regiments of a thousand men. They were to be disposed in military posts and in "station houses" not more than twenty miles apart all along the line. The men should produce their own supplies by tilling the soil about the posts and stations. In addition to his regular pay, each soldier would receive a section of land at the expiration of three years service.[2] This bill was similar in terms to a proposal made in the St. Louis and Memphis railroad conventions of 1849 as a desirable measure preliminary to the construction of a Pacific railway.[3] Douglas probably intended it to prepare the way for the construction of the railroad and for the opening of the Nebraska country to settlement, which

---

[1] *Cong. Globe*, 32 Cong., 1 Sess., 941, 1759.
[2] *Ibid.*, 1161, 1683.
[3] Above, pp. 50, 51.

he believed was a necessary concomitant. He presented his bill, however, as one calculated, in default of provision for a railroad, to secure similar objects: "Is there a man in this body," he asked, "who does not know that this Union cannot exist unless we have some means, either *this road or a railroad*, or some other means, of communication with the Pacific?" [4]

Douglas's emigrant route bill was not cordially received by the Senate. Bell, of Tennessee, thought it would be more economical to start the railroad directly. Others thought the measure would postpone the construction of a railway instead of hastening it. Finally on motion of Gwin, California, the bill was recommitted to the Committee on Territories with virtual instructions to report a Pacific railroad bill. [5] A few days later Douglas reported such a bill but apparently was not pleased with it. It authorized the President to enter into contracts with reliable parties making the most satisfactory bids for the construction of two railroads across the *territories*. The contractors were to select the routes, provided that one start on the western boundary of Arkansas not north of Memphis and run to the eastern boundary of California near the mouth of the Gila and the other start on the western boundary of Missouri or Iowa not south of St. Louis and run to "some safe and commodious harbor" in Oregon. The contractors were to be reimbursed by liberal grants of public lands, remuneration for carrying the mails and government supplies, as well as by the earnings of the railroad. Large grants of land were offered to the states of Iowa, Missouri, Arkansas, Louisiana, and California for one connecting branch each. [6] This bill went over to the short session.

Before the Senate resumed consideration of the Douglas Pacific Railroad bill in the short session a group of New York speculators headed by Ex-Secretary of the Treasury Robert J. Walker and Levi S. Chatfield, an ex-attorney general of New York, came forward with a proposal for building the Pacific railroad. They would build the road if the government would

---

[4] *Cong. Globe*, 32 Cong., 1 Sess., 1762.
[5] *Ibid.*, 1763, 1847.
[6] *Ibid.*, 1890, 2466.

permit them to select their own route, make a grant of lands, loan them its bonds to the amount of $30,000,000, and pay the interest thereon until the road should have been completed. They seem to have had the southern route in contemplation. This group soon secured a charter from the State of New York as the Atlantic and Pacific Railroad Company, with an authorized capital stock of $100,000,000. The majority of the stock was soon subscribed, although not paid in.[7] The Legislature of Missouri also amended the charter of the Pacific Railroad Company of Missouri to permit it to extend its line to the Pacific and requested Congress to confer upon it the right of way across the public lands and a strip of land sixty miles wide in aid.[8]

In the short session of the Thirty Second Congress, there seemed to be a rather general disposition in the Senate to try to frame and pass a Pacific railroad bill. The bill reported by Douglas at the last session was made the special order for January 10, 1853. When it was taken up, a bill introduced by Gwin was promptly substituted with the understanding that it was only a point of departure and that every detail would have to be threshed out.[9]

The Gwin bill was almost indentical with the Douglas bill except as to routes. It provided for a main trunk with six branches, designed to take care of all the contenders for termini. The main trunk was to run from San Francisco southeastward up the San Joaquin and Lake Tulare valleys, along the 35th parallel route to Albuquerque and thence southeastward on the north bank of the Red River to the boundary of Arkansas near Fulton. From some point near Albuquerque a main branch was to break off and follow the Santa Fe Trail to the Missouri boundary near Kansas City. This branch in turn was to throw off another to run to the boundary of Iowa at Council Bluffs. Still another branch was to depart from the main trunk near the source of the Red River and cross Texas

[7] Am. R. R. Jour., XXVI, 728, XXVII, 394-96; Chicago Daily Jour., Jan. 14, 1853; Daily Mo. Repub., Jan. 31, Apr. 8.
[8] Ibid., Feb. 1, 1853; West. Jour. and Civilian, IX, 340-44.
[9] Cong. Globe, 32 Cong., 2 Sess., 127, 280-87, 314.

via Austin to the Gulf. At the other end a branch was to connect San Francisco and Puget Sound. The contractors were to receive the alternate sections of public land for forty miles on each side of the routes chosen in the territories. In addition, twenty alternate sections per mile were to be given the State of Iowa in behalf of a connecting road from Dubuque to Council Bluffs, to Missouri for one from St. Louis to Kansas City, to Arkansas for a road from Memphis to Fulton, and to Louisiana for one from New Orleans to Fulton, while forty sections per mile were to go to California in aid of the portions of the road therein.[10] In all, Gwin estimated, the bill would provide for the construction of 5,115 miles of railroad and would grant 97,536,000 acres of the public domain. The federal government had no lands in Texas to grant, but Gwin proposed to grant $12,000 per mile in aid of the branch in that state.

Brooke, of Mississippi, immediately offered as a substitute a bill embodying the proposal of the Atlantic and Pacfic Railroad Company of New York. According to this bill the road should run from some point on the Mississippi or the Gulf of Mexico west of the river. It was clear that the company intended to employ federal money in states, but it was possible (and the bill so provided), if states should refuse to allow the company to locate its line within their borders, to locate the railroad entirely within the territories.[11]

A few days debate made it clear that neither the magnificent Gwin bill nor the New York company's measure could pass. Some of the friends of a transcontinental railway conceived the idea of referring the old Douglas bill to a select committee and continuing the debate on the Gwin measure for the committee's guidance. The President of the Senate, Atchison, of Missouri, appointed Rusk, of Texas, chairman, Bell, of Tennessee, Dodge, of Iowa, Davis, of Massachusetts, and Gwin. All were friends of a railroad. Three were Democrats, two Whigs. Three, Rusk, Bell, and Gwin, were favorable to a southern route.

10 *Ibid.*, 280-84.
11 *Ibid.*, 315.

The debate on the Gwin bill brought out certain facts. For one, the Senate would not vote for more than one main trunk line. Gwin's bill "is entirely too magnificent for me," said Cass.[12] This decision was a bitter pill to some of the Western men. Geyer, of Missouri, complained that without provision for branches in the territories, every other state would have to get permission from the state in which the road should start to make connection with it; and "How, I will ask, with the spirit that has prevailed in some of the States of the Union, is that to be obtained?" [13]

The decision to lop off all branches naturally intensified the struggle over the terminus and route of the main line. Test votes quickly demonstrated that no agreement could be reached and that an attempt to designate the route would defeat the bill. Bell thereupon suggested that the designation of the termini and general route be left to the President of the United States, and, in default of any better way out, this was agreed to.

There seemed to be a consensus of opinion also that grants of lands alone would not secure the construction of a railroad and that money aid also must be given. It was agreed that the contractors must not be named in the bill but the contract should be awarded to the best bidder in free competition. The debates also showed that extreme caution must be exercised to avoid offending the scruples of influential Democrats, such as Cass, against infringing upon states' rights.

Guided in part by the debate on the Gwin bill, the Select Committee drew up a bill which was much superior to any earlier one. The President was to designate the termini and general route at as early a date as practicable, employing army and civil engineers to supply him with the information necessary to a judicious choice. He was to receive sealed bids for the execution of the work and was to let the contract to the lowest and best bidders. Under proper safeguards against fraud, the contractors were to receive twelve sections of public land per mile in the territories and six sections in the states

[12] *Ibid.*, 285.
[13] *Ibid.*, 422.

through which the road might pass, in both cases on the familiar alternate-sections principle. They were also to receive United States bonds to an amount not in excess of $20,000,000. The railroad must be completed within ten years. It would be the property of the contractors, but the government might purchase it at any time after thirty years for ten per cent more than the actual cost of construction. The contractors must carry the mails and troops and military supplies for the federal government free of charge. Congress could authorize other railroad companies to make connections between their lines and the Pacific. The contractors would be incorporated as "The Pacific Railroad and Telegraph Company." The provisions of the Act were to have no effect within the limits of any state "without the consent of the Legislature of said state previously had and obtained" — a condition manifestly designed to meet constitutional scruples.[14]

The opponents of federal aid at once assailed the Rusk Bill, as it was called, at every possible point with every available weapon. Brodhead, of Pennsylvania, thought it absurd to provide for a railroad in advance of surveys. How was it known that any transcontinental railroad was practicable? He proposed as a substitute the appropriation of $100,000 for a reconnaissance of the several possible routes by the United States Topographical Engineers.[15] How, asked others, could a Pacific railroad be protected from the Indians? The grants in aid offered by the bill were too large. Private companies, if given time, would build the road without government assistance. Congress had no power to charter a company to operate within a state either with or without its consent. It had no power to appropriate money in aid of internal improvements within states. The Pacific Railway and Telegraph Company would be such a monster as the Second United Bank. The bill conferred too much power upon the executive and abrogated the powers of Congress. It put too great a load upon the incoming president in requiring him to select the route and termini. Any selection the president might make would make enemies of the

14 *Ibid.*, 469.
15 *Ibid.*, 471.

unsuccessful interests. "If this bill passes, Franklin Pierce
may well ask to be saved from his friends," said Pettit of
Indiana.[16] The bill would disrupt the Democratic Party, said
Mason and Butler.

The opponents of a Pacific railroad measure tried to stir up
strife over the route. In replying to objections to federal incorporation of a company to operate in a state Douglas unwise-
ly said it might not be necessary for any portion of the road
to lie in a state; ". . . if General Pierce should make the terminus . . . down near the Red river and then should select a
pass in the mountains of New Mexico, it might be necessary
to run across a barren waste in the corner of Texas." Charl-
ton, of Georgia, pounced upon the remark. "My honorable
friend from Illinois knows that General Pierce . . . is a strict
constructionist . . . and, therefore, never will consent to locate
this road through a State. Then I understand he will be compelled to locate the road through the South Pass. That will
bring it through the Nebraska Territory to the Missouri River,
at the point [Council Bluffs] which the Senator from Ohio
[Chase] first designated." — Only two days earlier, Douglas
as Chairman of the Committee on Territories had reported a
bill for the organization of Nebraska which had already passed
the House— Said Butler, of South Carolina, "I believe there
is a concurrent opinion that the Gila route is best; but . . . it
will not be adopted. I will make the prediction. The road
will go to the lakes." [17]

The friends of Pacific railway legislation held together quite
well for some time, although many were evidently nervous
about the provisions as to route.[18] They marshalled the arguments in favor of a Pacific railroad and of the particular provisions of the committee bill in an entirely competent manner.
They made much of the failures of our diplomacy to clear the
way for isthmian projects. "Since the ratification of the unfortunate Clayton-Bulwer treaty," said Toucey, of Connecti-

[16] J. B. Lamar advised Howell Cobb not to enter Pierce's cabinet on this
account. *Toombs, Stephens, Cobb Correspondence* (Am. Hist. Assn., *Report*,
1911, Vol. II), 324.
[17] *Cong. Globe*, 32 Cong., 2 Sess., 697, 708, 709.
[18] *Ibid.*, App., 186, 225 (remarks of Geyer and Bell).

cut, "which assures to Great Britain the ascendancy in Central America, I regard it as a measure of vastly increased importance" to build a transcontinental railroad.[19]

On February 18, Brodhead's substitute providing merely for a survey of routes was defeated by a vote of 22-34, and a motion by Mason, of Virginia, to recommit the bill was voted down 18 to 33.[20] These two votes show the full strength of the opponents of government aid for constructing a railroad to the Pacific. Of these opponents nine may be recognized as Southern strict-constructionist, states' rights men opposed to all measures calculated to increase the expenditures or expand the activities of the federal government. Two were Eastern Democrats of the strict-construction school who were also usually hostile to measures for developing the West. Six were Eastern or Southern Whigs who had often shown unfriendliness to Western measures. The Wisconsin senators voted for Brodhead's substitute; they favored the extreme northern route and knew there was little chance of its selection under the pending bill. Chase, of Ohio, also voted for the substitute; he was a strong anti-slavery man and was apparently determined to vote for no bill which did not expressly designate a northern route. Bright and Pettit, of Indiana, seem to have counselled with their fears for the effects of a Pacific railroad bill upon the fortunes of the Democratic Party. Bell and Geyer both asserted that the Panama Railroad Company, the Accessory Transit Company, the Pacific Mail Steamship Company, the Tehuantepec Railroad Company, and various shipping interests were bringing great outside pressure to bear against the railroad bill.[21] This may have been true, but no senator can be identified as having been influenced primarily or even largely by these interests except Soulé, of Louisiana, who was a supporter of the Tehuantepec project.

Following the defeat of Brodhead's substitute, it seemed that the Rusk Bill would surely pass, and its enemies well-nigh

[19] *Ibid.*, 681.
[20] *Ibid.*, 676, 680.
[21] *Ibid.*, App., 187, 227. *Cf.* J. A. McDougall, of California, *West. Jour. and Civilian*, IX, 97.

despaired. The sequel proved they had been unduly alarmed.

Various minor alterations to perfect the bill were made, various hostile amendments were voted down. The bill was just on the point of being reported to the Senate from the Committee of the Whole when Cass, who had voted favorably on every motion thus far, struck consternation among the friends of the measure by saying he could never support it so long as it provided for the construction of a railroad in a state whether with or without the state's consent.[22] The bill was nevertheless reported favorably to the Senate.

At this juncture Shields, of Illinois, *after consultation with Douglas and Geyer*, offered the following amendment: "Provided, That no portion of the $20,000,000 to be advanced by the United States, shall be expended in, or deemed to apply to, a road within the limits of any existing state of the Union; and so much of said road, if any, as shall be located within any State of this Union, shall be made under the authority thereof, to be derived from the State Legislature, and not otherwise." [23] A vote was taken almost immediately, and the amendment was adopted, 22 to 20. Rusk angrily exclaimed that the amendment had "disjointed" the bill. "Destroyed," said Gwin. "Yes, sir, destroyed," replied Rusk. Underwood, of Kentucky, pronounced it dead. Brodhead renewed his substitute for a preliminary survey of routes. Three days later Weller, of California, moved to reconsider the vote by which the Shields amendment had been adopted. The motion carried. Weller then offered a substitute which differed only slightly from Shields's proviso, and this was adopted by a vote of 27 to 25.[24]

Douglas, Weller, and others now pressed for the passage of the bill with the Weller amendment attached. Rusk, Borland, Bell, and other advocates of a Pacific railway declared their unwillingness to vote for the measure as amended. Gwin decided to support it in spite of the objectionable proviso. But its remaining friends were unable to bring the ill-starred measure to a final vote. A debate then ensued on the question,

[22] *Cong. Globe*, 32 Cong., 2 Sess., 711.
[23] *Ibid.*, 714, 744.
[24] *Ibid.*, 715, 755, 756.

Who killed cock robin and why?[25] Rusk *et al* contended that those erstwhile friends who had supported the proviso were responsible. The latter hotly denied the charge and insisted that those who had turned against their own because of the amendment were the culprits. Where lay the truth among these charges and counter charges?

The voting in the Senate is very suggestive in this regard. Nine Democrats and one Whig who had shown themselves friendly to the Pacific Railroad bill on earlier roll calls voted for the Shields-Weller amendment. The Democrats were Cass and Felch, of Michigan, Walker, of Wisconsin, Hamlin, of Maine, Downs, of Louisiana, Douglas, Shields, Atchison, and Weller. Geyer, the Whig, voted for the Shields version and against the Weller substitute but showed no grief when the latter was adopted. Of the ten, only Downs lived below St. Louis. Nine Democratic senators friendly to the Pacific Railroad bill refused to vote for the Shields-Weller amendment. They were Rusk and Houston, of Texas, Borland and Sebastian, of Arkansas, Brooke, of Mississippi, Dodge and Jones, of Iowa, Dodge, of Wisconsin, and Gwin. Six of the nine, including Gwin, favored a southern route. *All* the senators who withdrew their support of the bill after the adoption of the Shields-Weller amendment were from the Southwest or South and favored a southern route.

Senators favorable to a southern route believed the Shields-Weller amendment weighted the bill heavily against that route and in favor of a central or northern. Borland put it, thus, "The amendment . . . excludes the whole range of Southern states from participation in the bill." A Pacific railroad from the Mississippi by the Gila route must cross two states before entering the territory of New Mexico, a distance of approximately twelve hundred miles. On the California end the best route from San Francisco, which almost everyone thought must be the western terminus, to the crossing of the Colorado was about seven hundred miles long. Such long stretches of railroad in Arkansas or Louisiana, Texas, and California, it

[25] *Ibid.*, 740-45, 756, 766-75, 817, 838-39.

seemed certain, could not be constructed without the aid of the federal government in money or credit. On the central and northern routes the case was different. There was every prospect that the two Missouri railroads would be successfully completed with local support, state aid, and the congressional land grant, made in 1852. As the *Daily Missouri Republican* rather naïvely put it, "The amendment of Mr. Shields ought not to have received so much opposition. So far as the eastern end of the road is concerned, the Pacific [of Missouri] Road will be built through Missouri, and by the people of Missouri, quite soon enough to connect with the road to be built under the patronage of the General Government through the Territory." [26] It seemed reasonably certain that at least one railroad could be pushed across Iowa without other federal subsidy than a land grant like that made to Missouri; there were powerful railroad interests in the Northwest interested in Iowa projects. The Missouri River was navigable to any suggested starting point in the territories for a railroad by a central route. On the California end the distance from San Francisco to the eastern boundary was not half as great by the central route as by the southern. On a northern route a railroad could be built from the Mississippi to the Pacific without entering a state at all.

The Southwestern senators who had deserted the Pacific Railway bill after the adoption of the Shields amendment ascribed various motives to the sponsors of that amendment. They were especially bitter against Cass, whom they held chiefly responsible. He had given the bill a "side blow," said one. He had allowed himself to be "confounded" by the constitutional refinements of Mason and Butler, said another. Cass, Douglas, and others had been terrified by the threats against the solidarity of the Democratic party, said some of the Whigs. Other senators charged that the Shields amendment was a cleverly planned maneuver for the express purpose of insuring the selection of the central route. John Bell was

[26] Feb. 28, 1853. The *Republican* also quoted the N. Y. *Herald* to the same effect.

quite pointed: "On Saturday evening gentlemen interested in a particular section of the Union, whether with or without concert, with or without reference to sectional interests, or a determination to secure an eastern terminus of that road at a particular point on the western borders, had an amendment adopted, under which I do not choose to submit quietly." [27]

Shields, Douglas, and Weller defended themselves. They had only been insisting, they said, upon the good Democratic doctrine that the government can not constitutionally aid internal improvements within the states. They had no sectional motives in urging the amendment. There would be no trouble in getting private capital to build the road in the states. If the road should go through Texas, she could aid it with a large land grant. At any rate, under the bill, the same amount of federal aid was offered whatever the route which might be chosen. Douglas especially argued at length that a route through Texas was just as likely to be chosen under the amended bill as under the original. Borland considered his arguments "specious."

The senators who, while supporting the Pacific Railroad bill in general, voted for the Shields amendment may have persuaded themselves honestly enough that party principles and personal consistency required them to take the course they did. This was almost certainly the case with Cass, an ex-presidential candidate. It would be difficult to find any other explanation in the case of Downs, a Southerner — Tehuantepec is an outside possibility. But in the cases of the others there may have been and probably was a subtle connection between constitutional principles and the desire to influence the choice of the route.[28] It would be difficult indeed to show why constitutional scruples or fears for the future of the Democratic party should have weighed more heavily with Shields, Douglas, Atchison, Felch, Walker, Hamlin, and Weller than with Borland, Sebastian, Rusk, Houston, and Gwin. Usually Southwestern Democrats had more constitutional scruples than

[27] *Cong. Globe,* 32 Cong., 2 Sess., 744.
[28] *Cf.* George Fort Milton, *The Eve of Conflict: Stephen A. Douglas and the Needless War,* 101.

Northwestern. In the preceding session of Congress, constitutional scruples had not prevented Douglas, Shields, Cass, Walker, and Felch from voting for a rivers and harbors bill.[29] Geyer, who had voted for the Shields amendment, although not for Weller's substitute, was a Whig; and Whigs were not supposed to have constitutional scruples against voting for federal aid to internal improvements in states.

Until the adoption of the Shields amendment Southwestern senators appeared confident that the bill would, if passed, result in the choice of a southern route. Rusk had written the bill.[30] In a speech at Henderson, Texas, the following September he gave this version of what had occurred, with what degree of accuracy it is impossible to say: "A company of capitalists [the New York Atlantic and Pacific Railroad Company] after making the necessary examinations, made a proposition to build the road, if the government would loan them $30,000,-000, and let them select the route. They brought an engineer of great skill and ability [A. B. Gray], furnished him with all the data that could be obtained; he estimated the cost of the road on the Northern route at $125,000,000, and the profit it would pay at one per cent. He estimated the cost of a road on the Southern route at $39,000,000, and the profit it would pay at 20 per cent. This brought over nearly all the opponents of the bill. Upon a final hearing all the North and East voted for it, and it lost by only two votes." [31] He had in mind, of course, the vote on the Shields amendment.

After the abandonment of the Rusk bill, Gwin, wishing to salvage something from the wreck, proposed Brodhead's survey bill as an amendment to the Army Appropriation bill. The sum was raised to $150,000. An additional section authorized and required the Secretary of War to receive proposals from individuals or associations for the construction of a railroad to the Pacific and to lay the same before Congress at its next session. The group of irreconcilable opponents of Pacific railway legislation assailed this item as earnestly as if it had pro-

[29] *Cong. Globe,* 32 Cong., 1 Sess., 2329.
[30] *Ibid.,* 32 Cong., 2 Sess., 703.
[31] *Texas State Gaz.,* Sept. 24, 1853.

vided for the actual building of a railroad. It was passed, however, by a vote of 31 to 16,[32] and was accepted by the House except for the additional section in regard to receiving bids.[33]

A few hours after Brodhead's amendment was accepted by the Senate, Douglas offered a slightly modified version of his bill of the previous session for the protection of the emigrant route to Oregon and California as another amendment to the Army Appropriation bill. It was again opposed by nearly all the Southern and Southwestern senators, no doubt largely because they feared it would weigh in favor of the selection of a central route for a railroad. The amendment was accepted nevertheless by the Senate. It was rejected by the House because of objections to details.[34]

On March 2, Douglas and Weller tried to add to the Post Office Appropriation bill a measure providing for a line of telegraph from the western boundary of Missouri to San Francisco. According to the terms of the amendment, when the line should have been constructed in a satisfactory manner, the builders were to receive warrants for 1,500,000 acres of public lands to be located along the route. Southwestern senators objected on the ground that the location of a telegraph line would determine the choice of a route for a Pacific railroad. "I do not charge," said Bell, "that there is indirection pursued by the amendment . . . but the effect is precisely the same as if that mode were adopted for finally locating the route for the great railroad." Douglas thereupon offered first to leave the selection of the route to the contractors and then, that not sufficing, to let the objectors designate the eastern terminus themselves. But suspicions could not be allayed, and the bill was defeated by practically the same combination which had defeated the Pacific Railway bill after the adoption of the Shields-Weller amendment, that is the opponents of federal aid to a Pacific railroad of any sort and the champions of a southern route.[35]

[32] Cong. Globe, 32 Cong., 2 Sess., 798-99, 814-23, 837-41.
[33] Ibid., 996-98.
[34] Ibid., 845, 1001-002, 1035, 1056.
[35] Ibid., 536, 1010-12.

The friends of a Pacific railway the country over accepted the provision for a survey of the possible routes as genuine progress, and, while the surveys were being got under way by the Secretary of War, public interest remained at a high pitch. In June, 1853, the second session of the Southern Commercial Convention, meeting in Memphis, gave most of its time and thought to the Pacific railroad. "This," said the New Orleans *Delta*, "was the Aaron's rod that swallowed up all others." [36] Chicago newspapers felt constrained to propose a Chicago Pacific railroad convention to offset the impression of the Memphis gathering. [37] In August, the *American Railroad Journal* thought the interest in the Pacific railway was at "fever heat" in the West and a little later believed the country unanimously convinced that the road must be built and speedily. [38] A San Francisco gentleman was reported to have offered a prize of $10,000 for the best treatise on the "Great Pacific Railway." [39] A newspaper was launched in Texas styled *"The Pacific Railroad Advocate."*

Congress could not well take up the Pacific railway problem directly again until after the reports of the surveys should have been received. But various states and cities continued to push forward their projects for "first links" with whatever resources and energy they could command. Proponents of various routes sought to remove as many of the political obstacles in the way of the selection of their respective favorites as possible. In the case of the 32nd-parallel route the principal obstacle of the sort was Mexican ownership of a goodly portion. In the cases of other routes the chief political obstacle was that a wide stretch of territory athwart them was unorganized and not even open to white settlement.

[36] Quoted in Richmond *Enquirer*, Je. 24, 1853.
[37] *Daily Jour.*, Je. 11, 23, 1853; Weekly *Democrat*, Je. 18.
[38] XXVI, 545, 762.
[39] San Francisco *Placer Times and Transcript*, Je. 10, 25, 1853; *DeBow's Rev.*, XV, 214.

# CHAPTER VIII

# FIRST LINKS

IT WAS abundantly clear to all who were striving to bring the proposed Pacific railroad through their respective states or into their respective cities that the palm might well go to that community which should first successfully push iron rails a considerable distance out upon the plains. Congress might well be persuaded to attach the national road to the most promising "first link."

In position, population, and wealth St. Louis and Missouri seemed to have the advantage over their rivals in promoting first links.

The Legislature of Missouri had chartered the Hannibal and St. Joseph Railroad Company, February, 1847, and the Pacific of Missouri, March 12, 1849.[1] However serviceable the projected roads might prove as local railroads, both were possible first links. The *American Railroad Journal* hailed the chartering of the Pacific of Missouri as the "most important move yet made in reference to a railroad to the Pacific." [2]

The Missouri delegation in Congress labored diligently to secure grants of public land in aid of the construction of the two roads. In 1850 they failed, although Illinois, Alabama, and Mississippi received a munificent grant on behalf of the Illinois Central and the Mobile and Ohio. Stephen A. Douglas, the principal architect of this measure, had got together a stronger combination of interests than the Missourians could effect. Moreover the Missouri bills suffered from the repercussions of a congressional trade which had failed of completion: Western members in pursuit of land grants for rail-

---

[1] Accounts of early Missouri projects are in R. E. Riegel, "Trans-Mississippi Railroads during the Fifties," *Miss. Val. Hist. Rev.*, X (Sept., 1923), 153-72; "The Missouri Pacific Railroad to 1879," *Mo. Hist. Rev.*, XVIII (1923), 3-26; E. M. Violette, *Some Chapters in the Story of Missouri*; and J. W. Million, *State Aid to Railways in Missouri*. See n. 1, ch. iii, for more general references.

[2] XXIII, 120, 601, 647.

roads had come to an understanding with Eastern Whigs in pursuit of increased tariffs that they would allow a tariff bill to slip through the House if the Easterners would neglect to block the land grants. The Illinois Central and Mobile and Ohio bill came up first and passed. The tariff measure came up next and was defeated, the Western bargainers being either unable or unwilling to deliver the necessary votes to save it. Then the Missouri bills came up and were defeated, several Eastern Whigs who had supported the Illinois Central bill now voting the other way.[3]

Congressmen from the land states gave equal support to the Missouri and Illinois bills. They had to do so on the general principle that, unless they stuck together on land grants, none of them could get anything. There were four Western states, however, in which the federal government owned no lands, namely, Ohio, Kentucky, Tennessee, and Texas. Interestingly enough nine members from Ohio and Kentucky who had not voted for the Illinois Central bill did vote for the Missouri bills while two Texas congressmen who had voted for the former bill failed to vote for the Missouri measures: Ohio and Kentucky were favorable to a central route for the Pacific railroad, Texas preferred a southern.

The Missouri Legislature at its next session, 1851, extended considerable state aid to the Pacific and the Hannibal and St. Joseph. Construction was actually begun on both roads before the end of the year. In March, 1851, the Legislature chartered the Northern Missouri Railroad Company to build northwest-ward from St. Louis, "intercept" the Hannibal and St. Joseph at Macon, and continue to the Iowa line with the prospect of making connection with Iowa roads. In November, 1851, it chartered the St. Louis and Iron Mountain Railroad Company to build a road from St. Louis through the iron ore district with the prospect of extension to Little Rock, Arkansas,

---

[3] This explanation is based on an analysis of House votes, some little colloquies in that body, and the reports of Washington correspondents of certain Western journals. *Cong. Globe*, 31 Cong., 1 Sess., 1838, 1950-53; 31 Cong., 2 Sess., 130; St. Louis *Mo. Repub.*, Sept. 23, 1850; *West. Jour. and Civilian*, V, 37, 38; *Am. R. R. Jour.*, XXIII, 601, XXIV, 153. *Cf.* H. G. Brownson, *Hist. of the Ill. Cent. R. R. to 1870*, pp. 26-31.

as a part of a proposed chain of railroads between St. Louis
and New Orleans. It was suggested that, if the Pacific railroad
should be built from Memphis, the Iron Mountain would be
in an advantageous position to tap it.

In June, 1852, the Missouri delegation finally succeeded in
securing a congressional land grant in aid of two east and west
roads across the commonwealth. The companies used some
money judiciously, but it is not clear just how, and the congressmen seem to have done some judicious trading, although it is
not clear just what. The bill specified the Hannibal and St.
Joseph route but for the other merely required that the grant
be used for the benefit of *a* railroad from St. Louis to the
western boundary of the state. The omission of a more
specific description had been necessary to maintain harmony
within the Missouri delegation.[4]

The State Legislature was shortly called into special session
to confer the federal land grant upon appropriate railroad
companies. The Hannibal and St. Joseph got its share without
difficulty. The Missouri Pacific was not so fortunate.[5] People
of southwestern Missouri demanded that their section receive
some benefit from the grant. Some of them, notably J. S.
Phelps of Springfield, an influential congressman, contended
that the best route for a railroad to the Pacific was from St.
Louis via Springfield to Fort Smith, Arkansas, and thence over
the thirty-fifth parallel route.[6] The special session was unable
to effect a solution of the knotty problem; but the regular
session, in December, arranged a compromise acceptable to all
concerned. It happened that the lands along the route of the
Missouri Pacific were already pretty well taken up, and a land
grant there would not be very valuable. More of the lands
along the southwest route were still in federal possession, and
besides the route was longer. The Pacific Railroad Company,
therefore, consented to build a branch to the southwest corner
of the state and receive the land grant for its exclusive benefit.

    [4] *Cong. Globe*, 32 Cong., 1 Sess., 1832; *Mo. Repub.*, Je. 15, 18, Sept. 11, Oct.
15, 1852, Je. 7, 9, 1853.
    [5] *Ibid.*, Sept. 1–30, 1852.
    [6] *Ibid.*, Sept. 21; *West. Jour. and Civilian*, VII, 23.

The Legislature thereupon undertook to give extra aid in behalf of the main line from St. Louis to Independence.[7]

Congressman John S. Phelps now became almost as ardent a champion of the thirty-fifth parallel route as Thomas H. Benton was of the central and was supported by southwest Missouri.[8] Said Benton, ". . . an insidious attempt has been made . . . to draw off the southwestern counties from the interest and glory of Missouri and attach them to the fortunes of Arkansas and Texas."[9] Other St. Louisans were glad to have another anchor to windward. Said one, "Thanks to a wise policy . . . in three years we shall have a railroad striking to the South-west three hundred miles . . . and ready to intercept any Railroad which Congress may order to be commenced to the Pacific."[10] In fact St. Louis had still another line out, the Northern Missouri, which was to cross the Hannibal and St. Joseph at Macon. It might "after all be the true road from our city to the Golden Gate."[11] The various Missouri roads were slowly but persistently got under way.

Chicago's "first links" in her immediate vicinity were easily and rapidly acquired; those beyond the Mississippi came more tardily. Of those of the former class, most was hoped of the Chicago and Rock Island. It had been originally chartered as the Rock Island and La Salle to run from LaSalle, the western terminus of the Illinois-Michigan Canal, to the Mississippi. In 1851 its name was changed and it was given permission to build into Chicago. Construction was started the same year, and the road was in operation by July, 1854. Rock Island was reputed the best bridge site on the Mississippi. Next in line, in the estimation of Chicagoans, for the honor of being first link was the Galena and Chicago Union, which would connect Chicago with Freeport, whence the branch of the closely allied Illinois Central would carry on to a point on the river opposite Dubuque, Iowa. This connection was completed in 1854. A branch of the Galena and Chicago Union, known as the Mis-

[7] *Mo. Repub.*, Jan. 1, 3, Feb. 2, Je. 7, 1853.
[8] *Ibid.*, Jan. 31, Feb. 15, Je. 7.
[9] *Ibid.*, May 17.
[10] *Ibid.*, Je. 24. See also *West. Jour. and Civilian*, VII, 23, VIII, 338.
[11] *Mo. Repub.*, Jan. 16, 1854.

sissippi and Rock River Junction, was completed in 1855 to the Mississippi at Fulton, opposite Clinton, Iowa. A chain of five short roads, already closely allied, promised when complete to give Chicago connection with the Mississippi at a point opposite Burlington, Iowa, and at Quincy, only twenty miles above Hannibal, Missouri, the terminus of the Hannibal and St. Joseph. The Burlington connection was established in 1855 and that to Quincy the following year. Meanwhile the consolidation of the little roads into the Chicago, Burlington, and Quincy was practically completed. Still another road, the Chicago and Alton, was completed in 1854 between Alton, twenty miles above St. Louis, and Joliet on the Rock Island, while a branch to Illinoistown opposite St. Louis was under construction.[12]  (See the map opposite p. 174.)

Thus as early as 1854 there was scarcely a possible point of departure on the Mississippi for a central Pacific railroad with which Chicago did not have or was not about to have rail connections. These several rail connections came to Chicago without any public aid on her part, without state aid, and with the exception of the short section of the Illinois Central, mentioned above, without federal aid. The companies received the usual local aid from communities through which their roads ran, but the funds were supplied mostly by investors who had confidence in the economic future of northern Illinois. The roads would have been built just as readily if there had been no prospect of Pacific connections. The chief engineer of the Fort Wayne and Chicago, after describing the numerous tributaries of the city, put the Chicago viewpoint aptly: "I have made no allusion to the anticipated connections with the Pacific, preferring to enumerate only those advantages which are without contingency. When this shall have been accomplished, whatever may be the route, Chicago will be in a position to share largely in its benefits. She is stretching out her iron arms toward the setting sun, and these in their widening embrace will give a liberal proportion of the commerce of the Pacific, whenever this shall have been reached."[13]  Of course Chi-

[12] Summary in *Am. R. R. Jour.*, XXVII, 595-98. See n. 1, ch. iii.
[13] *Am. R. R. Jour.*, XXVII, 821.

cagoans were still concerned that the point of departure for a central road be in the latitude of Chicago rather than in that of St. Louis.

As early as 1853, Edwin F. Johnson, a prominent advocate of a northern route for the Pacific railroad, could describe the first thousand miles out of Chicago as authorized in existing railroad charters, namely, those of the Illinois and Wisconsin, from Chicago to the Wisconsin state line, the Rock River Valley Union, from the line by way of Madison to La Crosse and thence up the Mississippi to the Minnesota line near St. Paul, and the Minnesota Western, from the Wisconsin line via St. Paul to the Red River of the North.[14] Considerable work had already been done by the first two companies, and they were said to be in the process of consolidation. So rapidly had the possibilities of railroads been demonstrated within a few years that by 1853 or 1854 Chicagoans no longer feared the competition as a railroad center of any lake port to the northward except possibly that which might arise at the head of Lake Superior. As Johnson put it, "Chicago being near the southern extremity of Lake Michigan, is a point towards which the various lines of railway traversing the country west and northwest of the Great Lakes, must converge. . . ."[15]

Out in Iowa, Chicago's most assured hinterland, projects for railroads pointing toward the Pacific were somewhat slower to take form than in Missouri.[16] Iowa was a new state, the population was small, and there were no cities of wealth and influence. In 1848 Stephen A. Douglas and Congressman Lefler, of Iowa, introduced bills for a congressional land grant in aid of a railroad from Davenport, opposite Rock Island, to Council Bluffs on the Missouri, that is for a road which would continue the soon-to-be Chicago and Rock Island to the Missouri. The same year the Iowa Legislature instructed the state's delegation in Congress to support the measure and the

[14] *Railroad to the Pacific, Northern Route; Its General Character, Relative Merits*, 11 ff. Johnson later became the chief engineer of the Northern Pacific.
[15] *Ibid.*, 100.
[16] Accounts of early Iowa projects are in "Historical Sketch of Iowa Railroads," *Rept. of the Railroad Commission of Iowa, 1893*; and *H. Repts*, 34 Cong., 1 Sess., III (870), No. 349. See n. 1, ch. iii, for more general references.

following year chartered a company to build the road. In 1850 a land grant bill for the road met the same fate in the House that the Missouri bills did.[17] A railroad convention in Iowa City later in the year and another in October, 1851, gave considerable impetus to this and other railway projects. In January, 1852, the Legislature chartered the Burlington and Missouri Railroad Company to build a road across the state from Burlington on the Mississippi to the Missouri at or near the mouth of the Platte. In Congress, Iowa representatives presented the claims of this project for a land grant on the ground that it would continue in the direction of the Pacific a partially completed chain of roads from Philadelphia to the Mississippi via Pittsburgh, Columbus, LaFayette, Indiana, and Peoria, Illinois.[18] In fact this Iowa road was destined to become an integral part of the Chicago, Burlington, and Quincy.

A land grant bill for aid for the Iowa roads was defeated in the House, June 9, 1852, only two weeks after the passage of a similar bill for the Missouri roads. The defeat was not due to any hostility to Iowa railroad projects in particular but to the vicissitudes of party and sectional politics. The Eastern Whigs had decided to hold up all grants in aid of railroads for the time being in an effort to force the passage of a general distribution bill, which would give federal lands to the landless states as well as to those in which such lands lay.[19]

In spite of the rebuff in Congress, construction was begun on the Burlington and Missouri in May, 1854. By that date, the company was receiving encouragement and assistance from the Illinois roads which were soon to be consolidated as the Chicago, Burlington, and Quincy. February, 1853, the Legislature chartered the Mississippi and Missouri Railroad Company to build the road from Davenport to Council Bluffs. John A. Dix, of New York, was president. Construction was not begun until 1855. The company was at this early date little more than a subsidiary of the Chicago and Rock Island,

[17] See above, p. 110.
[18] *Cong. Globe*, 32 Cong., 1 Sess., App., 359, 672.
[19] *Ibid.*, 1536, 1603.

with which it was shortly to be consolidated. Meanwhile the Dubuque and Pacific Company had been organized, April, 1853, to build a road across the state from Dubuque to Sioux City. The Legislature requested Congress to give it a land grant, suggesting that it "appears favorable to form a link in the great chain of railroads destined sooner or later to connect the Atlantic seaboard with the Pacific coast." [20] This road was eventually built and consolidated with the Illinois Central. Another ambitious project which the Legislature commended to Congress was for a road by Asa Whitney's old route from McGregor, opposite Prairie du Chien, to the mouth of the Big Sioux. Still another road, the Chicago, Iowa, and Nebraska, was projected to run from Clinton, opposite the Fulton terminus of the Galena and Chicago Union, via Cedar Rapids and along the 42nd parallel to the Missouri. No company was organized to build this road, however, until 1856. Thus at an early date, by early 1854 at least, no less than five railroads were projected to cross the state from east to west, each looked upon as a possible link in a road to the Pacific and each connecting at its eastern terminus with a road, built or soon to be built, to Chicago. At least four of these five Iowa roads could readily make Council Bluffs their western terminus if that should be selected as the point of departure for San Francisco.

In the lower Mississippi Valley also there were numerous projects for "first links." If actual construction was less there than in the upper valley, it was not due to any dearth of popular interest but rather to the lack of wherewithal to build. In fact public interest in the Pacific railroad was greater in the Southwest; for attention was not so much distracted by actual railroad developments, and there was greater need for the stimulus which the Pacific railroad might give.

Arkansas was somewhat slower than other states to catch the railroad fever. By 1852, however, there were four well-defined projects. Of these three were presented to the public as the beginnings of a railroad to the Pacific and had little other *raison d'etre*. The earliest and sturdiest of these projects

[20] Memorial, Jan. 5, 1853, *Sen. Misc. Docs.*, 33 Cong., 1 Sess. (705).

was for the Arkansas Central from Memphis via Little Rock to Fulton (near Texarkana) in the extreme southwest corner of the state, that is to say over the Arkansas portion of the Memphis-El Paso route. This project received impetus from two railroad conventions in Little Rock, November, 1851, and July, 1852, which had met to outline an internal improvement program for the state.[21] Other projects were for two east and west roads, Helena to Fort Smith, on the 35th-degree or Albuquerque route, and Gaines Landing to Fulton, and a north and south road through Little Rock, the Arkansas section of a much discussed Mississippi Valley road from New Orleans to St. Paul.[22]

The Arkansas delegation made the usual effort to secure a federal land grant on behalf of the proposed railroads. In 1852, Senator Borland, in conformity, he believed, with the wishes of his constituents, secured the passage of bills in the Senate for a grant in aid of the proposed Memphis to Fulton and the Gaines Landing to Fulton roads.[23] In the House, where the real struggle over land grants always occurred, Representative Johnson asked for a grant for a road from St. Louis, Missouri, to Fulton by way of Little Rock with a "branch" from the latter to the Mississippi at a point not designated and another from Little Rock to Fort Smith. The Committee on Public Lands reported a bill, April 17, for these roads with the exception that Cairo was substituted for St. Louis as the terminus of the north and south road.[24] This bill remained on the calendar until August 27, near the closing day of the session, when Johnson secured a suspension of the rules for taking it up out of order. Debate was cut off, and the bill was passed within an hour.[25]

As we have seen an Iowa land grant bill had been defeated earlier in the session because of a determination on the part of landless-state Whigs to force through a general distribu-

[21] West. Jour. and Civilian, VII, 189-92, VIII, 282-83.
[22] Ibid., IX, 116, 121 ff.
[23] Cong. Globe, 32 Cong., 1 Sess., 782, 1686.
[24] Ibid., 1004.
[25] Ibid., 2387. Johnson's management won praise. Daily Mo. Repub., Oct. 15, 1852; Ark. State Gaz. and Dem., Feb. 18, 1853.

tion bill. Now either, having failed to secure the passage of
the Bennett distribution bill, they had relaxed their opposition
to land grants in aid of railroads or, what is much more probable, had no chance to voice their opposition because the bill
had been brought up unexpectedly, to them, in a thin house.

The bill was called up in the Senate August 30, by Borland.
Its passage was urged by Rusk, of Texas, the arch champion
of the Gila route to the Pacific. The Senate, however, refused
to consider it so near the end of the session, and it went over
to the short session with excellent prospects for passage.[26]

These moves in Congress were received in Arkansas with
divided feelings. Those sections of the state interested in the
roads omitted from the Johnson bill were critical of Johnson.
People in the northeastern corner of the state were pleased
with the Cairo provision. No one else was. A road to Cairo
had hardly been mentioned in previous discussions in Arkansas.
Aid for a road to St. Louis would have been much more
popular. The provision in the Johnson bill for a branch from
Little Rock to the Mississippi without the point being designated threatened warfare between the friends of the Memphis
terminus and the friends of Helena. The Legislature instructed the state's delegation in Congress to work for a grant
for the Memphis, Little Rock, and Fulton and the Gaines
Landing to Fulton roads, that is, the roads provided for in
Borland's bills, but failed to recommend the Cairo road.[27]
However, it chartered the Cairo and Fulton Railroad Company
as well as the Arkansas Central Railroad Company, the latter
to build a road from Memphis via Little Rock and Fulton to
a point on the Texas boundary "most favorable for continuation" through northeastern Texas and on a scale suitable to
"an integral portion of the main trunk or a southern branch of
the National Atlantic and Pacific Railroad." [28]

The reasons why Congressman Johnson did not work in the
House for the bills whose passage Borland had secured in the
Senate are understandable. The Senate would pass almost any

[26] *Cong. Globe*, 32 Cong., 1 Sess., 2463-64.
[27] *Ibid.*, 32 Cong., 2 Sess., 514, 672 ff.
[28] *Ark. State Gaz. and Dem.*, Feb. 18, 1853.

land grant bill introduced. Johnson had to frame a bill which would pass the House. Northern votes were needed. Provision for a northern connection might attract them. Borland's bills contained no such provision. Johnson lived in Little Rock. His bill offered aid for two roads through that little city; Borland's for only one. There were no strong interests outside Arkansas interested in the Gaines Landing to Fulton project. The branch to Fort Smith might attract friends of the Albuquerque route.

The substitution in the House bill of Cairo for St. Louis (which was designated in Johnson's original bill) as the northern terminus of the northeast-southwest road is more difficult to explain. Provision for a road to St. Louis was objectionable to many in that it would give Missouri aid for a third railroad, aid for two having been granted already in the Act of June, 1852. A road to Cairo would cross only a corner of Missouri and that in a locality where most of the lands had already been granted to the state under the Swamp Lands Act, of 1850. A Cairo terminus might secure favor in Kentucky where the mouth of the Ohio was being advocated as a compromise terminus for a Pacific railroad. It would secure the favor of the Illinois delegation, for it would give Chicago southwestern connections independent of St. Louis.[29] It is an interesting commentary that, although the attendance in the House was small when the bill was passed, every Illinois congressman was in his seat and voted for the bill. Professor Hodder has seen the "clever manipulation" of Stephen A. Douglas in the addition of the Cairo provision.[30] There seems to be only circumstantial evidence to prove his complicity. He was most certainly interested in the Illinois Central and its connections. There is plenty of evidence, however, that he had not despaired of having the Pacific railroad built on a central or northern route. Senator Rusk, of Texas, was probably the chief engineer of the Cairo provision. He was working hard at the very time for

[29] As to Johnson's motives, see Memphis *Daily Appeal*, Apr. 19, 1853; *Ark. State Gaz. and Dem.*, Feb. 18, Mar. 11, Apr. 8; remarks in the Senate, *Cong. Globe*, 32 Cong., 1 Sess., 2464; 32 Cong., 2 Sess., 421, 514, 672-75.

[30] F. H. Hodder, "The Pacific Railroad Background of the Kansas-Nebraska Act," *Miss. Val. Hist. Rev.*, XII, 13 (Je., 1925).

the southern route for the railroad to the Pacific, and he hoped
that the promise of Northern connections would help to secure
its selection.[31] The Cairo to Fulton road fitted his Pacific railroad scheme like a glove.

In the short session of Congress, Sebastian, the junior
Arkansas senator, contrary to a promise he had made to
Borland, called up the Johnson land grant bill when his colleague was not in his seat. In fact he misrepresented Borland's
position and probably that of his state also. Geyer, of Missouri, expressed a dislike of the Cairo provision but refrained
from offering an amendment lest it result in sending the bill
back to the House. Gwin, of California, and Rusk lent their
powerful support to the bill. It was then passed without a
division.[32]

Two weeks later, when the fight over a Pacific railroad bill
was at its height, Borland rose to make an explanation. He
discoursed on the sentiment in his state, excoriated the Cairo
project, and found fault that the land grant bill had not specifically designated Memphis as the Mississippi terminus of
even the branch from Little Rock. Said he: "How far this
making Cairo, a point so unnatural and remote, the river terminus of the Arkansas system of roads, instead of Memphis,
which is the natural and obviously proper key to the resources
of the State, may affect the question of fixing the Mississippi
terminus of the great Pacific railroad, and so far deciding the
question whether Arkansas or another State shall be the
thoroughfare of the eastern section of this great highway,
time alone perhaps will determine. Should it prove to have
been a stone even of an ounce weight cast in, however uninten-
tionally, to turn the scale against our State, I shall never covet
the honors, nor the reflections, of any man of whom it may be
said, 'He did it'." [33] After Borland had resumed his seat,
Sebastian rose also to explain. He stated that an adverse vote
in the House on the Wisconsin land grant bill on the day before he had called up the Arkansas bill had proven that to

[31] *Cong. Globe*, 32 Cong., 1 Sess., 2464; 32 Cong., 2 Sess., 675; speeches in
Texas, *Tex. State Gaz.*, Sept. 24, Nov. 8, 1853. See above, 95ff.
[32] *Cong. Globe*, 32 Cong., 2 Sess., 514-16.
[33] *Ibid.*, 672-75.

amend the bill and send it back to the House would mean its death. He had consulted with Atchison, the presiding officer of the Senate, and with Senators Rusk and Gwin, who had charge of the Pacific Railroad bill, and they had brought forward reasons which had induced him to call up the bill contrary to his understanding with Borland. He promised to make a detailed explanation at a later date; this he never did.

Borland, in his pique, no doubt made too much of the failure to designate Memphis as the terminus of the so-called branch from Little Rock to the Mississippi. There could be little doubt that the Arkansas Legislature would confer the appropriate land grant upon the Arkansas Central, which was to build from Memphis. People interested in the Central Railroad rejoiced greatly over the land grant. Albert Pike, of Arkansas, wrote from Washington to Trezevant, of Memphis, a promoter of the road, "We regard this as settling, in point of fact, the Pacific Rail Road question, and as securing the ultimate adoption of the southern route." [34] There was rejoicing in Memphis. [35] A proposal to subscribe $500,000 to the Arkansas Central was submitted to the voters in April and carried by an overwhelming majority. The Memphis *Appeal* supported the proposal on the ground that it would ensure Memphis a western feeder and would "materially determine the question as to whether or not we shall have a connection with the great Pacific road." [36]

Pressure was brought to bear upon Governor Conway to call the Arkansas Legislature into special session to confer the land grant upon the railroad companies and, thus, get the roads started. The Governor refused, for certain reasons of factional politics, [37] and the lands were not conferred until January, 1855. They were then conferred upon the Cairo and Fulton, the "Memphis and Little Rock," and the Little Rock and Fort Smith companies each authorized to build over the route suggested by its name. The companies made earnest

[34] *Ark. State Gaz. and Dem.*, Feb. 25, 1853.
[35] *Ibid.*, Mar. 4, 18, Apr. 18.
[36] *Daily Appeal*, Apr. 20, 1853. Also issues for Apr. 7, 9, 12, 13, May 2; and *Ark. State Gaz. and Dem.*, Apr. 8, May 13.
[37] *Ibid.*, Je. 3, 10, 17, July 12, 22, 29; *West. Jour. and Civilian*, X, 39.

efforts to raise funds and start construction but without early success.[38]

The people of New Orleans, after repeated warnings that in this railroad age they could not depend indefinitely upon the Father of Waters alone to bring to their city the "lifeblood of commerce," [39] at last awoke to the necessity of joining in the struggle for railroads. One road, the New Orleans, Jackson, and Great Northern, was projected to run northward in the direction of Cairo, Louisville, or Cincinnati to prevent rivals from drawing off the trade of New Orleans' rightful domain. Another, the New Orleans, Opelousas, and Great Western was to run by way of Opelousas and Alexandria northwestwardly to the Sabine at a point most favorable for intercepting the proposed road through Fulton, Arkansas, to El Paso and the Pacific, with a branch running northward from Alexandria. The project was formally launched at a railroad convention in New Orleans in June, 1851, and, together with the Great Northern and other projects in the Southwest, was given great impetus by the large Southwestern Railroad Convention held in New Orleans in January, 1852.[40] Meanwhile another road to be known as the Vicksburg, Shreveport, and Texas had been projected to cross the northern portion of Louisiana. Its supporters also aspired to make it a link in a railroad to the Pacific, continuing a "chain" from Charleston and Savannah through Macon, Georgia, Montgomery, Alabama, and Jackson, Mississippi.[41]

The people of New Orleans and Louisiana, having once caught the fever, pushed their railroads with vigor. To enable New Orleans as a municipality to aid her railroads, a new charter was granted, February, 1852, reorganizing the city government and making provision for the extinguishment of the city's debt and, thus, the restoration of her credit.[42] The people of New Orleans then voted to guarantee the interest

---

[38] *Am. R. R. Jour.*, XXIX, 485, 723, 778, 819, XXX, 197, 563, 632.
[39] See *DeBow's Rev.*, II, 39-48, VIII, 444-50.
[40] *Ibid.*, X, 473, XI, 74, 142-78, 217, 240, XII, 305-32, 543-68; *Am. R. R. Jour.*, XXV, 33, 65, 66, 484, 502, 516-17.
[41] *Ibid.*, XXVII, 818-20, 823.
[42] *DeBow's Rev.*, X, 690 ff., XI, 74-80; *Acts Passed at the Legislature* [of La.] *beginning Jan. 21, 1852*, p. 42.

upon $3,500,000 of railroad bonds, $1,500,000 for the Opelousas and Great Western, and in 1854 the city loaned its own bonds to the railroad companies.[43] Thanks to sad experiences during the Panic of 1837, Louisiana had a constitution which forbade state aid to corporations. On the same day the new charter was granted to New Orleans, the Legislature submitted to the people of the state the question of calling a convention to revise the constitution. The popular vote was favorable. A new constitution was promptly made and approved which permitted state aid to railroad companies. The first Legislature under the new constitution granted liberal charters to the three railroad companies and subscribed for one fifth the capital stock of each on behalf of the state to be paid in at that rate as rapidly as private subscriptions should be made.[44] The Louisiana delegation in Congress sought federal land grants in aid of the roads, advancing all the well-known arguments. But Louisiana was compelled to wait, along with Iowa and other states, until 1856. The New Orleans, Opelousas, and Great Western was organized in May, 1852, with an able president and, as agent, the energetic and eloquent Buckner H. Payne, whose enlarged views of the prospects of his road and its importance to the Crescent City we have had occasion to quote.[45] Construction was begun in 1853 and pushed forward about as rapidly as upon any other road west of the Mississippi.[46] The Vicksburg, Shreveport, and Texas Company was organized in January, 1853, and began construction the following year. But, not having the interests back of it that the other company had, it built westward very slowly indeed.[47]

Texas people were acutely aware that any railroad to the Pacific by the thirty-second parallel route would have to cross the Lone Star state and that, if they could make provision for the construction of the long link in Texas, it would go far

[43] West. Jour. and Civilian, IX, 127, 333.
[44] Acts Passed by the First Legislature of La. . . . Begun in Baton Rouge, Jan. 17, 1853, pp. 109, 142, 195.
[45] Above, p. 23.
[46] Am. R. R. Jour., XXV, 517, XXVIII, 179, XXIX, 155.
[47] Ibid., XXV, 823, XXVII, 455, XXIX, 824.

toward insuring the selection of that route. There were at an early date numerous projects in the state for building the link. The Texas Legislature of 1852 granted charters liberally.[48] Among others granted was one to the Texas and Western, which might build from any "suitable point" on the eastern boundary of the state to El Paso. This charter was destined to play quite a rôle several years later. The Legislature also offered a subsidy of eight sections of public lands to every railroad company for each mile of road it should construct within the state. This liberal offer did not give any immediate vitality to the Texas and Western, for at the time such a road could have no value except as part of a transcontinental line. More vitality was shown by companies which were trying to build from various Gulf ports into the settled portions of the state. Each of these avowed the intention of eventually intercepting any southern Pacific railroad that might be built. One of these, the Buffalo Bayou, Brazos, and Colorado, a generation later became a part of the Southern Pacific.[49]

In the fall of 1853 the time seemed more propitious to Texans for getting their link of the Pacific railroad started. The preceding winter, the United States Senate had come within an ace of passing a bill which they believed would have assured the selection of a southern route. The Arkansas land grant was expected to get connections started in that state. The provision in that grant for a Cairo, Illinois, terminus of one of the Arkansas roads was believed calculated to reconcile Illinois interests, at least, to a southern route. The new Pierce administration was certainly friendly to the South. It appeared to be getting ready to support Pacific railway legislation. Jefferson Davis, the secretary of war, had endorsed the measure in speeches in the President's hearing, and other members of the cabinet had expressed themselves favorably to it. Pierce had sent James Gadsden to Mexico with the object,

[48] Accounts of early Texas railroad projects are in C. S. Potts, *Railroad Transportation in Texas* (*Bul. of the Univ. of Tex.*, No. 119, *Humanistic Series*, No. 7); R. E. Riegel, "Trans-Mississippi Railroads during the Fifties," *Miss. Val. Hist. Rev.*, X, 153-72. See n. 1, ch. iii, for more general references.
[49] R. E. Riegel, *The Story of the Western Railroads*, 25, 120, 183; Potts, *op. cit.*, 27-29.

among others, of purchasing the strip of land south of the Gila containing the most eligible southern route. The influential Corps of Topographical Engineers was believed to be partial to this route. Jefferson Davis was in charge of the Pacific railroad surveys, authorized by the preceding Congress.[50]

Senator Rusk took the lead in the effort to provide the Texas link. He interviewed and interested directors of the Atlantic and Pacific Railroad Company of New York, the "one hundred million corporation" which had been organized in anticipation of opportunities. In the summer of 1853 he made a personal reconnaissance of the most likely route across the state.[51] In the fall, in a number of speeches, he proposed his plan.[52] The Legislature should offer a large grant of land on the alternate-sections principle to the company which would contract with the state on the most favorable terms to build a railroad near the thirty-second parallel from an eligible point on the eastern boundary to El Paso. If the proper terminus on the eastern border should be selected, he thought, it would be made the focal point of the Cairo and Fulton, the Vicksburg, Shreveport, and Texas, and the northern branch of the New Orleans, Opelousas, and Great Western. The Senator urged haste. Delay even a year, and the opportunity might be lost by the superior exertions of the friends of other routes.

Rusk's plan met with public favor. A mass meeting in Nacogdoches County endorsed it. A meeting in Cherokee County approved and suggested a loan of state funds at five per cent in addition to the land grant. The several railroad companies which had been struggling with slight success to raise money to build railroads up from the Gulf into the interior lent their support, feeling that the construction of the great Pacific railroad, with which their respective lines might connect, would enable them to sell their bonds. Senator Houston extended support to Rusk's plan, as did Governor Bell, whose term was about to expire.[53] The plan was pre-

[50] See above, 120, below, 138, 168, 187; N. Y. Herald, July 14, 18 31, 1853; Tex. State Gaz., Aug. 13, Sept. 24, Nov. 8.
[51] Ibid., Sept. 10, 24 (speech at Henderson), 1853.
[52] Ibid., Sept. 24, Nov. 8; Memphis Daily Appeal, Nov. 8.
[53] Tex. State Gaz., Sept. 3, 17, Oct. 15, 22, Nov. 15.

sented in the Legislature when it met in November. According
to the newspapers, agents of the Atlantic and Pacific Railroad
Company lobbied in its behalf.[54] A bill framed in accordance
with Rusk's suggestions was passed by large majorities in both
houses and signed by Governor Pease, December 21, 1853.[55]

By the provisions of the bill, the Governor was directed to
advertise for bids for the construction of the "Mississippi and
Pacific Railroad" to run from the eastern boundary of the state
not north of Fulton, Arkansas, to El Paso. The contractors
were to be incorporated with a capital stock of $20,000,000,
which might be increased. They must build not less than fifty
miles within eighteen months and not less than one hundred
miles each year thereafter until the road should be completed.
They might connect their line with roads in other states. They
must deposit $300,000 with the State Treasurer as evidence
of good faith. Under proper safeguards to protect the state
from fraud, they were to receive twenty alternate sections of
land along the route selected for each mile of railroad constructed. The lands along the possible routes were, by the act,
reserved from sale by the state until the contracting company
should have located its sections. No loan of money or state
credit was offered.

This bill was passed only at a price. Other companies insisted upon similar state aid.[56] Another act, approved January
30, 1854, offered to every other railroad company chartered
by the state sixteen sections of land for every mile of railroad
properly constructed.[57]

These two acts raised hopes high in Texas and were commented upon favorably throughout the nation. Railway ex-
perts, however, warned that land grants alone would not
insure the building of railroads.[58] The actual immediate results of the Texas legislation were disappointing.

[54] *Daily Mo. Repub.*, Jan. 18, 1854; N. Y. *Herald*, Jan. 15.
[55] *Tex. State Gaz.*, Dec. 13, 20, 27, 1853; *DeBow's Rev.*, XVI, 545; *Am. R. R.
Jour.*, XXVII, 23.
[56] *Tex. State Gaz.*, Nov. 29, Dec. 6, 1853.
[57] *Ibid.*, Feb. 21, 1854; *Am. R. R. Jour.*, XXVIII, 515-16.
[58] *Ibid.*, XXVII, 665; *DeBow's Rev.*, XVI, 473, 519; N. Y. *Herald*, Jan. 15,
1854.

When Governor Pease advertised for bids for building the Mississippi and Pacific, one of the bids came from Robert J. Walker, Thomas Butler King, and fifteen reputable Texas citizens who were associated with them. Governor Pease was not satisfied with any of the bids received and advertised for a second three months' period. Finally, August 1, 1854, he awarded the contract to Robert J. Walker, Thomas Butler King, and their associates, that is, presumably, to the great New York company.[59]

This highly speculative corporation, in anticipation of making satisfactory arrangements with Texas, had already engaged A. B. Gray to make a survey of the whole Gila route to the Pacific. Gray had recently been over the route as surveyor with the Mexican Boundary Commission. He soon submitted an elaborate and highly favorable report.[60] The company had also sent an agent to Mexico to negotiate for the right of way south of the Gila [61]— a negotiation soon rendered superfluous by the Gadsden Purchase. Walker and King had been sent to Texas with authorization not only to bid for the charter of the Mississippi and Pacific but also to buy up any other loose Texas charters which they might deem useful. They saw fit to purchase the charter of the Texas and Western Railroad Company, previously mentioned.[62] Meanwhile, there had been dissension and scandal within the family of the Atlantic and Pacific Company. The first set of officers had been ousted, and Walker and King had been elected president and vice-president. The ousted officials had then "exposed" the company's affairs. A number of stockholders had withdrawn and new money had not been attracted.[63] Meanwhile, too, the Pierce administration had apparently cooled toward the Pacific railroad project.[64]

[59] Am. R. R. Jour., XXVII, 541; Tex. State Gaz., Mar. 28, Apr. 15, Aug. 5, 1854.
[60] Ibid., Nov. 29, 1853; Cong. Globe, 33 Cong., 2 Sess., App., 74; A. B. Gray, Southern Pacific Railroad; Survey of a Route for the . . . Texas Western R. R. Co., (110 pp., 1856).
[61] Am. R. R. Jour., XXVII, 394.
[62] Ibid., XXVII, 395; Circular to the Stockholders of the Atlantic and Pacific R. R. Co. (N. Y., Jan. 31, 1855); Tex. State Gaz., Oct. 4, 1856.
[63] Ibid., Aug. 5, 1854, Je. 9, 1855; Am. R. R. Jour., XXVI, 728, XXVII, 394-96.
[64] See below, 187, 190.

Under the circumstances the company experienced great difficulty in raising even the $300,000 which it must deposit with the Texas authorities to retain the Mississippi and Pacific charter. It finally offered as security $2,000 of State of New York Bonds and the remainder in preferred stock of the Sussex Iron Company of New Jersey and common stock of the Mechanics Bank of Memphis. Governor Pease accepted the bonds and rejected the stock.[65] The New York company then gave over the attempt to qualify for the Mississippi and Pacific charter. Walker and King and such of their associates as could be induced to go along now, January, 1855, organized under the Texas and Western charter, purchased to meet eventualities, saddling upon the new company the debts of the old Atlantic and Pacific Company of New York.[66] The Texas and Western, it will be remembered, was authorized to build from any "suitable" point on the eastern boundary to El Paso. Under the general act of January 30, 1854, it would be entitled to sixteen sections of land for every mile of line it should construct. To retain its charter it must have started construction within five years and have completed not less than twenty miles of railroad within six years of the date of the charter.[67] The encumbered and discredited company did nothing immediately under this charter. Few people in Texas now expected that it ever would.

Of course Senator Rusk and other sponsors of the Texas railroad act did not seriously expect to secure the construction of the Texas section of a Pacific railroad across all but unsettled portions of the state in advance of construction of the links in Arkansas and Louisiana and in advance of provision by the federal government for continuation of the road to the Pacific. They had confidently hoped that the act would induce Congress to extend the further aid necessary to insure the construction of the railroad to the Pacific by the Gila route. In this they were doomed to disappointment, as shall presently appear.

[65] *Am. R. R. Jour.*, XXVII, 743, 775; *Tex. State Gaz.*, Jan. 6, 1855.
[66] *Ibid.*, Jan. 6, 20; *Circular to the Stockholders of the Atlantic and Pacific Railroad Co.*
[67] Text in *ibid.*

# CHAPTER IX

# REMOVING AN OBSTACLE FROM THE SOUTHERN ROUTE — THE GADSDEN PURCHASE

THE ratification of the Gadsden Treaty with Mexico removed a formidable obstacle to the construction of a railroad on the 32nd-parallel route. The treaty also contained noteworthy provisions in regard to the transit of the Isthmus of Tehuantepec. The treaty was the result of diligent efforts on the part of champions of the Gila route supplemented not a little by circumstances.

It will be recalled that during the negotiation of the Treaty of Guadalupe Hidalgo Commissioner Trist, under instructions from Secretary of State Buchanan, had tried unsuccessfully to get enough territory south of the Gila to insure possession of the most favorable railroad route in that quarter.[1] The boundary was fixed at the Gila, but it was stipulated that, if it should be found practicable to construct a road, canal, or railroad along that stream within a marine league of either bank, the two governments would make an agreement regarding such a work in order that it might serve both countries equally.

The boundary from the Rio Grande to the Gila, also through difficult country, was to follow the southern boundary of New Mexico to its western termination, thence run northward along the western boundary of New Mexico until it should intersect the first branch of the Gila, and thence follow said branch to the Gila, or, if it should occur that no branch should be crossed, run northward to a point nearest such branch, thence directly west to the branch and down the same to the Gila. The southern and western limits of New Mexico were to be as laid down in a certain map of the United Mexican States, "Revised edition, Published at New York, in 1847, by J. Disturnell."

[1] See above, 14.

The boundary provisions of the Mexican Treaty were not entirely satisfactory to advocates of the 32nd-parallel route at the time they were made. As geographical information accumulated in the years immediately following the Mexican War, it became apparent that the most difficult portions of the railroad route to locate would be the crossing of the Rio Grande and the ascent to the table lands west of it, then the passage or turning of the Sierra Madre, and finally some very rough country about the upper Gila and its tributaries. The impression early gained currency that a railroad would have to follow the road by which Colonel Cooke had taken General Phil Kearney's wagon train through to California. This road undoubtedly swung considerably south of the boundary line as described in the treaty.[2]

It soon became known in well-informed circles that J. Disturnell's map contained many errors, that the boundary of New Mexico had never been marked, and, therefore, that the survey might occasion controversy. The location of the line, it was understood, would involve the possession of some copper mines and otherwise valuable territory and, possibly, of the most eligible railroad route. Even before the United States boundary commission left Washington for the border, Major W. H. Emory, the chief astronomer, advised his superiors that securing the railroad route would, in his opinion, be facilitated by beginning the survey at the Rio Grande rather than at the Gila.[3] A year later Emory wrote Secretary of the Interior Ewing to the same effect. Surveying from west to east might cause the United States a loss "no less than the only practicable route for a railway over the Sierra Madre" near the 32nd parallel. Emory clearly hoped to find and make part of the boundary a branch of the Gila which swung far to the south and entered the main stream far to the west, below the rough lands along its upper course. The Disturnell map, he said, was notoriously inaccurate, and the boundary between New Mexico and Chihuahua had never been located on the ground. "In this condition of things the commissioners must

[2] See above, 41.
[3] *Sen. Exec. Docs.*, 31 Cong., 1 Sess., X (558), No. 34, pp. 13-17.

negotiate, and they may adopt the 32nd parallel of latitude until it strikes the San Pedro, or even a more southern parallel of latitude. This would give what good authority, combined with my own observations, authorizes me to say is a practicable route for a railroad — I believe the only one from ocean to ocean within our territory." [4]

The first United States boundary commission under the Treaty of Guadalupe Hidalgo was organized early in 1849 under the direction of Secretary of State Buchanan. It was headed by John B. Weller, of Ohio, as commissioner and A. B. Gray, of Texas, as surveyor. Major Emory was "chief astronomer." In his instructions to Weller, Buchanan said the United States wanted to gain no advantage over Mexico but to secure only what it was entitled to. The appropriation was not large enough to permit a survey of the railroad route, he said, but the President would be gratified if the commission could make examinations incidentally.[5] The portion of the line between the Pacific and the Colorado River was run first without particular difficulty. Then the commissions adjourned to meet at El Paso on the first Monday in November, 1850, or as shortly thereafter as possible.

During the interval, the United States commission was reorganized by the new Taylor administration. Weller was superseded by John R. Bartlett, of New York, and Major Emory by Brevet Lieutenant Colonel McClellan. Gray remained as surveyor. The staff was greatly enlarged to permit thorough reconnaissances of the country through which the line might run, and Bartlett was instructed to collect as much information about the railroad route and the mineral resources as possible.[6] As to the location of the boundary, Bartlett seems to have received no further instructions than those given by Buchanan to Weller, and he was not well supplied with maps and books that might afford him information.[7]

---

[4] *Ibid., loc. cit.*
[5] *Ibid.,* 3-6.
[6] *Sen. Exec. Docs.,* 32 Cong., 1 Sess., XIV (626), No. 119, pp. 87-90; John R. Bartlett, *Personal Narrative of Explorations and Incidents . . . Connected with the United States and Mexican Boundary Commission . . .* (2 vols., N. Y., 1854), II, 588-92.
[7] *Sen. Exec. Docs.,* 32 Cong., 1 Sess., XIV (626), No. 119, pp. 145-48.

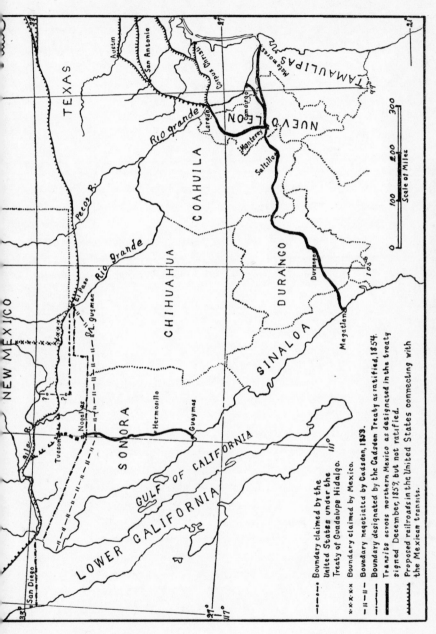

The Gadsden Purchase and Mexican Transits

Boundary claimed by the United States under the Treaty of Guadalupe Hidalgo.
Boundary claimed by Mexico.
Boundary negotiated by Gadsden, 1853.
Boundary designated by the Gadsden Treaty as ratified, 1854.
Transits across northern Mexico as designated in the treaty signed December, 1859, but not ratified.
Proposed railroads in the United States connecting with the Mexican transits.

Scale of Miles
0    100   200   300

Bartlett arrived at El Paso with part of his staff, November 13, 1850. Gray, the surveyor, did not arrive until the following summer, thanks to his illness and the mismanagement of Secretary of the Interior Stuart, who now had supervision of the boundary commission.[8] In Gray's absence, Bartlett's most competent technical adviser was Lieutenant Whipple, an assistant astronomer.

The first task was to locate the point where the southern boundary of New Mexico intersected the Rio Grande. On J. Disturnell's map the boundary was represented by a sinuous line with a mean latitude of 32°22′ extending to a point 3 degrees (175 miles) west of the river and crossing the river about 7 minutes (8 miles) above El Paso. It was immediately discovered, however, that the true latitude of El Paso was 31°45′ instead of 32°15′, as shown on the map, and that the true longitude of El Paso and the near portions of the Rio Grande was 2 degrees farther east than the map indicated.

This discrepancy between the map and actuality presented a difficult problem. If the southern boundary of New Mexico had been placed on the map according to latitude and longitude, it crossed the river at 32°22′, actually about 43 miles north of El Paso, and extended only one degree (58+ miles) west of the river. If, on the other hand, the boundary had been located on the map with reference to El Paso and the Rio Grande, it crossed the river at 31°52′, only 8 miles north of the town and extended 3 degrees, or 175 miles, beyond it. The Mexican commissioner contended for the former interpretation, and Bartlett, but apparently without strong conviction, contended for the latter. Finally they compromised. The Mexican contention as to latitude was accepted while the American view of the westward extension prevailed. The "initial point" was located and marked, and the survey begun. Bartlett appointed Lieutenant Whipple acting surveyor and had him sign the necessary papers.[9] Bartlett thus abandoned, in so far as he could, a claim to not less than 6,000 square

[8] *Ibid.*, 279 ff.; *ibid.*, 33 Cong., 2 Sess., VII (752), No. 55, pp. 1-3.
[9] *Ibid.*, 32 Cong., 2 Sess., VII (665), No. 41, pp. 2-4; *ibid.*, 32 Cong., 1 Sess., XIV (626), No. 119, p. 247; and citations in notes 7 and 8.

miles of territory while the Mexican commissioner abandoned a claim to possibly 3,000 square miles. (The precise amounts would depend upon where a branch of the Gila might be struck.)

When the surveyor, Gray, arrived upon the scene, in July, 1851, he refused to approve the compromise Bartlett had made and denied that it was binding without his signature. He persuaded Bartlett to suspend the survey of the New Mexican boundary.[10] The two commissions then proceeded amicably enough to survey the Rio Grande and Gila portions of the international boundary, while the Mexican commission completed the running of the disputed portion of the line as well. The American parties spent so much time looking for routes for a railroad and a wagon road that the Mexican government protested to the government of the United States against the delays and consequent expense caused thereby.[11]

Meanwhile Bartlett and Gray reported their actions and disagreement to the Secretary of the Interior. A new chief astronomer, Lieutenant Colonel Graham also reported, siding with Gray.[12] Bartlett thought he had secured valuable territory and surrendered worthless. The only settlement in the strip to which he had abandoned claim was Mesilla near the Rio Grande with a population of 800 or 1,000 Mexicans, most of whom would move out if the territory should come under the jurisdiction of the United States. He made no mention of the railroad route. Gray contended that the compromise sacrificed valuable interests particularly the railroad route. "I find," he wrote, "there is a strong possibility of striking a branch of the San Pedro river, as laid down upon Colonel Cooke's route through this country, if we finally get the line a short distance above El Paso."

Secretary of the Interior Stuart upheld Bartlett and instructed Gray to sign the necessary papers and thus give

10 Sen. Exec. Docs., 32 Cong., 1 Sess., XIV (626), No. 119, pp. 279-86.
11 De la Rosa to Webster, Mar. 11, 1852, ibid., 32 Cong., 1 Sess., XIV (627), No. 120, p. 1; Stuart to Acting Secretary of State Derrick, Apr. 5, ibid., 32 Cong., 1 Sess., XIV (626), No. 119, pp. 108-110.
12 Ibid., 145-48, 243-46, 298-300.

validity to the compromise line.[13] Gray still refused to sign.[14] Meanwhile Stuart had sent out Major Emory, once more, to supersede both Gray and Graham, the astronomer. Emory was instructed to sign the papers, if he should find that Gray had not done so. Emory, however, merely signed a map of the compromise line with the reservation that it was the "boundary line agreed upon by the two commissioners." [15] Stuart then decided that after all Lieutenant Whipple's signature had been sufficient, with Bartlett's, to make the agreement binding on the government, and Secretary of State Webster was of the same opinion.[16]

In March, 1852, the Senate, at the instance of J. B. Weller, now senator from California, formerly on the boundary commission, requested the Secretary of the Interior to submit the papers relating to the dispute on the border.[17] In May, Senator Rusk, of Texas, secured an amendment to an item in a deficiency appropriation bill asserting that Congress did not approve the Bartlett compromise.[18] In June, the entire Texas delegation in Congress signed a letter to President Fillmore protesting against Bartlett's "error" and requesting its correction. Unless it should be corrected, they said, the United States stood to lose a large extent of valuable territory and a "channel of communication" to the Pacific. About the latter they seem not to have been so sure, however, for they continued: "In connection with this subject, we ask leave, with great deference, to suggest that a much better route for a road than the one in view might be selected a few miles to the southward of the true boundary line . . . ; and that inasmuch as such a work would operate very beneficially for Mexico in protecting her northern frontier from Indian depredations, we are inclined to believe that for a consideration . . . Mexico might be induced to grant the right of way in question." They under-

[13] *Sen. Exec. Docs.*, 33 Cong., Special Sess., I (688), No. 6, p. 6.
[14] *Ibid.*, 116-19.
[15] *Ibid.*, 153. Gray and Graham were not removed because of their opposition to Bartlett's line.
[16] *Ibid.*, 7-13.
[17] *Cong. Globe*, 32 Cong., 1 Sess., 814, 816. The papers were submitted four months later.
[18] *Ibid.*, 1404.

stood that a minister from Mexico had arrived with powers
to treat in regard to Tehuantepec and thought it an opportune
time to discuss the boundary.[19] The President submitted a
report of Secretary Stuart in reply. The congressmen then
rejoined, expressing dissent from Stuart's views not only as to
the proper location of the boundary but also as to the binding
character of Bartlett's agreement.[20] A few days later, August
24, Senator Mason, of Virginia, submitted a report on the
matter from the Committee on Foreign Relations. The committee upheld Gray's views as to the line and the value of the
territory involved. Important as the territory was in other
respects, they said, it was far more important in relation to the
railroad route. The committee also took issue with the secretaries of state and interior as to whether Bartlett's act was
binding.[21] The Senate then, at the instigation of Mason, Rusk,
and others, added the proviso to the item appropriating for
the expenses of the boundary commission "that no part of this
appropriation shall be used until it shall be made to appear
to the President of the United States that the Southern boundary of New Mexico has not been established further north
of El Paso than is laid down in Disturnell's map." [22] The
House concurred in the proviso, and the President signed the
bill which contained it. President Fillmore then after examination of the evidence decided the appropriation for the boundary
commission could not be used and ordered the discontinuance
of the survey.[23]

Major Emory, having been some time on the ground, now
gave the opinion that "Neither line gives us the road to California . . ." and expressed his regret that the government
had not accepted his earlier advice and negotiated in the first
place.[24] Bartlett returned to Washington and submitted an
elaborate report justifying his course. He described a route
"admirably adapted for a railroad" which, however, entered

19 *Sen. Exec. Docs.*, 33 Cong., Special Sess., I (688), No. 6, pp. 141-43.
20 *Ibid.*, 148-53.
21 *Sen. Repts.*, 32 Cong., 1 Sess., II (631), No. 345.
22 *Cong. Globe*, 32 Cong., 1 Sess., 2402-07.
23 Richardson, *Messages*, V, 173.
24 *Sen. Exec. Docs.*, 33 Cong., Special Sess., I (688), No. 6, pp. 151-54.

well into Mexico. "By no possible means," he said, "could a line of boundary have been obtained that would give us a route to the Pacific, even for a wagon road, without entering the State of Sonora." [25] Lieutenant Whipple was of the same opinion. Gray was still of the opinion that a *practicable* route might be found, if the disputed area could be secured, without going farther into Mexican territory than the one marine league permitted by the Treaty of Guadalupe Hidalgo. However, he admitted that a more practicable route could be had by crossing some forty miles of Mexican territory and a "much more practicable and less costly route still" could be had by going farther into Mexico and following the general line of Cooke's wagon road.[26]

In the course of the controversy over Bartlett's compromise, it was charged that Bartlett had tried to sign away a thirty-five-mile strip for the express purpose of defeating the project for a railroad to the Pacific by a southern route. Some had it that he was inspired by someone in the Department of the Interior; others that he obeyed the wishes of Senator William H. Seward. No less a person than General James Gadsden, of South Carolina, repeated the charge publicly.[27] There seems to have been no justification for the accusations. Bartlett's motives are quite apparent from his own rather naïve reports. When he made the compromise, he had not given the railroad much consideration. Except for the copper mines, which he secured, or kept, he attached little value to the disputed territory. He was convinced by the Mexican commissioner that locating the boundary only eight miles above El Paso would give the United States considerable territory which the states of Chihuahua and Sonora had always regarded as their own. Such dismemberment had not been intended by Polk, Buchanan, and Trist when the Mexican treaty was negotiated. He wanted to be fair, even generous.

[25] *Ibid.*, 32 Cong., 2 Sess., VII (665), No. 41.
[26] *Ibid.*, 33 Cong., 2 Sess., VII (752), No. 55.
[27] Speech in Southern Commercial Convention, at Charleston, April, 1854, in *DeBow's Rev.*, XVII, 408. Bartlett's reply is in Charleston *Daily Courier*, Apr. 28, and N. Y. *Tribune*, Apr. 27. Senator Rusk repeated the charge two years later. *Tex. State Gaz.*, Oct. 4, 1856.

Shortly after President Fillmore had ordered the discontinuance of the Mexican boundary survey, he relinquished office to Franklin Pierce. The Democratic party had for some time been less conciliatory toward Mexico and more expansionist than the Whig. To some extent, too, Bartlett's conduct had become a party issue in Congress. Prominent members of the new administration were friendly to a Pacific railroad by a southern route. It was a foregone conclusion, therefore, that the Pierce administration would not consider itself bound by Bartlett's agreement but would try to make the boundary a subject for negotiation.

Very shortly the need for haste in settling the boundary dispute was made urgent by events on the border. Governor Trias of Chihuahua extended his jurisdiction over the disputed area and decreed that only Mexican citizens could hold land therein. Some Americans who had settled in the fertile strip along the Rio Grande appealed to Governor William C. Lane of New Mexico Territory for protection. This the governor promised with some bluster. People on the border took sides, and the newspapers began to discuss the possibility of a clash. President Pierce sent a less truculent man to supplant Governor Lane; but the incident no doubt served to expedite negotiations.[28]

As minister to Mexico, to supersede the Whig appointee, Conkling, Pierce selected General James Gadsden, of South Carolina. It was the understanding at the time that Gadsden owed his appointment to Jefferson Davis.[29] The new minister had been a nullifier and, more recently, a secessionist.[30] He had been president of the South Carolina Railroad Company from 1840 to 1850 and had been very active in promoting his road's western connections, especially the line from Chattanooga to Memphis. As chairman of a committee in the Southwestern Convention, in Memphis, 1845, he had described a "chain" of railroads and projected railroads from Charleston and Savannah to Memphis and suggested its extension to

[28] P. N. Garber, *The Gadsden Treaty*, 70-74; J. F. Rippy, *The United States and Mexico*, 115-23; N. Y. *Herald*, July 1, 1853.
[29] *Ibid.*, Jan. 20, 1854; Roy F. Nichols, *Franklin Pierce*, 266.
[30] For a short biography of Gadsden, see Garber, *op. cit.*, 74-82.

the Pacific by a southern route.[31]  He had written a letter to the
Pacific Railroad Convention, in Memphis, 1849, again advocating the railroad and the route.[32]  Upon announcement of
his appointment, United States newspapers at once assumed
that the object of his mission would be to procure the territory
which would afford the most practicable railway route.  Mexican journals made the same inference.[33]

Secretary of State Marcy's instructions to Gadsden, dated
July 15, 1853, dwelt at length upon the boundary dispute and
the government's desire to secure a new boundary embracing
the railroad route.  They also instructed Gadsden to secure
the abrogation of Article XI of the Treaty of Guadalupe
Hidalgo.  This article related to efforts of the two governments to prevent Indian incursions across the border and to
exact satisfaction for damages done if such raids should nevertheless occur.  The interpretation and execution of the article
had proven very difficult and aggravating.  Daniel Webster
also had sought its abrogation.  For a satisfactory boundary
and the abrogation of the troublesome article, Marcy said the
United States would pay a liberal sum, which he did not set
down in writing.  The complicated Tehuantepec matter which
had occasioned the Taylor-Fillmore administration so much
trouble was reserved for later negotiations.[34]

General Gadsden reached his post in the middle of August,
1853, and began negotiations at once.  Santa Anna was in
power again.  His financial necessities were great.  He understood that a new boundary to accommodate a railroad was a
*sine qua non* and raised no noteworthy objections.  In fact he
gave United States officers permission to survey the portions of
the route which lay on Mexican soil while the negotiations were
still far from completion.[35]  Gadsden, however, in excess of
his written instructions sought the cession of enough additional
territory to give us a "natural" frontier of mountain ranges

---

[31] *Jour. of the Proceedings* . . . , 29-41.
[32] *Minutes and Proceedings* . . . , 64.
[33] N. Y. *Herald*, Aug. 15, 1853 ; *Tex. State Gaz.*, Sept. 17.
[34] Garber, *op. cit.*, 83-85 ; Rippy, *op. cit.*, 128-30. The works of Garber and
Rippy describe Gadsden's negotiations competently and in great detail. A brief
summary is given here for the sake of clarity and completeness.
[35] Dunbar Rowland, *Jefferson Davis, Constitutionalist*, II, 284, 315.

and deserts. He had probably been influenced by the War Department view that such a frontier would render easier the task of preventing Indian raids across the border.[36] He may have hoped to acquire more "slave" territory. Pierce and Marcy, encouraged by evidence of Santa Anna's compliant spirit, countenanced Gadsden's efforts to make a large acquisition of territory. In October they sent additional instructions to Gadsden describing six acceptable boundary lines and the sum which might be paid in each case.[37] The most inclusive included the entire peninsula of Lower California and approximately 160,000 square miles of Coahuila, Chihuahua, and Sonora, that is, an area about the size of Texas.

The new instructions were not entrusted to writing but were carried verbally by "General" Christopher L. Ward, a Pennsylvania politician and *agent and counsel* for the claimants under the old Garay grant. How Ward got his job as messenger is not clear; but it is clear why he wanted it.

It will be recalled that Garay had a decade before secured a liberal franchise for building a railroad or canal across the Isthmus of Tehuantepec and had later assigned his rights to United States citizens. Daniel Webster as secretary of state had tried unsuccessfully to make a treaty with Mexico for the protection of the assignees. The Mexican government had annulled the grant altogether and made a new grant to A. G. Sloo. The Garay grantees denied the legality of the annulment and presented a big bill for damages. In March, 1853, Gadsden's predecessor, Conkling, acting without instructions, had negotiated a treaty for the protection of the Sloo grant, leaving the Garay claimants out in the cold.[38] This treaty, President Pierce had among his papers during the Gadsden negotiations; but, it seems, he had no intention of submitting it to the Senate.[39]

The new instructions General Ward was to carry to Gads-

---

[36] E.g., Gen. P. Smith to Davis, Dec. 22, 1853, *ibid.*, II, 338. See also Rippy, *op. cit.*, 130.

[37] Rippy, *op. cit.*, 137 ff.; Garber, *op. cit.*, 90-93.

[38] Above, 93.

[39] Richardson, *Messages*, V, 233; *Sen. Exec. Jour.*, IX, 265, 276; Roy F. Nichols, *op. cit.*, 266.

den embraced no new subject for negotiation. In fact they expressly stated that no new subject was to be introduced. But before Ward left Washington he managed to have a long conversation with President Pierce about the Garay claim, and he chose to construe what that amiable gentleman said as approval of his contemplated effort to get provision for his clients inserted in the forthcoming treaty. Upon reaching Mexico he succeeded, although with much difficulty, in persuading Gadsden that the President wished him to demand an indemnity for the Garay claimants.[40]

After receipt of his new instructions, Gadsden redoubled his effort to get a large cession of land. He blustered, talked of manifest destiny, and threatened war. Santa Anna refused to part with more than enough to give ample room for the prospective railroad; and Gadsden eventually had to close on that basis. He later asserted that he could have secured Lower California also if it had not been for William Walker's inopportune filibustering expedition into the peninsula while the negotiations were in progress.[41] Neither would Santa Anna make any allowance for the Garay claim. Bonilla, the negotiator for Santa Anna, suggested its inclusion with certain claims of American citizens against Mexico which the United States was to assume, and Gadsden finally assented. This solution satisfied Ward, having regard for his clients' interests, and it satisfied A. G. Sloo and associates as well, for it would free them of further litigation over their concession. It left the United States holding the bag.

The Gadsden treaty was signed December 30, 1853. It defined a boundary running from the Colorado River at a point two marine leagues above the head of the Gulf of California in a straight line to the intersection of the 31st parallel and the 111th meridian and thence in another straight line, with a deviation if necessary to include Lake Guzman, to a point on the Rio Grande about two miles above El Paso. The troublesome XIth article of the Treaty of Guadalupe Hidalgo was

[40] Garber, op. cit., 94-97; Ward's version, N. Y. Tribune, Apr. 14, 1854; President Pierce's version, Sen. Exec. Jour., IX, 276.
[41] Charleston Courier, Jan. 21, 25, 1854.

abrogated. For the additional territory and the release from obligations under the article the United States was to pay Mexico $15,000,000. The United States agreed to assume all claims of its citizens against the Mexican Republic "including the claim of the so-called concession to Garay, whose lawful existence Mexico does not recognize, even as implied," and to make satisfaction to an amount not in excess of $5,000,000. The Mexican Government likewise released the United States from all claims of Mexico or its citizens.[42]

The treaty was received by President Pierce on January 19, 1854. Its terms promptly became public property. The New York *Herald* published a summary on the 20th. The Charleston *Courier* gave a more detailed account the next day, probably from information supplied by Gadsden himself, who had just arrived in the city. Public discussion followed. Most Southern journals praised the treaty highly. There was general satisfaction that the railroad route had been secured. In the North, administration organs acclaimed the treaty as settling all outstanding disputes with Mexico in a peaceful manner, but thought the territory worthless except for the route. Opposition journals denounced the treaty. It gave Santa Anna $15,000,000 with which to maintain his dictatorship, they said; it rewarded speculators. Some said the territory was a barren waste; others that it would make two slave states.

The President submitted the treaty to the Senate February 10, after that body had passed the Kansas-Nebraska bill. He had made one important amendment. This struck out special mention of the Garay claim and provided simply that the United States would pay all claims of its citizens against Mexico "which may have arisen under treaty or the law of nations since the date of the signature of the treaty of Guadalupe." The designation of a limit ($5,000,000) to the sum which might be paid in satisfaction of claims was also eliminated. These changes, it appears, left the Garay claimants as well provided for as the original terms had done.[43]

[42] *Sen. Exec. Jour.*, IX, 312-15.
[43] *Ibid.*, 238; Richardson, *Messages*, V, 230.

The treaty was considered by the Senate in secret session, and the injunction of secrecy has never been removed. However, from the Executive Journal, unguarded allusions of senators in other debates and in their private correspondence, and from the newspapers, although their reports of "leaks" must be used with great caution, it can be discovered about what happened and why.

The treaty and the President's message were referred to the Committee on Foreign Relations. At the instance of Senator Bell, a Whig, the President was requested to transmit a copy of the Conkling Convention of March 21, 1853, for extending protection to the A. G. Sloo Tehuantepec project. The President complied, and this copy and accompanying documents were also referred. On March 9, the committee reported the treaty substantially as the President had submitted it except that the Garay claim was again specifically mentioned.[44]

Senator Bell now offered an amendment embodying the substance of the Conkling Convention. It stipulated that charges upon the persons and property of citizens of the United States in transit across the Isthmus of Tehuantepec should never be higher than those upon the persons and property of citizens of other foreign countries. Interest in the transit facilities might never be transferred to a third government. No duties should be collected upon goods in transit, and no passports be required of persons. The United States government might send mails in closed bags, munitions of war, and troops across the isthmus. Finally, the United States might "extend its protection as it shall judge wise to the company, in the construction and completion of the road and the enjoyment of their privileges when it may feel sanctioned and warranted by the public or international law." [45] To this move President Pierce replied with a message giving his reasons for not submitting the Conkling Convention to the Senate for ratification. It was made without instructions, he said; it was unjust to the holders of the Garay grant; it involved the United States in engage-

44 *Sen. Exec. Jour.*, IX, 240, 247, 260.
45 *Ibid.*, 264, 299.

ments too "comprehensive and embarrassing"; and it violated the Clayton-Bulwer Treaty, which, however "inconvenient" it might be, still bound the United States.[46] It is difficult to see that these objections could be fairly made against Bell's amendment, however applicable they may have been to the original Conkling Convention. The Committee on Foreign Relations reported Bell's amendment without modification or recommendation.[47]

Meanwhile rumors had got abroad of Christopher L. Ward's intrigues in behalf of the Garay claimants. Charges were made that the treaty had been secured in Mexico by corrupt methods and that the Garay and Sloo groups were maintaining lobbies in Washington, well supplied with funds.[48] Ward's instructions and, at the instance of Gadsden's friends, his correspondence with Gadsden were called for by the Senate.[49] The disclosure of the employment of Ward and of his presumptuous acts destroyed any chance there may have been for indemnity for the Garay assignees. When the article relating to claims was reached, it was stricken out by a unanimous vote. The Garay claim was left to plague the A. G. Sloo group for many more seasons.

The boundary provisions of the treaty encountered much opposition in the Senate. Little, if any, of this opposition can be accredited to disinclination to acquire a southern route for a Pacific railroad, however. About a dozen northern anti-slavery Whigs and Free-Soilers were opposed to the annexation of any territory which might enlarge the area open to slavery. To be sure, it was charged in the South that these men were animated by hostility to a southern route;[50] but only a few of them had ever taken more than a passing interest in the Pacific railroad question. Five Northwestern senators who strongly preferred other routes supported the Gadsden treaty; they were Douglas, Atchison and Geyer, of Missouri, Dodge, of Wisconsin, and Jones, of Iowa. There were a few Demo-

[46] Ibid., 265; Richardson, Messages, V, 233.
[47] Sen. Exec. Jour., IX, 266.
[48] N. Y. Herald, Jan. 6, 11, 30, Feb. 7, 16, Mar. 3, 1854.
[49] Ibid., Apr. 12; Sen. Exec. Jour., IX, 266, 268, 271, 276.
[50] Richmond Enquirer, Apr. 18, 1854; DeBow's Rev., XVII, 210.

cratic senators who were dissatisfied, or who professed to be dissatisfied, with the treaty because it gained too little territory. Gwin, of California, voted against ratification because we would not gain frontage on the Gulf of California. Shields, of Illinois, Pettit, of Indiana, and Stuart, of Michigan, voted consistently for motions to increase the territorial acquisition and finally voted against ratification. Their motives are doubtful. A number of Whig senators from the old South were unwilling to acquire more than enough territory to accommodate the proposed railroad. Their position was consistent with Whig views at the time of the Mexican War. A combination of these diverse groups succeeded in striking out the boundary provision.[51] To save the treaty, Rusk, of Texas, offered an amendment fixing the boundary approximately where it is now, thus reducing the Gadsden Purchase by several thousand square miles. This amendment received the support of all the Southern and border state Whigs and even of three of the more moderate anti-slavery Whigs and was accepted by all the Democrats who had voted for the original boundary provision except Butler, of South Carolina, who remained faithful to Gadsden. The amendment was carried, thus, in the Committee of the Whole, by the narrow majority of 32 to 14,[52] a two-thirds majority being required.

Another difficult hurdle was yet to come. On April 17, after all other changes had been made, Bell renewed his amendment to provide for the protection of the Sloo Tehuantepec project. By a vote of 22 to 17 the Senate, still in Committee of the Whole, rejected it. After the treaty had been reported to the Senate, Bell offered his amendment once more, this time omitting the name of "A. G. Sloo and others." Again it was defeated, 28 for to 18 against.[53] It received the votes of all the Southern and about half the Northern Whigs, all but three Southern Democrats, several Northern Democrats, including Douglas, and both California senators. It was defeated by a combination of foes of the treaty in any form and administra-

[51] *Sen. Exec. Jour.*, IX, 278.
[52] *Ibid.*, 284.
[53] *Ibid.*, 299, 302.

tion Democrats, most of whom had no deep interest in communication with the Pacific by any means. After the defeat of the Tehuantepec provision the whole treaty was brought to a vote and failed of ratification, the vote being 27 to 18. The newspapers announced the treaty's demise; its foes exalted. Their celebration came too soon. The following day the Senate voted to reconsider the treaty. A week later the Bell amendment was adopted 30 to 14 and the treaty itself ratified by a vote of 33 to 12.[54]

An analysis of the several votes shows what caused this sudden reversal. During the week seven senators who had been absent at the time of the earlier votes returned to Washington and voted both for the Tehuantepec amendment and the treaty. Senators Evans, Atchison, Everett, Pettit, and Shields, who had formerly voted nay on Bell's amendment, now voted for it; and all their votes were needed to carry it. Evans and Atchison, who were consistent supporters of the treaty, evidently changed to win support for the treaty. The motives of the other three, who continued to oppose ratification, can only be left to conjecture.[55] It would seem that the treaty could not have been ratified without the Tehuantepec provision.[56]

The Tehuantepec provision, indeed, improved the treaty. A. G. Sloo may have been a speculator, but the Tehuantepec project was a worthy one, of especial interest to the lower South, and provision for its protection was entirely proper.

Much was said in the papers about lobbying by General Alamonte, the Mexican minister to the United States, and by representatives of the Hargous and Sloo interests.[57] It can not be shown that such lobbying was effective. The clause which would have taken care of the Hargous assignees had been stricken out by a unanimous vote.

Friends of a Southern Pacific railroad and the Tehuantepec

[54] *Ibid.*, 306, 310.
[55] Sixteen senators did not vote. Judging by their earlier votes and expressed views, the outcome would not have been different if they had.
[56] This was the judgment of the Washington correspondent of the Baltimore *Sun.* Quoted in *Tex. State Gaz.*, Apr. 15, 1854. The Sloo people boasted of carrying the treaty. Charleston *Courier*, May 1.
[57] N. Y. *Herald*, Mar. 21, 1854; Memphis *Daily Appeal*, May 3; Garber, *Gadsden Treaty*, 132.

venture had watched the progress of the Gadsden Treaty in the Senate with great solicitude. The Southern Commercial Convention, sitting at Charleston while the treaty was before the Senate, was with difficulty dissuaded from passing a resolution requesting the Senate to ratify. Gadsden himself was present and spoke. He charged that Senate opposition was animated by hostility to a southern route for the railroad.[58] When the treaty was believed to have been defeated, the *Texas State Gazette* termed the rejection the most disastrous blow the South in general and Texas in particular had received at the hands of Congress in fifty years.[59] There was general rejoicing when the treaty was ratified. In Texas credit for the victory was given to Senator Rusk, and he largely deserved it.

Considering the several changes which had been made in the treaty and the publicity given to his own rather inglorious part in the Ward intrigue, President Pierce was somewhat loath to accept the instrument as it came from the Senate.[60] Santa Anna was even more reluctant. The compensation had been reduced from $15,000,000 to $10,000,000, and the addition of the provisions regarding Tehuantepec were highly objectionable.[61] But his need for money was as dire as ever. Ratifications were exchanged.

The House of Representatives had opportunity to debate the merits of the Gadsden Treaty in its final form when it became necessary to make an appropriation to meet obligations incurred under it. The debate was short. The vote on the appropriation reveals little as to the popularity of the treaty in the House; for undoubtedly a majority of the congressmen felt duty bound to faithfully execute a properly made treaty.

Those who spoke in favor of the appropriation enumerated the advantages gained for the United States by the treaty. Phillip Phillips, of Alabama, asserted that the railroad route secured had been demonstrated by instrumental surveys

[58] Proceedings in *DeBow's Rev.*, XVII, 408-10.
[59] May 6, 1854.
[60] Garber, *op. cit.*, 135-36; Charleston *Courier*, May 1, 10, 1854.
[61] Garber, *op. cit.*, 136-40.

to be the best which could be had.  He hailed the treaty and Texas' recent generous proffer of state aid [62] as insuring that the Pacific railroad would go by the southern route whether the federal government should give pecuniary aid or not.[63]  Bocock, of Virginia, expressed sentiments which must have been shared by most of the strict-constructionist Democrats of the old South.  He was opposed to a Pacific railroad at government expense.  The right of way across Tehuantepec would obviate the need for such a measure, thus saving the constitution from violence and the treasury from an enormous drain.[64]  T. H. Bayly, another Virginia strict-constructionist, was likewise opposed to government aid in the construction of a railroad but was willing to purchase a route, "for this much, at least, is within our constitutional authority." [65]

The opposition to the appropriation was led on by Thomas Hart Benton, who spoke in his usual violent manner.[66]  He was patently animated by hostility to the administration as well as by dislike of the terms of the treaty.  The railroad provision was his especial *bête noir*.  "We have a fine national route on the parallels of 38 and 39, by Coo-cha-tope, . . . ; a sectional route on the parallels of 34 and 35, corresponding with the centre of the southern States."  The Gila route was too far south even to be Southern.  It was a thousand miles off the way to San Francisco.  It was in the most difficult location for defense.  Robert J. Walker had been on the point of buying the right of way from Mexico for $6,500 in cash and $500,000 in Texas railroad stock, yet the administration had paid $10,000,000.  The purchase was made in the interests of a group of speculators interested in promoting a town of New San Diego, to be the terminus of the road, and of Walker's "one hundred million company . . . to enable them to sell lots and railroad shares in New York and London."  A group of army men were promoting New San Diego, including A. B. Gray, formerly of the Boundary Commission, and Major W. H. Emory "who

[62] Above, 127.
[63] *Cong. Globe*, 33 Cong., 1 Sess., App., 1020.
[64] *Ibid.*, App., 1049.
[65] *Ibid.*, App., 1044.
[66] *Ibid.*, App., 1031-36.

was of the Boundary Commission, and is in charge of the Pacific route surveys, and who is the brother-in-law of the president of the one hundred million company." Major Bartlett had told him often, he said, that the boundary survey had been delayed eight months waiting for the survey of New San Diego.

Major Emory resented Benton's attack. He denied emphatically that he had any direct interest in New San Diego.[67] He was shortly relieved of his duties in connection with the Pacific railroad surveys and appointed to the new Mexican boundary commission, required under the terms of the Gadsden Treaty. The other specific charges made by Benton were not denied; but, of course, even if they were all true, the Gila route could still be advocated with propriety upon its merits.

Benton was the only Western representative to speak against the appropriation to carry out the treaty. The others who spoke against it were either Eastern Free-Soilers, plainly animated by opposition to the extension of "slave" territory, or Whigs, acting in the supposed interest of their party, or New York Barnburners, warring on the administration for having bestowed favors upon a rival faction in that faction-ridden state.

[67] *Am. R. R. Jour.*, XXVII, 454.

CHAPTER X

# REMOVING AN OBSTACLE FROM NORTHERN ROUTES — THE KANSAS-NEBRASKA BILL

THE organization of Kansas and Nebraska territories, 1854, involving as it did the repeal of the Missouri Compromise, was another incident in the struggle over the location and construction of a railway to the Pacific. Those people who in 1854 wanted to have the Nebraska country opened to white settlement and territorial governments organized therein were animated by several motives and considerations; by no means the least of these was a desire to remove a serious obstacle to the construction of a transcontinental railroad by a central or northern route.[1] The opposition to opening the Indian Country to whites was likewise animated by various motives, but one was the disinclination on the part of the partisans of a southern route to contribute to the removal of such an obstacle. The fact that the repeal of the Missouri Compromise came to overshadow the Pacific railroad issue in popular interest and historical importance should not be allowed to obscure the logical relation.

Back in the administrations of Monroe, J. Q. Adams, and Jackson, the policy had been adopted of removing Indian tribes from the organized states and territories and relocating them in unorganized territory. In pursuance of this policy, numerous tribes from farther east were settled along the western borders of Arkansas, Missouri, and Iowa. These re-

---

[1] This thesis has been fully developed by the late Professor F. H. Hodder, of the University of Kansas, in two able articles, "The Railroad Background of the Kansas-Nebraska Act," *Miss. Val. Hist. Rev.*, XII, 3-22 (Je., 1925), and "The Genesis of the Kansas-Nebraska Bill," *Proceedings of the State Hist. Soc. of Wis.*, for 1912; and by Professor James C. Malin, of the University of Kansas, in his *Indian Policy and Westward Expansion* (*Bul. of the Univ. of Kans., Humanistic Studies*, II, No. 3). The writer is greatly indebted to both Professor Hodder and Professor Malin. The approach in this chapter is different from that of Professor Malin and the interpretation differs considerably from that of Professor Hodder.

located tribes in every case were guaranteed their new lands in perpetuity, and in a few cases they were further guaranteed that they should never again be included in any organized state or territory.[2] By the Indian Intercourse act, of 1834, all the unorganized territory of the United States was designated the "Indian Country," and white persons were forbidden to settle there or even trade with the Indians therein without a license issued by the proper federal agent.[3] Thus an immense block of territory, one thousand miles long and six hundred miles wide, extending from Texas on the south to the national boundary on the north and from Arkansas, Missouri, Iowa, and Minnesota Territory on the east to New Mexico, Utah, and Oregon on the west was closed to occupation by white people.

Western people considered the policy of the permanent Indian frontier a mistaken one from the start.[4] They knew the lands beyond the line were habitable and were confident that they would sooner or later be wanted by our advancing population.

The first proposals by responsible persons for opening portions of the Indian Country to white settlement were made with the object of affording protection to emigrants to Oregon. That seems to have been the object of Senator Atchison in introducing a bill, December 1844, for organizing all of the Indian Country and Oregon; of Douglas, then in the House, in the same session of Congress in proposing to organize as Nebraska territory the region between the thirty-eighth and forty-third parallels from the Missouri to the Rockies; and of Secretary of War Wilkins in recommending a similar measure in his annual report for 1844.[5] It was felt that a few thousand settlers scattered along the emigrant routes would afford protection to the emigrants and obviate the necessity of establishing military posts.

When the building of a railroad to the Pacific came to be a matter of public discussion, it was generally understood that

[2] Collection of extracts from the treaties, *Cong. Globe*, 32 Cong., 2 Sess., 556.
[3] *U. S. Statutes at Large*, IV, 729-35.
[4] J. C. Malin, *op. cit.*, 26-29, 78.
[5] *Cong. Globe*, 28 Cong., 2 Sess., 41, App., 44; *H. Exec. Docs.*, 28 Cong., 2 Sess., I (463), No. 2, p. 124.

construction would have to be preceded or accompanied by the settlement of land along the route. It was evident that, as long as the great Indian Country remained closed to white settlement, it would be extremely difficult to build and operate a railroad across it. All supplies for construction gangs and maintenance crews would have to be brought in from the outside, it would be difficult to protect the road from the wild Indians of the Plains, and, still more serious, there could be no prospect of any considerable way traffic in the region to contribute to the road's support. The southern route for a railroad ran all the way through lands open to settlement and partially settled and under organized governments.

Accordingly all the plans proposed prior to 1854 for building the Pacific railroad by a route north of Texas involved the opening of at least portions of the Indian Country to settlers. Asa Whitney would get funds to prosecute the work by selling the lands in a strip sixty miles wide the full length of the road. In the plan which Stephen A. Douglas published in 1845 as a rival to Whitney's, he proposed the organization of a Nebraska Territory "with land enough on both sides of the Platte for a good state." Both the St. Louis and Memphis Pacific railroad conventions, of the fall of 1849, recommended as a measure preliminary to building the road the establishment of a line of military posts along the route which might be selected and the encouragement of settlements about the posts by liberal grants of lands to settlers. Thomas Hart Benton's bill, introduced December, 1849, called for the extinguishment of the Indian title in a strip one hundred miles wide from Missouri to California and the opening of the lands to whites.[6]

There were of course other reasons why people in the West came to demand the opening of portions of the Indian Country to settlement and the organization of territorial governments there. People of a speculative turn, and all Westerners were, wanted to get land cheap which might some day bring a high price. City and commonwealth builders near the frontier wanted trade areas extended in their hinterlands. As Senator

[6] See above, 11-12, 46, 50, 51.

Borland put it, "We have now an outlet for our trade and travel only on one side; and so long as we remain in that condition, we will be unable to develop even the half of our resources. We want a market on both sides; we desire to see settlements made west as well as east of us." [7] Statesmen believed or professed to believe that the Pacific coast region could not be kept in the Union unless settlements were continuous across the continent. As Douglas once put it, "I have no faith that we can hold our settlements on the Pacific in connection with those on this side of the mountains, unless we have a line of settlements across the country." [8]

Officials of the Bureau of Indian Affairs, often Western men in touch with Western public opinion, read the signs early. In his annual report for 1848, Indian Commissioner Medill said that, if the policy of keeping the Indian wards segregated from the whites was to be maintained, some of the tribes would have to be moved "so as to leave an ample outlet for our white population to spread and pass towards and beyond the Rocky Mountains." He recommended the gradual removal of most of the border tribes between the Kansas and Platte rivers to the district south of the Kansas "as the convenience of our emigrants and the pressure of our white population may require." [9] Medill's successors, Orlando Brown and Luke Lea, repeated the recommendation.[10] In his report for 1851, Lea represented the removals to be an "imperious necessity, in view of the already imposing demonstrations of the public feeling in favor of the early organization of a territorial government on which these Indians reside." D. D. Mitchell, Superintendent of Indian Affairs for the St. Louis district, became convinced that the policy of trying to civilize the Indians by segregating them from whites, other than missionaries and Indian agents, was a failure. He proposed, 1851, organizing the territory without removing the Indians, permitting the whites to occupy lands to which the Indian title was extin-

[7] *Cong. Globe*, 32 Cong., 1 Sess., 1685.
[8] *Ibid.*, 1758.
[9] *Ibid.*, 30 Cong., 2 Sess., App., 32.
[10] *Ibid.*, 31 Cong., 1 Sess., App., 25-26; 31 Cong., 2 Sess., App., 27; *Sen. Exec. Docs.*, 32 Cong., 1 Sess. (613), No. 1, p. 286.

guished, and granting lands in severalty to the more civilized Indians.[11] Some of the Indians themselves were represented as being anxious to part with a portion of their lands in return for a larger annuity, and some, indeed, wished to become citizens of the United States.[12]

In September, 1851, commissioners of the United States government signed the Treaty of Fort Laramie with the chiefs of the wild tribes north of the Arkansas River. The chiefs consented to the establishment of roads and military posts in their country and promised to abstain from depredations upon the emigrants to the Pacific coast. The United States government agreed to pay the tribes annuities to the sum of $50,000 for a number of years to indemnify them for game destroyed by the emigrants and other losses.[13] This treaty was interpreted, and no doubt so intended when made, to cover railroads as well as wagon roads. In 1853 a similar treaty was made at Fort Atkinson with the wild tribes south of the Arkansas,[14] thus formally securing the right of way for emigrant trails or railroads by the thirty-fifth parallel route.

In the summer and autumn of 1852 there were so many manifestations of public sentiment in favor of the organization of Nebraska Territory, especially in Missouri, that the subject could no longer be sidetracked in Congress.

In September, 1852, some persons claiming to be residents of the Nebraska country organized a local government and elected one Abelard Guthrie territorial delegate to Congress. Guthrie agitated the cause in Missouri.[15] Then Thomas H. Benton, on the lookout for a popular issue, took up the Nebraska question.

Benton was engaged in a desperate attempt to return to the United States senate. Back in 1849 the Democratic party of Missouri had split into two wings, Benton and Anti-Benton, over aspects of the slavery question. This split had resulted

11 *Ibid.*, 322-326.
12 J. C. Malin, *op. cit.*, 71-75; *Daily Mo. Repub.*, Feb. 2, 1853.
13 Supt. Mitchell's reports, *Sen. Exec. Docs.*, 32 Cong., 1 Sess. (613), No. 1, pp. 288-90; 32 Cong., 2 Sess. (658), No. 1, pp. 335-38.
14 *Ibid.*, 33 Cong., 1 Sess. (690), No. 1, p. 363; *U. S. Statutes at Large*, X, 1013.
15 *Daily Mo. Repub.*, Sept. 30, 1852, Feb. 2, 1853.

in 1851 in the election of a Whig, H. S. Geyer, to succeed Benton. The latter thereupon began a campaign for the seat of David R. Atchison, the leader of the Southern Rights Democrats; and, although Atchison's term would not expire until 1855, the campaign was already warm in 1852.[16]

In speeches about the state, Benton posed as the champion *par excellence* of a Pacific railroad with St. Louis as a terminus and vehemently called for the organization of "Nebraska," representing the two measures to be complementary and interdependent.[17] He whipped up a demand for the organization of the territory among Missouri farmers by advising them that the lands in the Indian Country to which Indian tribes did not hold specific title were already open to preëmption under the federal laws [18] — a clear misrepresentation of the laws. However deep and abiding Benton's interest in the Pacific Railroad and Nebraska may have been — and there were those who doubted his sincerity — he undoubtedly hoped to put his rival in an embarrassing position.

Atchison was indeed embarrassed. During the long struggle over the organization of the territory acquired by the Mexican War, he had taken strong ground against the exclusion of slavery from the territories. According to the Missouri Compromise, of 1820, that portion of the Indian Country which lay north of 36°30' was to be forever "free." To Benton's claim of being the father of the Pacific railroad, Atchison replied, and truthfully, that he had done more of a practical character to insure its construction with a Missouri terminus than his rival for all the latter's grandiloquent speeches. As for route, he would await the results of the surveys before committing himself in favor of a particular one; he astutely remembered, as Benton did not, that Missouri offered three points of departure for the Pacific and that the people were divided three ways on the question of the route. As for the organization of Nebraska, Atchison and his friends tried for the time to stem the tide. They tried to persuade the farmers

[16] P. O. Ray, *The Repeal of the Missouri Compromise.*
[17] *Ibid.*, 75.
[18] *Letter . . . to the People of Missouri; Central National Highway from the Mississippi River to the Pacific* (Mar. 4, 1853).

that it was to their advantage to have the territory remain unsettled so that they could continue without competition to supply the California- and Oregon-bound emigrants and the detachments of the United States army on the plains.[19] Atchison's arguments were of little avail. Nebraska sentiment grew.

The [St. Louis] *Western Journal and Civilian*, of November, 1852, expected the territory between Missouri and Utah to be organized at the approaching session of Congress. Upon the consummation of this event, it said, the Missouri Legislature could authorize the Pacific Railroad Company to extend its line to the Pacific provided the assent of the territories of "Kansas" and Utah and the State of California could be obtained.[20] In his message, December 28, 1852, Governor King, friendly to Benton, asked the Legislature to memorialize Congress on behalf of a Pacific railroad "and also press the necessity of taking the incipient steps to extinguish the Indian title to the territory west of us, and through which the road must run, and finally to bring about the organization of such territory. . . ."[21]

When Congress met, Hall, of Missouri, introduced another bill for the organization of a "Territory of the Platte."[22] February 2, 1853, Richardson, of Illinois, chairman of the Committee on Territories, reported a substitute providing for the organization of the territory between the parallels of 36°30' and 42°30' under the name Nebraska. One section appropriated $50,000 to enable the Executive to extinguish Indian titles.[23] The bill said nothing about slavery; presumably the new territory would be free under the Missouri Compromise. A few days later Hall and Richardson succeeded in getting their bill taken up in the Committee of the Whole. It was debated briefly but in a creditable manner.[24]

---

[19] *Address of Senator Atchison to the People of Missouri* (Jan. 5, 1854); *Cong. Globe*, 32 Cong., 2 Sess., 1113.

[20] IX, 88.

[21] *Mo. Repub.*, Jan. 1, 1853.

[22] *Cong. Globe*, 32 Cong., 2 Sess., 7, 47.

[23] *Ibid.*, 474, 475.

[24] Entire debate is in *ibid.*, 542-44, 556-65.

The sponsors of the bill were pressed to state their reasons for wanting the territory organized. They advanced the arguments which already have been recounted. They wanted to protect the emigrant trains against Indians. They would afford emigrants the protection of officers and courts of law against their lawless fellows. They wanted to satisfy the demands of prospective settlers. There were "today," said Richardson, five, ten, or fifteen thousand people waiting upon the borders of Missouri for permission to go in. They wanted the territory settled to consolidate the Union and attach the Pacific coast settlements. They wanted to facilitate the building of the Pacific railroad. "Why, everybody is talking about a railroad to the Pacific Ocean," said Hall. "In the name of God, how is the railroad to be made if you will never let people live on the lands through which the road passes? Are you going to construct a road through the Indian territory, at the expense of $200,000,000, and say that no one shall live upon the land through which it passes?" [25]

The opposition to the bill was ostensibly based upon two grounds. Sutherland, of New York, especially, voiced the old familiar Eastern opposition to measures designed to promote Western expansion. "I can understand this policy of gentlemen coming from the old States who are afraid that their people will go away and settle in the new Territory," said Richardson. The attack centered chiefly, however, upon the alleged injustice being done the Indians and upon the violation of solemn treaties, which the bill was said to involve. The proponents of the bill denied that its terms violated the Indian treaties, and they assailed the whole policy of the permanent Indian frontier. They quoted officials of the Indian Department as recommending the proposed changes. They refused to believe that the professed solicitude for the Indians was sincere; it was designed to cover other motives of opposition.

Representative V. E. Howard, of Texas, was especially solicitous for the Indians and intent upon preserving the old Indian policy. Hall refused to accept his professions. He had

[25] *Ibid.*, 560.

understood that "according to Texas politics, and according to Texas morals, the Indians had no rights whatever." There might be other considerations. "If the gentleman can convince this House that the Territory of Nebraska shall not be organized. . . ; if the people of Texas can prevail upon the Government of the United States to drive the Indians of Texas, the Camanches and other wild tribes, into the Territory of Nebraska, it may have the effect of rendering your overland routes from Missouri and Iowa to Oregon and California so dangerous that the tide of emigration will have to pass through Texas — an object which Texas has most zealously sought to accomplish for many years past. In addition to that, if in the course of time a great railroad should be found necessary from this part of the continent to the shores of the Pacific, and the doctrine prevail that all the territory west of the Missouri is to be a wilderness from this day henceforth and forever, Texas being settled, the people of this country will have no alternative but to make the Pacific road terminate at Galveston, or some point in Texas." [26]

Practically nothing was said about slavery during the debate on the bill. It is reasonable to suppose, however, in view of the recent excitement over the question of slavery in the territories, that considerations in regard to it affected the voting upon the bill. No party issues were involved as yet in the Nebraska question.

The Hall-Richardson Nebraska bill shortly passed the House, the test vote standing 107 to 49.[27] The representatives from the Northwest, who would, presumably, wish the territory opened and organized for all of the reasons advanced during the debate, and who had no objections to the exclusion of slavery therefrom, voted 38 to 2 in its favor. The representatives from Missouri and Kentucky, who would favor the organization for all the reasons mentioned except that they might object to the exclusion of slavery, gave 9 votes for the bill and none against. The members from the other Southwestern states, who, presumably, would be loath to organize

[26] Ibid., 558.
[27] Ibid., 565.

a territory from which slavery would be excluded and which would develop into a "free" state and who would be reluctant to vote for a measure to facilitate the building of a railroad to the Pacific by a central route, gave 7 votes for the bill and 9 against it, while several members, including the two from Arkansas, abstained from voting. The favorable votes can probably be accounted for in part by the feeling current in the West that Western men must stand together on Western measures if any were to be adopted and in part by the favor which all proposed legislation calculated to open new opportunities to small farmers met among such men as Andrew Johnson, of east Tennessee, a great champion of the Homestead bill. The delegations of the old Southern states cast 27 votes against the Nebraska bill and only 5 for it. Four of the five came from Maryland and Virginia, whose railroad interests largely supported a Missouri terminus for the Pacific railroad and whose westward migrants moved largely in the same belt. The Eastern States voted 47 to 10 in favor of the bill. The lone California representative, of course, voted aye.

In the Senate the Nebraska bill was reported favorably by Douglas, from the Committee on Territories, while the debate on the Rusk Pacific Railroad bill was at its height and just the day before the adoption of the Shields amendment, which, per Rusk, Borland, Bell, *et al*, killed that bill.[28] On March 2 and 3, Douglas made earnest efforts to have the Nebraska bill taken up for consideration.[29] Atchison reluctantly gave his support. He explained that when he came to Washington for the session he was strongly opposed to the organization of the territory unless the Missouri Compromise should be repealed and slaveowners be allowed to take their slaves with them into the region. He had found, however, that there was no prospect of repealing the compromise, and he would bow to the wishes of his constituents, "whose opinions I am bound to respect." Rusk and Houston, of Texas, Adams, of Mississippi, Borland, and Bell threatened to talk the bill to death if it were taken up. They assigned reasons for their opposition similar to those

---

[28] *Ibid.*, 658; above, 99ff.
[29] Senate debate is in *Cong. Globe*, 32 Cong., 2 Sess., 1020, 1111, 1113-17.

advanced in the House; and, just as in the House, the friends
of the bill refused to accept the assigned reasons as the true
ones. "I also know," said Douglas, "that there is a large number using the argument of sympathy for the Indians simply for
the purpose of killing the bill."

The bill was laid on the table the last day of the session by
a vote of 23 to 17.[30] Except for Atchison and Geyer, of Missouri, not a single senator from a Southern state voted for
the bill. Gwin, of California, as usual voted with the Southerners. Of the five Eastern senators who voted to table, four
were inveterate opponents of measures calculated to build up
the West. The vote made it as clear as a pikestaff that a
Nebraska bill could not be got through the Senate unless a few
more votes could be gained in the South.

In the House meanwhile, Phelps and Hall, both of Missouri, secured an amendment to the Indian Appropriation bill
authorizing the president to extinguish Indian titles in the
proposed territory and appropriating $50,000 to be used for
the purpose.[31] This much was accepted by the Senate.

After Congress adjourned, the fight in Missouri between the
Benton and Atchison factions waxed warmer. Benton issued a
pamphlet letter to the people and made speeches.[32] He re-
ported progress: He had persuaded Secretary of War Davis
to survey his 38th parallel route. An appropriation had been
made for extinguishing the Indian title to lands along the route.
Nebraska was still to be organized; that must be attended to.
Benton men accused Atchison of reneging in voting for a
Nebraska bill which left the Missouri Compromise intact.[33]
Atchison was forced to define his position anew. In speeches at
Parkville, Platte City, and Weston he said he would vote to
ratify the treaties with the Indians (surrendering lands). He
would also vote to organize the territory if it were to be open
to slaveholders and non-slaveholders alike. He would vote to
*let the people of the territory decide whether slavery should*

[30] *Ibid.*, 32 Cong., 2 Sess., 1117.
[31] *Ibid.*, 825; *Mo. Repub.*, Mar. 30, Je. 7, 1853.
[32] [Weekly] *Jeffersonian Inquirer*, Aug. 4, 1855, republication of speeches
made at Kansas, Westport, and Independence, May 6, 7, 1853.
[33] *Mo. Repub.*, Je. 16, 1853.

*be permitted or not*; but he would never vote to make Nebraska a free territory. He ridiculed Benton's route for the railroad. When the surveys should have been made, he would vote to appropriate both land and money in aid of a railroad, and, if it were not entirely incompatible with the public interest, he would vote for a Missouri terminus, either at St. Joseph, Kansas, or the southwest corner, depending upon the findings of the surveyors.[34]

When Congress met in December, 1853, the Nebraska question came up again. The chairmen of the committees on territories could not have sidetracked it had they been of a mind to do so;[35] and there is no evidence that they were. In fact, in view of the way conditions and events were rapidly shaping or being shaped to make the southern route the inevitable choice, the Northwestern men must have felt there was no time to lose. At the preceding session of Congress, lands had been granted to Arkansas to aid in building a railroad diagonally across the state from Cairo to Fulton with a connection from Little Rock to Memphis. Texas was on the point of bestowing a large grant of land upon the imposing New York Atlantic and Pacific Railroad Company to extend the road from Fulton to El Paso. James Gadsden had been sent to Mexico by President Pierce to secure, among other things, the strip of land south of the Gila which held the most eligible route in that quarter. Jefferson Davis, as Secretary of War, was in charge of the surveys of the several routes for a Pacific railroad. Davis seemed to have become the President's closest adviser. The chiefs of the Corps of Topographical Engineers were believed to prefer the southern route. The Pierce administration was certainly friendly to Southern interests in general.[36]

The task of Douglas, Richardson, and their associates was quite precisely defined by the logic of circumstances. They must frame a Nebraska bill which would *pass both houses* and

[34] *Ibid.*, Je. 13, 22, 1853; *Address of Senator Atchison to the People of Missouri*, Je. 5, 1854, extracts from addresses of the preceding year; N. Y. *Herald*, Dec. 18, 1854.
[35] *Daily Mo. Repub.*, Jan. 7, 1854, Washington correspondence for Dec. 31. *Cf.* F. H. Hodder, "The Railroad Background of the Kansas-Nebraska Act," *Miss. Val. Hist. Rev.*, XII, 3-22.
[36] See above, 118-22, 124-27, 138, and below, 168ff.

receive Pierce's signature. As prominent politicians of the
Democratic party (and Douglas at least had presidential
aspirations with good prospects of attaining them), they must
frame a bill which would cause as little discord as possible in
the party ranks. The vote in the Senate at the preceding session demonstrated that they needed at least a few Southern
votes in that body. Considering Atchison's reversion in the
summer and the confidence being shown by the Southern wing
of the party, inspired by various marks of President Pierce's
favor, there appeared to be no possibility of reconciling Southern senators to the Richardson bill that had been defeated in
the Senate in March. To attempt to force it through was
certain to raise the slavery question in a way calculated to
split the party wide open. Shortly after the question had gone
to the Senate Committee on Territories, a Washington correspondent put the matter as follows: "This is one of the most
important questions of the session. It involves the Pacific railroad question, and the slavery question, and a number of local
questions, and questions in relation to our Indian relations. . . .
[The Committee] has a very delicate duty to perform in regard to the terms on which the territories are to come in. To
revive the old Missouri controversy is not desirable. How to
avoid it is the question." [37]

The committee attempted to solve its problem by adopting
the principle of the Compromise of 1850 with regard to
slavery in the territories, namely, leaving the decision to the
territorial legislature with provision for the appeal of slave
cases directly to the Supreme Court of the United States so
that a decision might be had from that tribunal as to the constitutionality of restriction: Southern Democrats professed to
believe that under the Constitution neither Congress nor the
territorial legislature had the right to prohibit slavery in a
territory. The Democratic Party had announced whole-
hearted acceptance of the Compromise of 1850 in its national
platform of 1852 and had won an overwhelming victory.
Southern men would have to vote for the territorial bill with

[37] *Mo. Repub.*, Jan. 4, 1854, quoting the N. Y. *Journal*, of Dec. 26.

the Compromise provision or run the risk of being considered unfaithful to the South's peculiar institution; for a vote against the bill would be equivalent to voting to retain the existing law excluding slavery as an unfit institution. Northern senators and representatives might be persuaded that the territories would actually become "free" by virtue of their soil and climate and that it was unwise to continue to exclude slavery by federal law just as "a taunt and a reproach to our Southern brethren." [38]

The Committee on Territories proposed to divide the territory to be organized into two, Kansas to extend from the 37th to the 40th parallel and Nebraska from the 40th parallel to the Canadian boundary. This division was made, as Professors Allen Johnson and F. H. Hodder have clearly shown, at the request of the Iowa delegation in Congress and of local interests in or near the portion of the Indian Country lying west of Iowa.[39] They feared that with only one territory, the valley of the Kansas, being somewhat more accessible than the valley of the Platte, would be somewhat earlier settled, would get the seat of government, and would, therefore, get a link in the Pacific railroad several years before the valley of the Platte. Douglas himself explained that the division had been made after consultation with the Iowa delegation and a part of the Missouri delegation.[40] Dodge, of Iowa, said: "Originally I favored the organization of one territory, but representations from our constituents, and a more critical examination of the subject — having an eye to the systems of internal improvement which must be adopted by the people of Nebraska and Kansas to develop their resources — satisfied my colleague [Jones], who was a member of the committee who reported this bill, and myself that the great interests of the whole country and especially of our State demanded two territories, otherwise the seat of government and leading thoroughfares must have fallen south of Iowa." [41]

[38] For a similar interpretation see Geo. F. Milton, *The Eve of Conflict*, 108 ff.
[39] Johnson, *Stephen A. Douglas*, 239; Hodder, *op. cit.*, 16-17.
[40] *Cong. Globe*, 33 Cong., 1 Sess., 221.
[41] *Ibid.*, App., 382.

There are reasons for believing that the committee seriously considered creating a third territory west of Arkansas, in what is now Oklahoma, but gave up the plan because "certain parties of influence" could not be reconciled to the ejection of the civilized tribes there." [42] As it was the southern boundary of Kansas was moved northward from the parallel of 36°30′, as provided in the Richardson bill of the preceding session, to the 37th parallel so as not to disturb the Cherokees in one half of their lands.[43] A territory west of Arkansas might have facilitated the extension of the "systems of internal improvement" of Arkansas and the Southwest Branch of the Missouri Pacific along the 35th-parallel route.

The northern boundary of Nebraska also was moved up to the Canadian boundary. No public explanation of this seems to have been made. The reason which most readily occurs is that it was as easy to put the boundary at one line as another and the slavery question might as well be settled for all the organizable territory at once. It should not be forgotten, however, that the northern route to the Pacific was being surveyed and had influential champions. Douglas himself had probably switched his personal interest to this route. He, Bright, of Indiana, Breckinridge, of Kentucky, and several other prominent Democratic politicians had acquired an extensive tract of land at the western end of Lake Superior, which was expected to be a terminus of a Northern Pacific railroad. Douglas had taken great interest in the survey of the northern route. Colonel Isaac I. Stevens, who was in charge of it, conferred with him as to route and reported his success.[44] In the same session of Congress that passed the Kansas-Nebraska bill, Douglas introduced a measure providing for three railroads

[42] Washington correspondence of the *Mo. Repub.*, Jan. 4, 13, 17, 1854; Washington correspondence of the N. Y. *Jour. of Commerce*, Dec. 30, 1853, cited in G. F. Milton, *op. cit.*, 109.

[43] *Cong. Globe*, 33 Cong., 1 Sess., 221.

[44] *Correspondence of R. M. T. Hunter* (Am. Hist. Asso., *Rept.*, 1916, II), 158, 168, 262; Geo. F. Milton, *op. cit.*, 104-06. Professor Hodder thought Douglas was interested only in the Platte Valley route (*op. cit.*); and Milton thinks he exerted his public influence only in behalf of the "central" route (p. 106). Different sections and interests in Illinois preferred different routes. Douglas was too shrewd to openly espouse only one of them while representing Illinois as senator.

to the Pacific, one by a northern route, one by a central, and one by a southern.

The details of the great debate over the repeal of the Missouri Compromise are not germane here. The extreme violence of the opposition had not been anticipated. It came mostly from the Free-Soilers and Northern Whigs, but not only. Had the Kansas-Nebraska bill not contained the provision repealing the Missouri Compromise, the debate would have been still more violent with Northern Democrats and Southern Democrats strongly arrayed against each other, and the bill would not have passed the Senate. As it was, few of those who voted for the bill did so with enthusiasm, but *the bill passed.*[45] As had been anticipated, Southern representatives mostly felt constrained to vote for the bill because of the concession as to slavery, but, considering the objects for which the Northwest wanted the territory organized and the strong probability that neither territory would become slaveholding,[46] it is not surprising that they could muster little fervor for the measure. It is noteworthy that both Senators Bell and Houston, members of the Committee on Territories, opposed the bill on the same grounds they had opposed the Richardson bill at the preceding session.[47]

The immediate purpose and larger implications of the Kansas-Nebraska bill certainly did not escape alert Southerners outside Congress. Albert Pike, of Arkansas, stated them in his speeches and addresses in behalf of his plan for building a Southern Pacific railway. "Not content," he wrote, "with the natural and regular growth towards manly stature of the great country lying in the North-west, they have resorted to the system of forcing, as men use hotbeds in horticulture; and we see new territories of vast size and comparatively unpeopled, organized and established on the line of a Northern Pacific Railroad — Oregon and Washington standing on the shores of the Pacific, and Nebraska and Kansas on those of

[45] In the Senate the Democrats voted 28 for, 5 against, the Whigs, 9 for, 7 against; in the House the Democrats voted 101 to 44 and the Whigs 12 to 52. *Cong. Globe,* 32 Cong., 1 Sess., 532, 1254.
[46] *Ibid.,* 279, App., 149; Geo. F. Milton, *op. cit.,* 149.
[47] *Tex. State Gaz.,* Dec. 1, 1855 (Houston's speech).

the Mississippi — each clasping hands with the other on the slopes of the rocky mountains. It needs no prophetic eye to see in the future a cordon of free States carved in succession off from these territories, extending with a continuous and swarming population across the continent, giving such power to the Northern vote in Congress as has hitherto been only dreamed of, and securing to their road, the Nile of this new Egypt, aid from the National Treasury, and countenance and encouragement from the general government." [48]

After the Kansas-Nebraska bill had become law, the people of Missouri and elsewhere in the Northwest remembered its original objects. An anti-Benton meeting in St. Louis con-demned Benton for opposing a measure "whereby the Great West, and especially St. Louis and Missouri, were to be largely benefited" [49] — Benton had opposed the bill because of its repeal of the Missouri Compromise. Senator Atchison right-fully regarded the passage of the bill in the form it took as a great victory for himself over Benton. In an *Address . . . to the People of Missouri*, dated June 5, 1854, he vindicated his record on the territories, the railroad, and other questions of interest to his state. [50] "The Douglas bill was a Western meas-ure," he said. "It was designed to add to the power and wealth of the West. . . . All of the railroad interests are largely interested, for a terminus on the Western frontier, blocked by an Indian wall, is very different from an indefinite exten-sion westward through new and rapidly opening settlements. Every interest of St. Louis was connected with the territorial question, and there can be no plausible excuse for the en-venomed hostility which the St. Louis representative [Benton] has manifested since the Senate first commenced to act on the subject during the present session of Congress." He hoped Congress would grant lands to the territories to extend the Hannibal and St. Joseph up the Platte, the Missouri Pacific up the Kansas, and the Springfield road (the Southwest Branch) across the Neosho and Arkansas rivers in the direc-

[48] *DeBow's Rev.*, XVII, 595.
[49] *Mo. Repub.*, May 29, 1854.
[50] *Ibid.*, Je. 21, 1854; also as a pamphlet.

tion of Albuquerque. Let all the roads be constructed to the foot of the Rockies and the one on the most practicable route extended to the Pacific. The roads would prove profitable even if they should never go beyond the mountains.

Opening the territories to settlement and organizing territorial governments therein did remove an obstacle to the building of a railroad to the Pacific by central and northern routes. The congregation of population along the Kansas and the Platte furnished arguments for selecting a route in the vicinity of one or the other. The territories promptly developed projects for "links" in the Pacific railroad and for other railroads and petitioned Congress for land grants in aid. On December 26, 1854, Mr. Whitfield, delegate from Kansas territory, introduced a bill for a land grant in aid of a road in Kansas.[51] In the next session of Congress grants were requested for Kansas, Nebraska, and Minnesota, and the following year for New Mexico as well.[52] Thereafter the territories had almost as many requests for land grants in aid of railroad projects as full-fledged states.

In an indirect way, however, the organization of the territories contributed strongly to delaying the great project its friends had hoped to advance. The bitter debate over the repeal of the Missouri Compromise and the subsequent struggle over whether Kansas should become a slave or a free state greatly exacerbated the sectional feeling of the time, which, in turn, rendered the federal government well-nigh impotent to take a national measure for a national purpose.

[51] *Cong. Globe*, 33 Cong., 2 Sess., 130.
[52] *Ibid.*, 34 Cong., 1 Sess., 1325, 1944; 34 Cong., 2 Sess., 341, 352, 357, 920, 1000, 1069.

# CHAPTER XI

## THE PACIFIC RAILWAY SURVEYS

I T FELL to Jefferson Davis as secretary of war in Franklin Pierce's cabinet to supervise the surveys of the routes for a Pacific railroad provided for in the closing days of the Thirty Second Congress.[1] With a reasonable degree of promptitude, Davis went about the task of putting surveying parties in the field. He received numerous suggestions as to where to survey and how. Governor Doty, of Wisconsin, and a few Illinois congressmen urged the claims of an extreme northern route.[2] Thomas H. Benton endeavored to have Colonel Frémont and a former assistant, Lieutenant E. F. Beale, put in the charge of the survey of his favorite thirty-eighth degree route. The other Missouri congressmen refused to support Benton's request, and Davis did not accede to it.[3] Yet for obvious reasons Davis had to assign a surveying party to this route and to every other which had commended itself to a considerable portion of the public. The $150,000 appropriation was apportioned fairly among the several routes. In selecting the head of each surveying party and his principal assistant, Davis seems to have been guided only by the advice of Colonel J. J. Abert, chief of the Corps of Topographical Engineers, and Major Emory of the same corps. It is an interesting and significant fact that all the heads of parties and their principal assistants and the officers who later examined and compared the reports were Northerners with the sole exception of Captain John Pope, who was from Kentucky, and all surviving served with distinction in the Union army during the Civil War. Except for the choice of his chief assistant, the head of each party was allowed considerable freedom in the

[1] Above, 100, 107.
[2] *Weekly Chicago Democrat*, Je. 18, 1853; *Daily Mo. Repub.*, Apr. 18.
[3] *Ibid.*, Apr. 12, May 4, Je. 1, 13, 16; Dunbar Rowland, *Jefferson Davis, Constitutionalist*, II, 191, 193.

choice of personnel. Each party was provided with a proper military escort. Six parties were put in the field.

The survey of the most northern route was entrusted to the charge of Colonel Isaac I. Stevens, the newly appointed governor of Washington Territory. Captain George B. McClellan was his chief assistant. Stevens was a native of Massachusetts. He had been an army engineer and had served with distinction in the Mexican War. Since the war he had been head of the Coast Survey office in Washington. His designation gave great satisfaction to the friends of the northern route.[4] McClellan had some experience in Western exploration, notably in an expedition to the sources of the Red River with Captain R. B. Marcy. The Stevens party was to start at St. Paul and proceed by way of the great bend of the Missouri to Puget Sound. Stevens was the first of the party chiefs to receive his orders, April 8, and the first to get his party in the field June, 1853. Haste was urgent because of the shortness of the season in such a high latitude. The sum of $40,000 was allocated to this route.[5]

Captain J. W. Gunnison, of the Topographical Engineers, with Lieutenant E. G. Beckwith as chief assistant, was charged with organizing the party and conducting the survey of portions of the 38th- and 41st-degree routes. The Gunnison party was to start at Fort Leavenworth, cross the Rockies by passes which might be found among the headwaters of the Arkansas, Rio Grande, and Green, and thence move westerly to the eastern base of the Sierra Nevada. It was not to cross this range but was to turn northeast to Great Salt Lake and search for a practicable route through the Wasatch and Uintah Mountains to Fort Bridger on the Oregon trail. Gunnison had been chief assistant of Captain Stansbury in his survey of the Salt Lake region, 1849 and 1850. The sum of $40,000 also was allotted to Gunnison's party.[6]

Lieutenant A. W. Whipple, of the Topographical En-

---

[4] *Am. R. R. Jour.*, XXVI, 216, 422.
[5] Davis's instructions to Stevens, *Sen. Exec. Docs.*, 33 Cong., 1 Sess., II (691), No. 1, Pt. II, 55.
[6] *Ibid.*, 57.

gineers, was charged with organizing and leading a party to survey the 35th-parallel route. Whipple was a native of Massachusetts. He had acquired a knowledge of the West while serving with the Mexican boundary commission. His party was to go by way of the valleys of the Canadian and Pecos rivers to the Rio Grande at or near Albuquerque, across the Zuni Mountains and the Colorado Plateau to the Colorado River near the 35th parallel, and thence by the most practicable route to the Pacific at either San Pedro or San Diego. Forty thousand dollars were allocated for the survey of this route.[7]

Lieutenant R. S. Williamson, Topographical Engineers, was to organize a party which should seek practicable routes in California to continue the 35th- and 32nd-degree routes from their crossings of the Colorado to San Francisco, San Pedro, and San Diego. This involved particularly the examination of passes in the Sierra Nevada and the Coast Range. Lieutenant Williamson was a native of New York. He had had experience in California explorations and surveys as assistant of Captain Warner. Williamson's chief assistant was Lieutenant J. G. Parke, Topographical Engineers, a Pennsylvanian, who also had an enviable record in connection with Western exploration. Lieutenant Williamson was allotted the remaining $30,000 of the appropriation.[8]

Provision for the survey of the 32nd-degree route, except for the portion Lieutenant Williamson was to cover, was considerably delayed. It was not until November, while Gadsden's negotiations were in progress, that the Mexican government gave its consent to the survey on that portion of the route which lay within what was soon to be the Gadsden Purchase. Then Davis instructed Lieutenant J. G. Parke, with a small party, to make a rapid reconnoissance from the Pimas Villages on the lower Gila via Tucson to the Rio Grande at Doña Ana. For this survey Parke was allowed $5,000 and what funds could be spared by Lieutenants Whip-

[7] *Ibid.*, 58.
[8] *Ibid.*, 60.

ple and Williamson.[9] Meanwhile, in October, Brevet Captain John Pope, Topographical Engineers, had been instructed to organize a party on the Rio Grande and explore a route across Texas from Doña Ana through the Llano Estacado to Preston on the Red River. He was to determine also the military usefulness of the route. This latter feature enabled Secretary Davis to finance the survey with unexpended balances of several military explorations. Pope had $15,000 at his command.[10] There was considerable complaint in the South about the delay in providing for the survey of portions of the 32nd-parallel route. Governor Bell, of Texas, went so far as to recommend that the state should undertake the survey of the portion of the route which lay within Texas.[11]

There were notable omissions from the list of routes whose survey was provided for. Only that portion of the 41st-parallel, or South Pass, route which lay between Salt Lake and Fort Bridger was to be examined. No provision was made for surveying a route for a branch to Oregon from Fort Bridger or other eligible point on the South Pass route. The survey of the 38th-degree route was to be carried only to the eastern base of the Sierra Nevada. A portion of the 32nd-parallel route that lay along the lower Gila was neglected altogether, and other portions were given only scant attention.

Most serious and least justifiable of the omissions was the lack of provision for continuing the survey of the two central routes across the Sierra Nevada to San Francisco. Davis justified it on the ground that earlier official explorations had shown that no railway pass could be found in the range north of about the 35th parallel. Having learned, he said, that the Mormons were making a survey to Walker's Pass, he had directed Captain Gunnison to procure a copy "thus connecting his line with the survey ordered to be made near the thirty-fifth parallel." [12] It is clear, though, that a failure to find a pass in

[9] *Ibid.*, 61-64.
[10] *Ibid.*, 64. In regard to funds see also Davis's report of Feb. 6, 1854, in *Sen. Exec. Docs.*, 33 Cong., 1 Sess., V (695), No. 29.
[11] *Tex. State Gaz.*, Sept. 3, 17, Nov. 15, 1853; Richmond *Enquirer*, July 1.
[12] *Sen. Exec. Docs.*, 33 Cong., 1 Sess., II (691), No. 1., Pt. II, 20. Davis's official reports are also in Rowland, *op. cit.*, II.

the Sierra Nevada considerably north of the 35th parallel would be fatal to both the central routes, especially the South Pass route. Moreover many people whose opinions were entitled to respect, including Lieutenant R. S. Williamson, believed a practicable pass could be found.[13] This omission was partly rectified later by an order, dated May 1, 1854, to Lieutenant Beckwith, then in charge of the surveys on the central routes, to continue the surveys westward from Salt Lake to San Francisco.

Jefferson Davis justified the neglect of the South Pass route east of Fort Bridger on the ground that the section was already well known, that Frémont had explored it "with proper instruments," and that Captain Stansbury had made a careful survey of it in 1849-50.[14] Considering how scant the appropriation was, this omission may have been justifiable. It was at least unfortunate. Captain Stansbury's report had raised considerable doubt of the practicability of building a railroad along the emigrant road up the North Fork of the Platte and the Sweetwater and through South Pass. He had contended strongly for the superiority of a little-known route up the South Fork and Lodge Pole Creek and through Cheyenne Pass, the route destined to be used, in the main, by the Union Pacific. The comparative neglect of the Gila route was probably amply justified by the great amount of reliable information which had come from numerous official explorations in the region, especially those of the Mexican Boundary Commission.

All of the six surveying parties were pretty much alike in organization and equipment and proceeded in about the same manner.[15] Each had a number of engineers or surveyors, one

[13] *Sen. Exec. Docs.*, 31 Cong., 1 Sess., X (558), No. 47, Pt. II, 17-22; *Cong. Globe*, 33 Cong., 1 Sess., 1796.
[14] *Sen. Exec. Docs.*, 33 Cong., 1 Sess., II (691), No. 1, Pt. II, 20; 32 Cong., Spec. Sess. (608), No. 3 (Stansbury).
[15] The following description of the conduct of the surveys is generalized from the reports of the several parties. The earlier reports of the parties already mentioned are in *H. Exec. Docs.*, 33 Cong., 1 Sess., XVIII (736, 737, 739), No. 129. They were republished with revisions and additions and with reports of subsequent surveys in a twelve-volume, beautifully illustrated series entitled, *Reports of Explorations and Surveys, to Ascertain the Most Practicable and Economical Route for a Railroad from the Mississippi River to the Pacific*

or more geologists, botanists, naturalists, astronomers, meteorologists, topographers, and artists, a physician, and a complement of instrument bearers, teamsters, cooks, etc. Each was accompanied by a very necessary military escort, usually about as large as the surveying party itself. At one time Governor Stevens had over one hundred men, including the military escort, under his immediate command, while Captain McClellan had a detachment of over sixty on another portion of the route. Stevens's was the largest expedition. On his rapid reconnoissance from the Pimas Villages to the Rio Grande Lieutenant Parke had only twenty-eight in his party, and the escort was of the same number. The usual equipment consisted of barometers for determining elevation, sextants, chronometers, and tables for determining latitude and longitude, odometers, attached to wagon wheels, for measuring distances, and the ordinary surveyors' instruments. Captain Pope was especially poorly provided with instruments in consequence of having to organize his party on the Rio Grande. Many instruments proved defective.

It is not to be supposed that these so-called Pacific railroad surveys were actual surveys. They were rather reconnoissances. The parties did not set stakes or make detailed calculations of grades, curves, excavations, embankments, bridging, etc. They moved too rapidly and covered too wide areas for that. The main wagon train in each case took a route determined upon from the information furnished by earlier explorations or reports brought in from day to day by reconnoitering parties sent in advance. This route had to be immediately practicable for wagons whether or not it seemed practicable for a railroad. Detachments were sent to either side of the route of the main train as occasion demanded to examine what might be more favorable ground. The route of the main train was plotted with care; other points were then located with reference to this trace as a base line. Barometric readings

---

*Ocean* . . . (1855-1861). There are both House and Senate editions. They are identical except that Vol. XII is missing from the latter. The series will be referred to hereafter as the *Pacific Railroad Surveys*.

were taken only at the main divides and depressions. Lieutenant Williamson alone ran a series of levels, and he only to test his barometers. Distances were measured with the odometer where possible or, in the absence of the wagon, estimated. The chain was seldom used.

The greatest degree of care was devoted to mountain passes, canyons, and bridge sites, since they would be determining points in locating a railroad and since their degree of practicability would largely determine the availability of the route as a whole. Inability to avoid the necessity of a long and expensive tunnel, for example, would be almost fatal to the claims of a route. Careful notes were made of the amount and location of timber, building stone, coal, and water which might be used in constructing and operating a railroad. Great importance was attached to the geology, soil, meteorology, and vegetation of the regions traversed, since they were indications of prospective ability to support a population. On the more northern routes great efforts were made to learn the depths of snow in the mountain passes in winter.

Considering the time and money at their disposal, the achievements of these surveying parties were truly remarkable.[16] Governor Stevens's parties operated in a region most of which had not been explored by trained men since Lewis and Clark had traversed it. In fact Stevens used Lewis and Clark's journal constantly. His parties accomplished wonders. They mapped two main lines of approach to the Rockies. They explored nine passes in that chain. They examined two routes from Clark's Fork of the Columbia across the Bitter Root Mountains to Spokane. They selected and explored two routes from Spokane across the Cascade Range, one via the Columbia to Vancouver, the other up the Yakima River and through Yakima Pass to Puget Sound. Both of these routes are followed substantially by the Northern Pacific. Several of the mountain passes were examined in winter. McClellan judged Seattle to be the best railway terminus on Puget

---

[16] The itineraries and experiences of the several parties are described in detail in G. L. Albright, *Official Explorations for Pacific Railroads.*

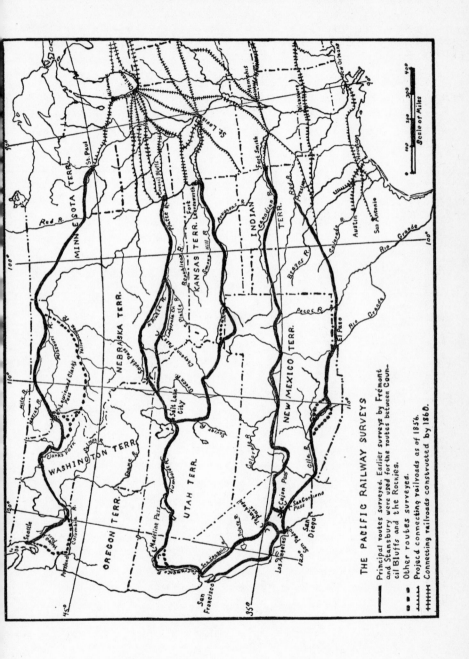

THE PACIFIC RAILWAY SURVEYS

Principal routes surveyed. Earlier surveys by Frémont
and Stansbury were used for the routes between Council Bluffs and the Rockies.

---- Other routes surveyed.

•••• Project connecting railroads as of 1856.

++++ Connecting railroads constructed by 1860.

Sound. This survey, begun the preceding June, was completed in March, 1854, except for the work of a few small detachments operating on a prospective deficiency appropriation.

Captain Gunnison's party operated in the most difficult country. They found a difficult but possible railroad pass from the headwaters of the Arkansas River to the headwaters of the Rio Grande and the Colorado. In October Gunnison and a small detachment were surprised near the Sevier River by a band of Paiute Indians and killed. The command devolved on Lieutenant Beckwith. Beckwith wintered the party at Salt Lake. In the early spring of 1854 he explored between Salt Lake and Fort Bridger finding two difficult but practicable routes through the Wasatch Mountains. Upon his own recommendation, he then received orders, May 1, to continue his survey westward to San Francisco. He found a practicable pass in the Humboldt Mountains, in the Great Basin. He explored several passes in the Sierra Nevada and concluded that Madeline Pass was the best. He explored also much of the difficult terrain between the Sierras and San Francisco. It is no reflection on his efficiency that he failed to designate a route through California which has been utilized by a transcontinental railway. Beckwith disbanded his party in California, July 26, 1854, and reported in Washington, D. C., in person, September, 1854.

Lieutenant Whipple's party, traversing ground which had already been partially explored by officers of the Topographical Engineers, made a rapid and efficient survey. The field work was begun at Fort Smith, Arkansas, in July, 1853, and completed at San Pedro, California, in March, 1854. The route Whipple recommended from the crossing of the Rio Grande to the Cajon Pass in the Sierra Nevada is followed in all its important features, including the crossing of the Colorado at Needles, by the present Atchison, Topeka, and Santa Fe Railroad.

Lieutenants Williamson and Parke explored passes in the Sierra Nevada and the Coast Range. They reported that there was no practicable route directly from the Colorado at the mouth of the Gila to San Diego, and to this day there is no direct railroad entirely on American soil between the two points. Williamson recommended as practicable a route from the mouth of the Gila through San Gorgonio Pass, San Bernardino, and Los Angeles to the Pacific at San Pedro. The route was later adopted in its essential features by the Southern Pacific Railroad Company. He also reported that the Cajon Pass, now used by the Santa Fe, would afford a practicable, though difficult, route to San Pedro for a road by the 35th-parallel route. He proved the Walker and Tejon passes, leading from the Great Basin through the Sierra Nevada into the Tulare Valley, to be impracticable. Their names had long been conjured with by advocates of a southern route. Williamson showed, however, that the Tehachapi Pass, hitherto dismissed, would afford a practicable route for a road crossing the Colorado at the Needles; it has been utilized by the Southern Pacific, and the Santa Fe uses the Southern Pacific line at this point. The field work of the Williamson party was begun in July and completed in December, 1853.

Only one of the surveying parties completed its field work before the date set by Congress for the reports to be in; and after the field work was done it still took much time to prepare reports, estimates, profiles, and maps. The reports were transmitted to Secretary Davis at various dates between February 1, 1854, in the case of Beckwith's report on the 38th-degree route, and December 31 of the same year, Williamson's. Congress had simply ordered something humanly impossible to accomplish.

Some of the party heads, particularly Stevens, Whipple, and Pope, by quite natural psychological reactions had become very enthusiastic over the merits of their respective routes, and their reports have the tone of special pleadings. Stevens played up the superior capacity of the region along his route to support a population.[17] Whipple insisted that only the 35th-parallel route was eligible; San Francisco, he said, must be the western

[17] *H. Exec. Docs.*, 33 Cong., 1 Sess., XVIII (736, 737, 739), No. 129, Rept. by Col. I. I. Stevens, 13, 42, 81.

terminus and nearly all the known passes in the Sierra Nevada were in the latitude of 35 degrees. "Should local interests secure the construction of the main road direct to a frontier harbor — San Diego or Puget's Sound — or to other smaller ports, trade could scarcely be forced from its natural channel." [18] Pope somehow found between the 32nd and 34th parallels a broad belt of well-watered, well-timbered country adapted in a high degree to agricultural purposes which projected for 354 miles "like a vast peninsula, into the parched and treeless waste of plains." [19]

Stevens's report was discredited to a degree and the public mind further confused by a report of one F. W. Lander, Civil Engineer. Lander had been an assistant with the Stevens party. He formed the opinion that a railroad by the northern route would be too expensive to be practicable in the near future and that Washington and Oregon would improve their chances of getting early railroad connection by supporting the construction of a road to California with a branch to Puget Sound. He was authorized by the Legislature of Washington Territory to make a reconnoissance from the Columbia by way of the Snake River Valley to Salt Lake. He reported finding a practicable route. It was rumored that Captain McClellan, also, disagreed with his chief. [20]

From the start it had been Jefferson Davis's intention, and properly so, to subject the various reports from field parties to rigid analysis and comparison before laying them before Congress. To assist him in this task he first unfortunately selected Major William H. Emory, of the Topographical Engineers. [21] Emory's designation was criticized by the watchful Thomas H. Benton and others on the grounds of his earlier participation in surveys on the Gila route, his alleged prejudice in its favor and in favor of San Diego as the Pacific terminus, and his family connection with Robert J. Walker, who, at the time,

---

[18] *Ibid.*, Rept. by Lt. A. W. Whipple, 10.
[19] *Ibid.*, Rept. by Brevet Capt. John Pope, 9.
[20] *Cong. Globe*, 37 Cong., 2 Sess., 2806; *Pacific Railroad Surveys*, II, Rept. by F. W. Lander, *passim.*
[21] *Ibid.*, I, Davis's "Report . . . on the Several Railroad Explorations" (dated Feb. 27, 1855), 30; *Am. R. R. Jour.*, XXVII, 451.

was interested in the Mississippi and Pacific in Texas.[22] Davis himself was not unsuspected of bias. The *American Railroad Journal* argued strongly for the submission of the reports to a commission of civil engineers experienced in railway building.[23] Senator Fessenden, of Maine, tried unsuccessfully to get a provision to this effect attached to an item appropriating money for continuing the surveys.[24] Fortunately Major Emory was appointed, August, 1854, to the Mexican boundary commission under the Gadsden Treaty, and Captain A. A. Humphreys, another capable officer of the Topographical Corps, was put in charge of the office work in connection with the surveys.[25]

After much tedious labor Captain Humphreys and Lieutenant J. K. Warren, his chief assistant, submitted to Davis a long "Examination . . . of the Reports of Explorations for Railroad Routes from the Mississippi to the Pacific . . . and of the Explorations made Previous to that Time which have a Bearing upon the Subject." [26] The document was dated February 5, 1855. With the "Examination" and the reports themselves before him, Secretary Davis prepared his "Report . . . on the Several Railroad Explorations." [27] This "Report" and the "Examination" with four volumes of documents [28] were submitted to Congress on February 27, 1855, the very end of the short session and over a year later than the law had stipulated.[29] A large general map of the western half of the United States showing the relative locations of the various routes was still to be completed.

Humphreys and Warren found merits in all the routes surveyed except that of the 38th parallel, Benton's. They found

---

[22] *Ibid.*, XXVII, 454; *Cong. Globe*, 33 Cong., 1 Sess., App., 1034. Also see above, 148.

[23] XXVII, 273, 451.

[24] *Cong. Globe*, 33 Cong., 1 Sess., 2189.

[25] *Pacific Railroad Surveys*, I, Davis's "Report . . . on the Several Railroad Explorations," 30.

[26] *Ibid.*, I.

[27] *Ibid.*, I.

[28] *H. Exec. Docs.*, 33 Cong., 1 Sess., XVIII (736-39), No. 129. See n. 15.

[29] However, most of the reports of the various surveying parties had been printed and put upon congressmen's desks several weeks earlier. *Cong. Globe*, 33 Cong., 2 Sess., 217, 281.

the principal favorable features of the northern route to be
its low profile and easy grades. Its most unfavorable features
were high costs of construction on the mountain sections, extremely heavy snowfall in Yakima Pass, and the great delay
which would be occasioned by the necessity of constructing a
long tunnel at either Cadotte's or Lewis and Clark's Pass in
the Rockies. They raised Stevens's estimate of the cost of a
road from St. Paul to Seattle by twenty per cent bringing it
up to $140,871,000.

Humphreys and Warren's "Examination" was quite favorable to the route near the 41st and 42nd parallels. The cost
of sections along the North Platte, if followed, in the Wasatch
Mountains, and down the canyon of the Sacramento River
would be very high. Coal and timber could be had only at
long intervals. The total cost for the whole distance from
the Missouri River to San Francisco was estimated at
$116,095,000.

The "Examination" dismissed the route near the 38th and
39th parallels with scant notice. The difficulties were enormous. There were no offsetting merits. Even the alleged
advantage of being in the latitude of San Francisco was illusory
since it would be necessary to go down to the 35th or up to the
41st parallel to cross the Sierra Nevada. It was not considered worthwhile to give an estimate of cost. These conclusions, it is believed, were amply justified by Gunnison's notes
and Beckwith's report. They have been justified since by the
course of actual railroad construction; for, while the Denver
and Rio Grande crosses the Rockies at about the place designated by Frémont and Benton, it does not continue westward
in the direction of San Francisco but veers off northwestward
to Salt Lake.

Humphreys and Warren found the 35th-degree route to be
unexpectedly favorable. It possessed timber and fuel, which
were lacking on the 32nd-parallel route. Its principal unfavorable features were great elevation and a high sum of
ascents and descents. Whipple's estimate of $169,210,000 for
the cost of a railroad from Fort Smith, Arkansas, to San

Francisco was considered to be too high but no other figure was offered. It was shown from reports of other explorations, especially that of Dr. Wislezenius, made in 1846, that a practicable route existed between Independence, Missouri, and Albuquerque, on Whipple's route.

The officers in their "Examination" were most favorably impressed by the 32nd-parallel route and accorded it the most space. They found it to be the shortest, 1,618 miles from Fulton, Arkansas, to San Pedro and 2,039 to San Francisco as against 1892 from Fort Smith, Arkansas, to San Pedro and 2,174 to San Francisco by the 35th-parallel route, 2,032 from Omaha to San Francisco by the central route, and 1,864 from St. Paul to Vancouver by the northern route. The actual distances by railroads now in use on the several routes between the points named are as follows, Davis's estimates in parentheses: on the 32nd parallel 1,720 (1,618) miles to San Pedro and 2,166 (2,039) to San Francisco; on the 35th parallel 1,722 (1,892) to San Pedro and 2,002 (2,174) to San Francisco; on the central route 1,775 (2,032); and on the northern route 1,814 (1,864) miles. Thus it appears the Topographical Engineers and Jefferson Davis underestimated the length of the Gila route by 102 miles and overestimated the lengths of all the others by 50 to 257 miles. It must be remembered, however, that the engineers of the 1850's tried to choose routes which would not require long tunnels while the later railroad builders preferred expensive tunnels to any considerable increase in the length of their lines. Moreover the surveying parties had not explored all the possible variations of route. Humphreys and Warren's estimates are justified by the reports. Therefore the evidence casts only the barest suspicion on the War Department of tampering with the figures.

The greatest advantage of the southern route, according to Humphreys and Warren, lay in long stretches on the Llano Estacado and the table lands of the Gadsden Purchase which would require scarcely any grading and where, indeed, the natural surface could be used for a temporary road. There would be few pieces of difficult construction on the whole length. Some of the grades would be heavy. Fertile soil seemed to extend farther west on this route than on any other, but the evidence was not conclusive on this point. The route was deficient in but two elements for cheap construction and operation, namely, fuel and water. There was no coal west of the Brazos. There were long stretches without sufficient water for working parties, but it could certainly be procured by means of artesian wells. The harbor of San Pedro was exposed and would require a breakwater. San Diego, which could best be reached by way of San Pedro, had an excellent but small harbor. However, "the great object of a Pacific railroad will not be accomplished unless a connected line can be had to the best harbor on the coast, that of San Francisco." There would be difficult sections with heavy grades along the 521 miles from San Bernardino to San Francisco; further surveys were needed to determine the best route. The cost of a railroad from Fulton to San Pedro was estimated at $68,970,000 and one from Fulton to San Francisco at $93,120,000.

Estimates of costs, it may be said, were made by "assimilating" various sections along the routes to railroads in the states whose costs were known and adding a percentage to cover the estimated differential between costs in the East and costs in a remote unsettled region. The estimates for mountain sections were often based on the costs of the Baltimore and Ohio and those for the canyon sections upon the costs of the Hudson River Railroad. As Davis properly pointed out, the estimates of costs were more valid for determining the relative costs of roads by the several routes than the absolute cost of constructing a railroad upon any of them.[30]

Captain Humphreys calculated that under the worst conditions the net earnings of a railroad on the 32-parallel route could not be less than $6,000,000 a year, a fair return on the prospective investment. If the government would pay the interest on the capital invested during the period of construction, he thought, private parties would probably build the road. Without at least so much aid, it probably never would be built.

[30] *Pacific Railroad Surveys*, I, Davis's Report, 29.

A land grant, which had been proposed so often, would be of comparatively little value. The captain apparently was considerably influenced in his preference for the southern route by the army view that a railroad was required primarily for military purposes, that its business would be confined for a long period to carrying troops, military supplies, mails, passengers, and express, and that, therefore, it should be cheaply constructed and would need only light equipment. The implication of the "Examination" is that, if a heavy freight business were to be anticipated, the Gila route would not be rated quite so highly in comparison with routes which had better access to coal and easier grades. No expectations were entertained in 1855 of development of any considerable amount of way traffic on any route between about the 100th meridian and the Sierra Nevada.

Jefferson Davis's "Report," another long document, followed Humphreys and Warren's "Examination" quite closely. Davis gave less credence than the two officers to Stevens's report of finding large areas on the middle portions of the northern route suitable for cultivation and grazing — such areas are there. He believed the upkeep of a railroad would be less on the 32nd-parallel route than upon any other. He asserted that snows would suspend the operation of trains on other routes except the 35th-degree during a portion of the year — this despite the fact that railroad engineers no longer considered snow a serious obstacle to the operation of trains. The Secretary, therefore, concluded that the route of the 32nd parallel was "of those surveyed the most practicable and economical route for a railroad from the Mississippi river to the Pacific ocean" and the "shortest and cheapest" to San Francisco itself.

Neither Davis nor Humphreys attempted any conclusions as to which route would best serve the commercial interests of the country. Davis did throw in the assertion that "the aggregate length of railroad lines" connecting the southern route at its eastern terminus with the Atlantic and Gulf was less than the aggregate length of connections with any other routes. Obviously the result of such a comparison would depend largely upon the list of seaports selected, and there was no justification for omitting interior cities from the calculation. With the exceptions noted, the conclusions of Davis and the two army officers were such as impartial, intelligent persons might draw from the reports submitted to them.

The reports of the surveys and Davis's and Humphreys' analyses thereof strengthened the partisans of the Gila route in their belief in its superiority. They certainly did not convert the partisans of other routes. Some questioned Davis's detachment. E. Haskett Derby, of the Boston bar, who reviewed the reports, Humphreys and Warren's analysis thereof, and Davis's summary for *Hunt's Merchants Magazine*, thought that, if the reader of Davis's summary would dip into the reports themselves, he would "inevitably find that the facts do not warrant the deductions of the Secretary, and will discover a little Southern proclivity in his report. Perhaps he might infer that a true son of the South, anxious for her supremacy, who has taken the extreme Southern view on the Kansas question, who has opposed that great link in Northern improvements, the Rock Island Bridge, might feel solicitous to secure to the South the great and perhaps sole route to the Pacific." [31]

The railroad surveys served to confirm the public in general in the judgment that a railroad to the Pacific was practicable by any of several routes at a cost great, perhaps, but not prohibitive.[32] In fact, the public had grasped this essential finding months before Davis submitted his summary. Those people who preferred another route than the thirty-second parallel could cogently argue on the basis of the reports that the cost of construction and operation on one route would not be sufficiently less than that upon any other to outweigh other considerations in making a choice. The surveys, then, did not abate the rivalry over routes and termini one jot. If anything, they intensified it, for all could now quote expert opinion.

[31] XXXV, 659-80.
[32] *DeBow's Rev.*, XVI, 507; *Daily Mo. Repub.*, Dec. 28, 1854, message of Gov. Price, of Mo.

The claims of one proposed route only were damaged beyond repair, namely, that near the 38th and 39th parallels. People of St. Louis and parties financially interested in the Pacific of Missouri were keenly disappointed by the verdict.[33] Colonel Thomas Hart Benton and his closest supporters refused to accept it. Benton had virtually staked his return to the United States Senate upon a railroad to the Pacific by "Coo-cha-to-pe" Pass. He and his friends denounced the report on the route as unfair, accused the Secretary of War of bias, and inveighed against the Topographical Engineers.[34] Benton's enemies, even in Missouri, rejoiced at his discomfiture.[35]

In December, 1854, Benton made a tour through the East in an attempt to rehabilitate his route in the public mind. He spoke eloquently to great audiences in Tremont Temple, Boston, and elsewhere.[36] He described the route in glowing terms, pictured five great states rising along it, and appealed to the solid men of the East to come forward and build the railroad. "For this purpose I come here," he said, "and go elsewhere, at much inconvenience to myself, and great cost of personal feeling. . . . But for this cause I could become . . . a *Peter the Hermit*! traversing the country and preaching a crusade." [37] He seems to have convinced many. The *American Railroad Journal* thought it worthwhile to publish a couple of articles calculated to "strip Mr. Benton of his gaudy plumage, of his vast assumption, and effectually dispose of a man who, as far as his influence goes, is really the most formidable obstacle to the execution of this great work." [38] The adverse report on Benton's route won much support in Missouri for the 35th-parallel route with a St. Louis connection either via

[33] *Weekly Jefferson Inquirer*, Sept. 22, 1855.
[34] *Daily Mo. Dem.*, Jan. 1, 12, 18, Feb. 15, Mar. 26, 1855; *Weekly Jefferson Inquirer*, Aug. 15, Sept. 8, 22; *Cong. Globe*, 33 Cong., 2 Sess., App., 73.
[35] *Daily Mo. Dem.*, Feb. 27, 1855.
[36] *Ibid.*, Jan. 4, 6, 1855; *Weekly Jefferson Inquirer*, Jan. 20; *Am. R. R. Jour.*, XXVIII, 2.
[37] *Discourse of Mr. Benton . . . before the Boston Mercantile Library Association, on the Physical Geography of the Country between the States of Missouri and California, with a view to Show Its Adaptation to Settlements, and to the Construction of a Railroad.*
[38] XXVIII, 2-4, 17-19.

Independence and the Santa Fe Trail or, as Congressman J. S. Phelps had been so energetically urging, via the Southwest Branch to a point in the valley of the Canadian.

Even before Jefferson Davis had submitted his summary report to Congress, he had taken action which implied a belief that only the two southern routes were deserving of further attention. Under the appropriation of August 5, 1854, for continuing the surveys he had sent Lieutenant Parke to search for a practicable route from Los Angeles to San Francisco west of the Coast Range and to explore further a route recommended by Lieutenant Whipple between Soda Lake (in Southern California) and the Colorado. Parke was also to go over the Gila route again from the Pimas Villages to the Rio Grande with a view, especially, to finding water for building and operating a railroad.[39] The Secretary had also instructed Captain John Pope, January 5, 1855, to organize a party and determine by borings whether or not water could be had by artesian wells on the Llano Estacado. Pope was also to make borings on the Gila route west of the Rio Grande.[40] Later, in May, 1855, Davis instructed Lieutenant Williamson to seek a practicable route between San Francisco and Oregon and to determine whether or not there existed a practicable pass in the Sierra Nevada near the source of the Carson River, the possibility of which had been suggested by Lieutenant Colonel Steptoe and others. Before the latter task could be undertaken, Williamson and party were recalled.[41] The neglect of the central route was, to say the least, in clear violation of the intent of Congressman McDougall, of California, who had taken the lead in securing the appropriation for supplemental surveys.[42]

Davis summarized the results of the later surveys and of the further office study of the earlier reports in his annual report of December, 1855.[43] Captain Humphreys stated them in

[39] *Pacific Railroad Surveys*, VII, Rept. by Lt. Parke, 13-15.
[40] *Ibid.*, VII, No. 2, p. 16, No. 4, p. 31.
[41] *Ibid.*, VI, Rept. by Lt. Abbot, 3, 9-10.
[42] *Cong. Globe*, 33 Cong., 1 Sess., 1271, 1796.
[43] *Ibid.*, 34 Cong., 1 Sess., App., 19-21; *Pacific Railroad Surveys*, VII, Conclusion, No. 1, pp. 7-10.

greater detail in a report which Davis transmitted to Congress.[44] Further study of the data on the 35th-parallel route had greatly improved its profile and had justified a reduction in the estimate of cost from $169,210,000 to $106,000,000. The route now compared quite favorably with either of the others. Lieutenant Parke's survey had much improved the aspect of the 32nd-parallel route. Parke had found an "eminently practicable" route from Los Angeles to San Francisco west of the Coast Range. He had improved the route from the Pimas Villages to the Rio Grande by avoiding one difficult section of eight miles, by passing it through certain cultivable valleys, and by bringing it into proximity to water. He had found an area of forty-five hundred square miles in the Colorado Desert which was irrigable and had good alluvial soil. Captain Pope's efforts to secure artesian wells on the Llano Estacado had been only partially successful, but "little doubt" was entertained of their ultimate success. No further information was submitted with regard to routes north of the 35th parallel.

The four-volume report submitted to Congress in February, 1855, was republished with revisions and additions in twelve volumes, the last of which did not appear until 1861.[45] The volumes were beautifully illustrated and contained a great store of information of scientific interest. It is, perhaps, an ironical comment on the working of democratic institutions that the publication of the reports cost twice as much as the actual surveying. A congressman calculated in 1859 that to date the surveys had cost $340,000 and printing of reports, $890,000.[46] To the $340,000 should be added $15,000 secured by transferring the unexpended balances of appropriations made for certain military surveys and $100,000 appropriated in 1857 for continuing Pope's search for artesian wells on the Llano Estacado, making a total of $455,000 for the actual surveys.

[44] Ibid., VII, Conclusion, No. 2, pp. 11-18.
[45] See n. 15.
[46] Cong. Globe, 35 Cong., 2 Sess., 239; San Francisco Herald, Apr. 4, 1859.

# CHAPTER XII

# CONGRESSIONAL DEADLOCK, 1853-1856

THE numerous manifestations of enthusiasm for a Pacific railroad in the summer of 1853 led the new Pierce administration to ponder the idea of making its construction a major objective. In July, 1853, the President accompanied by members of his cabinet made a good-will tour through the East. At Philadelphia and New York Secretary of War Jefferson Davis made speeches in the President's hearing strongly advocating a Pacific railway on the ground of military necessity, especially, finding in the war power constitutional authority for federal construction in the territories and grants of aid for sections lying within states.[1] Attorney General Cushing and Secretary of the Treasury Guthrie also were able to find constitutional sanctions.[2] Protests soon came in great numbers from strict-constructionist members of the Democratic Party and those opposed to "government in business." [3] Davis announced that he had been expressing only his own views.[4] Apparently the administration had been putting out a "feeler."

In his annual message of December, 1853, President Pierce spoke very cautiously. He dwelt at some length upon the "varied, great, and increasing claims to consideration" of a railway to the Pacific. The government should render aid by "all constitutional means" in the territories; but government construction and administration there were of doubtful constitutionality and more than doubtful propriety. Private enterprise, he thought, would construct the sections within states. ". . . no grandeur of enterprise and no present urgent inducement promising popular favor" would induce him to disregard

---

[1] Dunbar Rowland, *Jefferson Davis, Constitutionalist*, II, 242, 246; N. Y. *Herald*, July 14, 18, 1853.

[2] *Ibid.*, July 18, 31; *Ark. Gaz. and Dem.*, Aug. 5; *Tex. State Gaz.*, Aug. 13, Sept. 24, Nov. 8.

[3] *Ibid.*, Sept. 24; N. Y. *Herald*, July 31, Aug. 5, Dec. 2.

[4] Rowland, *op. cit.*, II, 277; *Ark. Gaz. and Dem.*, Nov. 25, 1853.

"lights of the Constitution as expounded and illustrated by those whose opinions and expositions constitute the standard of my political faith" or depart from the path which experience had proved to be safe.[5] Clearly Pierce had decided not to make the Pacific railroad an administration measure and was advising Congress that it must proceed circumspectly if it was to avoid a presidential veto.

Secretary Davis, in his annual report, advised Congress to delay action until after it should have received and studied the reports of the surveys and indicated that the reports could not be submitted in time for consideration at the session.[6] With the long and bitter struggle over Kansas and Nebraska and with the Gadsden Treaty, Canadian reciprocity, public lands, and other weighty matters before it, Congress could have little time or inclination for the Pacific railroad matter anyway. Under the circumstances Pacific railroad members in both houses had to be content to await a more convenient season for bringing forward their great measure. The Congress made a deficiency appropriation of $40,000 for the surveys and voted $150,000 for continuing them and completing the reports.[7] It adjourned in the summer of 1854 with the general understanding that the Pacific railway question would be taken up in earnest at the next session.

In the South disappointment caused by the failure of well-laid plans to secure federal approval for a road by the southern route and the growing sectional feeling of the day led to the formulation and wide approval of a plan for building a sectional Pacific railroad. The author was Albert Pike, of Arkansas, orator, poet, and Pacific railroad enthusiast. He first presented his scheme in the Southern Commercial Convention meeting in Charleston, April, 1854,[8] while the Kansas-Nebraska bill was still before Congress and the fate of the Gadsden Treaty still in the balance.

[5] Richardson, *Messages*, V, 220-22.
[6] *Sen. Exec. Docs.*, 33 Cong., 1 Sess., II (691), No. 1, p. 21 ; Rowland, *op. cit.*, II, 310-18. See also *Sen. Exec. Docs.*, 33 Cong., 1 Sess., V (695), No. 29.
[7] *Cong. Globe*, 33 Cong., 1 Sess., 820, 1271, 1340, 1796, 2189, 2234.
[8] Proceedings in *DeBow's Rev.*, XVI, 632-41, XVII, 91-99, 200-13, 250-61, 398-410, 491-510.

Pike proposed that one of the Southern states charter a company to build the road by the Gila route and that Southern states, cities, and loyal Southerners subscribe the stock. The subscribing states should be equally represented on the board of directors. The company should be authorized to negotiate with Mexico for the right of way, where the route lay on her soil, in case the Gadsden Treaty should fail. Branches should be built from various points along the lower Mississippi. Texas should be requested to confer her proffered land grant upon the company, but no federal aid should be sought.[9]

The resolutions embodying Pike's plan were opposed by several of the ablest men in the convention.[10] They tried to show that the scheme was impracticable and even unconstitutional. It was the duty of the federal government, they said, to aid in the construction of a Pacific railroad by the most practicable route. The southern route was the most practicable, and the federal government should be expected to adopt it.

Pike defended his plan in a couple of eloquent speeches.[11] People talked, he said, about building the road with land grants. He had been over the route and knew that most of the lands were worthless. Only money could build the road. Someone must supply it. Southerners had constitutional scruples against federal grants. The southern route, he agreed, was cheapest, shortest, and most practicable; but, if they depended upon the federal government to build the road, it would go to the North. He invited attention to the great Northwest which Southern men seemed never to take into consideration. It was being filled at a prodigious rate and was giving the North a preponderance over the South. The North was bidding for foreign immigration to settle the region. Grants of the privileges of citizenship to persons who had not even declared their intentions of becoming citizens were one bid. The Homestead bill, which had already passed the House, was another. The Kansas-Nebraska bill was a third. With this continued increase of the foreign and Northern influence,

[9] Ibid., XVI, 636-37.
[10] Ibid., XVII, 212, 409-10, 491-99.
[11] Ibid., XVII, 208-12, 500-06.

was it not obvious that the prospect of the South ever getting
the Pacific railroad from Congress was growing beautifully
less every year? His plan might prove impracticable. There
could be no harm in trying it. He wanted to demonstrate that
the South could unite in its own interest. He believed Congress
should help, but he did not want to ask it for aid. He wanted
his resolutions to be "a sort of declaration of independence on
the part of the South."

Albert Pike's eloquence and the strong sectional feeling of
the delegates carried the day. His resolutions were adopted
by a unanimous vote of the convention, voting by states.[12]
California was invited to unite in the proposed organization.
A committee of one member from each state represented was
appointed to draft a charter for the contemplated company
and lay it before the governors of the several states and the
councils of "the Cherokee, Creek, and Choctaw nations." [13]

The plan did not evoke as much enthusiasm outside the
Southern Commercial Convention as in it. Thomas H. Benton
denounced the Charleston gathering as an assemblage of dis-
unionists and the railroad plan as a plan for the dissolution
of the Union.[14] Southern comments were diverse.[15] In general
the Southern advocates of a Pacific railroad thought it wiser
to continue the contest over route along lines already laid
down. However, Pike's plan was kept under advisement. It
was again endorsed by the thinly-attended session of the
Southern Commercial Convention that met in New Orleans in
January, 1855,[16] and the very large assemblage at Savannah,
December, 1856.[17] The Legislature of Louisiana eventually
granted a charter, but no company was organized under it.[18]

When Congress met for the short session in December,
1854, President Pierce had clearly turned entirely cold to the
project of a Pacific railroad.[19] Railroad securities were tem-

[12] Ibid., XVII, 506.
[13] Ibid., XVII, 593-99, memoir of the committee.
[14] Ibid., XVIII, 523.
[15] Daily Mo. Repub., Apr. 25, 1854; Tex. State Gaz., Je. 3.
[16] DeBow's Rev., XVIII, 353-60, 520-28, 623-35, 749-60.
[17] Ibid., XXII, 81-105, 216-24, 307-18.
[18] Ibid., XXI, 472.
[19] Richardson, Messages, V, 291; San Francisco Alta California, Jan. 3, 1855.

porarily under a cloud, the result of over expansion. The reports of the surveys were not all in, although their general
tenor was known.[20] The reports were submitted at intervals
during the session. In spite of these unfavorable auspices the
proponents of a railroad determined to put through a measure
at all hazards.

Each house had a select committee which had been appointed
in the long session, and each had a bill before it reported by its
select committee. Both bills were impossible. It was therefore agreed informally that both committees would support a
bill presented by Senator Douglas in the Senate select committee, but not approved by it, in the long session.[21]

The Douglas bill instructed the secretaries of the Interior,
War, and Navy and the Postmaster General to advertise for
bids for building one or more of three lines of railroad and
telegraph, one to run from the western boundary of Texas to
the Pacific at a point not designated, one from the western
boundary of Missouri or Iowa to San Francisco, and the other
from the western boundary of Wisconsin to the coast in either
Oregon or Washington Territory. The bids must stipulate the
period within which the contractors would complete the roads,
provided it be not over ten years, the time when the roads
would be surrendered to the government, and the sum for
which the mails and military supplies and materials would be
carried, provided that the compensation for carrying the mails
be not greater than $300 per year per mile of road for a daily
mail both ways. The four cabinet members named, under the
direction of the President, were to open the bids and award
the contracts. The contractors were to be entirely free to
locate the road or roads within the designated limits. They
were to receive twelve sections of public land per mile of road
according to the familiar alternate-sections principle. The
government would survey the lands and extinguish Indian
titles. Adequate safeguards were provided against fraud, non-
performance, poor construction, and too prolonged withhold-
ing of lands from sale. Connections with other roads could be

[20] See above, 176, 183.
[21] *Cong. Globe*, 33 Cong., 2 Sess., 281, 287, 289, 318, App., 150.

made only under the direction of the states or territories in which such connections might be located, and the consent of California must be obtained for passage through her territory. Whenever a railroad built under the terms of the bill should revert to the federal government it would be turned over to the states in which it lay.[22]

The bill was adroitly framed to forestall opposition. Its sponsors probably did not expect it to secure the prompt construction of three transcontinental railroads. They hoped that satisfactory bids would be received for at least one. By leaving the choice of routes and termini to the "lynx eye of capital," they would avoid futile attempts to secure agreement in Congress. The friends of every route, it was thought, should be willing to accept the judgment of persons who would be guided only by the prospect of returns upon capital invested. The federal aid promised was of varieties in accord with Democratic principles. States' rights were severely guarded.

It will have been observed that the bill, by failing to mention the western boundary of Arkansas along with the boundaries of Texas, Missouri, Iowa, and Wisconsin as a permissible eastern terminus, would virtually preclude the choice of the thirty-fifth parallel route with Fort Smith as its point of departure. This exclusion, it transpired, was made at the instance of Southern men who believed the South had no chance to get a road which would not go through Texas.[23]

The House moved first. The original select-committee bill was taken up as a special order in Committee of the Whole, January 9, 1855. Debate was desultory until Colonel Thomas H. Benton started the fireworks. He gave his Tremont Temple speech over again with embellishments. He charged that the administration was hostile to the central route and wanted only "foreign and frontier" roads along the Mexican and Canadian borders or through Tehuantepec and intimated it was trying to play into the hands of certain speculators, whom he named. He renewed his feud with the Corps of Topograph-

[22] *Ibid.*, 281, 749.
[23] *Ibid.*, 330.

ical Engineers and attacked the Gadsden Treaty again.  He asserted that he had found solid capitalists, not mere speculators like Robert J. Walker, who were ready to build the road by the central route and that not even a land grant was necessary as inducement.[24]  John McDougall, of California, replied effectively, pointing out Benton's inconsistencies and ridiculing his extravagances.[25]  Yet Benton's speech seems to have made a strong impression on the House and to have prepared the way for what followed.

As soon as opportunity afforded, the Douglas three-road bill was offered as a substitute for the original House bill.[26] Hendricks, of Indiana, moved to amend the substitute by striking out the southern route; he hoped someone would do the same for the northern route, leaving only the central.  His motion received only thirty-nine votes.[27]  The next day Davis, also of Indiana, proposed an amendment to the substitute providing for one trunk line with its eastern terminus on the Missouri or Iowa boundary between the 39th and 41st parallels (Kansas City or St. Joseph) with branches to Memphis and Lake Superior.  At the request of an Iowa representative he changed the limits of the eastern terminus to the 37th and 43d parallels (thus including Omaha and Sioux City).[28]  McDougall, who was presumably in charge, declared the amendment would kill the bill.  However, it was adopted, 80 to 52, most of the opponents of Pacific railway legislation of any sort voting aye along with the strong partisans of a central route.[29] McDougall then moved to strike out the enacting clause.  The motion was carried.  The bill was then reported from the Committee of the Whole to the House.  McDougall again offered the Douglas bill as a substitute, and its friends secured an adjournment that they might have time to collect their scattered forces.[30]

[24] Ibid., 278, App., 73-82.
[25] Ibid., 279, App., 148-51.
[26] Ibid., 279-281.
[27] Ibid., 286, 287, 289.
[28] Ibid., 290, 316, 317.
[29] Ibid., 317.
[30] Ibid., 317-19, 330.

Apparently they could not get together. When, the next day, Davis prepared to renew his amendment in the House, some of the friends of the Douglas measure wanted to serve notice that they would vote against the bill if Davis's proposal should be adopted. McDougall hesitated. He thought it might be well to try first one plan and then another to see if any commanded a majority. Perhaps the Davis amendment had better be tried first. He warned, however, that the amendment might be adopted and still the bill be defeated, "Because those gentlemen from Virginia, and other portions of the Union, who are opposed to the entire project, will vote to amend the bill in that shape. . ." in the hope of impairing its strength.[31]

Davis thereupon renewed his amendment for a single main trunk with branches and supported it with cogent arguments. The central route was the most national. Bids were more likely to be made if only one road was to be built than if three might be; for, in the latter case, capitalists might hesitate to bid for any one lest the other two be built in competition. Branches were less costly than main lines, said Davis. Many members who would vote for the construction of one road because of the great national necessities would balk at providing for three.[32] At the request of J. S. Phelps, Missouri, Davis altered his amendment to permit the main trunk to start as far south as the 36th parallel,[33] thus letting in the possibility of a choice of the thirty-fifth parallel route with a connection with the Southwest Branch of the Pacific of Missouri near Springfield, Phelps's home town. Benton put in his oar. The friends of the central route had finally got it in, he said, but the Douglas bill was still unfair. "Secret bidding, and three gentlemen to decide, two of them carefully selected from the South, I fear for the result. . . ." [34] Benton and Taylor, of Ohio, tried to get the bill referred to a new select committee with the former as chairman, and were frustrated only by an adjournment.[35] The following day, January 20, the Davis amendment

[31] *Ibid.*, 329-32.
[32] *Ibid.*, 330, 333.
[33] *Ibid.*, 334.
[34] *Ibid.*, 335.
[35] *Ibid.*, 334, 336-38; N. Y. *Times*, Jan. 20, 1855.

was adopted 104 to 91, and a motion to reconsider was defeated.[36]

An analysis of the vote by which the Davis amendment was adopted is illuminating. Of members friendly to a Pacific railroad, the amendment received the votes of the two from Iowa, five of six from Missouri, six of eight from Illinois, eight of ten from Indiana, ten of fifteen from Ohio, nine of eleven from Pennsylvania, and three from Tennessee. It received no votes from friends of a railroad in the delegations of Arkansas, Texas, and other Southern states, excepting the three from Tennessee, no votes from Wisconsin or Michigan, and only scattering votes from New York and New England. Ominously, it received the votes of almost all of the irreconcilable opponents of any Pacific railway legislation.

The Davis amendment having been adopted, McDougall took charge again and tried to secure the passage of the substitute as amended. There followed a display of parliamentary maneuvering which is almost bewildering.[37] Only an outline can be given here. The substitute as amended, that is, the Douglas bill with Davis's amendment for one road with branches, was adopted 122 to 79. Then the bill as amended was ordered engrossed and read the third time, 104 to 97; the previous question was ordered on the passage of the bill; and then the House adjourned. Sunday intervened, giving an opportunity for intrigue as well as devotion.[38] On Monday, after nearly every dilatory motion in the House's repertoire had been defeated, the bill was passed, by a vote of 109 to 97. But it did not stay passed. The House now voted 100 to 94 to reconsider this vote and, finally, recommitted the bill by a vote of 105 to 91. There were about one hundred thirty members in the House who wanted to extend federal aid to a Pacific railroad; only seventy-five or eighty who were opposed. Yet no bill was finally adopted.

An analysis of the votes just given, together with reports sent home by "Long John" Wentworth, a Chicago congress-

[36] *Cong. Globe*, 33 Cong., 2 Sess., 339.
[37] *Ibid.*, 339-40, 352-56, 368.
[38] *Daily Mo. Dem.*, Feb. 21, 1855.

man, and others, enable us to know approximately what happened and why.[39] Most of the friends of the Douglas measure
who had at first tried to defeat the Davis amendment, once
the latter had been adopted, joined McDougall in supporting
the bill as amended. All such representatives from Arkansas,
Tennessee, and Kentucky came over, as did those from Michigan and two of the three from Wisconsin. But some seventeen
men from the lower South who were for the Gila route first,
last, and all the time voted consistently against the amended
bill, as did all those who wanted no railroad at all. This left
the balance of power to a little bloc of five or six thick-and-thin
partisans of the Stevens route, headed by Wentworth and
Israel Washburn, of Maine. By voting first on one side and
then on the other, this little band prevented the bill with the
Davis amendment from being finally defeated or finally passed
and at length forced its recommitment to the Select Committee, "the very committee that originally reported three
routes and will do so again." Newspapers had it that Wentworth *et al* advised with Douglas and acted in accord.

Many were inclined to attribute failure to poor leadership
on the part of McDougall.[40] Advocates of the one central
route with branches asserted that, if he had taken a stronger
stand in its behalf after the Davis amendment had been
adopted on Saturday and had insisted upon a vote on the bill
before the over-Sunday adjournment, it would have become
law. A careful reading of the debates and an analysis of the
votes do not disclose where the few extra votes required
could have been picked up. Moreover, even if the central-route
measure by good fortune had passed the House, it could not
have passed the Senate, for there the South's representation
was proportionally greater. Advocates of three routes, on
their part, asserted that, if McDougall had taken a determined
stand against the Davis amendment, it could have been defeated, and then the Douglas bill could have been passed.
This contention, too, seems to have been unfounded. The

[39] *Ibid.*, Feb. 26; *Weekly Chicago Dem.*, Feb. 3.
[40] *Ibid.*, Feb. 3; N. Y. *Times*, Jan. 20; *Daily Mo. Dem.*, Feb. 21, 26, 27,
Apr. 6; Memphis *Eagle and Enquirer*, Feb. 3; *Daily Alta California*, Apr. 19.

single fact that, after the Douglas bill passed the Senate and came to the House, it was not even brought to a vote is sufficient evidence that its friends knew they did not have the votes to carry it. In short Congress was hopelessly deadlocked. A large majority was rendered impotent to enact a great national measure by conflicting local and sectional interests.

For a reason already suggested — the greater proportionate strength of the lower South and the extreme Northwest in that body — the Senate preferred the three road measure, and the Douglas bill was carried through by a vote of 24 to 21 in a thin session,[41] the first Pacific railroad bill to pass either house of Congress.

One speech in the Senate illuminates a ramification of the contest which the House debates leave to conjecture. Geyer, of Missouri, said that his "insuperable objection" to the Douglas, three-road bill was that it presented inducements to form combinations against his state so that there was scarcely a possibility that she would get the terminus of either road. It would be to the interests of both the contractors and California to have the central road enter the state near the northern end and proceed southward to San Francisco and the southern road to enter at the southwest corner and proceed north: thus California would get a railroad the length of the state and the contractors much valuable land. A route from St. Louis via Albuquerque would not be chosen because it would be too near the southern road. A road via Salt Lake would have a Chicago terminus. "The South, and the contractors for the southern road, the States of California and Illinois, and the capitalists who own the roads from Lake Erie, by Chicago, to Rock Island, and through Iowa, are invited to co-operate in securing the eastern terminus of the central road on the western boundary of Iowa."[42] Clearly Geyer considered Benton's route impossible.

In the long session, the Senate had passed a bill to grant the right of way and 2,000,000 acres of public land to Messrs.

[41] *Cong. Globe*, 33 Cong., 2 Sess., 814.
[42] *Ibid.*, 749, 751, 808, App., 198-200.

Alden and Eddy, of Maine, to aid them in constructing a "subterranean" telegraph from some point on the Mississippi to the Pacific. In return for privileges granted, the government was to receive a limited amount of free service per year for ten years.[43] The bill came up in the House during the short session shortly after the railroad bill had been recommitted. It met the bitter opposition of Benton, Delegate Joe Lane, of Oregon, and others. Plainly they feared the location of a telegraph line would influence the location of a railroad. To save the measure in any form, its friends had to accept a substitute which simply authorized the construction of the telegraph, granted the right of way, and offered protection.[44] The Senate accepted this substitute also and it became law.[45] But in this form it offered no inducement to promoters.

McDougall, having failed to get provision for a railroad, bent his efforts to get provision for a daily overland mail in coaches. The House was in no mood to listen.[46] Somehow Benton and others slipped a small item into the Post Office Appropriation bill for a monthly overland mail from Independence to Stockton, California, by the 38th-degree route. Benton's satellites hailed this as a great victory and the forerunner of a railroad;[47] but it took three and one half years to even find a contractor.[48] Such was the legislative grist of the 33d Congress.

Divided and discomfited in one congress, the supporters of improved communication with the Pacific could only repeat their efforts in the next.

Franklin Pierce had now lost whatever modicum of interest in the railroad project he had ever possessed. Jefferson Davis attempted to provide the leadership which his chief denied. In his annual report of December, 1855, and a letter to John M. Sandidge, chairman of the House Committee on Military

[43] *Cong. Globe*, 33 Cong., 1 Sess., 1593, 1681, 1791.
[44] *Cong. Globe*, 33 Cong., 2 Sess., 472-83, 504.
[45] *Ibid.*, 697.
[46] *Ibid.*, 446, 615, 691, 1062.
[47] *Daily Mo. Dem.*, Mar. 12, 1855.
[48] P. M. Gen. Holt, quoted in *Cong. Globe*, 36 Cong., 1 Sess., 2458; San Francisco *Herald*, Aug. 31, 1860.

Affairs, he presented probably the most imposing argument for the railroad as a military necessity ever presented.[49]

In case of war with a strong naval power, said Davis, communication with California by sea could not be relied upon. At existing rates, it would cost $20,000,000 and require from four to six months to transport overland a year's supplies for an army large enough to defend the Pacific coast. A railroad would reduce the cost to $3,000,000 and the time to seven days. In wartime the cost without a railroad would be from $60,000,000 to $80,000,000. Indeed, without a railroad, it might be impracticable to send the requisite troops and supplies overland at all. It was doubtful that there was enough water and grass on the way for the great number of draught animals which would be required. It would cost about $100,000,000 to lay down on the Pacific coast in time of peace a sufficient stock of military supplies to defend it in war. In time of peace it would cost only about two thirds as much to send troops to the Pacific by railroad as by the isthmus.

With a transcontinental railroad, said the Secretary, it would cost only one sixth as much to send troops to interior posts along the way as it would without and would take only one twentieth of the time. The construction of the railroad would lead to settlement of the region traversed and would, thus, break the power of the Indian tribes in a wide area and relieve the government of the necessity of maintaining army posts therein. If located near the southern boundary, the railroad would eventually protect it and northern Mexico' from Indian depredations and enable the government to dispense with 5,000 men on the Mexican frontier at a saving of $4,000,000 per annum. This amount alone was about equal to the annual interest on the initial cost of building the railroad.

Congress did not respond to Davis's proffered leadership. The deadlock continued. The majority in the House was of the new Republican party and distrustful. Bleeding Kansas and other exciting sectional questions and the impending presidential election absorbed most of the time and attention. In

49 Rowland, *Jefferson Davis, Constitutionalist*, II, 567-70, 588-90.

the House a select committee of thirty-one did not succeed in reporting a Pacific railroad bill until the very close of the session.[50] In the Senate, the select committee could not agree on a bill at all but allowed the chairman, Weller, of California, to report a bill of his own.[51] This provided for one road with the choice of the route left to the contractors.[52] Senators Douglas and Bright, whose support was almost indispensable, opposed on the ground that they wanted three roads. Southwestern senators were unfriendly. Weller could not get his bill considered. It was finally taken up at the close of the session and tabled on a test vote, 25 to 23.[53] "Again are our hearts doomed to 'the sickness of hope deferred' " said the San Francisco *Morning Globe*.[54]

People of California were becoming more vociferous in their demands for improved communication with the rest of the Union. They voiced demands for wagon roads and an overland mail as more immediately practicable than a railroad. In the winter of 1856, seventy-five thousand citizens of the commonwealth signed a petition to Congress for a wagon road from Missouri. The petition was handsomely bound in two great volumes weighing about one hundred pounds with a title page illuminated with California gold leaf.[55] California representatives labored as earnestly for the more modest measures as they did for the railroad.

Weller managed to get a bill through the Senate appropriating $300,000 to build a military road from Missouri by way of South Pass and Salt Lake to Carson Valley and to establish military posts and wells along the line. A companion bill appropriated $200,000 for a road from El Paso to Fort Yuma.[56] Republicans in the House, where the Republicans were in the majority, objected to these bills because Jefferson Davis would direct the expenditure of the money. In an effort to conciliate

---

[50] *Cong. Globe*, 34 Cong., 1 Sess., 1787, 1913, 2188.
[51] *Ibid.*, 699.
[52] *Ibid.*, 962, 1720, App., 477.
[53] *Ibid.*, 963, 1719, 2023, 2056; "Address of John B. Weller to the People of California," in San Francisco *Morning Globe*, Oct. 23, 1856.
[54] Sept. 1, 1856.
[55] N. Y. *Herald*, May 22, 1856; *Cong. Globe*, 34 Cong., 1 Sess., 1297-98.
[56] *Ibid.*, 1298, 1299, 1304, 1485, 1964.

and to pay them an indemnity. Lord Clarendon offered to settle the Mosquito question on the terms of the Webster-Crampton Basis, of 1852, or of Lord John Russell's note of January 19, 1853. He would concede nothing as to the Bay Islands or Belize. He professed to attach little importance to the control of transit routes but insisted that British *honor* would not permit his government to be forced from positions once occupied.[10]

The British government was plainly disturbed by the numerous expansionist activities of the Pierce administration — in Cuba, Santo Domingo, Mexico, and Hawaii — and by American filibustering proclivities in general and was determined to oppose them all along the line. In this Britain had the support of France.[11] A foothold in Central America might prove useful. Marcy wrote Buchanan: "The allies have placed themselves in our path and attempted to obstruct us in whatever direction we have attempted to move." [12]

Lord Clarendon clearly was disposed to protract the negotiations until after the contemporary quarrel with Russia and, then, the Crimean War should be over and Britain's bargaining position stronger. He entered only a mild protest when in April, 1853, he learned that Captain Hollins of the U. S. Sloop *Cyane* had landed marines at Greytown to protect the property of the Accessory Transit Company against the authorities of the "free city," who were attempting to force the company to move its terminus to Greytown from the opposite bank of the San Juan River.[13] Clarendon's protest was not much stronger when in July, 1854, the *Cyane* bombarded Greytown and utterly destroyed it for refusal of the authorities to apologize for an insult to the United States Minister to Nicaragua, to pay reparations to the company for losses occasioned, and to give assurances of future good behavior.[14] Buchanan, on his part, hesitated for some time to press Claren-

[10] *Ibid.*, 50, 52-55, 92.
[11] *Works of James Buchanan*, IX, 267-73.
[12] *Ibid.*, IX, 354.
[13] *Parl. Papers*, 1856, LX, Nos. 156, 159, 160, 162, 165, 169, 171.
[14] Richardson, *Messages*, V, 280-84; *Sen. Exec. Docs.*, 35 Cong., 1 Sess., I (918), No. 9; *Works of James Buchanan*, IX, 298-99, 335.

don too hard lest he rouse resentment by seeming to take advantage of Britain's involvement with Russia.[15] Buchanan's suggestion to Pierce to bring matters to a head by publishing the correspondence was not heeded.[16] Apparently the President was little more willing to have a show down than Clarendon. When finally Buchanan pressed Clarendon too closely, the latter threw out suggestions of arbitration and held on.[17] The tone of the British government was thought to have stiffened a little when Lord Palmerston succeeded Lord Aberdeen as prime minister, February, 1855.[18]

While negotiations were dragging on in London, the position of the United States in Central America was not greatly improved. Borland labored hard and with a degree of success to restore Nicaraguan confidence in his government. He negotiated a commercial treaty with Nicaragua by which the United States was to guarantee her territory.[19] Pierce did not choose to send the treaty to the Senate; it was too likely to involve us with Great Britain. Borland soon resigned and was succeeded by J. H. Wheeler, of North Carolina. Honduras remained friendly to the United States because of the dispute with Great Britain over the Bay Islands and because of the influence of the Honduras Interoceanic Railway Company. The company was composed of American citizens. In the summer of 1853, it had secured a franchise to build the proposed railroad from Puerto Caballos on the Gulf of Honduras to Fonseca Bay. E. G. Squier was the agent of the company and chief promoter. He became an unofficial adviser of the Honduran government.[20] In Costa Rica, Salvador, and Guatemala, British influence continued to predominate and British agents were active. (See the map opposite p. 64.)

Deadlock and stalemate might have continued indefinitely had not new factors entered the situation. The advertising Nicaragua received from the thousands of Americans who had

[15] *H. Exec. Docs.*, 34 Cong., 1 Sess., I (840), Pt. I, No. 1, pp. 52, 70.
[16] *Works of James Buchanan*, IX, 185, 288, 333.
[17] *Ibid.*, IX, 278, 445, 456.
[18] *Ibid.*, IX, 297, 319, 338.
[19] M. W. Williams, *Anglo-American Isthmian Diplomacy*, 168-69.
[20] Williams, *op. cit.*, 168-71.

crossed it, its large areas of vacant lands, the prospects of the establishment of a great international highway, and the disordered state of its politics began to attract settlers and adventurers from its great northern neighbor. Governments concerned had to formulate policies with regard to colonization and filibustering.

A Colonel Kinney, of Philadelphia, was the first to move. He had bought a claim to a large tract of land which the Mosquito King had granted a certain Shepherd family of Georgia, back in 1839. In 1854, Kinney organized a "Central American Agricultural and Mining Association" for the avowed purpose of colonizing his tract. Ex-Senator Cooper, of Pennsylvania, accepted the presidency. President Pierce's private secretary, Sidney Webster, and A. O. P. Nicholson, editor of the Washington *Union*, the administration organ, were indiscreet enough to become involved. The Accessory Transit Company was friendly, at least at first. Marcoleta, the Nicaraguan minister to the United States, believed filibustering to be the object and protested to Marcy. Crampton, the British minister, also evidenced concern. Marcy moved tardily. He inquired the object of the venture and received assurances from Colonel Kinney that it was peaceful emigration. He informed Kinney that, if the object was peaceful, the government would not interfere but could not offer protection. He warned Kinney that neither the Central American states nor the United States recognized the validity of a grant of lands made by the King of the Mosquitos. Finally when evidence became conclusive that the enterprise was to have a military character, the government interfered and gave orders for the detention of any vessel Kinney might attempt to use for the purpose of his proposed expedition. Kinney eventually reached his land grant with only a few followers and was unable to pursue his scheme further.[21] Evidently the State Department had not been averse to letting the British Foreign Office have something to worry about.

One incident succeeded another. In May, 1855, the notori-

[21] *Ibid.*, 186-93; *Harper's Mag.*, X, 542; Wm. O. Scroggs, *Filibusters and Financiers*, ch. ix.

ous William Walker began his fiilibustering activities in Nicaragua.[22] One of that republic's numerous civil wars was raging. In this case the struggle was between the "Legitimists," or "Serviles," and the "Liberals," or "Democrats." At the outset the Legitimists seemed to hold the advantage. The Liberals sought to bolster their cause by enlisting adventurous citizens of the United States by promises of land to be granted at the close of a successful campaign. Walker was one of several men who signed contracts to supply military aid. He had already led a filibustering expedition from California into Sonora. Walker and fifty-eight companions sailed from San Francisco, ostensibly as peaceful colonizers. Arrived in Nicaragua, Walker augmented his force by new enlistments from California and by recruiting among the Americans who were crossing the peninsula. He and his men fought with considerable success. In October, following negotiations between the contending factions, Patricio Rivas, a moderate, became president with Walker as general in chief of the army and virtual dictator.

Walker could not have reached this eminence and could not have maintained his position long had it not been for the support of the Accessory Transit Company. For several years the company had been engaged in a quarrel with successive Nicaraguan governments over payments alleged to be due Nicaragua and over other matters. It had paid $10,000 a year as stipulated in the charter but had not paid 10% of the net profits, if any — it refused to show its accounts. There had been complicated negotiations. The government had frequently threatened to annul the charter. At the time of Walker's arrival on the scene, the company was engaged in negotiations with the Legitimists and was, therefore, hostile to him. After the filibuster had begun to win victories, the company saw a chance of using him to escape its obligations and so began to curry his favor. It advanced him $20,000 cash in hand, transported his troops gratis in its steamboats, which it could not have avoided doing, perhaps, and brought hundreds of volun-

---

[22] Of the voluminous literature on Walker, Scroggs, *op. cit.*, seems most authoritative.

teers from New York and San Francisco. In some cases, it seems, the company furnished transportation free of all charges, in other cases it charged the amounts to the Rivas government to offset the debt owed by the company. The company acted entirely on its own responsibility and according to what it considered its interests.[23]

The United States government made rather futile but probably honest efforts to prevent recruits being sent to Walker. It refused to receive Parker H. French, one of the filibusters, whom the Rivas government appointed as minister. Marcy instructed Wheeler, in Nicaragua, not to present himself to Rivas. The attitude of the United States government was, therefore, technically correct.[24] Private citizens in this country were divided in their sympathies, but the majority seem to have been sympathetic to Walker at this stage of the episode. People hoped that their countrymen would contribute a stable element to the population of the turbulent little republic, insure the security of the transit route, checkmate the wicked machinations of England in that quarter, and pave the way for Nicaragua's eventual annexation to the Union.

The governments of the other little Central American states and the British government protested to the State Department against the recruiting being done in this country for Walker, charging lax enforcement of the neutrality laws.[25] They evidently suspected connivance on the part of federal officials. The British government reinforced its fleet in the Caribbean; and the London *Times* announced that Britain was "determined to supply the ability which the American government lacks to enforce its own laws." [26] Buchanan tried to get the

[23] Accounts of the relations between the Accessory Transit Company and the Nicaraguan government are very conflicting. Vanderbilt's version is in letters to Marcy, *Sen. Exec. Docs.*, 34 Cong., 1 Sess., XIII (822), No. 68, pp. 80-82, 120-21. The Costa Rican version is in Molina to Marcy, *ibid.*, 57-59. A Walker-inspired version appeared in N. Y. *Herald*, Je. 11, 1856. Other accounts are in *ibid.*, July 16, Dec. 18, 26, 1853, Feb. 10, Mar. 23, Apr. 30, 1854; W. V. Wells, *Walker's Expedition to Nicaragua* (N. Y., 1856), 203-24; and Scroggs, *op. cit.*, ch. xii.

[24] *Sen. Exec. Docs.*, 34 Cong., 1 Sess., XIII (822), No. 68. *Cf.* Wells, *op. cit.*

[25] *Sen. Exec. Docs.*, 34 Cong., 1 Sess., XIII (822), No. 68, pp. 21-22, 46-49, 131, 137; *Works of James Buchanan*, IX, 433-36.

[26] Oct. 25, 1855. See also *Harper's Mag.*, XII, 253; *Works of James Buchanan*, IX, 433-36.

ships recalled. Lord Clarendon replied that the object of the fleet was to intercept privateers which, it was alleged, had been fitted out in New York on Russian account.[27]

As luck would have it, just as the British government was making its righteous complaints against filibustering, Crampton, the British minister, was caught beyond peradventure of a doubt participating in recruiting American boys, in violation of our laws, to fight in the Crimea.[28] Pierce and Marcy were quick to seize upon the tactical advantage afforded by Walker's early successes and Crampton's plight to attempt to bring the Central America dispute with Great Britain to some conclusion.

In September, 1855, Buchanan communicated the President's "conclusions" to Lord Clarendon. Clarendon replied that Her Majesty's Government adhered to their position.[29] Pierce then reviewed the whole history of Anglo-American isthmian relations in his annual message and submitted the correspondence, which was immediately published in the Washington Union.[30] "This international difficulty," said the President, "can not long remain undetermined without involving in serious danger the friendly relations which it is the interest as well as the duty of both countries to cherish and preserve."

The President's message and the related events and circumstances precipitated a lively debate in the Senate. Several of the speeches were very belligerent in tone. Wilson, of Massachusetts, would abrogate the Clayton-Bulwer Treaty and let the peninsula be colonized; if England should interfere, he would take Canada.[31] A few senators criticized the policy of the administration, notably John Bell, of Tennessee. He suggested that Britain may have been made more stubborn in her stand by the administration's expansionist activities in Cuba, the Hawaiian Islands, Mexico, and elsewhere.[32] In general Southern senators were less belligerent than Northern. They always were when England was the prospective foe: They

[27] Ibid., IX, 438-40, 463; London Times, Dec. 1, 11, 1855.
[28] H. B. Learned, William Learned Marcy (in S. F. Bemis, ed., The Am. Secretaries of State and Their Diplomacy, VI), ch. vii.
[29] H. Exec. Docs., 34 Cong., 1 Sess., I (840), Pt. I, No. 1, pp. 73-78.
[30] Richardson, Messages, V, 328-31; Washington Union, Jan. 3, 1856.
[31] Cong. Globe, 34 Cong., 1 Sess., App., 84-87.
[32] Ibid., App., 109-15.

feared the interruption of the cotton trade and the acquisition of Canada with its anti-slavery sentiment. In general there was more sympathy for Walker at this time in the North than in the South. The idea had not yet strongly seized upon the imagination of Southerners that Walker might be an instrument for extending slave territory. Public opinion outside Congress as reflected in the press was also divided, but the President and Marcy seem to have been pretty well supported in the position they had taken.[33]

In Great Britain, Walker's filibustering, the dispatch of a fleet to the West Indies, the President's strong language, the Senate debates, and the threatened dismissal of Crampton aroused widespread public interest in the Central American matter for the first time. There was a mild war scare. While public opinion was divided, the prevailing view was that Britain's interests in Central America were not worth risking war. Mosquito Indians, Bay Islands, and the region between the Sibun and Sarstoon meant little to most Englishmen.[34] A number of influential people including, so it was reported, Bulwer himself, professed to be convinced of the correctness of the American interpretation of the Clayton-Bulwer Treaty.[35] When Parliament convened the government's policy was condemned by the former prime minister, Aberdeen, Richard Cobden, and others. Cobden forced Lord Palmerston to consent to the publication of the correspondence.[36]

The British ministry did not, however, abandon its efforts to balk William Walker. In the autumn of 1855 Costa Rica, Guatemala, and Salvador determined to make war on Walker; and in March, 1856, Costa Rica actually began the war. Wallerstein, Consul General in England for Costa Rica and Guatemala, asked for and received promise of arms for Guatemalan troops and a visit of English cruisers to the coasts of Costa Rica "for the protection of British interests."[37]

Wallerstein's correspondence with the Costa Rican govern-

[33] *Harper's Mag.*, XII, 255; London *Times*, Dec. 11, 1855, Jan. 29, Feb. 1, 2, 1856, quoting American journals.
[34] London *Times*, Jan. 21, 1856.
[35] *Works of James Buchanan*, X, 12, 19, 31, 52, 60.
[36] *Ibid.*, X, 60-61; Williams, *op. cit.*, 204-06.
[37] *Parl. Papers*, 1856, separately numbered; London *Times*, May 13, 1856.

ment was intercepted by Walker's men and given to United States newspapers. Its publication, early in May, caused a stir.[38] Walker was shrewd enough to see an opportunity to bolster his fortunes and began to pose as the champion of the Americanization of the isthmus, a rôle he had theretofore been careful to disclaim in Nicaragua.[39] He now sent Father Vijil to the United States as minister. The United States government could have no personal objections to Father Vijil, and his nationality semed to indicate that the Walker regime had popular support.

Meanwhile the transit across Nicaragua had been closed. The Accessory Transit Company had been faction ridden. When it first gave aid to the filibusters, C. K. Garrison was the San Francisco manager and Charles Morgan was the New York manager; together they controlled the policies of the company. Early in 1856 opposing interests bought up enough stock to turn out Morgan and Garrison and elect Cornelius Vanderbilt president. Newspaper gossip had it that this coup was made by parties interested in the Panama route and it was Vanderbilt's intention to close the Nicaragua route in the interests of its rival. However that may be, Morgan and Garrison fought back, and Walker made the fatal mistake, as it proved, of abetting them. At their instigation Walker secured the revocation of the company's charter and the confiscation of its property. The next day, February 19, a new charter to operate a transit was granted to Morgan and Garrison, and somewhat later the confiscated property of the Accessory Transit Company was "sold" to them.[40] Vanderbilt appealed to Marcy for protection and promptly withdrew his steamers from the Atlantic leg of the route. For about six weeks the route could not be used.[41]

During the interval the Panama route also was closed for a short time as the result of a riotous attack upon the Panama

---

[38] N. Y. *Herald*, May 3, 1856.

[39] Letter to Sen. Weller, N. Y. *Herald*, May 3, 1856; *Cong. Globe*, 34 Cong., 1 Sess., 107; Scroggs, *op. cit.*, 172.

[40] Wm. O. Scroggs, "William Walker and the Steamship Corporation in Nicaragua," *Am. Hist. Rev.*, X, 792-811; London *Times*, Apr. 8, 1856. See citations in n. 24 above.

[41] Scroggs, *Filibusters and Financiers*, 152.

Railroad by people of the vicinity.[42]  For the time all communication with California was cut off; it was a startling object
lesson.

Revelation of British aid and comfort to Walker's enemies
and the interruption of communication with the Pacific Coast
caused quite an outburst of feeling in the United States.
Walker's true character had not yet been revealed, and many
people imagined him to be another Sam Houston.  In New
Orleans a meeting of sympathy for Walker was addressed by
Pierre Soulé, recent minister to Spain, and a subscription was
raised.[43]  A great meeting was held in New York City, May 9,
1856.  The flag of Nicaragua was displayed.  Muskets were
pledged.  Speakers demanded the recognition of Walker, the
abrogation of the Clayton-Bulwer Treaty, and the enforcement
of the Monroe Doctrine.  Secretary of State Marcy was
criticized for enforcing the neutrality laws, and the right of
every man to emigrate and take his rifle with him was asserted.
One speaker said he expected some day to see William Walker
sitting in the United States Senate as a member for the State
of Nicaragua.[44]  John B. Weller defended Walker in the
United States Senate.[45]

The Pierce administration now moved fast.  On May 14,
Pierce received Father Vijil.  The following day he sent a
special message to Congress explaining his action.[46]  With it
he submitted the correspondence relating to Walker and the
war in Central America.  The President reviewed the various
efforts made by the United States to assure suitable means of
"commercial transit" across Panama, Tehuantepec, and Nicaragua and told how Great Britain had continually thrown
obstacles in the way.  He defended the conduct of the administration with regard to Walker and his reception of Father
Vijil.  The Rivas government was now the government *de facto*
and, insofar as such existed, the government *de jure* of Nicaragua.  It had always been the established policy of the United

---

[42] Richardson, *Messages*, V, 374, 416; N. Y. *Herald*, May 2, 1856.
[43] *Ibid.*, May 7.
[44] *Ibid.*, May 10.
[45] *Cong. Globe*, 34 Cong., 1 Sess., 1069-72.
[46] Richardson, *Messages*, V, 368-74.

States to recognize *de facto* governments, especially in Spanish American states, where revolutions were so frequent. Recognition was likewise called for by the most imperative special exigencies, namely, the revocation of the charter of the Transit Company and its claim for protection and redress and the interruption of the transit, neither of which matters could receive due consideration without resumption of diplomatic intercourse with Nicaragua. The President referred to the temporary obstruction of the Panama railroad. "It would be difficult to suggest a single object of interest, external or internal, more important to the United States than the maintenance of the communication, by land and sea, between the Atlantic and Pacific States and Territories of the Union. It is a material element of the national integrity and sovereignty."

On May 28, the British minister, Crampton was dismissed for complicity in violating the American neutrality laws. The matter had been handled with great discretion by Marcy, and he was morally certain that Great Britain would not take the dismissal as a cause of war. He would not have been surprised had Dallas been dismissed in retaliation.[47]

The President's action seems to have been approved by the country. A Nicaragua sympathy meeting in New York on May 23 was said to have drawn 20,000 people.[48] The Democratic National Convention, meeting early in June, put strong language in the party platform. The principles of the Monroe Doctrine, it said, should be preserved with "unbending rigidity." The construction of a great highway across the isthmus should be secured by a "timely and efficient exertion of the control which we have the right to claim over it, and no power on earth should be suffered to impede or clog its progress by any interference" with the relations between the United States and isthmian states. The platform expressed sympathy with the efforts of the "people" of Central America to "regenerate" their portion of the continent.[49] The Americans had held their convention in February, *before* Pierce had recognized Walker.

[47] *Sen. Docs.*, 56 Cong., 1 Sess., XI (3853), No. 161, pp. 33-37; London *Times*, Je. 13, 16, 17, 1856.
[48] N. Y. *Herald*, May 24, 1856.
[49] *Ibid.*, Je. 5; K. H. Porter, *National Party Platforms*, 46.

They accused the administration of "a truckling subserviency to the stronger, and an insolent and cowardly bravado toward the weaker powers." [50]  The Republican platform neither condemned nor approved; it contained no reference whatever to foreign relations.

The British government now decided, at long last, to show a more conciliatory spirit. It did not take umbrage at the recognition of Walker's government and did not dismiss Dallas in retaliation for the dismissal of Crampton.  It showed a real disposition to settle the Central American question on lines not unsatisfactory to the United States if it could do so without appearing to be coerced.  Marcy and Dallas were approachable to say the least.  Dallas suggested to Clarendon that they forgo arguments about the meaning of the Clayton-Bulwer Treaty.  Clarendon assented.[51]  Thereafter negotiations proceeded smoothly and rapidly.[52]

As had been anticipated, the Mosquito Indians question gave least difficulty.  Dallas and Clarendon incorporated in their draft treaty a set of proposals to be submitted to Nicaragua and Costa Rica similar to those of the Webster-Crampton Agreement of 1852.[53]  The Mosquitos were to be given a reservation within which they might govern themselves. They might not cede or grant their land to any foreign state without the consent of Great Britain and the United States; they might if they chose be incorporated into Nicaragua.  Remaining lands which had been claimed for the Mosquitos would revert to Nicaragua or Costa Rica as the case might be.  Greytown was to be a free city with a free port under the sovereignty of Nicaragua.  It must pay an annuity for a period of years to the Mosquito Indians.  Costa Rica would enjoy free navigation of the lower San Juan.  If Costa Rica and Nicaragua could not settle their differences amicably by negotiations, they must submit them to the joint arbitration of the United States and Great Britain.  In case either little power or both refused to accept the propositions made to them, the United States and

[50] *Ibid.*, 40.
[51] *Sen. Docs.*, 56 Cong., 1 Sess., XI (3853), No. 161, pp. 37-40.
[52] They may be followed in *ibid.*, 10-60, *passim.*
[53] Above, pp. 77-78.

Great Britain would not consent to more favorable terms for the refusing party or parties.

The Bay Islands matter was more difficult. A way out was suggested by E. G. Squier, who had become the unofficial adviser of the Honduras government, as has been noted, and was now in England as adviser to Señors Herran and Alvarado, ministers to Great Britain and the United States respectively. He had succeeded in interesting British capitalists in his Honduras Interoceanic Railway Company, notably a Mr. Brown, member of parliament for Liverpool. Squier saw that "honor" would not permit Britain to withdraw from the Bay Islands at the request of the United States but she might be willing to surrender them by direct negotiations with Honduras. He therefore proposed that Señor Herran negotiate with Clarendon doing nothing not approved by Dallas. Dallas fell in with the suggestion. Brown, M. P., saw Clarendon. The Clarendon-Herran Treaty resulted. Great Britain thereby recognized the sovereignty of Honduras over the Bay Islands; but the people thereof were to have their own government, and Honduras might not tax them, exact military service of them except for their own defense, erect fortifications, nor introduce slavery.[54] Dallas was not entirely pleased but thought that, if Honduras was satisfied, the United States would have no cause to oppose the treaty.[55] Accordingly only the simple statement was put in the Dallas-Clarendon Convention that "the two contracting parties do hereby mutually engage to recognize and respect in all future time the independence and rights of the said free territory as a part of the Republic of Honduras."

As regards Belize, or British Honduras, the Dallas-Clarendon Convention stated that Great Britain would make a treaty with Guatemala defining the boundaries as they existed April 19, 1850, the date of the Clayton-Bulwer Treaty. Dallas and Clarendon signed their Convention on October 17, 1856.[56]

While the Dallas-Clarendon Convention did not secure all

[54] *Sen. Docs.*, 56 Cong., 1 Sess., XI (3853), No. 161, pp. 27-28, 30-33, 42, 46, 49-51.
[55] *Ibid.*, 55.
[56] Text in *ibid.*, 60-65.

that Pierce and Marcy had set out to accomplish, the President submitted it to the Senate, in December. It was not taken up for consideration, however, until the special session of the Senate early in Buchanan's administration. Buchanan disliked the provision regarding the Bay Islands. On his advice, the Senate ratified the convention with an amendment which substituted for the description of the Bay Islands as a "free territory" under the sovereignty of Honduras a simple statement that the contracting parties recognized the Bay Islands "as under the sovereignty and as a part of the said Republic of Honduras." [57] Honduras, on its part, refused to ratify the Clarendon-Herran Treaty.[58] Thereupon the British government refused to accept the Senate's amendment to the Dallas-Clarendon Convention, and the Convention fell to the ground.[59] The Dallas negotiations had not been a total loss, however, for they pointed the way to the final settlement which was made a few years later and they insured that the terms thereof would be no less satisfactory from the American point of view.

Clarendon and Herran had also signed a commercial treaty whereby Honduras granted to the government and people of Great Britain full use of the proposed Honduras Interoceanic Railway and Great Britain, in consideration thereof, guaranteed the road's neutrality and engaged, when it should have been completed, to protect it against interruption, seizure, or unjust confiscation from any source whatsoever. This treaty was in accord with the principles and intent of the Clayton-Bulwer Treaty. Señor Alvarado applied to Dallas to negotiate a similar treaty between Honduras and the United States. Dallas, unfortunately, did not do so; and the commercial treaty also fell with the other for the time being.[60]

After Clarendon had offered to negotiate with Dallas, the United States government, as was to be expected, gave no further encouragement to William Walker. Walker then rode

[57] Ibid., 106-07.
[58] Parl. Papers, 1860, LXVIII, 39, 40.
[59] Works of James Buchanan, X, 115-16; Sen. Docs., 56 Cong., 1 Sess., XI (3853), No. 161, pp. 108-111.
[60] Ibid., 43-47, 49-51.

rapidly to his fall. He quarreled with President Rivas. Rivas recalled Father Vijil from Washington and sent another to replace him. In July, 1856, Walker had himself counted in as president and sent still another minister to Washington. Marcy refused to receive either one. He recalled Wheeler from Nicaragua when the minister made the blunder of presenting himself to Walker. Walker tried desperately to attract more Americans to his standard by various expedients. In August Pierre Soulé visited him. On Soulé's advice Walker issued, September 22, 1856, a decree preparing the way for the introduction of slavery into Nicaragua. This was a desperate bid for the support of those Southerners who were desperately seeking more slave territory to maintain the South's equality of strength in the United States Senate. Hot-headed Southerners rose to the bait. Walker was played up in Southern journals as the "grey-eyed man of destiny," a fanatically patriotic Southerner. Walker was in fact an utterly selfish and unprincipled adventurer of mediocre ability whose sole virtue was courage cold as steel. The South could do little for Walker. Commodore Vanderbilt gave him the *coup de grace*. He found ways and means of closing the transit again after Morgan and Garrison had succeeded in reopening it. This cut off all possibility of getting recruits from the United States and extinguished Walker's last hope. In May, 1857, Walker sought and, unfortunately for the United States, was accorded refuge on board a United States war vessel in the harbor of San Juan del Sur.[61]

The Nicaragua route to California now remained closed. The Panama Railroad Company and the steamship companies whose lines connected with the railroad raised rates and passages, imposing an estimated additional cost of about $1,500,-000 a year upon the American public. The Panama Railroad Company even raised the rates for carrying the United States mails across the isthmus.[62] Insofar as the object of Pierce's Central American diplomacy was to keep the transit route open, it had failed utterly.

---

[61] *Ibid.*, 35; Scroggs, *Filibusters and Financiers*, chs. xv–xix.
[62] *Am. R. R. Jour.*, XXVIII, 426; *Cong. Globe*, 34 Cong., 3 Sess., 31.

# CHAPTER XIV

## PARTY AND SECTIONAL SNIPING, 1856-1859

AS THE 1850's wore on the congressional stalemate on the route of and method of financing the proposed Pacific railroad continued. The battle in Congress degenerated into party and sectional sniping.

During the presidential campaign of 1856 the friends of a Pacific railroad undertook to put all the political parties and their candidates on solemn record in favor of government countenance and aid for their project.

California's delegates to the Democratic National Convention went to Cincinnati pledged to get a satisfactory railroad plank and to work for the nomination of James Buchanan. In the Committee on Resolutions, Colonel Inge, California's member, offered a resolution recognizing the national importance of the road and declaring it to be the duty of the federal government to exercise promptly "all its constitutional powers" to promote its construction. The resolution appears guarded enough for any party platform, but it caused a big row. The committee finally consented to report it but as a sort of appendix to the platform rather than an integral part thereof. The convention voted separately upon the Inge resolution and tabled it 134 to 122, the Pennsylvania delegation, which was supposed to reflect Buchanan's wishes, voting to table. On the day nominations were to be made, Inge made an effort to have the resolution taken up but failed. Thereupon he put Lewis Cass in nomination, and the California delegation supported him to the last. When the nomination went to Buchanan, Colonel Inge pledged California's support in a lugubrious speech on the Pacific railroad. Later in the day a Missouri delegate moved to suspend the rules to permit the consideration of the Pacific railroad resolution. Another quarrel ensued. Finally with the aid of the big New York delegation, which had not participated in previous votes, the rules were suspended and the resolution adopted by a vote of 205 to 77. The insertion of the word "proper" into the phrase "all its constitutional powers" somehow enabled six of the twenty-seven Pennsylvania delegates to vote for the resolution.[1] Buchanan endorsed the platform.

The new Republican party, having no Southern adherents to appease, found no difficulty in resolving "That a railroad to the Pacific Ocean by the most central and practicable route is imperatively demanded by the interests of the whole country, and that the Federal Government ought to render immediate and efficient aid in its construction, and, as auxiliary thereto, the immediate construction of an emigrant road on the line of the railroad."[2] The nomination of John C. Frémont, while made because of other considerations, was calculated to greatly strengthen the pledge. The platforms of the American and Whig parties did not mention the Pacific railroad, but Fillmore's record was asserted to be sufficient assurance to Pacific railroad advocates in those parties.[3]

With so many other exciting issues before the people, only in California did the Pacific railroad question play a large part in the campaign after the conventions.[4] There it was the principal issue. The Republicans inscribed "Freedom, Frémont, and the Railroad" on their banner and insisted that, since their man had explored the route, he was the very man to build the road.[5] Both they and the Americans asserted that Buchanan and his party were hostile to the railroad and cited the equivocal proceedings at Cincinnati as proof. The Democrats were hard put to it to make effective reply. They ridiculed Frémont's "great experience in following Kit Carson." They quoted a polite little speech which Buchanan had made in Philadelphia three years earlier approving Jefferson Davis's

[1] N. Y. *Herald*, Je. 4-7, 15, 1856; San Francisco *Morning Globe*, July 21; Sacramento *Dem. State Jour.*, Sept. 22; *Letter of Hon. John S. Phelps, of Missouri, to his Constituents* (pamphlet, dated July 8, 1856); Kirk H. Porter, *National Party Platforms*, 46.
[2] *Ibid.*, 49; N. Y. *Herald*, Je. 17-20, 1856.
[3] Porter, *op. cit.*, 38-40, 50-51.
[4] Allan Nevins, *Frémont, the West's Greatest Adventurer*, II, chs. xxvii, xxviii; Andrew W. Crandall, *The Early Hist. of the Republican Party*, Part IV.
[5] Sacramento *Dem. State Jour.*, Aug. 29, 1856.

argument for the constitutionality of government aid.[6] Finally, Buchanan was prevailed upon to write a letter to Colonel B. T. Washington, chairman of the Democratic state committee, in which he declared himself to be "decidedly favorable" to government aid for a railroad and found constitutional authority in the war power. He said Congress had the same power to aid in constructing the road that it had "to erect fortifications at the mouth of the harbor of San Francisco." The letter was nicely timed to permit wide publicity in California before election day but not to give time for any inkling of it to get back to the South and East until after the election should be over.[7] As it transpired, Buchanan carried California by such a large plurality that the letter probably had been an unnecessary commitment.[8]

James Buchanan and all parties in Congress, then, had been put under pledge to take measures to promote the construction of a railroad to the Pacific. Buchanan had a much greater mandate, however. That was to check the alarming drift in the South toward "disunion." The President's conception of the proper way to fulfill his mission seems to have been to accede to every demand of the "fire-eaters." This he did in the matter of Kansas, and in the matter of Mexico,[9] and was prepared to do in the matter of Cuba. This, with qualification in the case of Nicaragua,[10] he was ready to do in the matter of communication with the Pacific.

In the short session which followed immediately after the election, Congress showed a disposition to redeem recent party pledges. Senator Rusk succeeded in getting another appropriation, of $100,000, for continuing the search for artesian wells on the Staked Plains of western Texas.[11] Two bills for wagon roads which had passed the Senate at the preceding session [12] were now accepted by the House with changes. One

[6] The campaign in California has been followed in *ibid.* and the San Francisco *Morning Globe* and *Daily Alta California.*
[7] Dated Sept. 17, 1856. In *Morning Globe*, Oct. 17.
[8] *Cong. Globe*, 35 Cong., 1 Sess., 1642, Broderick's interpretation.
[9] See the next chapter.
[10] See chapter xvi.
[11] *Tex. State Gaz.*, Mar. 28, 1857; *DeBow's Rev.*, XXII, 438; *Cong. Globe*, 34 Cong., 3 Sess., 1047.
[12] See above, 200.

road was to run from Fort Kearney, Nebraska, to Honey Lake, on the boundary of California, the other from El Paso to Fort Yuma. They were to be built under the direction of the secretary of the interior.[13] Moreover, the Post Office Appropriation bill carried provisions for establishing an overland mail.

The overland-mail act provided that the postmaster general was to advertise for bids for carrying the letter mails in good four-horse coaches between some point on the Mississippi and San Francisco. The time was not to be over twenty-five days each way. The contract was to be for six years. The compensation was to be not over $600,000 for a semiweekly mail, not over $450,000 for a weekly mail, or not over $300,000 for a semimonthly mail. The contractor was to select the starting point on the Mississippi and the route thence to San Francisco. It was clearly the intention of Congress that the postmaster general should exercise no discretion as to the choice of route. The reason for denying such discretion was also clear: It was believed that emigration would follow the mail route, settlements would spring up along it, and they in turn would influence the location of the railroad. With such a matter at stake, Congress was unable to agree upon a route, and, unwilling to leave the choice to a government official, adopted the expedient of several Pacific railroad bills, namely, leaving the choice of route to the "eagle eye" of business.[14]

Immediately upon the advent of the Buchanan administration the duty devolved upon the new Postmaster General, A. V. Brown, of Tennessee, of advertising for bids for carrying the letter mails overland as provided in the bill just described. The act presumably left him no discretion as to route, but Brown was resourceful, to say the least. He received numerous bids with various routes designated. The lowest bid for a semiweekly mail was $520,000 with a route from St. Louis via Independence and Fort Laramie. No bidder designated Brown's favorite route; so he designated it himself. He pre-

[13] *Am. R. R. Jour.*, XX, 156, 213, 260; *H. Exec. Docs.*, 35 Cong., 2 Sess., IX (1008), No. 108; *Cong. Globe*, 34 Cong., 3 Sess., 610-12.
[14] *Ibid.*, App., 307-20.

scribed a bifurcated route starting at St. Louis and Memphis, converging at Little Rock, and running thence via Preston, Texas, El Paso, Fort Yuma, and Los Angeles to San Francisco. He then prevailed upon all regular bidders (throwing out one bid as irregular) to apply their bids to his route. Then he awarded the contract to John Butterfield and associates for $595,000, a sum soon changed to $600,000, the maximum permitted by the law.[15]

Butterfield *et al* protested against the route they were forced to accept. Champions of other routes bitterly criticized the Postmaster General and charged him with violation of the law.[16] Brown stood his ground, however, consenting only, upon request of Congressman John Phelps, of Springfield, Missouri, and others, to let the St. Louis branch go by way of Springfield and Fort Smith to a junction with the Memphis branch farther to the southwest than Little Rock.[17]

In his annual report, December, 1857, the Postmaster General stoutly defended his action at length.[18] He denied that the appropriation bill required him to leave the selection of the route to the contractor. Experience had shown, he said, that mails could not be carried regularly on the Laramie route. The Gila route was superior topographically to the Albuquerque route and better fitted for travelers and emigrants. The act of congress looked not only to the carrying of mail. "It looks expressly to the comfort of passengers in stages, and doubtless to the millions of emigrants and others who, for ages, might pass to and from our Pacific States." Congress had appropriated $200,000 to build a wagon road from El Paso to Fort Yuma. (He neglected to say that Congress had also appropriated $300,000 to build a road from Fort Kearney via Fort Laramie to California.) He had been mindful of the fact that the mail route might be "a pioneer route for the first great railroad" to the Pacific. Jefferson Davis had determined

[15] Rept. of P. M. Gen. Brown, *Cong. Globe*, 35 Cong., 1 Sess., App., 25.
[16] *Ibid.*, 35 Cong., 1 Sess., 350, App., 422; 35 Cong., 2 Sess., 262-63, 305, 360; *Daily Mo. Repub.*, Feb. 19, 1858.
[17] *Letter of Hon. John S. Phelps to Citizens of Ark. in Relation to a Pac. R. R.* (pamphlet, dated Dec. 26, 1857); *Cong. Globe*, 35 Cong., 1 Sess., App., 25.
[18] *Ibid.*, App., 26-28; *Tex. State Gaz.*, Mar. 27, 1858.

that the Gila route was the most practical and economical for a railroad. If all or the greater part of the railroads east of the Mississippi had concentrated at one point on that river, he would have selected that as the terminus of the overland mail. But they concentrated chiefly at St. Louis, Cairo(!), and Memphis. So he had found a common concentration point for all farther west (in Texas). Moreover, said Brown, the stage road would "open a vast agricultural and mining region in Missouri; lend a helping hand to the young, growing, and unappreciated State of Arkansas; and conduct the hardy pioneers to the delightful woodlands and prairies of Texas." Especially if followed by a railroad, the southern location of the mail route might serve a valuable purpose in reference to Mexico.

The charming frankness, or naïveté, of the Postmaster General must have made his critics writhe. When all is said, however, in regard to motives, the route selected seems to have been the best adapted for a stage line which must run regularly in winter as well as in summer.

The Butterfield Company showed commendable energy in locating the line, establishing its relay stations, and accumulating supplies and livestock.[19] The route was opened September 15, 1858, within the period required by law. There were celebrations at San Francisco and St. Louis when the first mails arrived. Butterfield seldom failed to get the mails through in the allotted twenty-five days. The usual time came to be under twenty-two. However, Eastern news seldom reached the coast by the overland route more than a few days before it arrived by steamer from Panama; although this advantage was increased as the telegraph followed the road farther and farther beyond St. Louis. Between Los Angeles and San Francisco mails were often carried more rapidly by steamers than by the stages.[20] Although the letter mail was often so heavy as to almost exclude passengers from the coaches, the postages did not begin to recompense the government. For

[19] F. S. Paxson, *Hist. of the Am. Frontier*, 462-65; *Last Am. Frontier*, ch. xi; F. A. Root and W. E. Connelley, *Overland Stage to California*; L. R. Hafen, *The Overland Mail, 1849-1869*, ch. iv.
[20] San Francisco *Herald*, Jan. 14, 16, Mar. 26, Nov. 15, 1859.

example, for the first fourteen months of operation they amounted to only $27,229.94. Nor did the establishment of the overland mail materially change the course of travel and emigration to California. The emigrants continued to go principally over the Platte River road. Heavy freight for New Mexico continued to utilize the Santa Fe Trail.

Even before Postmaster General Brown let the contract for the great overland mail, he had let, June, 1857, a contract to one, James E. Burch, for a semimonthly mail on horseback from San Antonio, Texas, to San Diego, California, for $149,800 per annum. Brown at that time expected Burch to be the successful bidder for the contract which Butterfield got. But Burch was killed. His contract was transferred to George H. Giddings. When the Butterfield company began to carry mail, Brown annulled the Giddings contract insofar as it applied to the section between El Paso and Fort Yuma but continued it for the two ends, San Antonio to El Paso and Yuma to San Diego, substituted a weekly for the original semimonthly mail, and increased the compensation. Thus the Postmaster General took care of the Southwest.[21]

As far back as October, 1856, a contract had been let to one Hiram Kimball for carrying the mail monthly in covered wagons between St. Joseph and Salt Lake; Kimball and a successor, Miles, failed, and it was not until the contract was relet to J. M. Hockaday for a weekly mail in covered wagons or carriages that a reasonably satisfactory service was secured, May, 1858. In July a weekly mail was established between Salt Lake and Placerville, California, with George Chorpenning as contractor. Over these two connecting routes the mails were carried from St. Joseph to Placerville in thirty-eight days. In October, 1858, a contractor was finally found to carry a monthly mail in wagons between Independence, Missouri, and Stockton, California, as provided in an item in the Post Office appropriation of March 3, 1855, sponsored by Thomas H. Benton. Contrary to Benton's anticipations, the route turned

[21] *Ibid.*, Aug. 31, 1860; letter of P. M. Gen. Holt, Mar. 22, 1860, in *Cong. Globe*, 36 Cong., 1 Sess., 2458. Brown also took care of the Tehuantepec project. See below, 237.

out to be that of the thirty-fifth parallel. The compensation was fixed at $79,999 per annum. In December, 1859, Postmaster General Joseph Holt, who had succeeded on A. V. Brown's death, reported that there had been only four arrivals on this route in nine months and that the whole matter received in Kansas City from Stockton was two letters and twenty-six newspapers.[22]

Meanwhile the small appropriations made by the last Congress for the Fort Kearney, Fort Laramie, and Honey Lake and the El Paso and Fort Yuma roads were being spent under the direction of Secretary of the Interior Jacob Thompson. Under an efficient chief engineer the appropriation for the former was spent mostly on the actual road and resulted in some improvements. The appropriation for the southern road seems to have been largely exhausted in the work of organization and preliminary survey.[23]

President Buchanan showed some disposition to redeem promises with regard to a Pacific railroad. He commended the project in his inaugural. He forbore from expressing an opinion as to how Congress might best lend aid but remarked dryly, "I believe that many of the difficulties in the way . . . will in great degree vanish as soon as the nearest and best route shall have been satisfactorily ascertained." [24] In his first annual message, Buchanan "without finally committing" himself expressed a strong preference for the Gila route.[25] Secretary of War John B. Floyd, of Virginia, thought the superior eligibility of that route had been established beyond controversy.[26] Postmaster General Brown's predilection for the route had been made clear. It soon came to be the settled impression in the country that the thirty-second parallel route was the administration route.[27] As time passed there were those who thought the President preferred to wait until northern Mexico

[22] Cong. Globe, 36 Cong., 1 Sess., App., 22.
[23] H. Exec. Docs., 35 Cong., 2 Sess., IX (1008), No. 108; E. Douglas Branch, "Frederick West Lander, Road Builder," Miss. Val. Hist. Rev., XVI, 172-87.
[24] Richardson, Messages, V, 434-35.
[25] Ibid., V, 456-57.
[26] Ann. Rept., Cong. Globe, 35 Cong., 1 Sess., App., 35.
[27] Ibid., 349, 1642, App., 421, 422; N. O. Picayune, Feb. 5, 1858; Tex. State Gaz., Aug. 8, 1857.

could be annexed and then extend aid to a road to Guaymas or Mazatlan.[28]

Sectional and party interests and jealousies rendered Congress when it met, 1857-58, wholly impotent to act upon the matter of a railroad to the Pacific. There was long fencing in the House before that body could even agree to authorize the Speaker to appoint a select committee. The Republican minority, fearful of packing in favor of the southern route, supported a motion stipulating how the members should be apportioned among sections and regions.[29] Washburn, of Maine, served notice that he would support no bill which should leave the administration any discretion as to route.[30] The select committee, finally appointed, were unable to agree upon a bill during the session.

The Senate started out more auspiciously. A select committee of nine with Gwin as chairman was appointed. The committee set itself the task of framing a bill which would command the votes of 32 senators and 118 representatives, that is a bare majority in each house.[31] It decided Congress would stand for only one road.[32] San Francisco was agreed upon as the western terminus. The four Northern members (Douglas, Bright, Seward, and Foot) and Gwin agreed that the eastern terminus must be somewhere on the Missouri River between the mouths of the Big Sioux and the Kansas (Sioux City, Omaha, St. Joseph, or Kansas City). Within these limits the choice was to be left to the contractors. The four Southern members demanded that the road be required to swing down to a southern pass in the Rockies but were overruled.[33] Federal aid was to consist of twenty alternate sections of land per mile and not over $500 per mile per annum for transportation of mails, troops, and government supplies, such compensation to be paid in advance as the road should be constructed to an amount not exceeding $25,000,000. Details

[28] Cong. Globe, 35 Cong., 2 Sess., 356; San Francisco Herald, Jan. 21, 1859.
[29] Cong. Globe, 35 Cong., 1 Sess., 349, 350.
[30] Ibid., 350.
[31] Ibid., 1584.
[32] Ibid., 1645; Am. R. R. Jour., XXXI, 45.
[33] Cong. Globe, 35 Cong., 1 Sess., 1299, 1643.

were well worked out.[34] The bill was approved with amendments of detail in the Committee of the Whole and reported
to the Senate. Then, as on former occasions, counsels of discord prevailed.

Southern senators made a concerted attack upon the bill.
Said Johnson, of Arkansas, "the intention and will seem to be
to drive a road across a northern route at any expense to the
national treasury to which we contribute equally, and yet we
are to be excluded from any fair opportunity to participate
in it. We cease almost to be considered as a part of the
Union." [35] Senator Iverson, of Georgia, moved to amend to
provide for two roads, a northern and a southern, and grant
each but one half the compensation for services provided in the
bill for a single road.[36]

Southern attacks had been anticipated. But opposition and
lack of co-operation appeared where support was to be expected. Broderick, of California, showed jealousy of Gwin's
leadership, found fault with the bill and its management, and
tried to bring Lecompton animosities into the debate.[37] Green,
of Missouri, moved to fix the terminus at the mouth of the
Kansas, while his colleague, Polk, in the interests of the Albuquerque route moved to permit the choice of a terminus anywhere on the western boundary of Iowa, Missouri, and Arkansas, between Sioux City and Fort Smith.[38] But the unkindest
cut of all came from Eastern Republicans. The bill seemed
almost made to order to fit the Republican national platform
of 1856. Yet Hale, New Hampshire, and Wilson, Massachusetts, opposed on the ground that the treasury would not
stand the strain in view of the existing depression, following
the panic of 1857.[39] On motion of Benjamin, of Louisiana,
whose main interest was Tehuantepec, further consideration of
the bill was postponed until the short session, the motion receiving the votes of six Eastern and one Western Republican,

[34] Ibid., 1535; Am. R. R. Jour., XXXI, 67-68.
[35] Cong. Globe, 35 Cong., 1 Sess., 1641.
[36] Ibid., 1582-83.
[37] Ibid., 1537, 1641-42; San Francisco Daily Globe, May 22, July 31, 1858.
[38] Cong. Globe, 35 Cong., 1 Sess., 1580, 1586, 1598.
[39] Ibid., 1603, 1643.

one Eastern Democrat and all the Southern senators present except Bell, of Tennessee, Kennedy, of Maryland, and Henderson, of Texas.[40]

In the short session, 1858-59, the Senate spent about six weeks threshing over the old straw. Never before had a Pacific railroad bill been debated so thoroughly and apparently so earnestly. Of course there could be little new in the arguments. Gwin made effective use of a table which showed that the government was already paying $2,200,000 per year for the transportation of the mails to and from the Coast; a railroad would carry a daily mail, instead of a semiweekly and semimonthly, for considerably less.[41] Douglas and others drew an argument from the recent "Mormon War," which, it was estimated, had cost the government $5,000,000. If there had been a central Pacific railroad, they said, either the rebellion would not have occurred or could have been crushed in much less time and at far less cost.[42] Recent favorable treaties with China and Japan and British discussion of a transcontinental railway across Canada were utilized in argument.[43] But arguments availed little *pro* or *con*. Strife over routes and party politics again stymied action.

Iverson renewed his proposal of the preceding session for two roads, a northern and a southern, and accompanied it by a disunion speech. He described the signs and portents which convinced him that the time was near when the Southern states would secede and form a new confederacy. "What I demand, therefore," he said, "is that the South shall be put upon an equality with the North, whether the Union lasts or not; that in appropriating the public lands and money . . . the South shall have an equal chance to secure a road within her borders, to inure to her benefit whilst the Union lasts, to belong to her when, if ever, the Union is dissolved." [44] Jefferson Davis offered a substitute for the committee bill which, while osten-

[40] *Ibid.*, 1641, 1647; N. O. *Picayune*, Apr. 28, 1858; San Francisco *Daily Globe*, May 31, July 31.
[41] *Cong. Globe*, 35 Cong., 2 Sess., 51.
[42] *Ibid.*, 52; San Francisco *Herald*, Jan. 15, 1859.
[43] *Am. R. R. Jour.*, XXXII, 370; *Cong. Globe*, 35 Cong., 2 Sess., 55, 108, 305.
[44] *Ibid.*, 242-44.

sibly putting all routes on a fair competitive basis, was clearly designed to make the choice of any other than the Gila route impossible.[45]  Doolittle, of Wisconsin, and the senators from the recently admitted State of Minnesota pleaded for a three-road bill, one road to go by the extreme northern route.[46] Green again tried to have the eastern terminus fixed at the mouth of the Kansas and offered two branches to accommodate other contenders.[47]

Harlan, of Iowa, adverting to a report that the New England senators had caucused and agreed to let the railroad bill die, demanded that New England come up to scratch or expect no Western support for Eastern measures.  However, he himself offered an amendment calculated to further divide the West: he proposed to restrict the road to the region between the 37th and 43d parallels.[48]  Douglas protested earnestly. The Albuquerque route was probably the best, he said.  Its exclusion would alienate support from the bill.[49]  Broderick supported the amendment: He was from San Francisco and feared that a railroad by a southern route would terminate at Los Angeles or San Diego.  Not many Southerners would vote for any railroad bill, he said.  Why be considerate of the South?[50]  Republican leaders announced that without further restriction of the route the bill would not get many Republican votes.  They professed to fear that, without such restrictions, the administration would somehow manage to take the road down to the Mexican border as it had the overland mail.[51]  All the Republicans voted for Harlan's amendment except two, all the Democrats but three voted against it.  It was defeated by a vote of 19 to 35.  An amendment offered by Wilson, of Massachusetts, to restrict the railroad throughout its length to the region between the forty-third and thirty-fourth parallels, thus permitting the use of the thirty-fifth degree route with Kansas City as its eastern terminus, received a few

[45] Ibid., 72, 310-14, 356, 477-83, 578.
[46] Ibid., 74, 139, 260-61, 325, 330, 415, 487, 607-09.
[47] Ibid., 76, 326, 415-16.
[48] Ibid., 156, 310, 315, 332.
[49] Ibid., 333, 358.
[50] Ibid., 357.
[51] Ibid., 75, 156, 239, 262-64, 305.

**PARTY AND SECTIONAL SNIPING, 1856-1859    231**

more Democratic votes than did Harlan's but was likewise defeated.[52]

The Senate now made minor changes in the bill and voted down various proposed amendments designed to encumber it. It accepted an amendment offered by Doolittle authorizing the Secretary of the Interior to receive bids for roads along the northern and the southern route and to report the same to Congress.[53] Now, if the bill were to be passed at all, was the psychological time to pass it. At this juncture, Simmons, a Republican, from Rhode Island, offered a substitute, previously offered by Bell and defeated, requiring the President to advertise for bids for building a railroad along each of three routes and to submit such bids as he should receive to Congress. This substitute was now adopted by a vote of 38 to 20, receiving the votes of the Eastern Republicans, the opponents of any sort of government financial aid, and the partisans of the extreme northern and southern routes.[54] "We have now undone all our work for the last six months," said Pugh.[55] Mason, of Virginia, taunted the friends of the road upon their inability to agree, just as he had done on a similar occasion six years before.[56]

The committee bill as it had been perfected in the Senate was undoubtedly the most adequate and carefully worked out Pacific railroad bill that had appeared thus far; in fact it was superior to the Pacific railroad bills which Congress enacted in 1862 and 1864. Had the bill passed through Congress, if the attitude of Senator Bigler, of Pennsylvania, and of the Washington *Union* may be taken as indications, President Buchanan probably would have signed it.[57] Whether its enactment would have assured the construction of the railroad or not is highly problematical. One thing is clear, the provision for a single railroad by a central route against the bitter opposition of the lower South already on the verge of secession

[52] *Ibid.*, 373, 374.
[53] *Ibid.*, 623.
[54] *Ibid.*, 603-09, 627; San Francisco *Herald*, Sept. 4, 1859.
[55] *Cong. Globe*, 35 Cong., 2 Sess., 627.
[56] *Ibid.*, 631.
[57] *Ibid.*, 304.

would not have been an act of statesmanship. It is a sad commentary on the sectionalism of the times that, while the Southerners opposed the bill because, among other reasons, it did not provide for a southern road as well as a northern, the Republicans opposed it because it gave even an outside chance for the selection of the southern route, and Northern Democrats were willing to give the South little more than an outside chance of getting the road.[58]

[58] *Cf.* Chicago *Daily Press and Tribune*, Feb. 3, 1859; San Francisco *Herald*, Aug. 31, 1860, Gwin's speech.

# CHAPTER XV

# TRANSITS ACROSS MEXICO DURING BUCHANAN'S ADMINISTRATION

I N THE opening weeks of Buchanan's administration prominent Southerners sought his support for an ambitious Mexican policy. Their plans envisaged (1) the construction of a railroad across the Isthmus of Tehuantepec and a treaty more effective than the Gadsden for its protection, (2) securing a charter for a railroad across northern Mexico from the Rio Grande to Mazatlan or other point on the Gulf of Lower California, and (3) the acquisition of another large slice of Mexican territory. Senator Robert Toombs, of Georgia, who had a conference with President Buchanan on Mexican policy in March, 1857, wrote W. W. Burwell, of Virginia, another insider: "If we can do this [get Cuba] and get a charter from the Rio Grande to Tiberon from Mexico *before* we buy Sonora and secure the Tehuantepec route, we shall do pretty well for four years. The charter, etc., must be gotten before we buy, to get ridd of grants for the Northern and Central Pacific routes which the North will insist on before they would give us such a charter and proper grant." [1] Buchanan was anxious to satisfy any reasonable Southern demands.

The Tehuantepec project had undergone many vicissitudes during the several preceding years. Under the A. G. Sloo grant of February 5, 1853, it had shown little sign of vitality, notwithstanding the protection afforded it by the Gadsden Treaty. [2] Sloo and associates had bound themselves to pay the Mexican government $600,000. Having no means of their own, they borrowed this sum of F. de P. Falconnet, a British subject, giving a lien upon the grant as security. Then they entered into a contract with Sykes, DeBergne, and Company,

[1] *Toombs, Stephens, Cobb Correspondence* (Amer. Hist. Assoc. *Rept.*, 1911), II, 399.
[2] Above, 94, 140ff.

of England, to open the route. Sykes and Company assumed the debt to Falconnet and agreed to accept the bonds of the Tehuantepec Company for their services. But Sykes and his principal assistants were lost at sea while on the way to the isthmus.[3] Falconnet transferred his lien, November, 1855, to Peter Hargous, of New York, the very same who earlier had owned the ill-fated Garay grant. When Hargous found himself unable to collect from Sloo, he entered a claim for all the rights and privileges of the grant.[4] The Tehuantepec Company succeeded, however, in getting a new contractor, one W. J. Smith, and made a desperate effort to complete the plank road before February 5, 1857, the date set in the charter. But investors refused to put money into the enterprise as long as Sloo was connected with its management. With Sloo doomed to lose his charter, a new company was organized in New Orleans for the purpose of getting a new grant and building the railway. Emile la Sére was president, Judah P. Benjamin was attorney, and John Slidell, a close political associate of Buchanan, was an active figure.[5] It was in behalf of this new company that the good offices of the Buchanan administration were sought.

The possibility of extending Texas railroads across northern Mexico to the Gulf of California, thereby substantially shortening the Pacific railroad, had been considered in the South for years. There were Texas charters in existence which authorized the building of railroads from Houston, Austin, or San Antonio to points on the lower Rio Grande and thence across Mexico to Mazatlan.[6] The few inhabitants in Arizona felt that their best route to the sea lay through Sonora. It would appear, however, that railroads across northern Mexico were desired not so much to solve the problem of communication

[3] DeBow's Rev., XXII, 193-96; N. Y. Herald, Jan. 19, 1854; Am. R. R. Jour., XXVI, 842, XXIX, 533.

[4] Sen. Exec. Docs., 35 Cong., 1 Sess., XIII (930), No. 72, pp. 33-36.

[5] Am. R. R. Jour., XXIX, 532-33, 587, 826, XXX, 165, 329, 331; DeBow's Rev., XXII, 193-96; San Francisco Morning Globe, Dec. 12, 1856; San Francisco Herald, Mar. 16, Aug. 15, 1859.

[6] Am. R. R. Jour., XXXI, 827, XXXIII, 215, XXXIV, 370; Tex. State Gaz., Nov. 6, 13, 20, 1858; Albert M. Lea, A Pacific Railway (pamphlet, 1858); C. S. Potts, Railroad Transportation in Texas (Bul. of the Univ. of Tex., No. 119), 33. See below, 272. See the map opposite p. 132.

with California and Oregon as to facilitate the settlement and utilization of the territory whose acquisition was sought.

The Southerners' primary reason for wanting another large slice of Mexico was to expand the area of slavery. They were engaged in a desperate struggle to maintain a balance of power in the United States Senate, which would enable them to fend off legislation hostile to their peculiar institution, and they hoped that Coahuila, Chihuahua, and Sonora could be brought into the Union, each with two friendly senators. There were minerals in Sonora. Some people may have felt that the international boundary was a little too close to the overland mail route for comfort.[7] Of course it was not overlooked that the acquisition of the territory would give us the shorter railroad routes.

Robert Toombs and colleagues had some difficulty in persuading Buchanan to adopt their ambitious Mexican policy. There were cabinet meetings on the subject.[8] Eventually the policy was agreed to. Southern demands were reinforced by the opportunity annexation would afford of satisfying numerous claims of American citizens against the Mexican government. Furthermore, the payment of a sum of money to Mexico for territory and transit privileges would obviate any excuse for intervention in Mexico by Great Britain, France, and Spain, which were also attempting to collect claims. As time passed and the shadow of Europe lengthened, this latter object of Buchanan's Mexican policy became paramount.[9]

On July 17, 1857, Secretary of State Cass sent instructions to John Forsyth, Minister to Mexico, embodying the new policy. Forsyth was to offer Mexico twelve million dollars or, if necessary, a maximum of fifteen millions for Lower California, nearly all of Sonora, and so much of Chihuahua as lay

[7] J. F. Rippy, The U. S. and Mexico, 88, 91, 194; W. O. Scroggs, Filibusters and Financiers, 19.
[8] Jno. B. Floyd to W. W. Burwell, Apr. 30, 1857, in Wm. W. Burwell Letters (Lib. of Cong.); Am. R. R. Jour., XXX, 474.
[9] Buchanan's Mexican policy is discussed in J. F. Rippy, The United States and Mexico, chs. x-xii; J. M. Callahan, "The Mexican Policy of Southern Leaders under Buchanan's Administration" (Am. Hist. Assoc., Rept., 1910, pp. 135-51); and Lewis Einstein, Lewis Cass (S. F. Bemis, ed., The American Secretaries of State and Their Diplomacy, VI), ch. iii. No attempt has been made here to retraverse the ground except insofar as transit privileges were involved.

north of the thirtieth parallel together with the perpetual
right of way and privilege of transit over any line of interoceanic communication across Mexico which might be established. Not more than two million dollars of the sum to be
paid Mexico might be retained by the United States to satisfy
the claims of its citizens. Forsyth was to aid La Sére and
Benjamin, who had already gone to Mexico, to get a new
grant for building a railroad across the Isthmus of Tehuantepec and was to make use of them in conducting the negotiations for a cession of territory and for other concessions. He
was to get more satisfactory provisions with regard to the
transit across the isthmus than those contained in article VIII
of the Gadsden Treaty. That treaty only by implication, not
in express terms, granted the United States rights of transit.
Cass insisted that the transit was "to be used and enjoyed in
the same manner and upon equal terms by both Republics"
and desired that there be a "perfect equality of the citizens
and subjects of all nations with the citizens of Mexico in regard to charges and tolls. . . ." The Gadsden Treaty stipulated
that the United States might extend its protection to the
transit "as it shall judge wise . . . when it may feel sanctioned
and warranted by the public or international law." Cass instructed Forsyth to get a more specific statement and one less
likely to involve the government in controversy with Mexico.[10]

Forsyth, a Pierce appointee, who had succeeded Gadsden in
1856, knew that it was hopeless to approach the Comonfort
government with an offer for a purchase of territory and did
so with reluctance. He resented being instructed to make use
of La Sére and Benjamin in the negotiations and refused to
co-operate with them.

La Sére and Benjamin succeeded, however, in getting a new
contract for building a railroad across Tehuantepec, dated
September 3, 1857. Forsyth criticized the contract; it was
unfair to Sloo, he said, and secured no advantages for the
United States government. He claimed that its separate conclusion prevented him from getting a treaty with Mexico which

[10] Rippy, *op. cit.*, 214; Callahan, *op. cit.*, 138; Einstein, *op. cit.*, 325-30.

would have secured practically all he was instructed to get.[11] President Buchanan and his cabinet seem to have made no particular objection to the contract, although it did not meet their expectations in all respects.

The new grant stipulated that a railroad must be commenced within 18 months and built at the rate of not less than 26 miles per year until completed. The company was to build the necessary wharves, moles, etc. at the termini. It was to deliver the mails along the line and carry officers, troops, and other employees of the Mexican government gratis and transport government property at 20% less than the regular rates. The line of transit was to be open to the people of all nations on equal terms, provided that citizens of belligerent nations were to be charged rates 25% higher than the regular rates. No duties were to be levied by the government upon persons or goods in transit except 12 cents for each passenger and package. Foreign mails might go through in sealed bags. The Mexican government was to receive 15% of the declared dividends of the company. The company was to have the exclusive right of transportation along the route for 60 years. The government undertook to protect the line. The Sloo contract was annulled on condition that the new company pay the Falconnet-Hargous loan of $600,000 with interest and damages.[12]

The organization of the new company was now completed, and a charter was secured in Louisiana under the name *The Louisiana Tehuantepec Company.* The capital was fixed at $10,000,000. The claims of the Sloo group and of the old Garay grantees, who had never ceased to contest the legality of the annulment of their contract, back in 1852, were quieted by $2,000,000 of fully paid stock.[13] Work was promptly begun upon the railroad. High hopes were fixed upon the enterprise in the South and in California. It was given a great impetus when Postmaster General A. V. Brown, who had put

[11] Callahan, *op. cit.*, 139.
[12] *Am. R. R. Jour.*, XXXI, 651; *Harper's Mag.*, XV, 832.
[13] N. O. *Daily Picayune*, Apr. 21, 1858; San Francisco *Herald*, Mar. 16, 1859.

the overland mail on the Gila route, awarded the company a contract for carrying the mails for a year, beginning October 1, 1858. An attempt to secure a special act of Congress authorizing such a contract having failed, authority was found under an act of March 3, 1855.[14] An act of Congress, dated June 14, 1858, stipulated that the compensation on an ocean route should not be greater than the combined sea and inland postages on the mails carried thereon. However, fortified by an opinion of the Attorney General, Brown ruled that the Tehuantepec route was a coastwise route and fixed the compensation at $286,000.[15] The postages on the route for the year it was used proved to be $9,435.98.[16] An association of Southern railroad companies took steps to induce the government to send the New York-California mail by rail to New Orleans and thence via Tehuantepec.[17]

Ground was broken for the railroad on March 5, 1859. Jefe Político Don Porfirio Diaz was present and made an appropriate speech.[18] A temporary transit was established at once. Passengers were taken up the Coatzocoalcos River on the Atlantic side for twenty miles in ocean steamers, thence for a distance in small river steamers, thence on mules for forty miles, twenty-five of which were over execrable roads through dense tropical jungle, thence by wagons to the Pacific. The steamers of the Pacific Mail Steamship Company called at the Pacific terminus.[19] The route was not improved thereafter. Misfortune had dogged every Tehuantepec project, and this one was not to be an exception. In May, 1859, came the failure of Hargous and Brother of New York, who in spite of previous unsatisfactory experience with Tehuantepec grants had made considerable advances to the new company.[20] Postmaster General Joseph Holt, who had succeeded upon the death of

[14] *Ibid.*, Jan. 1, Mar. 16, 18, May 12, 1859; *DeBow's Rev.*, XXV, 232, XXVI, 206, 340; *Cong. Globe*, 35 Cong., 2 Sess., App., 22; N. Y. *Herald*, May 15, 1858; N. O. *Picayune*, May 28, Je. 16; San Francisco *Daily Globe*, May 16, Je. 30.
[15] San Francisco *Herald*, May 26, 1859.
[16] Rept. of P. M. Gen. Holt, *Cong. Globe*, 36th Cong., 1 Sess., App., 22.
[17] N. O. *Picayune*, May 28, 1858.
[18] *Am. R. R. Jour.*, XXXII, 231.
[19] San Francisco *Herald*, Jan. 1, Feb. 1, 1859.
[20] N. O. *Daily True Delta*, May 27, 1859.

Brown, refused to renew the contract for carrying mail on the gound that the condition of the route at the time rendered it comparatively useless for mails or travel. "Were the Gulf and the Pacific connected at this point by a railroad," he said, ". . . no doubt the route would become a favorite thoroughfare both for travel and the mails, and, in the judgment of many, there are political and commercial considerations which would justify the government of the United States in assisting the company . . . to construct such a road." But, if assistance was to be given, he thought, Congress should make a direct appropriation from the treasury.[21] The failure to secure a renewal of the mail contract virtually ended the Tehuantepec venture.

The Buchanan administration had persisted meanwhile in its efforts to secure a cession of territory and a grant of transit privileges. In the fall of 1857, Forsyth asked permission to offer Mexico $12,000,000 for a treaty of transits and commerce. Such a treaty he argued would not only sustain the Comonfort government and prevent European intervention, but would also prepare the way for the other objective, namely, acquisition of territory. The President refused permission because, he said, the advantages to be gained did not justify so large an expenditure. Forsyth then requested authority to offer a larger sum for territory, but the President refused to raise his maximum.[22]

In January, 1858, General Comonfort was driven from office by a rebellion, and a Conservative government was established with General Zuloaga as president and, shortly, General Miramon as dictator. Chief Justice Juarez refused to countenance the new regime and proceeded to form a "Constitutional" government. Civil war ensued between the two governments, with constantly changing fortunes. Forsyth, along with other members of the diplomatic corps, at first recognized the Zuloaga-Miramon government. He felt it out in regard to a territorial cession but was rebuffed. He soon had reason to become bitterly hostile to that government and

[21] *Cong. Globe*, 36 Cong., 1 Sess., App., 22.
[22] Callahan, *op. cit.*, 139-40; Rippy, *op. cit.*, 215.

broke off diplomatic relations with it. His action was approved by Buchanan and Cass, but he was called home.[23]

In the spring and summer of 1858 officials of the Buchanan administration and Southern leaders began to test out public sentiment with regard to armed intervention in Mexico.[24] The response was not gratifying.

In his annual message of December, 1858, the President described in strong language the numerous gross injuries to the persons as well as the property of United States citizens in Mexico, "unredressed and even unnoticed." Abundant cause existed, he said, for war against the Zuloaga-Miramon government; but, if the Constitutional government should prevail, there was reason to believe it would be less unfriendly toward the United States. But for this expectation, he said, he would have recommended that Congress grant him the power to take possession of "a sufficient portion of the remote and unsettled" territory of Mexico to hold as a pledge for the redress of our grievances. As it was he recommended only the establishment of a temporary protectorate over the northern portions of Chihuahua and Sonora for the purpose of ending a "state of anarchy and violence" on that "distant frontier" and protecting the newly established overland mail. Such action he believed would be welcomed by the people of Chihuahua and Sonora.[25]

The Senate Committee on Foreign Relations reported a bill, January 11, 1859, authorizing the President to employ the armed forces of the nation to protect American citizens in Mexico. There was considerable debate, but the Senate refused by a vote of 31 to 25 to formally take the bill up for consideration.[26] The debates convey the clear impression that the Republicans and some of the Democrats in Congress believed that the President had overdrawn our grievances against Mexico and that the object of the bill was to enable him to

[23] Ibid., 216-17; Callahan, op. cit., 141; Einstein, op. cit., 331-32; Richardson, Messages, V, 512, 563-64.
[24] W. W. Burwell to R. M. T. Hunter, Aug. 22, 1858, in Correspondence of R. M. T. Hunter (Am. Hist. Assoc., Rept., 1916, II), 264; Cong. Globe, 35 Cong., 1 Sess., 2529, 2630.
[25] Richardson, Messages, V, 511-14.
[26] Cong. Globe, 35 Cong., 1 Sess., 1118-43.

seize territory. The Republicans were inflexibly opposed to further acquisitions until the question of slavery in the territories should have been finally settled their way.

Late in December, 1858, President Buchanan had sent a special agent, William Churchwell, to Mexico to determine whether the time was ripe to recognize the Constitutional, or Juarez, government. Churchwell sent back favorable reports and a memorandum signed by Juarez which intimated that, under certain conditions, he might be willing to cede Lower California and grant perpetual rights of way over the Isthmus of Tehuantepec and across northern Mexico by two proposed railroads.[27] Thereupon Buchanan sent Robert M. McLane, of Maryland, to Mexico as minister with instructions to recognize the Juarez government if its prospects warranted. After having recognized this government, if he found it willing to negotiate, McLane was to offer $10,000,000 for Lower California and the right of way across the Isthmus of Tehuantepec and over the two contemplated railroads, one from the Rio Grande via Monterey, Saltillo, and Durango to Mazatlan, the other from Nogales, on the boundary of Arizona, via Hermosillo to Guaymas. The United States must have the right to land troops to protect the transits. Part of the purchase price should be reserved to satisfy claims of United States citizens against Mexico.[28] (See the map opposite p. 132.)

McLane promptly recognized the Juarez government; but he found it more difficult to negotiate a treaty than he had been led to expect. There was strong public sentiment in Mexico against the alienation of territory or the granting of discretionary power to the United States to introduce troops into the country to protect transit routes which Juarez, great as were his financial necessities, hesitated to offend. Juarez steadily refused to cede territory under any circumstances. Eventually McLane was instructed to offer $4,000,000 for merely a treaty of transits and commerce, of which sum $2,000,000 was to be reserved to satisfy claims. As regards the transits, Juarez insisted that the United States should not

[27] Callahan, op. cit., 142; Rippy, op. cit., 219.
[28] Ibid., 219-31; Callahan, op. cit., 142.

have the right to use force for their protection without the previous consent of Mexico. Cass finally consented to this with the proviso that such consent would not be necessary "in cases of sudden emergency." To this proviso Juarez would not agree. The Juarez government on its part sought a military alliance with the United States which would not only have obligated the latter to defend Mexico against intervention by European powers but to aid the Constitutional government in extending its authority over the whole of Mexico.[29]

By the latter part of 1859 the danger of intervention in Mexico by Great Britain, France, and Spain seemed serious enough that Buchanan thenceforth subordinated his concern for territory and transits and even redress for injuries received to the great objective of preventing European intervention. In his annual message of 1859, he asked Congress for authority to use force to help the Constitutional government extend its power over the whole republic. That government would then satisfy our claims and redress our grievances and remove the occasion for possible intervention from abroad, he said.[30]

Buchanan had already instructed McLane to negotiate with Juarez for a treaty providing for armed intervention in Mexico at the request of the Mexican government and granting to the United States the commercial and transit rights and privileges which the administration had been insisting upon. The necessities of the Juarez government were now very great; the renewed negotiations resulted promptly in the signing, December 14, of a treaty and a convention in accord with the minister's instructions.[31]

By the treaty Mexico granted the United States the perpetual right of way across the Isthmus of Tehuantepec and by two routes across northern Mexico for its citizens and their merchandise and for the mails. One route ran from Matamoras, Camargo, or other convenient point on the lower Rio Grande via Monterey to Mazatlan, the other from Nogales to

[29] Ibid., 142-46; Einstein, op. cit., 335-39; Harper's Mag., XIX, 696.
[30] Richardson, Messages, V, 563-68.
[31] Rippy, op. cit., 223-26; Callahan, op. cit., 146-47; San Francisco Herald, Jan. 14, 1860; Harper's Mag., XX, 690.

Guaymas. The transit privilege extended to any kind of road or roads which might be provided. Mexico undertook to provide free ports or right of deposit at the termini of all three routes and to impose no tolls or restrictions of any kind on persons or goods in transit. The United States government might transport troops, munitions, and military supplies over the Tehuantepec and Nogales-Guaymas routes. The two governments jointly guaranteed the neutrality and security of the transits; and the United States might employ force to protect them upon the request of the Mexican government or, in case of imminent danger to the lives and property of American citizens, upon its own initiative. There were some commercial and other provisions. The United States was to pay Mexico $4,000,000, of which sum one half was to be retained to satisfy claims of United States citizens. The convention in effect pledged the United States to assist the Juarez government to establish its authority over the whole of Mexico. It was the price the United States had to pay for the treaty.

On January 4, 1860, the President submitted the treaty and the convention to the Senate,[32] and they were at once referred to the Committee on Foreign Relations. All of the Senate's proceedings in relation to them were carried on in executive session, and the injunction of secrecy has never been removed. However, the Senate seems to have given them serious consideration. On May 31, they failed of ratification by a vote of 18 to 27. This vote was reconsidered on June 27, but subsequently further consideration was postponed until the short session of Congress.[33] They were never again taken up. Of the eighteen senators who had voted for ratification all were Democrats and all but four were from the South; of the twenty-seven who had voted against ratification twenty-one were Republicans and all but four were from the North.

Meanwhile the request made by the President in his annual message for authority to employ force in Mexico had received scant notice in Congress. The Northern majority was still

[32] Richardson, *Messages*, V, 578.
[33] *Sen. Exec. Jour.*, XI, 115 ff.; Rippy, *op. cit.*, 226; San Antonio *Ledger and Texan*, Mar. 10, 17, 1860.

unwilling to trust James Buchanan with the armed forces of
the nation beyond the Rio Grande and either did not want
Mexican transits at all or, at least, did not want them if they
were to facilitate the acquisition of more slave territory.[34] For
the remainder of his term Buchanan was forced to confine himself, insofar as Mexican policy was concerned, to commendable
and dignified diplomatic protests against the impending intervention of Great Britain, France, and Spain.[35]

[34] *Ibid., loc. cit.*; H. L. Wilson, "President Buchanan's Proposed Intervention
in Mexico," in *Am. Hist. Rev.*, V, 698-99.

[35] Einstein, *op. cit.*, 340-47; Callahan, *op. cit.*, 149-51; Rippy, *op. cit.*, 226-29.

# CHAPTER XVI

# BUCHANAN'S ISTHMIAN TRANSITS POLICY

THE Buchanan administration had to take up various isthmian matters in the unfinished state in which they had been left by its predecessor.[1] President Buchanan and Secretary of State Cass showed a somewhat better grasp of the various problems and issues than Pierce and Marcy had done and, perhaps because of different circumstances, for which they were in no wise responsible, achieved a somewhat greater measure of success. Its isthmian diplomacy constitutes one of the more creditable chapters in the history of the Buchanan administration. However, the administration accomplished nothing whatever in the way of actually providing improved facilities of travel and commerce.

President Buchanan was well prepared by experience to deal with the isthmian problems. Cass was appointed secretary of state for reasons of party politics. He was, or had been, an ardent expansionist, had lent moral encouragement to William Walker's first venture in Nicaragua, and was known as an Anglophobe. His appointment was likely to cause concern in Great Britain. Buchanan understood this and attempted to quiet fears in advance. Before his inauguration he wrote Lord Clarendon that no Englishman need feel the least uneasiness with regard to Cass. "His Anglophobia, as you used facetiously to term it, if it ever existed, no longer exists." He intimated that he would personally keep in close contact with foreign relations. This he did.[2]

One of the first isthmian matters to be handled concerned Panama. New Granada had attempted to collect tonnage duties on foreign vessels in Aspinwall and Panama, the termini of the Panama Railroad, and to tax the mails in transit. The

---

[1] See ch. xiii.
[2] *Works of James Buchanan*, X, 102-03; Lewis Einstein, *Lewis Cass* (in S. F. Bemis, ed., *The Am. Secretaries of State and Their Diplomacy*, VI), ch. i.

United States government had objected to these acts as contrary to the Treaty of 1848 and the railroad charter. More serious had been a riotous attack made by the inhabitants of the City of Panama on the railroad and passengers, April 15, 1856, in which several American citizens had been killed and much property destroyed. Pierce had sent naval vessels to Aspinwall and Panama to protect lives and property and demanded reparations. He had appointed a special commissioner to negotiate with New Granada and had empowered him to make a treaty acquiring control of the Panama Railroad and sovereignty over islands in the harbor of Panama.[3] The negotiations continued into Buchanan's administration. The British government became suspicious. Lord Napier, the new British minister, protested to Cass, observing that for either power to exercise exclusive control over the Panama route would be contrary to article VIII of the Clayton-Bulwer Treaty. Cass gave the desired assurance, without committing himself as to interpretation. The British cabinet then proposed a tripartite guarantee of the Panama route by Great Britain, France, and the United States. Cass rejected this as against established policy of avoiding alliances and unnecessary in view of the Treaty of 1848 guaranteeing the neutrality and protection of the route.[4] The dispute with New Granada was easily settled.

Buchanan had to decide early what to do about William Walker and filibustering in Nicaragua. In May, 1857, Walker was expelled from Nicaragua and was brought to the United States on an American vessel. He claimed still to be the rightful president of the little republic, avowed his intention of returning, and sought recognition from President Buchanan.[5] Buchanan probably had not the slightest intention of giving Walker any countenance. To do so would destroy any possibility of making a satisfactory arrangement with Great Britain and further weaken the standing of the United States in Central America. Walker, however, still had many sympa-

[3] Richardson, *Messages*, V, 415-16; N. Y. *Herald*, May 2, 1856; *Harper's Mag.*, XIV, 836, XV, 116; *Sen. Exec. Docs.*, 56 Cong., 1 Sess., XI (3853), No. 237, pp. 25-34.
[4] M. W. Williams, *Anglo-American Isthmian Diplomacy*, 233-34, 237-38.
[5] *Harper's Mag.*, XV, 402; W. O. Scroggs, *Filibusters and Financiers*, 334.

thizers in the South, where Buchanan was especially anxious to please. So the President went so far as to grant Walker an interview and to delay for a time the recognition of the new government in Nicaragua.[6] But, when Walker began to make preparations for another expedition, the President gave stringent orders to prevent its escape; and, when Lord Napier sought assurances in regard to it, they were promptly given.[7]

The expulsion of the filibusters seemed to promise a speedy reopening of the Nicaragua transit. The Martinez government was at once approached by several parties who desired the privilege. Among them were the old Atlantic and Pacific Ship Canal Company, with H. G. Stebbins as president and Joseph White as chief manipulator, the Accessory Transit Company (Vanderbilt), which claimed its charter had never been legally annulled, and Morgan and Garrison, to whom Walker had granted the concession. Yrisarri, who was commissioned Nicaraguan minister to the United States, signed a contract with the Stebbins group, June 27. Costa Rica also claimed jurisdiction over the route and signed a contract with an English adventurer named Webster. The United States government was very anxious to have the transit opened in order to have competition with the Panama route renewed. While it took no part in negotiations, it looked with favor on the Stebbins contract. The other interested parties tried to defeat confirmation of the Stebbins contract by Nicaragua. Webster joined forces with Morgan and Garrison.[8] Lord Napier saw President Buchanan in their behalf.[9] Buchanan and Cass denied the right of Costa Rica to have a finger in the pie. The President wrote privately to Lord Clarendon. "I think you ought to keep your protegé, Costa Rica, in hand." She claimed the right to sell the canal route to the highest bidder. "To this I shall not submit. She has got hold of the greatest scamps as purchasers. . . ."[10] Lord Napier soon be-

[6] *Ibid.*, 334 ff., 355.

[7] *Sen. Exec. Docs.*, 35 Cong., 1 Sess., I (918), No. 13; *Sen. Exec. Docs.*, 56 Cong., 1 Sess., XI (3853), No. 161, p. 113; *Harper's Mag.*, XV, 831.

[8] *Ibid.*, XV, 112; Scroggs, *op. cit.*, 353-55.

[9] *Parl. Papers*, 1860, LXVIII, 46, 47.

[10] *Works of James Buchanan*, X, 122-24; *Sen. Exec. Docs.*, 56 Cong., 1 Sess., XI (3853), No. 161, p. 112.

came convinced that Webster, Morgan, and Garrison were "equally devoid of character and pecuniary means." After gaining a promise of concessions for Costa Rica, he acquiesced in the Stebbins contract, which was eventually confirmed.[11]

Buchanan was determined that the transit should have other protection than what Nicaragua might afford. He, therefore, deferred the formal reception of Señor Yrisarri until a satisfactory treaty of "friendship, commerce, and navigation should be signed." The Cass-Yrisarri Treaty was signed November 16, 1857, and Yrisarri was received the same day.[12]

According to the terms of the treaty, Nicaragua granted to the United States government and citizens the right of transit by any route on equal terms with her own citizens. The United States undertook to protect the transit routes and their neutrality and to attempt to get other nations to do the same. Nicaragua agreed to establish a free port at either end of one route. This was as close as the treaty came to containing recognition by the United States of Nicaragua's sovereignty over Greytown. The United States might send troops and munitions across by any route. There were provisions designed to prevent excessive charges or discrimination in tolls or services. The concessions to Costa Rica which Cass and Yrisarri had promised Lord Napier amounted only to a simple statement that nothing in the treaty should be construed to affect the claims of Costa Rica to free passage by the San Juan River to and from the sea. There was nothing in the treaty contrary to the letter or spirit of the Clayton-Bulwer Treaty; in fact it was the sort of treaty that that covenant had obligated the United States and Great Britain to make.

To hasten negotiations with Great Britain regarding outstanding isthmian issues, Buchanan and Cass intimated to Lord Napier that they might favor abrogation of the Clayton-Bulwer Treaty. If they did not take the lead, they said, Congress might do so at the next session.[13] Lord Napier advised his government that, if it wished to save the treaty, it had better

11 *Ibid.*, 117; *Parl. Papers*, 1860, LXVIII, 52; Scroggs, *op. cit.*, 355.
12 *Sen. Exec. Docs.*, 56 Cong., 1 Sess., XI (3853), No. 161, pp. 117-25.
13 *Ibid.*, 112; *Works of James Buchanan*, X, 122; Williams, *op. cit.*, 231.

come to an agreement on terms acceptable to the United States before Congress should meet. He suggested that an able commissioner be sent to Central America to negotiate agreements with the several little states for which the informal approval of Washington should be sought and secured in advance.[14] This procedure would enable the two governments to avoid further fruitless wrangling over the meaning of the Clayton-Bulwer Treaty.

The British government fell in with Lord Napier's suggestion and appointed Sir William Ouseley, an intimate acquaintance of Buchanan, as commissioner.[15] Buchanan approved the line of procedure and promised not to recommend abrogation of the Clayton-Bulwer Treaty nor to countenance moves in Congress to abrogate it if Ouseley's instructions should prove satisfactory. The British minister gave assurance that his government would not support Webster, Morgan, and Garrison and their Costa Rica franchise for a transit by the Nicaragua route. Buchanan gave assurance that he would enforce the laws against filibustering.[16]

In his annual message of December 8, 1857, the President outlined and endorsed the arrangement which had been made. He severely denounced filibustering and asked for more effectual laws against it. The United States was more deeply interested than any other nation in preserving the freedom and security of all the communications across the isthmus, he said. It was our duty, therefore, "to take care that they shall not be interrupted either by invasions from our own country or by wars between the independent States of Central America." We were bound by treaty to protect the neutrality of the Isthmus of Panama and New Granada's sovereignty over it. He, therefore, recommended legislation "authorizing the President, in case of necessity, to employ the land and naval forces of the United States to carry into effect this guaranty of neutrality and protection" and to maintain the security "of any other route across the Isthmus in which we may acquire an

14 *Ibid.*, 231-33.
15 *Sen. Exec. Docs.*, 56 Cong., 1 Sess., XI (3853), No. 161, pp. 114-17.
16 *Ibid.*, 113-17; *Works of James Buchanan*, X, 124-28.

interest by treaty." [17]  The request seems reasonable and statesmanlike.

The new method of approach did not bring quick results. Ouseley's instructions, when he appeared in Washington, did not prove acceptable to Buchanan and Cass.[18] The British government, still suspicious of Buchanan's intentions and uncertain as to what Congress might do, instructed Ouseley to move cautiously.[19] Lord Napier, fearful of the outcome, offered to submit the dispute over the Clayton-Bulwer Treaty to arbitration.[20] Events in Central America and reactions in Congress and among the American people added complications.

On November 16, the very day of the signing of the Cass-Yrisarri Treaty, William Walker had escaped from Mobile with a party of 158 men to return to Nicaragua. On December 8, the day Buchanan sent in his annual message, Commodore Paulding had landed sailors and marines at Puenta Arenas, on what the United States recognized as Nicaraguan soil, and captured Walker and his filibusters. He brought them back to the United States. The President decided Paulding had violated the proprieties in seizing Walker on Nicaraguan soil and ordered Walker released, though not returned to Nicaragua. Paulding was not punished, and Buchanan was obviously relieved by Walker's discomfiture.[21] Far from taking umbrage, the Nicaraguan minister wrote Cass thanking the United States government for arresting Walker.[22]

The President sent a special message to the Senate explaining his action.[23] He gave a scathing denunciation of filibusterism, which could not have been put in stronger language. "The truth is that no Administration can successfully conduct the foreign affairs of the country in Central America or anywhere else if it is to be interfered with at every step by lawless military expeditions 'set on foot' in the United States." The

[17] Richardson, *Messages*, V, 442-45, 447-48.
[18] *Parl. Papers*, 1860, LXVIII, 48-51, 70-72.
[19] *Ibid.*, 64.
[20] *Sen. Exec. Docs.*, 56 Cong., 1 Sess., XI (3853), No. 161, p. 128.
[21] Richardson, *Messages*, V, 466-69; *Sen. Exec. Docs.*, 35 Cong., 1 Sess., I (918), No. 13; *Harper's Mag.*, XVI, 401. Walker was brought to trial in New Orleans, but the jury disagreed, and the case was then dropped.
[22] *Cong. Globe*, 35 Cong., 1 Sess., 357.
[23] Richardson, *Messages*, V, 466-69.

documents make it perfectly clear that negotiations with Great Britain could not have continued had Walker been allowed to invade Nicaragua again.[24] Some of Buchanan's statements, however, could hardly have been reassuring to Central American states or other foreign powers. "It is beyond question the destiny of our race," he said, "to spread themselves over the continent of North America, and this at no distant day should events be permitted to take their natural course." Then, "Liberty under the restraint of law will preserve domestic peace, whilst the different transit routes . . . will have assured protection." Nothing had retarded this happy event more than filibustering. Had one half the number of American citizens who had perished miserably in Walker's expeditions gone to Nicaragua as peaceful settlers, this object would already have been accomplished in a great degree.

The arrest of William Walker precipitated a lively debate in Congress not only upon Commodore Paulding's action in arresting Walker upon Nicaraguan soil but also upon filibusterism and isthmian policy in general.[25] The debate showed that isthmian questions, like every other national issue, were being drawn into the destructive vortex of the sectional struggle over slavery. One group, nearly all Democrats from the deep South, especially the Southwest, condemned Paulding, defended filibustering, and demanded less stringent neutrality laws rather than stronger. They were disinclined to grant the President the authority he had requested to employ land and naval forces for the protection of the transit routes lest he use it to suppress filibusters. This group had comparatively little interest in isthmian transits but were clearly animated by a desire to get more slave territory. A few from the lower South, to be sure, spoke out in honorable fashion against filibustering. L. Q. C. Lamar, of Mississippi, said he would "never consent to submit the fate of our noble [Southern] institutions to the hands of marauding bands, or violate their sanctity by identifying their progress with the success of unlawful expedi-

---

[24] E. g., *Sen. Exec. Docs.*, 56 Cong., 1 Sess., XI (3853), No. 161, p. 142.
[25] The majority and minority reports of the H. Com. on Naval affairs are in *H. Repts.*, 35 Cong., 1 Sess., I (964), No. 74.

tions." [26] The majority of the Democrats, from the North and the upper South mostly, took the same position as the President. They denounced filibustering but looked forward to the Americanization of the isthmus by peaceful colonization or as the result of "honorable war." They mostly, but by no means all, favored the abrogation of the Clayton-Bulwer Treaty because of its self-denial clause.

The Republicans defended Paulding and, of course, condemned filibusterism. They opposed abrogation of the Clayton-Bulwer Treaty, not so much because they approved its principles as because they feared it would lead to a scramble for territory and they opposed further expansion until the slavery question should have been settled. They mostly opposed granting the President authority to employ military forces in protecting the isthmian crossings, professing to believe he would abuse it and seize territory into which slavery might be extended. They apparently expected the President by unaided diplomacy, somehow, to keep the transits open. One Westerner, Curtis, of Iowa, spoke out against the whole policy of trying to secure transit routes across foreign territory. Central America could not be settled by citizens of the United States, he said; conditions there could not be stabilized. The best route to the Pacific was transcontinental.[27] A resolution requesting the President to take steps to abrogate the Clayton-Bulwer Treaty was ordered to a third reading in the House by a vote of 97 to 86.[28] The Republicans cast only 3 votes for the resolution and 70 against it. The sixteen Democrats and Americans who voted against it represented widely scattered districts. There was no vote on the President's request for authority to use military forces in protecting the isthmian routes, but the majority was clearly opposed. Lord Napier must have duly noted how the Executive's position was weakened by internal divisions. It was another case of sectional animosities interfering with the effective operation of the government in a highly important matter.

[26] *Cong. Globe*, 35 Cong., 1 Sess., 279.
[27] *Ibid.*, 273-74.
[28] *Ibid.*, 1945, 2203.

In Central America matters continued to go wrong from the point of view of the Buchanan administration. On January 28, 1858, the Nicaraguan government revoked the contract with the Stebbins group for the operation of the transit and on March 8 transferred it to Vanderbilt.[29] The latter made no attempt to reopen the route. According to the newspapers he received $56,000 a month from the steamship companies connected with the Panama route to keep it closed.[30] Later in the year, when the Stebbins people attempted to reopen the transit, the Nicaraguan government refused to allow passengers to cross and seized two of the company's steamers.[31] Meanwhile the Cass-Yrisarri Treaty had come up for consideration in Nicaragua. There was serious opposition to the provision which permitted the United States to use force to protect the transit. Vanderbilt's agents worked against ratification, fearing, it would appear, that the United States government preferred the Stebbins interests. The Assembly, however, ratified. Thereupon President Martinez refused to exchange ratifications.

President Martinez had fallen under the influence of M. Felix Belly, a French adventurer, who both understood and possessed the Latin temperament. He represented that he had the approval of the Emperor of France. He made Martinez believe that the Buchanan government approved filibustering, which was not difficult to believe, and that, should the Cass-Yrisarri Treaty be ratified, the United States would dominate the isthmus. He was instrumental in getting Nicaragua and Costa Rica to sign a treaty settling their boundary dispute. The treaty recognized Costa Rica's claim to a considerable portion of the canal route. M. Belly then persuaded the two governments to grant him the exclusive privilege of building and operating a canal. He assured them that the French government would protect the canal. One provision of his contract gave France permission to keep two war vessels on Lake

[29] Scroggs, *Filibusters and Financiers*, 357, 368.

[30] *Ibid.*, 365; *Cong. Globe*, 35 Cong., 1 Sess., 1973; San Francisco *Herald*, Aug. 15, 1859.

[31] Scroggs, *op. cit.*, 366; *Parl. Papers*, 1860, LXVIII, 213; *Harper's Mag.*, XVIII, 257.

Nicaragua while the canal should be under construction. Finally M. Belly induced the presidents of the two republics to sign a joint manifesto putting their countries under the joint protection of Great Britain, France, and Sardinia and alleging in justification that an armed expedition was threatening under the patronage of the United States, which, they said, desired to annex the whole isthmus. Belly then went home, wrote a book entitled *Percement de L'Isthme Americaine*, and tried to organize a company.[32]

These events in Central America caused Buchanan and Cass no little vexation. Cass wrote at length to Lamar, United States minister to Nicaragua, outlining the views of his government. The United States government would not tolerate the proposed tripartite protectorate. It would not deny the right of Nicaragua and Costa Rica to make a contract with M. Belly; but it would insist that any contract made be on such terms as to render the routes free and safe to all nations with moderate and reasonable tolls and not subject to the control of any one nation. American citizens claimed to hold contracts from Nicaragua. Unfortunately there were disputes among American interests which he would not pass upon. But the United States government would insist that when fair contracts were fairly entered into with American citizens they should not be wantonly abrogated. As for the treaty between Nicaragua and Costa Rica, his government would recognize no settlement which interfered with existing contracts with regard to transit.[33] Lamar secured what amounted to a retraction of the offensive manifesto of the two presidents, August, 1858, but he failed to secure ratification of the Cass-Yrisarri Treaty. Cass secured from the French government a disavowal of any connection with M. Belly. No one in the United States expected M. Belly to build a canal, but his contract stood for the time being.[34]

Through the summer and autumn of 1858 Walker made

[32] *Ibid.*, XVII, 403, 546; Scroggs, *op. cit.*, 358-62; *Sen. Exec. Docs.*, 56 Cong., 1 Sess., XI (3853), No. 161, pp. 133-37.
[33] *Ibid., loc. cit.*
[34] *Works of James Buchanan*, X, 317; Scroggs, *op. cit.*, 362, 364.

desperate efforts to get to Nicaragua again. He sold bonds, enlisted men as "emigrants," secured a ship, and set a date for sailing. By a ruse he got his ship to sea with 150 men on board. Fortunately it was wrecked on the coast of Honduras and, ironically enough, Walker and his men were brought back to Mobile by a British war vessel.[35]

With the American government beset by so many difficulties, the negotiations with Great Britain inevitably dragged. The British government waited to see if Buchanan would act effectively against the filibusters. Then it waited on the debate in Congress. It raised objections to the Cass-Yrisarri Treaty. In February, 1858, Napier sent a note to Cass saying his government would accept that treaty and was ready to send Ouseley on his mission but first desired a reply to its offer of arbitration. Then, when Cass delayed formal reply, it decided to accept abrogation of the Clayton-Bulwer Treaty and a return to the *status quo ante*.[36] Apparently it was prompted to take this tack by Buchanan's refusal to approve Ouseley's instructions and by the evidences that the President could not command congressional support for a strong isthmian policy. Lord Malmesbury, a Tory, somewhat less friendly to the United States, had succeeded Lord Clarendon as foreign secretary. On April 6, Cass formally rejected the offer of arbitration and also rejected abrogation of the Clayton-Bulwer Treaty unless Great Britain would first give up the territory she occupied in the Central American region. He insisted that Ouseley perform his mission and again asked to be informed of the details of his instructions.[37]

The question arises why Buchanan and Cass did not accept the British offer to abrogate the Clayton-Bulwer Treaty. Had they been bluffing when they had talked of abrogation earlier, and had Great Britain called their bluff? That is the most likely explanation. It may well be, however, that they had really seriously considered abrogation and a resort to a direct

[35] *Ibid.*, ch. xxiii; Richardson, *Messages*, V, 496; *Harper's Mag.*, XVI, 544, XVIII, 113, 401.

[36] *Sen. Exec. Docs.*, 56 Cong., 1 Sess., XI (3853), No. 161, pp. 128-33.

[37] *Ibid.*, 143-44; *Parl. Papers*, 1860, LXVIII, 87-90, 99.

assertion of the Monroe Doctrine but had found their position too greatly weakened at home by the involvement of the isthmian question in the sectional controversy and in Central America by filibustering.

In July Malmesbury instructed Ouseley to proceed to Central America but withdrew authority to treat for the relinquishment of the Bay Islands. A few weeks later he also withdrew authority to negotiate in regard to the Belize boundary. In August he tartly instructed Napier to tell Cass that no further explanations would be made about Ouseley's mission. Furthermore the British and French governments sent war vessels to Central American waters to guard against filibusters during the negotiations and refused to recall them despite Cass's vigorous protests.[38] Once in Central America, Ouseley gave it out that Great Britain was not going to give up anything and that British influence would predominate on the isthmus.[39]

Buchanan and Cass held on doggedly, however, and eventually surmounted their difficulties. Lord Napier was helpful; all along he had shown a disposition to settle on terms satisfactory to the United States government. The termination of the long quarrel over visitation and search also helped to clear the atmosphere.[40] By the end of the year, 1858, a working understanding was reached. Cass consented to modify his treaty with Yrisarri to the extent of abandoning the right to send troops across Nicaragua in case of hostilities against a power with which that nation was at peace. Great Britain was to make a treaty of commerce and transits with Nicaragua identical in essential respects with the Cass-Yrisarri Treaty. She was also to make a treaty with Nicaragua surrendering the Mosquito protectorate along the lines of the Dallas-Clarendon Convention. The United States treaty was to be ratified in Nicaragua before the British treaties, a necessary precaution because of the bitter feeling of the Nicaraguans toward this

---

[38] *Ibid.*, 99-120, 123-24, 134, 137-44, 154, 159, 161.
[39] *Ibid.*, 215-17, 229-33; Scroggs, *op. cit.*, 377.
[40] Lewis Einstein, *Lewis Cass* (in S. F. Bemis, ed., *The Am. Secretaries of State and Their Diplomacy*, VI), 316-23; *Parl. Papers*, 1860, LXVIII, 144-47.

country — and there had already been four abortive treaties, those of Hise, Squier, Borland, and Wheeler. The United States was to make a treaty with Honduras guaranteeing the neutrality and protection of the proposed Honduras Interoceanic Railway similar to the treaty between Great Britain and Honduras, signed August 26, 1856. Cass tacitly acquiesced in the retention of British and French war vessels in Central American waters during negotiations. The two governments instructed their agents in Central America to co-operate.[41]

The agents on the ground were unable to change their rôles so suddenly. Sir William Ouseley especially failed to rise to the occasion. For example, he had been instructed to sign both treaties with Nicaragua at the same time. Instead, he signed the treaty of commerce first and then found that Nicaragua was in no haste about the Mosquito protectorate, preferring that Great Britain retain it for a time and guard the coast against filibusters. Again, Sir William had consented to the inclusion of a provision in the treaty of commerce that Her Majesty's government would take care to enforce its laws against piratical expeditions. Nicaragua then demanded that a similar provision be put in her treaty with the United States. This was highly offensive to the United States government. Cass complained of Ouseley to the British government. Lord Malmesbury first scolded Ouseley and then removed him and appointed Charles Wyke, an able diplomat who had been entrusted with the negotiations with Guatemala and had brought them to a speedy and successful conclusion.[42] He performed the new tasks assigned him with efficiency and dispatch. In England Lord John Russell succeeded Malmesbury as Secretary for Foreign Affairs and was somewhat more accommodating to the American point of view.

The treaty between Great Britain and Guatemala, ratified by the latter, April, 1859, fixed the boundaries between that republic and British Honduras where the British had contended they were and described them as being the boundaries

[41] Ibid., 127-28, 133-35, 154-57, 160-61, 171, 215, 265.
[42] Ibid., 186-205, 209, 211, 215-17, 224, 263-66, 268-82; Works of James Buchanan, X, 315-18, 322-23.

"as they existed previous to and on the 1st day of January, 1850." [43] By treaty with Honduras, ratified by Honduras in February, 1860, Great Britain relinquished claim to the Bay Islands; Honduras engaged never to transfer the islands to another power and specifically guaranteed certain civil rights to their British inhabitants. Great Britain recognized that the portion of the Mosquito protectorate lying within the limits of Honduras belonged to the republic, and Honduras agreed to pay the Indians an annuity. [44] The United States minister signed, February 28, 1860, a treaty with Honduras guaranteeing the protection and neutrality of the proposed Interoceanic Railroad in about the same terms as did the British treaty relating to the same subject. [45]

In Nicaragua Lamar had succeeded in getting a treaty signed March 16, 1859, which was substantially the same as the Cass-Yrisarri Treaty for the use, protection, and neutrality of the transit route. [46] The British treaty of commerce and transits, which Ouseley had negotiated, was modified to conform. The French government also signed an identical treaty with Nicaragua. [47] In January, 1860, Wyke signed a treaty with Nicaragua, ratified by Nicaragua in April, for the relinquishment of the Mosquito protectorate. It followed closely the provisions of the Dallas-Clarendon Convention. The Indians were given a reservation under Nicaraguan sovereignty, within which they might have the rights of self-government if they chose. Nicaragua was to pay them an annuity. Greytown was made a free port under Nicaraguan sovereignty. [48] The ratification of the British-Central American treaties and exchange of ratifications were all complete by August, 1860.

President Buchanan could properly say in his annual message, of December, 1860, "The discordant constructions of the Clayton and Bulwer treaty between the two governments,

[43] *Sen. Exec. Docs.*, 56 Cong., 1 Sess., XI (3853), No. 161, pp. 146, 162-64.
[44] *Ibid.*, 148-51; *Parl. Papers*, 1860, LXVIII, 307-10, 320.
[45] Richardson, *Messages*, V, 585; text in Wm. M. Malloy, Comp., *Treaties Conventions, International Acts*, etc. I, 952-58.
[46] Text in *ibid.*, II, 1279-87.
[47] Richardson, *Messages*, V, 587; *Parl. Papers*, 1860, LXVIII, 318.
[48] *Ibid.*, 314-18; *Sen. Exec. Docs.*, 56 Cong., 1 Sess., XI (3853), No. 161, pp. 151-54.

which at different periods of the discussion bore a threatening aspect, have resulted in a final settlement entirely satisfactory to this Government." [49] The United States had not secured all it had ever claimed; for Great Britain retained Belize with its extended boundaries and converted it into a crown colony of the standard type. The United States probably had secured all any responsible official had ever seriously expected to secure. This result in all probability could have been achieved earlier had it not been for filibustering. The Clayton-Bulwer Treaty was presumably preserved in full vigor; the two governments were committed to the commendable principle that the isthmian transit routes should be open to all nations on fair and equal terms, that no one power should gain exclusive control over any of them, and that all powerful nations should join in guaranteeing their protection and neutrality.

By 1860 the United States had quite satisfactory treaties, two yet unratified, with all four of the states having practicable isthmian transit routes, New Granada, Nicaragua, Honduras, and Mexico.[50] By treaty with New Granada the United States guaranteed not only the security and neutrality of the Panama route but also the sovereignty of New Granada over it. In the other three treaties no such guarantee of sovereignty was given. The treaties with Mexico and Nicaragua expressly gave the United States the right to send troops and munitions across their borders at will, except that in case of Nicaragua it might not send troops designed to be used against a power with which Nicaragua was at peace. The treaties with Mexico and Nicaragua also gave the United States the right to land troops for the protection of the routes. The Mexican treaty said the United States might exercise the right when it should judge "wise" and when "it may feel sanctioned and warranted by the public or international law." The Nicaraguan treaty required the United States government to obtain first the

[49] Richardson, *Messages*, V, 639.
[50] Buchanan briefly summarized and compared them in a message to the Senate. *Ibid.*, V, 585-88. Because of amendment by the Senate, the Honduras and Nicaragua treaties were not completed. They were later renegotiated with minor changes and went into effect in 1865 and 1868 respectively. *Ibid.*, VI, 257, 581, 687.

consent of the proper Nicaraguan authorities except in "the exceptional case . . . of unforeseen or imminent danger. . . ." The treaties with New Granada and Honduras gave the United States rights to transport troops and munitions over the transits and to land troops to protect the routes only by implication. The treaties with Honduras and Nicaragua contained provision safeguarding the United States government and citizens against excessive or discriminating tolls and charges by the parties which should operate the transportation facilities.

Congress had not yet enacted legislation giving the President the power to employ the land and naval forces to protect the isthmian transits when necessity should arise. President Buchanan had requested such authority in each of his annual messages and in a special message. In his second annual message especially he put the matter strongly. The executive, he said, could not legally resort to force without the direct authority of Congress, except in resisting and repelling hostile attacks. "It would have no authority to enter the territories of Nicaragua even to prevent the destruction of the transit and protect the lives and property of our own citizens on their passage. It is true that on a sudden emergency of this character the President would direct any armed force in the vicinity to march to their relief, but in doing this he would act upon his own responsibility." [51] But Congress was too jealous of the war-making power to heed the President's requests, and Republican members in particular were too fearful of giving such authority to a president so sympathetic to the South's desire for more slave territory.

In 1860, despite a decade of effort and the establishment of correct principles, the Panama Railroad was the only isthmian transit. In the summer and autumn of 1859 both the Stebbins group (the Old Atlantic and Pacific Ship Canal Company) and Vanderbilt (the Accessory Transit Company) announced intentions of reopening the Nicaragua route but neither did so.[52]

[51] *Ibid.*, V, 516.
[52] San Francisco *Herald*, May 26, Je. 2, Aug. 15, Oct. 5, 1859; *Works of James Buchanan*, X, 328; Scroggs, *op. cit.*, 367.

From time to time during the next several years there were
projects for reopening this transit but none of them reached
the stage of realization. Had it not been for William Walker
this route might have seen many years of useful service, prior
to the opening of the first transcontinental railroad, in 1869.
The Tehuantepec project slumbered for years. The Honduras
Interoceanic Railroad project failed. In the fall of 1859
Vanderbilt's Atlantic and Pacific Mail Steamship Company
and the Pacific Mail Steamship Company came to an agreement whereby the former withdrew its steamers from the
Pacific side and the latter withdrew its steamers from the
Atlantic side.[53] Thus not only did the Panama route have a
monopoly as against other isthmian routes, but the Panama
route was in the control of three monopolistic companies, the
two steamship companies named and the Panama Railroad
Company.

[53] *Am. R. R. Jour.*, XXIII, 443.

# CHAPTER XVII

# NATIONAL DEVELOPMENT WEIGHTS THE BALANCE IN THE PACIFIC RAILWAY STRUGGLE

THE Pacific railroad issue was a perennial one, but it was not unchangeable. While Congress debated it and various groups and interests maneuvered and intrigued with regard to it, its form changed under the impact of national developments and events. The progress of the country would not wait upon a divided legislative body.

One national development which changed the form of the issue was the uneven advance of the frontier. Thousands of settlers flocked into Kansas in spite of civil strife, or perhaps in many cases because of it, and settled principally along the Kaw and the lower courses of its affluents. The census of 1860 showed a population of 107,206. Settlers even found their way to the comparatively inaccessible valley of the Platte in considerable numbers. There were 28,841 of them in 1860. A Pacific railroad by a central route would now find supporting settlements extending far out upon the plains. Railroad builders in Missouri and Iowa now had actual traffic to tap beyond the borders. Almost as soon as the territories were organized the legislatures of Kansas and Nebraska began chartering railway companies, designating routes, and petitioning Congress for land grants in aid. After January 31, 1861, Kansas had two United States Senators and a representative who participated most actively in congressional maneuverings.

In the autumn of 1858 gold was discovered on Cherry Creek, a branch of the South Fork of the Platte, in what was then part of Kansas Territory. The following spring a rush set in for the "Pike's Peak region" — Pike's Peak was ninety miles away — comparable to the rush to California in '49. The town of Denver sprang up. Soon long mule trains were carrying supplies across the prairies from St. Joseph, Leavenworth, and Independence. The Leavenworth and Pike's Peak Express was established by Jones, Russell, and Company. The Post Office Department had to establish a mail route. The settlers organized a government in the autumn for the "Territory of Jefferson" and applied to Congress for legalization. The people looked forward to early statehood. The expectation was not realized. Jefferson did not prove to be another California. Thousands of prospectors soon returned to the States. There was a residue, however. In February, 1861, Congress organized the Territory of Colorado. Congressmen could now say that whoever should build the Pacific railroad would want to go as near Denver as possible.[1]

In the summer of 1858, silver was discovered near Lake Tahoe at the western edge of the Great Basin in the present Nevada. Soon there was a rush from California and elsewhere to the "Washoe" mines. Carson City sprang up. Settlers petitioned for a territorial government and then for statehood. Congress organized the Territory of Nevada, March 2, 1861. Statehood came, prematurely, as it proved, in 1864.[2] The Mormon settlements about Salt Lake grew slowly and prospered. California continued to grow rapidly, and about three fourths of the population continued to be north of the latitude of San Francisco. These numerous developments on or near the central route to the Pacific gave that route claims to consideration on the score of prospective way traffic that no other route could rival.

Dramatic evidence of the attractions of the central route was the establishment thereon of the Pony Express, in April, 1860.[3] It was a strictly private venture of the Central Overland California and Pike's Peak Express Company, better known as Russell, Majors, and Waddell, although it seems to have been undertaken at the suggestion of Senator Gwin and may have been designed in part to demonstrate the feasibility

[1] L. R. Hafen, *The Overland Mail*, ch. vii; F. L. Paxson, *Hist. of the Am. Frontier*, 441-47.
[2] *Ibid.*, 449-51.
[3] Glenn B. Bradley, *The Story of the Pony Express*; W. L. Visscher, *The Pony Express*.

of the central route for a daily overland mail.[4] The terminal
points were St. Joseph and Sacramento. The Express carried
letters, on very thin paper, at the rate, originally, of $5.00
per half ounce for the entire distance. The service was weekly
at first but was made semiweekly in June. The time schedule
was ten days in summer and fifteen in winter; the schedule was
well kept to in the summer but not so well in winter. The
route was the emigrant road to Salt Lake, the mail route
thence to Carson City, and the route south of Lake Tahoe to
Placerville and Sacramento. The Pony Express, for all its
efficiency, did not prove a financial success.

The attractiveness of the northern route was also improved
but in lesser degree. Minnesota prospered and harbored many
railroad projects. Her admission to the Union, May 11, 1858,
gave her a freer hand to aid internal improvements and added
two able senators and a representative to the northern-route
contingent in Congress. The great Red River Valley was
already marked for land speculation on a large scale and
rapid occupation if only a railroad could be brought within
striking distance.[5] At the western end of the route, a portion
of the original Oregon Territory had been lopped off and
organized as Washington Territory, 1853. In 1859 a portion
of the remainder became the State of Oregon; and two more
senators and another representative were added to the ardent
little northern-route bloc in Congress.

By the late 1850's railroads and railroading were far different from what they had been when projects for a railroad
to the Pacific were young. It had now been well demonstrated
that railroads could carry great quantities of heavy freights for
long distances at rates far lower than had been foreseen. Companies were now building railroads hundreds of miles in
length. The gap between the Mississippi Valley and the Pacific
did not appear so formidable as formerly. The process of
consolidation also was well under way. Short end-to-end roads
were being pieced together into "trunks," and side roads were

[4] F. L. Paxson, *Hist. of the Am. Frontier*, 465-66; *Last Am. Frontier*, 182-85;
W. J. Ghent, *The Road to Oregon*, 194-99; L. R. Hafen, *op. cit.*, ch. viii.
[5] *Am. R. R. Jour.*, XXXI, 650, 712.

annexed thereto to form "systems." Great railroad systems were engaging each other and the waterways in "mighty rivalry." Powerful companies could bring great pressure upon Congress and legislatures. These great corporations wished to see one or more transcontinental railroads built; and several of them were interested in particular "first links" in the tier of states west of the Mississippi. Most of the railway systems and the more powerful of them lay north of the Ohio.

By the late 1850's some of the "links" in the states beyond the Mississippi were well beyond the paper stage. The first to span a state was the Hannibal and St. Joseph, completed February 22, 1859, just in time to make St. Joseph the chief jumping-off place in the Pike's Peak gold rush.[6] The road traversed a rich country, had benefited by a federal land grant and liberal state aid, and had been favored by enterprising management. Its eastern connections were as yet imperfect. Steamboats connected Hannibal with Quincy, Illinois, twelve miles up river. Before the end of the year the short Palmyra and Quincy was completed from Palmyra on the Hannibal and St. Joseph to the river opposite Quincy.[7] Quincy was a terminus of the Chicago, Burlington, and Quincy. The Northern Missouri Railroad from St. Louis intersected the Hannibal and St. Joseph at Macon. Early in 1861 a person could buy a through ticket in St. Louis for St. Joseph, Kansas City, Omaha, or Denver good on the Northern Missouri, Hannibal and St. Joseph, and connecting steamers and coaches.[8] The Pacific of Missouri had labored under greater difficulties than its neighbor. Its length was greater and the route more difficult. The company had agreed to use the federal land grant only in aid of the Southwest Branch, which ran toward Springfield. At the end of 1860 the Pacific still fell 114 miles short of Kansas City while only 47 miles of the branch were open to traffic.[9] (See the maps opposite pages 174 and 298.)

Several Iowa railroads were making steady progress west-

[6] *Ibid.,* XXXII, 359, XXXIII, 45.
[7] *Ibid.,* XXXII, 277, 722.
[8] *Ibid.,* XXXIV, 404.
[9] *Ibid.,* XXVIII, 115, XXIX, 465, XXXIII, 2.

ward toward the Missouri.[10] They were aided by federal land grants, finally secured in 1856, and some of them were assisted by strong companies in Illinois of whose lines they were extensions. The Burlington and Missouri was completed to Ottumwa, 93 miles, by September, 1859. There it halted for a time. A considerable portion of its stock was held by the Chicago, Burlington, and Quincy, which was destined to absorb it later (1872) and which was itself the product of recent consolidations.[11] The Mississippi and Missouri was open for 123 miles by January, 1861. It connected at Davenport over the Rock Island Bridge — first to span the Mississippi — with the Chicago and Rock Island, with which it was closely affiliated, the same men owning a controlling portion of the stock of each. The president was John A. Dix, of New York, a prominent Democratic politician, who did not hesitate to use his influence on behalf of the road.[12] A little farther north, the Chicago, Iowa, and Nebraska was completed from Clinton to Cedar Rapids, 80 miles. It was a continuation of the Chicago and Dixon Air Line. The latter was soon to be absorbed into the Chicago and Northwestern, as was eventually the Chicago, Iowa, and Nebraska also.[13] The Cedar Rapids and Missouri was organized, June, 1859, to continue the latter westward.[14] The Dubuque and Pacific or, after 1860, the Dubuque and Sioux City experienced unusual financial difficulties but extended about 80 miles by 1861. Its interests were identified with those of the Illinois Central and its affiliate, the Galena and Chicago Union.[15]

Railroad projects in Minnesota were given great impetus by a federal land grant in aid, secured March 3, 1857. The Legislature promptly conferred the lands upon three companies, two of which were building possible first links. The Minnesota and Pacific, later the St. Paul and Pacific, and event-

[10] There is a useful historical sketch of early Iowa railroads in the *Rept. of the Railroad Commission of Iowa* for 1893.
[11] *Am. R. R. Jour.*, XXIX, 260, 385, 593, XXX, 258, 485, XXIV, 2.
[12] *Ibid.*, XXXII, 675, XXXIII, 521, 772, XXXIV, 2; *Memoirs of John Adams Dix*, I, 306-10.
[13] *Am. R. R. Jour.*, XXXII, 407, 410, XXXIII, 719.
[14] *Ibid.*, XXXIII, 304, 719, 773, XXXIV, 484, XXXV, 469.
[15] *Ibid.*, XXIX, 276, XXXIII, 746, XXXIV, 2, 222.

ually the Northern Pacific, was authorized to build from Still-water on the eastern boundary via St. Paul and Minneapolis along the Stevens route to Breckenridge on the western boundary and thence on to the Missouri, with a branch to the extreme northwestern corner of the territory. William B. Ogden, of Chicago, was president. The Transit Company was to build from Winona across the southern end of the territory.[16] The companies were soon paralyzed by the Panic of 1857. Minnesota was determined to have railroads, however. In March, 1858, after a bitter contest, the Legislature voted $5,000,000 of bonds in their aid.[17] Prospects looked bright for eastern connections. In 1858 the Milwaukee and LaCrosse, shortly to become the Milwaukee and St. Paul and eventually the Chicago, Milwaukee, and St. Paul, was completed across Wisconsin. The same year the Detroit and Milwaukee was completed through Michigan, a branch of which was to connect at Sarnia with the Grand Trunk of Canada.[18] In 1859 William B. Ogden and others interested in the Minnesota and Pacific revived the defunct Chicago, St. Paul, and Fond du Lac as the Chicago and Northwestern and pushed it forward energetically in the direction of St. Paul.[19] Efforts were made to interest British capital in the Minnesota and Pacific by presenting a vision of a great chain of roads embracing the Grand Trunk, the Michigan and Wisconsin roads mentioned, and, from the corner of Minnesota, a road on Canadian soil to the Pacific along a route near the 50th parallel.[20] In spite of federal and state aid and promising connections, however, the Minnesota companies were unable to raise enough money to do more than a little grading before the Civil War.[21]

Arkansas struggled in vain to make any noteworthy headway on a link in a Pacific railroad. The most promising aspirant, the Memphis and Little Rock, beneficiary of a land grant and started with great fanfare, met one difficulty after

[16] *Ibid.*, XXX, 305, 346, 385.
[17] *Ibid.*, XXX, 443, 445, 469, 587, XXXI, 125, 160, 204, 265.
[18] *Ibid.*, XXIX, 105, XXXI, 633, 731, XXXIV, 89.
[19] *Ibid.*, XXVIII, 626, 700, XXXII, 389, 438.
[20] *Ibid.*, XXXI, 705, XXXIII, 511.
[21] *Ibid.*, XXXII, 862, XXXIII, 520, 550, 710, XXXIV, 515, 867.

another. A locomotive was run over the first section in 1857; and the Memphis *Bulletin* announced that its echoes "will not be stilled until the decree which civilization has proclaimed shall find its fulfilment on the shores of the far-off Pacific." The next year and the year following the section was over-flowed. About 38 miles were in operation when war came.[22] In 1859 the Arkansas Legislature permitted the Little Rock and Fort Smith Company to consolidate with the Memphis and Little Rock under the name the Central Pacific. No work was done between Little Rock and Fort Smith.[23] The Cairo and Fulton, another land-grant road, was begun in 1856 with the more or less active support of persons connected with the Illinois Central. The next year Missouri gave it some swamp lands and $650,000 of state bonds. The officers were able and energetic. About 26 miles were constructed before war inter-rupted.[24] Arkansas was too poor to build railroads. Con-struction would have to wait until developments in Texas or federal provision for a Southern Pacific should bring in outside capital.

Texas strove manfully to forward the great enterprise as well as other roads which would develop her vast internal resources. In 1854 the state had offered 16 sections of public land to its railroad companies for every mile of road built. When this offer failed to give the anticipated impetus to construction, the Legislature, August, 1856, offered to loan the state school fund to the companies at the rate of $6,000 per every mile completed in a workmanlike manner.[25]

One of the companies stirred into activity by this generous offer and by the manifest preference of the Buchanan admin-istration for the southern route was the Texas and Western, originally the Atlantic and Pacific, of New York. Since its

[22] *Ibid.*, XXIX, 819, XXX, 563, XXXI, 405, XXXII, 395, XXXIV, 330; *Ann. Rept. . . . of the Memphis and Little Rock R. R. Co.*, Feb. 20, 1860.
[23] *Am. R. R. Jour.*, XXXI, 248, 376, XXXII, 873.
[24] *Ibid.*, XXIX, 485, 723, 778, XXX, 197, 468, 492, 541, 632, XXXII, 210, 385, XXXIII, 176-79, XXXV, 10, 321.
[25] See above, 127; Austin *Tex. State Gaz.*, Apr. 14, 1855, Feb. 2, Apr. 5, July 12, 19, 26, Oct. 25, Nov. 22, 1856; *DeBow's Rev.*, XX, 640; *Am. R. R. Jour.*, XXIX, 601-02.

great fiasco of 1853-54,[26] the company had been moribund and had lost popularity. Now, rechristened the Southern Pacific, it resumed its highly speculative career.[27] In an effort to raise funds, it attempted to capitalize on Southern sectional feeling. On the condition, which was met, that Southern people subscribe $12,000,000 of the stock (only 5% to be paid in), the South was given a majority of the board of directors. A Mississippian, George S. Yerger became president, and the domicile was changed from New York to New Orleans. Stock subscriptions were made in Nashville, St. Louis, Memphis, Vicksburg, Natchez, Shreveport, New Orleans, and other Southern towns. An arrangement was made for connection with the Vicksburg, Shreveport, and Texas, of Louisiana. Speculators began to buy up lands along the route. The enterprise received favorable comment in the North.[28]

High hopes were soon dashed. The panic of '57 came. The new officers found the company saddled with debts of which they had not been informed in advance, and there was strong suspicion of fraud. In October, President Yerger and a portion of the directorate, probably acting in the interest of the trustees, executed a deed of trust for the road and all its franchises in order, it was alleged, to raise enough money to complete the first 20 miles by February 16, 1858, and save the charter, which otherwise would be forfeited under its terms. The company then proved unable, or at least failed, to repay the trustees, and the latter advertised the road to be sold at auction, June 1. It was bought for only $40,000 by a group of the stockholders, of whom L. T. Wigfall, shortly to be a United States senator, was most prominent. The purchasers, organized a "new" company.[29] Meanwhile certain stockholders of the "old" company refused to recognize the deed of trust and the sale as legal and reorganized with one Jeptha

<hr/>

[26] See above, 124-29.
[27] *Tex. State Gaz.*, Sept. 13, 1856, Nov. 14, 1857, May 29, 1858; *Am. R. R. Jour.*, XXX, 235-36, 320.
[28] *Ibid.*, XXX, 235-36, 292, 320, 340, 410, 417, 460, 718; *DeBow's Rev.*, XXII, 509-13.
[29] *Tex. State Gaz.*, Nov. 14, 1857, May 29, Je. 12, 1858; N. O. *Picayune*, May 16, 19, 1858; *Am. R. R. Jour.*, XXX, 796, XXXI, 27, 232, 314, 339, 706.

Fowlkes, of Tennessee, as president. Fowlkes sued for an injunction in a Texas court to prevent the new company from taking possession. Governor Runnels also took a hand and instituted suit for forfeiture of the charter on grounds of non-compliance with its terms.[30]

After much parleying, the old and the new companies effected a compromise out of court. Fowlkes became or remained president. The state's suit for forfeiture of the charter was successfully defended. Somehow Fowlkes raised money to pay the debts. Then J. Edgar Thompson, president of the Pennsylvania Railroad and one of the foremost railroad men in the country, was prevailed upon to accept the presidency, which Fowlkes voluntarily relinquished.[31] Apparently Thompson had reason to believe that Congress would provide aid for extending the Southern Pacific to California during the session then convened. When Congress failed to act, he resigned, August, 1860, and V. K. Stevenson, president of the Nashville and Chattanooga, took his place. With good management, the Southern Pacific began to make progress. Late in 1860 the company entered into encouraging negotiations with French capitalists.[32] Until the War came to interrupt, there was every prospect that the road would be built, slowly if Congress should continue to delay, rapidly if Congress should promptly vote aid for its extension to California. After the War the road was built as the Texas and Pacific.

The conservatively managed Vicksburg, Shreveport, and Texas, which was to connect with the Southern Pacific at the Texas line, was pushed slowly across Louisiana with state aid and a congressional land grant, secured in 1856. Some 54 miles were complete by 1861, and other sections were under construction.[33] Work had been begun also on the Memphis, El Paso, and Pacific. It started on the Red River in the extreme

[30] *Ibid.*, XXXI, 339; *Tex. State Gaz.*, May 29, Je. 5, 12, 19, July 3, Oct. 2, 1858; N. O. *Picayune*, May 11, 12, 13, 16, Je. 1, 10, 11, 13, 16, 26, 30, 1858; *DeBow's Rev.*, XXV, 584.
[31] *Ibid.*, XXV, 721, XXVII, 725; *Tex. State Gaz.*, Jan. 1, Feb. 12, 19, Aug. 6, 20, Sept. 24, Oct. 20, Nov. 12, Dec. 10, 1859; *Am. R. R. Jour.*, XXXI, 729, 811, 813, XXXII, 26, 362, 425, 660, 807-08, XXXIII, 66.
[32] *Ibid.*, XXXIII, 603, 637, 796, 869, 929, 1083, XXXIV, 283.
[33] *Ibid.*, XXX, 676, XXXI, 228, XXXII, 439, XXXIII, 93, XXXIV, 203.

northeast corner of Texas where the Cairo and Fulton was supposed to terminate and was designed to connect with the Southern Pacific at Dallas.[34]

Greater vitality was shown by several projects farther south than the Southern Pacific and the Vicksburg, Shreveport, and Texas and in a better settled region. The New Orleans, Opelousas, and Great Western, chartered in 1852, was built slowly with city and state aid. A federal land grant in 1856 gave impetus. By March, 1857, it had arrived at Berwick Bay, 80 miles, whence steamer connection with Galveston was established. A branch was projected to run from New Iberia, 125 miles west of New Orleans, to the Sabine in the direction of Houston, Texas.[35] Meanwhile the Texas Legislature had chartered the Sabine and Galveston Bay Railroad and Lumber Company, September, 1856, to carry on to Houston. Later this company, under the name Texas and New Orleans was empowered to build the Louisiana link to New Iberia. By January, 1861, the Texas section was completed, and part of the Louisiana section was under construction and part under contract. The whole road was expected to be completed by autumn.[36] As early as 1850 the Buffalo Bayou, Brazos, and Colorado had been chartered to run from the Bayou through Houston to Columbus on the Colorado, about 85 miles in the direction of San Antonio. Of this road 32 miles were in operation in 1861. The Columbus, San Antonio, and Rio Grande was chartered to continue the chain westward as indicated by its name.[37] The four roads just described eventually became sections of the main line of the post-war Southern Pacific.

The Houston and Texas Central, organized as early as 1848, was building northwestward from Houston. It was calculated to intercept any east and west road which might be

[34] Ibid., XXX, 410, 586, XXXIII, 188, XXXIV, 284; C. S. Potts, R. R. Transportation in Tex. (Bul. of the U. of Tex., No. 119), 33.
[35] Tex. State Gaz., Mar. 7, 1857; DeBow's Rev., XXIV, 332; Am. R. R. Jour., XXX, 145, 477, XXXII, 379, 841, XXXIII, 93.
[36] Ibid., XXX, 355, 477, XXXI, 827, XXXII, 379, XXXIII, 233, 505, 590, 673, 1037, XXXIV, 141, 361; Potts, op. cit., 27, 31; Tex. and N. O. R. R. Co., A Letter on the Sabine and Galveston Bay R. R. and Lumber Co. . . . (N. Y., 1859).
[37] Potts, op. cit., 27-29; Am. R. R. Jour., XXX, 477, XXXI, 827, XXXIII, 2.

built across Texas. About 80 miles had been built by the end of 1860. From Hempstead on this line the Washington County Railroad was completed, 20 miles, to Brenham, and the Austin Air Line had been chartered to connect Brenham and Austin. Austin also looked to the west with paper railroads.[38] The Houston Tap and Brazoria was being built from Houston to Wharton sixty odd miles to the southwest on the Colorado. It was almost completed when the War interrupted.[39] The Texas and Mexico Railroad Company was authorized by its charter to build from either Wharton or Corpus Christi across the lower Rio Grande and thence across Mexico to Mazatlan. A Mexican charter also was in existence for a road from the Rio Grande to Mazatlan.[40]

If the deplorable War for Southern Independence had not occurred, Texas would have become the scene of railroad building, land speculation, and settlement in the 1860's such as the South, or, indeed, any part of the Union, had never seen. It is highly probable that the first railroad to the Pacific would have been a continuation of one of the Texas lines, whether the federal government aided or not.

In California, also, the means were accumulating and the will was being displayed to do something in behalf of a Pacific railroad other than to petition Congress. The first railroad projects there were intended primarily for local purposes, but all were located to serve as "links" if opportunity should present.

The first California railroad to be started was the Sacramento Valley. It was to run eastward from Sacramento to Negro Bar on the American River and then turn north skirting the foothills. It would carry supplies to the mining camps from navigable water at Sacramento, and it could be "extended to the east into the mountains, so as to connect with any other rail or wagon road that may be under construction by the General Government, or by a responsible company."[41] The

[38] Ibid., XXXI, 827, XXXIII, 2, 395; Tex. State Gaz., Mar. 3, Apr. 21, 1860.
[39] Am. R. R. Jour., XXXI, 827, XXXIV, 2; Potts, op. cit., 30.
[40] Ibid., 28; Tex. State Gaz., Nov. 6, 13, 1858; Albert M. Lea, A Pac. Ry. (pamphlet, 1858); Am. R. R. Jour., XXXI, 827, XXXIII, 215, XXXIV, 370.
[41] Ibid., XXVIII, 109.

company was chartered in 1852, work was begun in 1855, and the road was opened to Folsom, 23 miles, in 1856.[42] "The construction of railroads on the Pacific coast cannot fail to exert a strong influence on promoting the construction of a great line spanning the continent," commented the *American Railroad Journal.*[43]

In 1857 the California Central Railroad Company was organized to build northward from Folsom to Marysville. This road was put under construction in 1859. Its promoters asserted that their road, while being built for another purpose, "as far as it goes occupies the route for the future railroad across the continent" — an assertion not justified by events.[44] The California Northern which was being constructed from Marysville northward through Oroville did become a section in the modern Western Pacific.[45] A company was organized also to construct a railroad from Benicia, at the north end of San Francisco Bay, to Sacramento. The four short roads just named when and if all were completed would give a continuous line of railway to the head of the Feather River Canyon, then considered in California to be the most practicable pass in the Sierras on the Central Route. Still another company, "The California Great Trunk of the Pacific and Atlantic Railroad Company," was organized, 1857, to build from San Francisco around the southern end of the Bay to Stockton and north to near Oroville.[46]

In the spring of 1859, after Congress had failed to agree upon a Pacific railroad bill, Californians determined to do something in the premises. The Legislature considered a bill to create a state improvement fund to aid in the construction of a railroad from San Francisco to the east boundary of the state, but failed to approve it.[47] The Legislature did, however, call a Pacific Railroad Convention to meet in Sacramento, September 20, "to promote the interests and insure the pro-

[42] *Ibid.,* XXVIII, 52, 109, 555, 596, XXIX, 73, XXXIII, 232, 813.
[43] XXIX, 73.
[44] *Am. R. R. Jour.,* XXXII, 706, XXXIII, 232, 813.
[45] *Ibid.,* XXXII, 706, 813.
[46] *Ibid.,* XXX, 828, XXXIII, 2, San Francisco *Herald,* May 15, 1859.
[47] *Ibid.,* Apr. 6, 21.

tection and security of the people of the States of California and Oregon and the territories of Washington and Arizona, and especially to consider the refusal of Congress to take efficient measures for the construction of a Railroad from the Atlantic States to the Pacific, and to adopt measures whereby the building of said Railroad can be accomplished. . . ." [48] An agitation was begun for the establishment of a steamship line to Japan and China. With such a line, said the San Francisco *Herald*, "nearly the whole Chinese and Japanese trades will fall into our hands"; that in turn would constitute one of the greatest arguments in favor of a transcontinental railway.[49] In the summer of 1859 subscriptions were sought to the stock of a company to build a line of telegraph from San Francisco to Salt Lake by way of Placerville.[50] Another company, the Pacific and Atlantic Telegraph Company, was building a telegraph southeastward along the route of the Overland Mail.[51] Great interest was manifested in a Russian project for building a telegraph to New York across Siberia, Bering Sea, and North America.[52]

The Pacific Railroad Convention met in Sacramento in September, 1859. Delegates were present from south California, Oregon, and Washington Territory, but those from north California predominated. The sessions lasted five days.[53]

The lengthiest debates were upon routes. The convention finally recommended one Pacific railroad by the central route, "without reference to any particular pass" in the Sierra Nevada, with two branches, one terminating at San Francisco, the other on the Columbia River or Puget Sound. The handful of delegates from southern California bitterly opposed the endorsement of the central route and, when they were defeated, withdrew from the convention.[54] A meeting held later

48 *Ibid.*, Sept. 19.
49 *Ibid.*, May 18, 19, Aug. 12, 28.
50 *Ibid.*, Aug. 9.
51 *Ibid.*, Sept. 28, 1859, Jan. 30, 1860.
52 *Ibid.*, Aug. 9, Oct. 31, 1859.
53 Proceedings in *ibid.*, Sept. 21-25; brief notice, *Am. R. R. Jour.*, XXXII, 705.
54 San Francisco *Herald*, Sept. 25, Oct. 1, 1859.

in Washington Territory to review the work of the Sacramento Convention refused to endorse its action in regard to routes and declared in favor of two roads, a northern and a southern.[55] The committee that the convention appointed to address the people in its behalf concisely summarized the considerations which had induced the recommendation of the central route. Although the 32d-degree route, it said, presented fewer engineering difficulties, congressional aid was more likely for the central. Of $961,074,000 invested in railroads in the United States, $818,817,000 were invested in northern roads, including those of Missouri. Even if Congress should render no aid, the great northern railroad interests would eventually push a line up the valley of the Kansas or the Platte. A road from San Francisco to Fort Yuma, where the 32nd-parallel route intersected the California boundary, would be as long as one to Salt Lake.[56] The *American Railroad Journal* understood the situation; the convention did not endorse the southern route because a road thereby might stop for some time at Los Angeles.[57] Even in San Francisco there were people, perhaps influenced by sympathy with the South, who believed endorsement of the central route to have been unwise.[58]

The convention was quite specific in its proposals with regard to procedure. It requested the legislatures of California, Oregon, and Washington Territory to cause accurate surveys of routes and estimates of costs to be made. It asked the legislatures of the two states to establish internal improvement funds which should include swamp and overflowed lands and other lands which might be donated to the states and all revenue from internal improvements which might be constructed; to authorize counties to vote aid to the road; and, in case of California, to authorize the contraction of a $15,000,000 state debt in behalf of the railroad. It recommended that the constitution of California be amended to

[55] *Ibid.*, Dec. 30.
[56] *Pac. R. R. Conv., Address to the People of the States and Territories on the Pacific*, 14-16.
[57] XXXIII, 705.
[58] San Francisco *Herald*, Sept. 25, 26, 28, 30, 1859.

permit the state to subscribe to the stock of railroad companies. It requested Congress to make a grant of lands to California in aid of her branch, to guarantee the interest on the bonds of a company which would build the section of the railroad lying in territories, and to remit the duties on railroad iron imported for the road. The convention appointed a permanent executive committee of 35 to prepare memorials and to secure subscriptions of stock with a view to the organization of a company in each state.

The executive committee of the convention took its duties seriously. It sent one of its members, T. D. Judah, who had been chief engineer of the Sacramento Valley Railroad, to Washington to further the views of the convention among congressmen. He seems to have had some success.[59] The $15,000,000 debt proposal was not cordially received in California.[60] In February, 1860, the Pacific Railroad Convention reassembled at Sacramento with members of the California Legislature listening in.[61] The $15,000,000 proposal was the principal subject of discussion. It was again approved although there was stronger opposition in the convention. Governor Latham had refused to recommend it to the Legislature, and that body did not adopt it.[62] Apparently the general public was less inclined to assume bonded indebtedness than were the Pacific railroad enthusiasts of northern California.

[59] Ibid., Oct. 26, Nov. 10, Dec. 30, 1859, Feb. 10, 1860; Stuart Daggett, Chapters on the Hist. of the So. Pac., 5-6.
[60] San Francisco Herald, Sept. 25, 30, Oct. 29, Nov. 4, 10, 11, 18, Dec. 30, 1859.
[61] Ibid., Feb. 7-10, 12, 21, 1860.
[62] Ibid., Jan. 8, 11.

# CHAPTER XVIII

# THE PACIFIC RAILROAD STRUGGLE IN THE SHADOW OF SECESSION

THERE was probably no good reason to believe that the 36th Congress, 1859-61, would be any more successful than its predecessors in breaking the deadlock over Pacific railway legislation. The principal novelty in the situation was that the Republicans were in complete control of the House. Inasmuch as the party was pledged to render "immediate and efficient" aid to a railroad by the "most central and practicable" route and, "as auxiliary thereto," the immediate construction of an emigrant road on the line of the railroad, and inasmuch as 1860 was a presidential election year, the Republican House might reasonably be expected to pass bills for political purposes at least.

President Buchanan, perhaps rather for the purpose of keeping his own record clear than with the expectation that his advice would be heeded, devoted a short paragraph to the Pacific railroad in his annual message, reiterating his views.[1] On the vexed question of routes, he maintained a discreet silence. On the subject of overland mails he said nothing. The mails proved to be the subject of the most intricate haggling between sections and localities.

The Congress which adjourned March 4, 1859, had failed to pass the regular Post Office appropriation bill for the fiscal year ending June 30, 1860. President Buchanan did not choose to call a special session of the new Congress.[2] Postmaster General Joseph Holt accordingly found it desirable to keep expenditures within receipts or nearly so. He proceeded to cut the extravagant cost, as he considered it, of the Pacific mails. The contract for carrying the semimonthly New York-

[1] Richardson, *Messages*, V, 572-73.
[2] *Ibid.*, 572.

San Francisco mail via Panama for $738,250 per annum ex-
pired October 1. Holt let a nine-months contract to Cornelius
Vanderbilt at the rate of $351,000 per year for a semi-
monthly mail via Panama or for $50,000 less if the Commo-
dore should succeed in reopening the Nicaragua transit. He
refused to renew the temporary contract for the Tehuantepec
route. He discontinued the San Antonio-El Paso-San Diego
service where it covered a portion of the Butterfield route and
reduced it from a weekly to a semimonthly one on the remainder. He discontinued services between Neosho, Missouri, and
Albuquerque and between Independence and Stockton via
Albuquerque altogether. He reduced the St. Joseph-Placer-
ville service from a weekly to a semimonthly. He was dissuaded from reducing service on the Butterfield route only by
an opinion of Attorney General Black that the contract would
not permit him to do so. By his various retrenchments and
reductions Holt reduced the cost of the Pacific coast mails from
$2,184,697 to $1,276,000.[3]

In his annual report of December, 1859, the Postmaster
General requested authority to discontinue the Butterfield contract. He declared roundly that "until a railroad shall have
been constructed across the continent the conveyance of the
Pacific mails overland must be regarded as wholly impracticable." He conceded that certain great national political and
commercial objects might be advanced by subsidies but thought,
not unreasonably, that, if Congress desired to subsidize, it
should do so by direct appropriation from the treasury and
not by a deficiency appropriation for the Post Office Department.[4]

Californians complained strongly of Holt's retrenchments.[5]
In fact the success of the Butterfield Company in carrying a
semiweekly mail in less than twenty-two days had only whetted
their appetite for improved postal facilities. They were, of

[3] Ann. Rept., in *Cong. Globe*, 36 Cong., I Sess., App., 22-23, 26-27; Holt's
letter to Sen. Latham and his correspondence with the Attorney General, quoted
in *ibid.*, 2458-59; letters of Buchanan to Holt, May 28, July 6, 16, 1859, *Joseph
H. Holt Papers* (Lib. of Cong.).
[4] *Cong. Globe*, 36 Cong., I Sess., App., 23, 26.
[5] San Francisco *Herald*, May 9, 10, Oct. 11, 1859, Jan. 25, 30, 1860.

course, not animated solely by a desire for quicker and more frequent news from the old states.

Governor Latham advised the California Legislature, January 1, 1860, to request Congress to establish a daily overland mail and discontinue all other mail contracts. The passage of a daily mail, he said, would make the route the common highway of immigration because of the protection which would be afforded on its account and because of the settlements which would spring up along the way. Such a highway would soon relieve the state of the "greatest blight to her prosperity — the want of a large permanent population." More than that, "it would — sooner than all other efforts now used, combined — bring about the much longed-for . . . building of the Great Atlantic and Pacific Railway." Latham would leave the selection of the route to the contractors.[6] The Legislature acted in accord with the Governor's suggestion and also elected him to the United States Senate.

In Washington, the entire Pacific coast delegation caucused and, taking into account existing mail contracts and local and sectional interests and jealousies, agreed upon a set of demands.[7] They were in brief: (1) changing the terminus of the Butterfield route from St. Louis and Memphis to Vicksburg or New Orleans and the service from semiweekly to triweekly; (2) a triweekly letter mail from St. Joseph to Placerville in not more than 18 days; (3) a weekly letter mail from St. Paul and Superior to Oregon; (4) a six-days-a-week mail from San Francisco to Portland; (5) a thrice-a-month steamer mail, which would include all printed matter, in not over 21 days. With proper dovetailing of times of departures, this scheme would have given California an overland letter mail six days a week.

The Republican House of Representatives under the leadership of Schuyler Colfax, of Indiana, chairman of the Committee on Post Offices and Post Roads, disregarding the Pacific coast plan, rushed through a bill requiring the Postmaster General to advertise for bids for the carrying of the entire

[6] *Ibid.*, Jan. 11, 1860.
[7] *Cong. Globe*, 36 Cong., 1 Sess., 2458.

Pacific mails upon one line, either overland or isthmian. The contractor was to be free to select his own route; and the bids were to be laid before Congress. While not openly avowed, it was the evident intention to secure a daily overland mail on the central route. The bill was opposed, therefore, by all those whose localities or interests might be better served by the Butterfield or other route.[8]

In the Senate the Democrats were in a majority. There was not such a preponderant sentiment for the central route. Agents of the Pacific steamship companies and the various contractors were in the lobby.[9] The Committee on Post Offices and Post Roads could not agree. The Republicans were out to annul the Butterfield contract; they had never forgiven the administration for the maneuver by which it had been instituted. Finally as a way out of an impasse a majority of the committee authorized Gwin to report a bill, May 10, for the carriage of mail of all classes from St. Joseph to Placerville semiweekly in 20 days. The intention was to have this bill passed separately and then give other routes further consideration. The plan failed. Sponsors of the other routes were unwilling to vote for the bill and thereby lose their bargaining power.[10]

On May 24, Gwin, for a majority of the committee, reported the House bill with a substitute. It provided for a semiweekly letter mail on each of the three overland routes, northern, southern, and central. The Butterfield service between Memphis and Fort Smith, Arkansas, was transferred to San Antonio-El Paso, giving thus, with routes already established between San Antonio and New Orleans,[11] a semiweekly mail between New Orleans and San Francisco. The St. Louis terminus of the Butterfield route was not disturbed. The act was not to go into effect unless the Postmaster General could contract for the transportation of the printed matter and franked documents by the isthmus for not more than $150,000.

[8] *Ibid.*, 1065, 1131.
[9] *Ibid.*, 3148, 3154, 3233; San Francisco *Herald*, Aug. 31, Sept. 8, 1860.
[10] *Ibid.*, Aug. 31; *Cong. Globe*, 36 Cong., 1 Sess., 1628, 1647-49, 2029.
[11] See above, 225.

This last provision bade fair to render the whole act futile. Hale, of New Hampshire, apparently on behalf of the Republican members, offered a substitute providing for a daily mail on the central route, a weekly mail on the northern, and a thrice-weekly mail from New Orleans to San Francisco. It would leave the Butterfield Company operating only between El Paso and San Francisco if the company would accept the change, otherwise not at all. St. Louis would, of course, lose its southern connection. Latham, of California, complicated matters further by offering a substitute embodying the proposals agreed upon in the caucus of the Pacific coast members.[12]

With such diverse counsels prevailing among the friends of overland mails, all these measures fell to the ground. The senators from Missouri, Arkansas, and Texas would not vote for any bill which would abandon the St. Louis and Memphis to El Paso route. The Republicans generally would vote for no bill which left it intact. The Missouri senators contended that a St. Joseph terminus for the central route was equivalent to a Chicago terminus, although Polk was almost won over by the offer of a Kansas City branch.

When the regular appropriation bill for the Post Office Department came up in the House, the Republicans added an amendment prohibiting payment in excess of the postages for transportation of mails by an isthmian route.[13] The obvious intent was to force the Postmaster General to send all the mails overland. The Senate accepted the provision without particular comment,[14] and President Buchanan signed the bill. Postmaster General Holt promptly protested. The steamship companies would not carry the mails for the postages, he said, and it was impracticable to send twenty or thirty tons of mail overland monthly. He asked for corrective legislation.[15] In the Senate a reasonable compromise was worked out. The Republicans gave way in the matter of the Butterfield route and contract and they were unmodified. The Postmaster Gen-

[12] Cong. Globe, 36 Cong., 1 Sess., 2338, 2339, 2458, 3146, 3152, 3157, 3194; San Francisco Herald, Aug. 31 (Gwin's account), Sept. 8, 11, 1860.
[13] Cong. Globe, 36 Cong., 1 Sess., 2842.
[14] Ibid., 2979, 3234, 3236.
[15] Ibid., 3232 (letter to Sen. Yulee).

erál was directed to contract with the lowest responsible bidder
for a daily mail of all classes on the central route between St.
Louis and San Francisco in not more than 20 days, service to
commence July 1, 1861. Meanwhile he might provide a temporary service by the isthmus for not over $350,000 per annum.
There was to be a weekly mail on the northern route. The
entire cost was put upon the treasury as the Postmaster General had requested.[16] The Senate bill went to the House in the
closing rush of the session, and that body refused to consider
it.[17]

The whole matter was thus left in status quo except that the
compensation for carrying mails by isthmian routes could not
exceed the postages. Nobody was satisfied with the outcome.
Senator Gwin went to President Buchanan and persuaded him
to restore weekly service on portions of the St. Joseph-Placer-
ville route but failed in his effort to get the time reduced.
Cornelius Vanderbilt consented to carry the isthmian mail for
the postages until March 4, 1861, on the express assurance of
the President that he would recommend to Congress to make
further allowance. The Postmaster General improved the
service between New Orleans and El Paso somewhat.[18]

Proceedings with regard to Pacific railroads were in character. It was not until March 9, 1860, that a select committee
on a Pacific railroad was appointed in the House. Samuel R.
Curtis, of Iowa, was made chairman. On April 13, he brought
in a report and a bill which had the approval of a majority of
the committee. Aldrich, of Minnesota, and Hamilton, of
Texas, presented separate reports, and three members could
not agree with either report.[19]

The Curtis bill provided for one line of railroad and telegraph to San Francisco with two short branches or prongs at
the eastern end, one starting on the western border of Missouri, and the other on the western boundary of Iowa, the

16 *Ibid.*, 3232, 3242, 3292; San Francisco *Herald*, Aug. 31, 1860.
17 *Cong. Globe*, 36 Cong., 1 Sess., 3302.
18 Holt's Ann. Rept., Dec., 1860, *Cong. Globe*, 36 Cong., 2 Sess., App., 13-14;
San Francisco *Herald*, Aug. 31, 1860.
19 *H. Repts.*, 36 Cong., 1 Sess., III (1069), No. 428; Chicago *Press and Tribune*, Apr. 19, 27, 1860.

precise spots not being designated, and uniting to form the
main trunk not more than 200 miles from the Missouri River.
The road was to run "by the vicinity of Great Salt Lake."
Subject to these restrictions only, the company was to select
the route. Forty-five persons were named in the bill who with
their associates were to form the company. The bill offered
in aid one alternate section of land per mile and a loan of
30-year, 5% bonds to a amount not greater than $60,000,000.
The loan was to be secured by a first mortgage on the road and
repaid only in services, that is, the transportation of mails,
troops, and supplies. It was estimated that about $60,000,000
of private funds in addition would be required to build the
road. This plan of financing foreshadowed the plan eventually
adopted and showed that speculative investors were finally
beginning to gather about the flesh pots.

Curtis and others stated quite frankly the considerations
which had shaped the bill. The committee had considered three
roads and two roads but had decided the House would not vote
for more than one. A road by a central route would accommodate more people at either end than any other. It offered
possibilities of way traffic that no other did. With a thousand
people a day going to the gold diggings about Denver, the
company would want to build as near that point as practicable.
There were forty thousand people about Salt Lake. The
Washoe mines were on the same parallel. The two branches
at the eastern end were necessary to reconcile divergent interests. The eastern termini were not more precisely designated, for, if they were, said Curtis, "some individuals on the
frontier would not be sure they had got the Pacific railroad."
Iowa and Missouri were given equal opportunities to have the
main trunk, he said; the Platte Valley route had some advantages in practicability, on the other hand, the Kaw Valley ran
directly to Denver.[20]

Hamilton, of Texas, in his minority report, proposed that
Congress, in addition to providing for a central road, should
aid the Southern Pacific Railroad Company, of Texas, to

[20] *Cong. Globe*, 36 Cong., 1 Sess., 2330-33; *H. Repts.*, 36 Cong., 1 Sess., III
(1069), No. 428, p. 3 and *passim*.

extend its line to San Francisco via El Paso and Fort Yuma and provide a branch from Fort Smith, Arkansas, to some point in Texas. Hamilton argued forcefully that both roads were necessary. The central road would "no more meet the wants of the southwest for development than the southern railroad would answer to develop the latent energies and wealth of Utah, Nevada, and Jefferson." The railroad systems of the South demanded extension along a southern route to the Pacific just as Northern systems demanded extension along a central route. The proposition to push forward one of these main lines and not the other was "immensely unwise under the circumstances by which the Congress is now [April, 1860] surrounded," and its adoption might "impress the public mind painfully with an idea that the domination of a sectional representation has begun already to become oppressive. . . ." [21] In debate Hamilton was still more outspoken. He charged that the majority bill was designed not so much to effect military and commercial objects as to give "supremacy to one section of the country to the detriment and injury of the other." The House majority had passed the Morrill Tariff bill, a homestead bill, and had refused to let the President use troops to protect American interests in northern Mexico. If, in addition, Congress should pass the majority railroad bill, he for one would favor secession. [22]

In reply to Hamilton's arguments and reproaches, the Republicans could say little except that the country could not afford two roads and the attempt to aid two would defeat the construction of any. Unfortunately for the effectiveness of Southern arguments and threats, far too many Southern congressmen were disinclined to vote aid for any Pacific railroad whatever.

The small contingent which preferred a road by the Stevens route adopted their usual tactics of demanding provision for three roads. Phelps and Noell, of Missouri, put in their oar for the thirty-fifth parallel route. Several Democratic members thought provision for more branches would strengthen

[21] *Ibid.*, 29-43.
[22] *Cong. Globe*, 36 Cong., 1 Sess., 2445-48.

the bill. There were objections to the plan for financing the construction of the railroad.

Eventually those who favored Pacific railway legislation but disliked features of the Curtis bill united with the opponents of aid to any railroad to recommit the bill.[23] The select committee now accepted Hamilton's amendment for a southern road and made minor changes in detail. A short while before the close of the session, Curtis reported the bill with the proposed changes and had consideration postponed to the short session.[24]

The vote by which the bill had been recommitted was 101 to 87. Twenty-one Republicans united with 80 Democrats and Americans to carry the motion. Outside the Missouri and California delegations, only 6 Democrats voted against recommital. Northern Democrats favorable to a Pacific railroad obviously were disinclined to offend their Southern colleagues. It is evident that, had the Republicans been reasonably well united, they could have passed the original Curtis bill with the aid of those Western Democrats who supported it because of advantages it promised to their localities. It is just as evident that the original Curtis bill would not have been acceptable to the Democratic Senate or to President Buchanan. The precise motives of the 21 Republicans who voted to recommit the bill are not discernible except in the cases of several strong partisans of the northern route. It would appear from the spirit shown in the debates on the railroad and other questions of the day that a disinclination to antagonize the South was not one of them. Had the Republicans consented, a bill for two roads could have been passed in both houses and in all probability would have been signed by Buchanan. Such a measure might have allayed to some extent the dangerous sectional feeling in the South. However, when a large majority of Southern Democrats would vote for no Pacific railroad bill of any sort, it was too much to expect that Northern Republicans would vote the South a road merely as an act of justice or good will.

[23] *Ibid.*, 2452.
[24] *Ibid.*, 2982; *H. Repts.*, 36 Cong., 1 Sess., III (1069), No. 428, p. 66.

One measure only to facilitate communication with the Pacific coast negotiated successfully the passage perilous through the first session of the Thirty-Sixth Congress. That was a bill to extend a modicum of aid in the construction of a transcontinental telegraph, approved June 16, 1860. The Legislature of California had offered a bonus of $60,000 to the parties first completing such a line.[25] St. Joseph already had telegraphic communication with St. Louis and thence with all points east and was a logical starting point. A line was being built from St. Louis southwestward along the Overland Mail route. In California a line had been extended from San Francisco to Carson City and another from San Francisco southeastward along the mail route.[26] The act of Congress instructed the Secretary of the Treasury to contract with the lowest responsibile bidder to transmit government messages between San Francisco and some point or points on the western boundary of Missouri for ten years at not more than $40,000 per annum. The line must be completed before July 31, 1862. The contractors were allowed to use the public lands. Some congressmen thought that even the location of the telegraph line might influence the choice of a route for a Pacific railroad, and there was considerable sparring over the designation of the initial point at the eastern end, especially between repre- sentatives of St. Louis and St. Joseph.[27] The company chose to start at neither St. Joseph nor St. Louis but at Omaha. The route was the Oregon Trail to Fort Bridger and thence via Salt Lake. The line was completed October 26, 1861, to the great joy of the Californians.[28]

Before the long session of Congress adjourned, June 28, 1860, the last of the national party conventions had been held. Both factions of the divided Democratic party pledged aid to a Pacific railroad; the Douglas wing offered "such Constitu- tional Government aid" as would insure its construction at the

[25] *Cong. Globe*, 36 Cong., 1 Sess., 2857, 3039.
[26] *Ibid.*, 2249, 2251-52; San Francisco *Herald*, Aug. 9, Sept. 28, Nov. 3, 1859, Jan. 16, 30, 1860.
[27] *Cong. Globe*, 36 Cong., 1 Sess., 1693, 2251-52, 2279-81.
[28] *Cong. Globe*, 37 Cong., 2 Sess., 6; F. A. Root and W. E. Connelley, *The Overland Stage to California*, 133-38.

"earliest practicable period," the Breckinridge wing promised aid to the extent of "the constitutional authority of Congress." The Republicans without paying respects to the Constitution resolved, "That a railroad to the Pacific Ocean is imperatively demanded by the interests of the whole country; that the federal government ought to render immediate and efficient aid in its construction; and that, as a preliminary thereto, a daily overland mail should be promptly established." This was essentially the plank of 1856 with specific endorsement of the central route omitted.[29]

The slavery question and threatened secession overshadowed all other issues during the campaign of 1860; but it would seem that primarily economic issues turned enough votes to the Republicans in some of the doubtful states to insure Lincoln's election. The promise of a protective tariff was most effective in Pennsylvania. The proffer of free homesteads to actual settlers appealed strongly in the Northwest.[30] The unequivocal plank on the railroad and daily overland mail probably gave the margin of victory in California.[31]

In the short session of Congress between Lincoln's election and inauguration the all-absorbing topic was how to save the Union. But time was found to consider the Pacific railroad and overland mails. In fact these matters were not unrelated to saving the Union.

On December 18, the Curtis bill as amended to provide for a southern road as well as a central came up as the special order in the House. It was evident that it commanded the support of a majority, and the majority proceeded to push it through virtually without discussion or opportunity for proposal of amendments. It was passed on the very day South Carolina seceded; the vote stood 94 to 72.[32] Of the Republicans 67 either voted for the bill or were paired in its favor, and 18 voted against it. Of those voting nay, several were

---

[29] Kirk H. Porter, *National Party Platforms*, 53-58.

[30] Wm. E. Dodd, "The Southern Struggle for the Northwest," *Am. Hist. Rev.*, XVI, 774.

[31] *Cong. Globe*, 36 Cong., 2 Sess., 619, 1111 (interpretations of Scott and Latham, of California).

[32] Proceedings in *ibid.*, 125-31, 162-71. John P. Davis, *The Union Pacific Railway*, 92-94, describes the tactics employed.

partisans of the northern route. Nine Republicans supported the bill who in the long session had seemed to be opposed to the original Curtis bill providing for only a central road; only ten opposed the bill who had formerly supported the original one-road bill. Of the Democrats and Americans, 35 supported the bill, while 63 either voted nay or were paired against it; 16 supported the bill with the provision for a southern road included who had opposed it when it provided only for the central road. It is noteworthy that only 10 representatives from the South, exclusive of Missouri, voted for the bill upon its passage, and of these only one was from a Gulf state.

The willingness of so many Republican congressmen (about 60) to vote aid to a road by the southern route in December who in the previous May had seemed so determined to provide for only a road by the central route is rather remarkable. In most cases probably they were influenced by the very practical consideration that, if they were to enact a bill, they must win over some Democratic votes. Members must also have seen the utter folly of pressing a measure so unfair to the South as the original Curtis bill at a time when one state was in the very act of seceding and there was grave danger that others would follow. Some of them must have hoped that a manifestation of fairness or liberality at this time might allay sectional feeling.

The Pacific railroad bill, having passed the House, was promptly taken up in the Senate. No less than seven days of this short and critical session were devoted principally to it. Seward spoke first and hailed the provision for a Southern road as a "great measure of conciliation, of pacification, of compromise, and of union." He was prepared to grant a road to the South at once, he said, "as their right, as their due, as equal and just, and as only an equivalent" for what the bill gave the North.[33] Seward's pronouncement did not secure smooth sailing for the bill. Savage attacks were made upon it by Rice and Wilkinson, of Minnesota, who wanted provision for the northern route, and by Joe Lane, of Oregon, who also

[33] *Cong. Globe*, 36 Cong., 2 Sess., 250-51.

wanted that or, at least, a branch to Oregon. Rice complained
bitterly of the disposition already shown in the House and
now by "high authority" in the Senate to give the South a
railroad while neglecting the Northwest. He thought it remarkable that Seward supposed the passage of the bill would
save the Union.[34]   Polk and Green, of Missouri, objected to
the provision which permitted the company to start the Missouri branch anywhere on the western boundary of the state.
They wanted Kansas City designated as the terminus. If that
were not done, they feared, the road would go to St. Joseph
to the disadvantage of St. Louis and the Pacific Railroad Company of Missouri. Polk contended that the names of the incor-
porators in the bill indicated the selection of St. Joseph unless
Kansas City were specifically named.[35]

Gwin, Latham, Seward, and others asked that all proposed
amendments be rejected. Amendments would kill the bill, they
said, for the House would not accept them. But the majority
refused to heed. First came Polk's amendment to terminate
the Missouri branch at Kansas City. It was supported by
senators from localities interested in roads pointing toward
St. Louis, senators who wished to conciliate the border slave
state of Missouri in view of the political crisis, senators who
had amendments of their own to offer, and senators who hoped
to defeat the bill altogether.[36]   Lane succeeded in getting a
land grant in aid of a branch from Sacramento to Portland.[37]
Finally the persistent Minnesota senators got their amendment for a road from Lake Superior to Puget Sound with a
branch to Oregon. In aid there were offered 12 alternate
sections of land in the states and 20 in the territories and a
loan of bonds not to exceed $25,000,000 in amount. This
amendment was adopted by the close vote of 22 to 19.[38]   A
motion of Grimes, Iowa, to strike out provision for both the
northern and southern roads leaving only the central was
defeated 22 to 25.[39]   Wilson, Massachusetts, tried ineffectually

[34] *Ibid.*, 251.
[35] *Ibid.*, 252, 253, 259.
[36] *Ibid.*, 252-59.
[37] *Ibid.*, 427, 521.
[38] *Ibid.*, 611-13.
[39] *Ibid.*, 613.

to get the aid offered for the southern road cut down to the same amount as for the northern. Then the bill as amended was adopted by the large vote of 37 to 14.[40]

Sixteen Republican senators voted for Wilkinson's amendment putting in the northern road and then turned right about and voted for Grimes's amendment to strike out all but the central road. Clearly, as, indeed, some of them avowed, these men were unwilling to aid a southern road unless two northern roads were added at the same time and a loan of $36,000,000 was offset by loans amounting to $85,000,000. Seward and Dixon, of Connecticut, were the only Republicans who stood firmly for the bill as it came from the House. The votes were taken after the senators of six cotton states had withdrawn from the Senate and their states had seceded. Whether or not the Republican senators would have been more conciliatory toward the South if the votes could have been taken before the six states seceded can only be conjectured. It is certain that if the votes had been taken before the withdrawal of the twelve senators, Wilkinson's amendment would have been defeated; Republican senators would have had to choose between a two-road bill and none at all. In that case, in all probability, enough of them would have voted for the bill to ensure its passage, and it would have become law. Of the Democrats only Gwin and Polk voted for Grimes's motion to strike out provision for the other roads and leave only the central. Latham explained his vote against it: ". . . the people of the state that I represent want a road, and not roads; and the only reason why, heretofore, I have advocated the establishment of two roads . . . is that it better reconciled all conflicting interests than any other scheme which could possibly be proposed." [41]

When the Pacific railroad bill as amended returned to the House, Curtis urged concurrence in the Senate's amendments as the only way to save it so late in such a busy session. The House, however, accepted an amendment offered by Craig, of Missouri, providing for a branch from St. Joseph connecting with

[40] *Ibid.*, 638.
[41] *Ibid.*, 613.

the branch from Kansas City. After that there was little hope of securing agreement between the two houses, and all efforts to that end were abandoned.[42] It was just as well; with seven states out of the Union and the secession of four others and civil war impending, provision for a southern road would have been futile even as a gesture of conciliation and the times were inauspicious for starting either of the other roads.

If at any time during six or seven years prior to secession Southern congressmen in general had been as willing to vote federal aid for Pacific railroads as were Northern congressmen in general, two railroads would have been provided for and their construction begun. Such an event might to a degree have allayed the passions of sectional controversy. But too many Southerners were obsessed with the idea that the South paid more than its share of the federal taxes and, therefore, would have to help pay for the northern road. Too many believed that, if there were two roads, the northern one would get the greater share of the traffic and the North would reap the greater benefits. Too many feared that, if the constitution were construed liberally enough to permit federal aid, such construction would somehow weaken the constitutional position of the section with regard to slavery. It is one of the ironies of history that it was largely this dog-in-the-manger attitude of the South with regard to the Pacific railroad and other measures which Northerners had come to look upon as essential to the economic development of their section that ensured the Republican victory in 1860 which, in turn, was the occasion for secession, war, and the destruction of slavery.

The proceedings of the Short Session with regard to Pacific Coast mails closely paralleled those on the railroad. When the session opened, the House had before it a bill which had come from the Senate in the closing hours of the long session.[43] The bill directed the Postmaster General to contract with the lowest responsible bidder for a daily mail of all classes over the central route between St. Louis and San Francisco in not more than 20 days. Until this service should be established,

[42] *Ibid.*, 877-82, 908.
[43] Above, 281.

the Postmaster General might contract for a temporary isthmian service at not more than $350,000 per year. The bill also provided for a weekly mail from St. Paul and Superior to the Dalles and left the much-controverted Butterfield service undisturbed. The House modified the provision for a daily mail on the central route, substituting a St. Joseph for a St. Louis terminus, struck out the northern route altogether, and on motion of Hamilton, of Texas, added a semiweekly mail between New Orleans and a point on the Butterfield route, thus providing a semiweekly mail between New Orleans and San Francisco.[44] Members interested in the northern route again complained of the disposition of the House to do almost anything for the Southwest but nothing for the Northwest.[45] Clearly the House was trying to conciliate the South in matters of appropriations. A few days earlier it had passed an appropriation for a regiment of mounted volunteers to defend the frontier of Texas. Hamilton promised to tell the people of his state that they had been well treated and should remain in the Union.[46]

Before the Senate could act upon the House amendments to its Post Routes bill, all the cotton states including Texas had seceded and the Butterfield mails had been interrupted. Nevertheless the Senate concurred in the House amendments, but with the understanding that supplemental legislation would be put in the regular Post Office appropriation bill.[47] When the latter appeared, the Senate adopted a proposal of Wilson, of Massachusetts, which achieved about what the Republicans had been contending for for several years. The Postmaster General was directed to discontinue service on the southern, "ox-bow" route and to require the Butterfield Company to carry the entire letter mail by the central route between some point on the Missouri River having Eastern connections and Placerville, California. The service should be six days a week and the time not over 20 days for eight months in the year

[44] *Cong. Globe*, 36 Cong., 2 Sess., 547-50, 618-20, 647-48, 671.
[45] *Ibid.*, 647-48.
[46] *Ibid.*, 462, 548.
[47] *Ibid.*, 1109-12, 1126-30, 1208-11.

and not over 23 days during the other four. The company was to be required also to carry the printed matter either overland on a less frequent and expedited schedule or via the isthmus and to operate a semiweekly pony express until the transcontinental telegraph should be completed. The last requirement was designed to subsidize the already established Pony Express, which, as we have seen, was being operated at a loss to its promoters.[48] Compensation was fixed at $1,000,-000 per annum. The Butterfield Company was given until July 1 to change routes and was to be adequately compensated for accepting changes in its contract. The House approved the Senate's provisions.[49]

The Butterfield Company accepted the changes in route and contract and made the transfer to the central route without especial difficulty. It made a working arrangement with the Central Overland and Pike's Peak Express Company (Russell, Majors, and Waddell), which had come to have a near monopoly of coaching and freighting by several central routes. Russell, Majors, and Waddell were to operate the mail coaches and the Pony Express as far as Salt Lake, and the Butterfield Company was to operate them on the remainder of the route. St. Joseph was selected as the starting point; but later Atchison was substituted. The route was at first through the South Pass. The Pony Express ceased to operate upon the completion of the telegraph, October 24, 1861. The mail coaches continued to go through with a reasonable degree of regularity.[50] Thus one of the first fruits of secession was a daily overland mail to California by a northern route.

[48] See above, 263.
[49] *Ibid.*, 1267-71, 1275-78, 1416-22.
[50] *Ibid.*, App., 6; F. A. Root and W. E. Connelley, *The Overland Stage to California*, ch. iii; F. L. Paxson, *Last Am. Frontier*, 184-91; San Francisco *Evening Bulletin*, Jan. 7, Mar. 19, 27, Apr. 8, 1862; L. R. Hafen, *The Overland Mail*, ch. x.

# CHAPTER XIX

## THE PACIFIC RAILROAD ACT OF 1862

FEDERAL provision for a railroad to the Pacific was finally made during the bitter years of internecine war. Secession, by taking from the halls of Congress most of the opponents of federal aid and all the partisans of the thirty-second degree route, probably enabled Congress to enact Pacific railway legislation several years earlier than it otherwise could have done. Secession certainly contributed to the triumph of the central route and, with the war and its aftermath, held back Southern railroad development for a decade and destroyed prospects for federal aid for a Southern Pacific road for at least that long. But secession and civil war did not still the rivalry in the North over routes and termini. The various interests concerned played as desperately for advantages over their rivals as if the fate of the Union had not been hanging in the balance.

Public discussion during the war years added little to the arguments in behalf of a railroad to the Pacific either on the score of necessity or convenience. Indeed, little could be added to the arguments of two decades.

When secession first occurred there had been a little talk in California of the establishment of a Pacific republic in case the South should gain her independence. Advocates of the railway gazed solemnly on this cloud little bigger than a man's hand.[1] They made much also of the crisis in the relations between this country and Great Britain over the seizure of the Trent. It was duly observed that the United States could not have defended the isthmian routes against the British navy if war had occurred; and it was alleged that during the Trent Affair the British government had sent orders to the fleet in

[1] San Francisco *Herald*, Jan. 10, 11, 17, 25, 1861; *Cong. Globe*, 37 Cong., 2 Sess., 1948.

the Pacific to strike at San Francisco as soon as news should arrive of the commencement of hostilities. The British fleet in the Pacific was said to be twice as large as the American.[2] The French intervention in Mexico was also used to point a moral. The company that was chartered to build the main trunk was patriotically styled the Union Pacific. It is extremely doubtful, however, that military and political arguments won a single vote in Congress for Pacific railway legislation. They were not very convincing. The danger of successful foreign attack upon the now populous Pacific coast was very small. Said Owen Lovejoy, of Illinois: "This road is not a military necessity. It is simply a commercial and social necessity to the people of the country." [3]

The growth of trade with China and Japan and other parts of the Orient and projects and schemes elsewhere in the world which might become rivals for carrying that trade no doubt strengthened the demand for a transcontinental railroad. Canadian projects were beginning to take tangible form.[4] The French had a scheme for a railroad across Mexico.[5] A company of English and French speculators revived the project of a Nicaragua Ship Canal, secured a contract from Nicaragua and Costa Rica, and issued a prospectus. A British naval officer got a concession from the government of Nicaragua for building a railroad across the isthmus.[6] The long discussed Suez Canal was finally put under construction. As a rival project British interests were planning a railroad from the Mediterranean Sea to the Euphrates River and the Persian Gulf.[7]

Several Eastern men objected to the enactment of Pacific railroad legislation in wartime on the ground that the treasury was already strained to the limit by the enormous costs of the war. The argument was met by the contention that the war

[2] *Ibid.*, 1579-80, 1590, 1594-95, 1949, 2677; San Francisco *Evening Bulletin*, Apr. 4, July 10, 1862; *Am. R. R. Jour.*, XXXV, 720-21, 786.
[3] *Cong. Globe*, 37 Cong., 2 Sess., 1699.
[4] *Ibid.*, 1578; *Am. R. R. Jour.*, XXXVI, 664, 956.
[5] *Ibid.*, XXXVI, 751.
[6] *Ibid.*, XXXVI, 689, XXXVII, 513, XXXIX, 1181.
[7] *Ibid.*, XXXV, 778, 866, XXXVI, 31; *Cong. Globe*, 37 Cong., 1 Sess., 1593, 1701.

would be over before construction could be sufficiently advanced to entitle the companies to federal aid.[8] The argument that the high prices of wartimes would greatly increase the cost was met in a similar fashion. Proponents of railroad measures also argued that the building of the great project would help absorb the thousands of young men who would be seeking employment when the war should end. By accustoming congressmen to appropriations of vast proportions, the war probably enabled the railroad to receive more liberal aid than it could have received if peace had prevailed. It was a matter of pride with many to demonstrate that the Union was strong enough to crush rebellion and take measures to insure its future prosperity at the same time.

More than one congressman and publicist expressed satisfaction that the preponderant North was given an opportunity by secession to legislate in behalf of its interests unhampered by Southern opposition in Congress. They did not propose to delay until after Southern delegations should have returned to their seats. Said Thaddeus Stevens: "But there is another consideration which, above all others, sways my judgment to immediate action. When in process of time [Southern representatives should return] we shall find them, with the same arrogant, insolent dictation which we have cringed to for twenty years, forbidding the construction of any road that does not run along our southern border. The result will be no road, or, by necessary compromise, three roads the whole way. This would be too heavy to bear. I am, therefore, for passing this law, and making it so irrevocable as to require all the branches of the Legislature to undo it before those halcyon days shall arrive." [9]

When Pacific railway bills came up for consideration in the Thirty-Seventh Congress little time was spent in debating the need for or the convenience of the road or the necessity of federal aid. It was generally understood that legislation of some sort would be enacted. Congressmen showed their sense of the realities by coming to grips at once with the intricate

[8] *Ibid.*, 1706, 1708, 1727, 1947, 1949, 2677, App., 307.
[9] *Ibid.*, 1950. See also *Am. R. R. Jour.*, XXXV, 509, 786.

problem of adjusting differences over routes and termini and the character and extent of the aid to be offered. Lobbyists were on hand to give moral, or immoral, support and practical advice.

During the crowded special session in the summer of 1861 there was little time for other than war measures. However, Samuel R. Curtis managed to have a modified version of the bill which had so narrowly failed of enactment at the preceding session referred to a select committee, of which he was appointed chairman. Latham, of California, introduced a similar measure in the Senate. Early in the regular session, December, it was likewise referred to a select committee of which McDougall, California, was chairman. A bill was also introduced in each house to authorize the People's Pacific Railroad Company, a Maine corporation, to build the road and to adequately aid the company in its great enterprise. The company had been organized in 1860 by a group of Eastern speculators who saw opportunity impending to serve the public advantage at a private profit. The company originally preferred the central route but was willing to build on the northern if Congress should give the requisite assistance.[10] In the regular session Rollins, of Missouri, offered a bill in the House which was carefully weighted in favor of St. Louis and allied interests. In the Senate, Pomeroy, of the patriotic new State of Kansas, introduced a similar bill with special provision for a local railroad company of which the distinguished senator happened to be president. Meanwhile Curtis had entered the army and had been succeeded by Campbell, of Pennsylvania, as chairman of the House select committee, a circumstance favorable to the St. Louis combination of interests as against the Chicago.

The select committee eventually reported a bill which Campbell said was based upon the Curtis bill of the preceding Congress. If so, the committee had strayed a considerable distance off base; for, whereas the Curtis bill tipped the balance in favor of the Chicago interests, the committee's sub-

[10] *People's Pac. R. R. Co., Charter, Organization, Address of the President, Joshiah Perham*, etc., (pamphlet, Boston, 1860) ; *Cong. Globe*, 37 Cong., 2 Sess., 1710.

stitute was more like the Rollins bill and weighted the scales, if ever so gently, in favor of the St. Louis-Ohio Valley combination. The infant state of Kansas was taken care of most generously.[11]

The committee's bill offered aid in the form of land grants and loans of the public credit to several railroad companies either already chartered or to be chartered to construct one main transcontinental line of railroad and telegraph and several branches. The loans were to be repaid in services to the government. A Kansas corporation, the Leavenworth, Pawnee, and Western was proffered aid to build a line from the Missouri boundary at Kansas City, toward which the Missouri Pacific was being built, to the 102d meridian, that is, to the western boundary of Kansas or an extension thereof, and also a branch from Leavenworth to Topeka, the state capital. The Hannibal and St. Joseph, of Missouri, was offered aid for the first 100 miles of a line running westward to a junction with the Leavenworth, Pawnee, and Western. The Hannibal and St. Joseph and the Missouri Pacific were authorized to aid the Leavenworth, Pawnee, and Western. The four principal east and west roads of Iowa or any one or more of them were offered aid to build a branch from some point of junction which they might agree upon not east of the meridian of Kansas City to connect with the Leavenworth, Pawnee, and Western at a point not more than 300 miles west of Kansas City and not more than 300 miles east of the 102d meridian, that is, roughly between 100 and 300 miles west of Kansas City.

A corporation to be styled the Union Pacific Railroad Company was to be chartered to build the portion of the main line from the terminus of the Leavenworth, Pawnee, and Western on the 102d meridian by the "most direct, central, and practicable" route to the eastern boundary of Nevada. Aid was offered to the Nevada Railroad Company, of Nevada, to build across that territory and to the Central Pacific, of California, to construct the portion of the road from the Pacific coast "at or near" San Francisco or the navigable waters of the Sac-

[11] Ibid., 1577-80 (Campbell's summary and explanation).

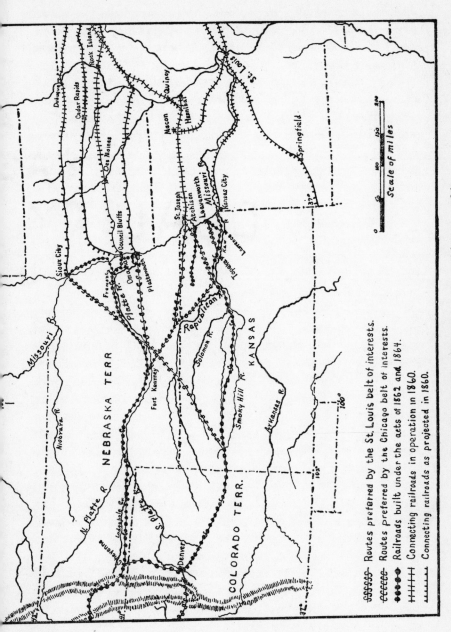

THE PACIFIC RAILROAD ACTS OF 1862 AND 1864

〰〰〰〰 Routes preferred by the St. Louis belt of interests.
ᄃᄃᄃᄃᄃ Routes preferred by the Chicago belt of interests.
●━●━●━ Railroads built under the acts of 1862 and 1864.
+++++ Connecting railroads in operation in 1860.
------- Connecting railroads as projected in 1860.

ramento River to the Nevada line. Companies which California and Oregon might charter thereafter were tendered aid for building a branch from the line of the Central Pacific to the Columbia River at Portland. No provision was made for a Northern or a Southern Pacific. No one even suggested providing for the latter.

The Leavenwoth, Pawnee, and Western and the Nevada Company had reached only the prospectus stage. The Central Pacific had been organized in 1861. It was a responsible company with considerable paid in capital. It had financed a competent survey to the Nevada line. Its able chief engineer, T. D. Judah, who had conducted the survey and discovered the so-called Dutch Flat route, said to be the best yet found, was in Washington in its interests.[12]

It would appear that the committee members representing the St. Louis-Ohio Valley-Baltimore-Philadelphia belt visualized a main line running from Kansas City up the Kaw Valley, then up either the Smoky Hill, the Solomon, or the Republican fork to Denver, thence across the Rockies by the lately-discovered Berthoud's Pass [13] or other pass in the vicinity with a branch running in from Leavenworth at Topeka, another from St. Joseph at Fort Riley (Junction City), and a third starting at Omaha, running up the Platte, and crossing over to a junction at about the 100th meridian. It was even possible under the terms of the bill that the road should run up the Smoky Hill, cross over to the Arkansas, and go through the Rockies by a pass at the head of that stream (Benton's old route).[14] Committee members representing the Iowa-Chicago-Great Lakes belt seem to have believed that the bill offered an even chance for the main line to go from Omaha up the Platte and through South or Cheyenne Pass with a Kansas branch crossing over from the Republican to the Platte at Fort Kearney.

In debate, Wilson, of Iowa, representing, he said, not mere-

[12] *Ibid.*, 1580, 1597; San Francisco *Evening Bull.*, Jan. 8, May 6, 1862; *Am. R. R. Jour.*, XXXIII, 1127, XXXVIII, 83.
[13] *Ibid.*, XXXV, 19, 419; *Cong. Globe*, 37 Cong., 2 Sess., 2754, 2780, 2784.
[14] *Ibid.*, 1702, 2754; *Am. R. R. Jour.*, XXXV, 345-46, 419.

ly "Iowa interests" but the "interests of all those great lines of railroad leading from the Northeast through the middle and western States to the western boundary of Iowa," subjected the terms of the committee bill as regards routes to rigid analysis and found them heavily weighted against the Platte Valley route.[15] He showed that under the terms of the bill it was really not the Union Pacific Railroad Company but the Leavenworth, Pawnee, and Western, a Kansas corporation, which would determine the initial point of the Union Pacific on the 102d meridian, for the Union Pacific could not be begun until the other road should have been completed. The four Iowa roads could not form a junction on the meridian of Kansas City without modification of their charters and their plans and without losing their federal land grants. It was too much to expect that four rival companies could agree on a common junction point within six months. At any rate, he said, an Iowa branch could not unite at all with the Leavenworth, Pawnee, and Western within the three hundred miles limit imposed by the bill if the latter road should be built upon the direct line to Denver. Wilson demanded that one company be authorized to *locate* and build the whole road including the Iowa and Missouri branches. This he could not obtain; the Kansas and Missouri companies were too well supported to be dislodged. However, he did very well. He secured an amendment authorizing and requiring the Union Pacific Company to construct the Iowa branch from "a point on the western boundary" of Iowa to connect with the main line, not the Leavenworth, Pawnee, and Western, "at some point not further west than" the 102d meridian. This would give the Union Pacific some leverage over the Leavenworth, Pawnee, and Western. The Iowa "branch" might easily become the main line. Another amendment further strengthened the Union Pacific Company by authorizing it to build the section across Nevada Territory.[16]

Efforts of Aldrich, of Minnesota, and others to get provision for a Northern Pacific railroad were defeated. The votes of

[15] *Cong. Globe*, 37 Cong., 2 Sess., 1704-05.
[16] *Ibid.*, 1846, 1889-90, 1912, 1943-46.

the friends of the northern road were not needed, as they had been in earlier congresses. Even the Oregon branch was stricken out. However, Aldrich finally succeeded in getting provision requiring the Union Pacific to build a branch from Sioux City to the "main line" not more than three hundred miles from the Missouri River "whenever there shall be a line of railroad through Minnesota or Iowa to Sioux City." [17]

A little group of congressmen who, for reasons not entirely clear, had espoused the cause of the People's Pacific Railroad Company, of Maine, made most vicious and persistent attacks upon the committee bill. Chairman Campbell retorted that the People's Company was "well known as the scheme of a celebrated lottery-ticket projector," and another representative intimated that the gentleman in question had supplied members of Congress with free railroad tickets.[18] Thaddeus Stevens, of Pennsylvania, got a provision put in requiring that all the iron used in the construction and equipment of the road be "of American manufacture of the best quality." [19] Some of the many loosely drawn provisions of the bill were improved somewhat. The bill was then passed as amended, 79 to 49.[20] There were no votes cast against it from states west of the Mississippi. From states east of the river, Republicans were mostly for it, Democrats largely against. Neither of the two belts, with rival groups of railroad interests, showed noticeably less favor than the other.

Upon the arrival of the House bill in the Senate, it was referred to a select committee of five, with McDougall, of California, as chairman. Upon motion of Lane, of Kansas, four more members were added to the committee, Lane being one of them. The committee at first reported the bill without change as far as routes were concerned. Harlan, of Iowa, objected seriously to the provisions on routes and virtually forced his own appointment to the committee as a tenth member. As McDougall put it: "It was suggested that the Iowa interest and the interests running along the head of Lake

[17] *Ibid.*, 1945, 1946, 1948.
[18] *Ibid.*, 1698-1700, 1706, 1708, 1710-11, 1944.
[19] *Ibid.*, 1909.
[20] *Ibid.*, 1971.

Michigan had not been properly consulted. Then, at my own suggestion, and with the consent of the Senator from Iowa, one additional member was added to the committee, and that gentleman was appointed." [21] After due discussion the committee reported amendments fixing the initial point of the Union Pacific main line at a point on the 100th meridian "between the south margin of the valley of the Republican river and the north margin of the valley of the Platte river," rather than on the 102d meridian at the terminus of the Leavenworth, Pawnee, and Western, as in the House bill.[22]

This was a fair arrangement between the two great conflicting interests. Chairman McDougall made a very clear explanation of the matter,[23] and a glance at a map of the region will confirm it. Near the 100th meridian the Platte and Republican rivers approach within about thirty-five miles of each other. The Platte then flows off to the northeast to join the Missouri at Plattsmouth, near Omaha, and the Republican flows to the southeast to unite with the Smoky Hill at Fort Riley to form the Kaw or Kansas. If, under the bill as the Senate select committee proposed to amend it, the Union Pacific should choose to build by the Platte-South Pass (or the Cheyenne Pass) route, the Leavenworth, Pawnee, and Western could run up the Valley of the Republican, cross over to the Platte, and make junction without increase of distance and without change of direction. The St. Joseph branch also could be connected advantageously without deviating from the general direction of the Hannibal and St. Joseph. If, on the contrary, the Union Pacific Company should decide to build by way of Denver and a pass in the Rockies west of that city, the distance from Kansas City would be little if any greater by way of the Republican than by way of the Smoky Hill or Solomon, and the Iowa branch could run up the Platte Valley, cross over to the Republican, and make a junction without substantial increase in length or change of direction. The St. Joseph branch could connect as favorably in this case as in the

[21] *Ibid.*, 2217, 2394, 2654, 2750.
[22] *Ibid.*, 2654, 2679, 2749.
[23] *Ibid.*, 2750.

other. Only the choice of the route through the Rockies at the head of the Arkansas was rendered virtually impossible by the committee's limitation of the junction point; and few senators believed this route was practicable anyway.

Senator Harlan considered this arrangement an improvement over that of the House bill but was still not satisfied. He offered an amendment fixing the junction point at or near Fort Kearney. Fort Kearney is on the Platte at about the 99th meridian. Its designation would have given a distinct advantage to the Iowa interest; for, if the Union Pacific should choose a route through Denver, the Kansas City branch would have to swing about seventy miles out of its course to make the junction. Harlan explained lamely that his sole object in proposing the amendment was, by shortening the branches to reduce the amount of government aid required. Every senator understood the real point at issue, however. A long, acrimonious debate ensued.[24] Harlan insisted on bringing his amendment to a vote and demanded the yeas and nays. His amendment was defeated, 18 to 21. The vote was almost strictly by geographical belts. All the senators present from New England, New York, Iowa, and Wisconsin voted for it, except one. All the senators present from Delaware, Maryland, Virginia, Kentucky, Missouri, and Kansas voted against it. Of the senators present from the middle belt of states, New Jersey, Pennsylvania, Ohio, Indiana, and Illinois, three voted for the amendment and four against it. The senators from the Pacific states, who presumably wished only to frame a bill which would pass, voted against the amendment. Howard, of Michigan, and Rice, of Minnesota, also voted against the amendment, for reasons not stated and not apparent. If any two of these last six senators had voted for Harlan's amendment it would have been adopted; and its adoption would probably have killed the bill.

Trumbull, of Illinois, had raised the objection to the compromise just described that it might permit a company chartered by the federal government to operate within a state,

24 Ibid., 2679-80, 2749-56.

Kansas in this case. He thought this would violate the constitutional principles of Democratic senators and of those Republicans who, like himself, had come over from that party. Such scruples seemed to sit more lightly on senators than before the war; but Trumbull's scruples were respected by making the amendment read on the 100th meridian "between the south margin of the valley of the Republican river and the north margin of the valley of the Platte river, *in the Territory of Nebraska.*" [25] The Republican River was many miles north of the Kansas-Nebraska line where it crossed the 100th meridian, and there would be no topographical reason why a railroad should swing back into Kansas between that point and Denver. The senators from Missouri and Kansas later tried to have the provision regarding the junction point changed so as to permit a location as far south as the Solomon or the Smoky Hill, but their motion was rejected.[26]

Clark, of New Hampshire, and other Eastern senators, in the interests of economy, undertook to lop off the numerous branches one by one with a view to leaving only one main stem.[27] McDougall opposed; if all the branches were stricken off no bill could be passed, he said. "The great railroad interests, and the great interests of the country had to be consulted." [28] The Western senators stood together pretty well in defense of their branches; the Eastern senators, also having "great railroad interests" to serve, were not solidly opposed. Aid to the little Leavenworth branch was first cut down from the amount for 50 miles of road to the amount for 30 (enough to permit it to be built to Lawrence instead of Topeka) and then stricken out altogether. The road would further no great railroad interest and had few friends outside of Kansas. The other branches were saved.

A proposal, by Clark, to give the St. Joseph branch aid for only 50 miles instead of for 100 as in the House bill was defeated by a narrow margin. It received the support of the Kansas senators, Lane and Pomeroy, and of Harlan, of Iowa,

[25] *Ibid.,* 2654, 2679, 2756.
[26] *Ibid.,* 2780-81.
[27] *Ibid.,* 2783-85, 2805-13, 2833-35.
[28] *Ibid.,* 2806.

while Grimes, of Iowa, refrained from voting. If the branch should receive aid for only 50 miles, it would in all probability have to run southwest and make a junction with the Kansas City branch at Topeka; if it should receive aid for 100 miles it would in all probability be built west or northwest to a junction high up the Republican. In the latter case, as far as direction was concerned, this branch would stand at least an even chance with the Omaha branch and the Kansas City branch of becoming the main line; the fact that the Hannibal and St. Joseph was the only railroad which had reached the Missouri would give it an initial advantage. Lane and Pomeroy wanted to make it run through their state capital and make it serve the interests of Kansas. Harlan and Grimes no doubt could not resist the impulse to strike down a rival to the Iowa branch.

The Kansas senators did succeed in securing an amendment in the Committee of the Whole requiring the St. Joseph branch to run down the Missouri River 21 miles to Atchison, Kansas, Pomeroy's home town, before proceeding westward. The Missouri senators attempted to have the amendment defeated in the whole Senate. Lane and Pomeroy threatened that the Kansas Legislature would not allow the road to enter the state unless it passed through Atchison. In support of their position they raised the issue of border ruffianism, in the time of "bleeding Kansas," and compared the war records of the two states. Their arguments were effective. The best their Missouri colleagues could do, under such handicaps, was to get authorization for the St. Joseph branch to be built "with the consent of the Kansas Legislature on the most direct and practicable route . . . if actual survey shall render it desirable." [29] The Kansas senators also tried to have the eastern terminus of the Kansas City branch put at the little town of Wyandotte (now Kansas City, Kansas) north of the Kaw River, thus compelling the Missouri Pacific to bridge that stream to make connection. The Missouri senators opposed and, for once, were allowed to have their way.[30] The House bill had made the

[29] *Ibid.*, 2760, 2776-78, 2837-39.
[30] *Ibid.*, 2758-59.

route of the Leavenworth, Pawnee, and Western subject to the approval of the President of the United States; as it came from the Senate committee, of which Lane was a member, the route was subject to the President's approval "west of the meridian of Fort Riley." The change, in effect, gave assurance that the Kansas City branch would be built through Lawrence and Topeka.[31] The Kansas senators had done quite well; persistence and patriotism paid.

The supporters of the northern route attempted to have a complete bill for a Northern Pacific railroad added as an amendment. Their bill called for a land grant of forty sections of land per mile but no loan of credit. The amendment was defeated, 15 - 23, principally, it appears, because senators feared it would embarrass the passage of the main bill in the House.[32]

The House bill required the several railroad companies that were to be beneficiaries to construct lines of telegraph along their respective roads. A Senate amendment authorized the railroad companies to meet this requirement by contracting with the three telegraph companies that operated the transcontinental telegraph to move their lines upon or along the railroad lines. In case of failure to make such contracts, the railroads must construct their own telegraph lines, but the telegraph companies might, for better protection, transfer their lines anyway. At the instigation of the telegraph companies, the select committee added the proviso that, in case the railroad companies built their own telegraph lines, they should be "confined to the business of the railroad companies, and the transmission of messages for the Government of the United States, and shall not enter into competition for the commercial business." This bold attempt to preserve a monopoly was thwarted by the vehement protests of Senator Latham, of California, and a 31 to 5 vote of the Senate.[33]

The various amendments in regard to routes and other matters having been made, the Senate passed the Pacific Railroad

[31] *Ibid.*, 2759.
[32] *Ibid.*, 2814-16.
[33] *Ibid.*, 2760, 2780-83.

bill by the vote of 35 to 5. Two senators were paired and one was excused from voting. The House, surprisingly enough, considering the gains made by the Iowa-Chicago interest, concurred in all the Senate amendments without debate by the vote of 104 to 21.[34] President Lincoln signed the bill July 1, 1862. The Senate passed the Northern Pacific bill as a separate measure without further discussion and without division.[35] The House did not even take it up for consideration.

The Union Pacific and the other companies that were beneficiaries under the Pacific Railway Act were to receive a right of way 400 feet wide through the public lands. They were to receive ten sections of land per mile on the alternate-sections principle. They were also to get loans of thirty-year, six-per cent United States bonds to the extent of $16,000 for each mile of railway constructed east of the eastern base of the Rockies and west of the western base of the Sierra Nevada, $48,000 per mile for 150 miles in the Rockies and 150 miles in the Sierra Nevada, and $32,000 for each mile in the Great Basin, provided that the total amount issued for the main line should not exceed $50,000,000. There were detailed and proper provisions to insure construction and equipment within reasonable limits of time and in a first-class manner. To secure the loans, the United States government was to hold a first mortgage on the roads. The companies were to transmit dispatches over the telegraph and to transport mails, troops, munitions, supplies, and public stores for the government at rates not exceeding those charged private persons. Compensation for such services was to be applied to the payment of the interest and principal of the bonds until they should be extinguished; in addition, after completion of the several roads, they were to apply at least 5 per cent of their net earnings each year to the payment of the bonds and interest.

The law provided that, if the Union Pacific should arrive at the California boundary before the Central Pacific did, it might continue building into California, the state consenting, to a junction with the other road. Likewise, if the Central Pacific

---

[34] *Ibid.*, 2840, 2905.
[35] *Ibid.*, 2941.

should arrive at the boundary first, it might continue building eastward; indeed it might even build the branches if they should still be uncompleted when the junction points were reached. After building their own lines, the Central Pacific and the Leavenworth, Pawnee, and Western companies or either of them might unite with the Union Pacific in building its lines. Likewise the Union Pacific, the Hannibal and St. Joseph, and the Pacific of Missouri, or either of them, Kansas consenting, might unite with the Leavenworth, Pawnee, and Western in building its road. All of the companies or two or more of them might consolidate into a single company without loss of government aid. If there should not be a continuous line of railroad from the Missouri River to Sacramento by July 1, 1876, the whole of all the railroads contemplated in the act should be forfeited to the United States. Thus Congress sought to make at least three railroad companies severally and collectively responsible for building a railroad to the Pacific.

The Pacific Railroad bill having become law, it remained to be determined whether the road and its branches would be built under its provisions and, if so, where, within the limits set by the law, they would be built. The public generally expected the law would result in the speedy construction of the roads. The California Central, especially, and the Leavenworth, Pawnee, and Western companies proceeded to act under its provisions. Public attention centered principally upon the Union Pacific.[36]

[36] San Francisco *Evening Bull.*, Je. 26, July 10, 1862; *Am. R. R. Jour.*, XXXV, 498, 565, 766; R. Riegel, *The Story of the Western Railroads*, 72.

# CHAPTER XX

# THE PACIFIC RAILROAD ACT OF 1864

THE Pacific Railroad Act of 1862 did not prove to be definitive. The powerful St. Louis-Ohio Valley combination could not accept as final the results of a single encounter. Minor interests hoped to come off somewhat better another time. Railroad builders were not convinced that they could build the road with the aid offered them.

The Pacific Railroad Act of 1862 had named 158 prominent railroad men, bankers, politicians, etc., who, with five commissioners to be appointed by the President of the United States, were to constitute a "Board of Commissioners" for completing the organization of the Union Pacific Railroad Company. The commissioners met in Chicago, September 2, 1862, with other prominent railroad men, politicians, and speculators also in attendance.[1] There was much patriotic oratory. Congress was praised for its wisdom in entrusting the great work to private enterprise instead of constructing it as a public work. The consensus was that the railroad act was in general well calculated to secure its object but required a few amendments to make the enterprise more attractive to investors. A committee was appointed to apply to Congress for such amendments. The commissioners met again later in New York and discussed the proposed amendments; the tone was not so sanguine.[2] The principal amendment demanded was the elimination of the provision for the reservation of a percentage of the subsidy bonds until the entire system of roads should have been completed.

Senator McDougall, who had attended the Chicago meeting, undertook in the short session that followed to get the amendments the commissioners requested. His bill passed the

---

[1] *Am. R. R. Jour.*, XXXV, 705, 719-22, 799-802.
[2] *Cong. Globe*, 37 Cong., 3 Sess., 1245.

Senate but arrived in the House too late for action.[3] An innocent-looking item was somehow slipped into the bill providing that, if the main line should not go through Denver, the Union Pacific Company might build a branch to that place and receive the same aid in its behalf as for comparable portions of the main line. Obviously it was designed to facilitate the selection of the Platte Valley-South Pass Route. The Kansas senators pounced upon it and demanded that it be stricken out. The Senate retained authorization of the branch but struck out the subsidy, without which the authorization was an empty gesture.

The Pacific Railroad act required the Union Pacific and all the branches to be of a uniform gauge, which was to be set by the President of the United States. The California Legislature had prescribed a five-foot gauge for all the railroads in the state. The Pacific of Missouri had a gauge of five feet six inches. The Ohio and Mississippi, between Cincinnati and St. Louis, had a gauge of six feet. Practically all the other railroads that could connect with the Pacific railroad had the now standard gauge of four feet eight and one half inches. Various delegations waited upon President Lincoln with advice. Lincoln sought expert counsel. The Secretary of the Interior sent out a questionnaire to railroad men and engineers. The matter is said to have been discussed in full cabinet meetings. It was said that Lincoln was influenced chiefly by Attorney General Bates, of St. Louis. Finally, January, 1863, he, rather ineptly, settled upon the California gauge.[4] Thereupon, Senator Harlan introduced a bill, January 24, prescribing the standard gauge. The California and Missouri representatives opposed but found little support in other states. The bill became law. The change was most acceptable to the Chicago interests.

Subscriptions to the stock of the Union Pacific came in very slowly. Investors found many more promising avenues during the war years. There may have been a feeling among them also that it would be better to hold off until it should be seen

[3] Cong. Globe, 37 Cong., 3 Sess., 837, 1179-81, 1240-47, 1277-78.
[4] Ibid., 958-60, 1046-49; Am. R. R. Jour., XXXVI, 134.

whether more aid could be wrung from a generous government. It was feared, also, that insiders were anxious that the stock be not widely distributed and not get into the wrong hands.[5] After considerable patriotic urging enough of the stock was subscribed to "save the charter," that is, over 2000 shares of $1000 each. Subscribers had to pay in only 10% at the time. Thus the company could be organized with $200,000 cash in hand to build a $100,000,000 or, some said, $200,000,000 railroad. The company was formally organized in October, 1863, with General John A. Dix as president and Thomas C. Durant as vice-president.[6] Dix remained pretty much a figurehead; the management fell mainly to Durant.

Dix had been president of the Mississippi and Missouri, of Iowa, a subsidiary of the Chicago and Rock Island, of which it was a continuation and soon to be a part. Thomas C. Durant and his brother Clark were directors of the Rock Island Company, and another brother, Charles W., was president. Omaha, the terminus toward which the Mississippi and Missouri was being built, was selected as the starting point for the so-called Iowa branch. It was clear enough, therefore, what interests were in control.[7] Ground was broken at Omaha in December, 1863. But the company probably had no serious intentions of constructing the road unless and until Congress should hold out greater financial inducement. The company was able somehow to maintain an active and expensive lobby in Washington.[8]

The Central Pacific Company and the Leavenworth and Western proceeded with reasonable speed. A road from San Francisco to the mining district of Nevada might prove profitable even if it should stop there. Likewise the Kansas branch might pay for itself as a local road for a few score miles. The first section of the Central Pacific was put under contract in

[5] *Ibid.*, XXXV, 865-66, XXXVI, 31, 189, 925-26, XXXVII, 705-06; *Cong. Globe*, 37 Cong., 3 Sess., 1245.
[6] *Cong. Globe*, 38 Cong., 1 Sess., 3149, 3151; *Am. R. R. Jour.*, XXXVI, 925-26, 1047.
[7] *Ibid.*, XXXVI, 926, 1125, 1199, XXXVIII, 490.
[8] A graphic description is in *Cong. Globe*, 40 Cong., 2 Sess., 2135.

December, 1862, and completed in February, 1864.[9] Work was begun on the Leavenworth, Pawnee, and Western in September, 1863. It was soon bought up by New York parties, of whom General John C. Fremont and Sam Hallet were the most noteworthy. They had the company rechristened "Union Pacific, Eastern Division," a name sufficiently indicative of the company's aspirations.[10] The Hannibal and St. Joseph, considering the aid offered by the act of 1862 for its western extension to be worthless because of the proviso that it build via Atchison, assigned its privileges to the Atchison and Pike's Peak Railroad Company, a Kansas corporation in which Senator Pomeroy, of Atchison, was principal stockholder.[11]

When the 38th Congress met in December, 1863, the Pacific railroad companies, especially the Union Pacific, were there hats in hand demanding greater financial aid and the removal of many restrictions. They asserted that the roads could not and would not be built under the Pacific Railroad act as it stood. The Kansas-St. Louis-Ohio Valley interests were ready to reopen the question of routes; they refused to regard the act of 1862 as a closed chapter in that regard.

Large majorities in both houses of Congress were prepared to offer greater inducements to the companies. Considerable minorities opposed. They charged that the companies had fallen into the control of Wall Street speculators and gamblers who were trying to hold the government up for all they could. They insisted that the aid proffered in the Pacific Railroad act of 1862 was adequate and the guarantees of performance only reasonable. They intimated that congressmen were being improperly influenced. One of them, Pruyn, of New York, contended that, inasmuch as the government would have to bear the entire cost of the road, or more, if private companies should build it, it would be wiser for the government itself to build the road. Other congressmen defended the companies

[9] Cong. Globe, 38 Cong., 1 Sess., 2355; Am. R. R. Jour., XXXVI, 232, 904, 1144, XXXVIII, 83.

[10] Ibid., XXXVI, 494, 589, 592, 871, 926, 1143, XXXVII, 460, 507, XXXVIII, 844.

[11] Ibid., XXXVIII, 654, 661, XXXIX, 1179; Cong. Globe, 38 Cong., 1 Sess., 3180.

and thought further aid was necessary. Thaddeus Stevens believed, he said, that the Union Pacific Company was composed of "pure men." [12]

Of the merits of this controversy it is impossible to write with assurance. The men who controlled the companies were probably as responsible as railroad men of that day in general. It was as naïve then as it is today to expect private corporations to subordinate private profits to considerations of the public advantage. The cost of such a railroad was most difficult to estimate, especially amid the deranged financial conditions of wartime; exaggerated estimates may have been made with perfect honesty. It is most easy now not to share congressmen's convictions of the need for haste, later events having shown that the need was not so great. It is easier now to recall the rapid development of the Trans-Missouri West, which soon made railroads profitable there, than it was to foresee it in 1864. The railroad lobby may have overpersuaded some congressmen; it also antagonized others.

The Senate framed a Pacific railroad bill. The House, under the masterful leadership of Thaddeus Stevens, refused to even consider the Senate bill and passed one of its own. The Senate amended the House bill by substituting its own measure. Differences were adjusted in conference, and a few provisions were slipped in there which had appeared in neither the Senate nor the House bill. The conference report was accepted in both houses without change.

The Senate was the more generous of the two.[13] Its bill increased the subsidy, or loan, from $16,000 per mile on the plains and west of Sierra Nevada, $32,000 in the Great Basin, and $48,000 in the difficult mountain sections to $24,000, $48,000, and $96,000 respectively. The subsidy was to be $48,000 per mile also for a 15-mile section in the Coast Range in California. Instead of receiving a loan of government bonds, as provided in the act of 1862, the companies were to be allowed to issue their own bonds for 30 years at 6 per cent,

[12] Principal debates in *ibid.*, 2327-32, 2351-58, 2376-84, 2395-2404, 2417-24, 3021-24, 3148-56, 3180-82.
[13] Text in *ibid.*, 2327-31.

and the government would pay the first year's interest as a gratuity and guarantee the interest for the nineteen subsequent years. Government advances would be secured by a deed of trust. The great advantage of the new arrangement was that the principal and interest of the companies' bonds, unlike the government bonds, would not have to be paid in gold but could be paid in "lawful" money. Paper currency was not then redeemable in specie, and was worth only about 57 cents on the dollar in gold. The Senate bill left the land grant unchanged at 10 sections per mile.

The subsidy provisions of the House bill differed from those of the Senate bill in two important respects.[14] The land grant was doubled. The government was to loan the companies its bonds in the amounts specified in the act of 1862; but the companies were authorized to issue their own first mortgage bonds in like amounts and the government's loans were to be secured by only a second mortgage. "I confess to a sort of admiration of the sublime audacity which parties must have to come here and ask Congress to enact such a provision into a law," said Elihu Washburne, of Illinois.[15] But Price, of Iowa, chairman of the select committee on the Pacific Railroad, assured the House that the increased aid was necessary and that the second mortgage did not lessen the government's security; and Thaddeus Stevens prophesied that both mortgages would be paid in time. As for the lands, there was a general feeling in Congress that the government would never get anything for them in any case and might as well give them to the railroads. In conference committee the House conferees led by the masterful Stevens had their way, and the House subsidy provisions were accepted in toto.

Several other provisions of the bill, on which there had been no material differences between the houses, offered further inducements to the railroad builders. Only one half the compensation for services rendered to the government need be applied to reimbursing it for advances instead of the entire amount as in the act of 1862. The provision of the act of

[14] *Ibid.*, 3151-52.
[15] *Ibid.*, 3152.

1862 by which the government was to reserve a considerable percentage of the subsidy bonds until the entire system of roads should have been completed was omitted. Provisions regarding delivery of lands and bonds as sections of the road should be constructed were greatly liberalized. The penalty of forfeiture in case the roads should not be completed within the time limits set was eliminated. So also was the unwise clause of the act of 1862 making each other company responsible, on pain of forfeiture, for the construction of the main line in case the Union Pacific failed to build it. The par value of the shares in the Union Pacific was reduced from $1000 to $100 in the hope of increasing their attractiveness to public-spirited citizens. The limitation upon individual stock holdings was removed. The time limits for designating routes, filing maps, and completing construction were extended one year in each case. Only a few minor provisions were designed to further safeguard the public treasury. Of these the principal one required that subscription books of the Union Pacific be kept open until all the capital should have been subscribed ($100,-000,000) and assessments on stockholders, payable in money only, of not less than $5 per share should be made at least every six months until the par value should be fully paid. The provision was designed to give assurance that the owners of the road would put at least a little of their own money into it. The management proved able to circumvent the requirement in large part.

The Pacific railroad bill of the Senate as reported by the new standing committee on the Pacific railroad, Howard, of Michigan, chairman, fixed the initial point of the main line at the 100th meridian "between the south margin of the valley of the Smoky Hill fork of the Republican or Kansas river, in the State of Kansas, and the north margin of the valley of the Platte river, in the Territory of Nebraska." The phrasing of the act of 1862 had been, it will be recalled, "between the south margin of the valley of the Republican river and the north margin of the valley of the Platte river, in the Territory of Nebraska." The new wording plainly permitted a location in Kansas whereas the old phraseology would permit it to be only in Nebraska. Howard explained that the change had been made upon the representation of interested persons that no timber, iron, or coal could be found on the more northern route.[16] Harlan, of Iowa, insisted upon restoring the language of the original, and it was done. Howard then moved to strike out the phrase, "in the Territory of Nebraska." This would have permitted a location well into Kansas, even though it might not be capable of demonstration that the Smoky Hill was indeed a "fork of the Republican." Howard's motion was defeated, 15 to 17.[17] Again the vote was almost strictly by belts. By such a close margin the Iowa-Chicago interest held its ground.

In the House the Kansas-St. Louis interest adopted a different tack. It had Dawes, of Massachusetts, introduce an amendment allowing any branch line to connect with the line of the Union Pacific west of the initial point, provided it should receive no increase of subsidy on that account. That is to say the Kansas City branch might go up the Smoky Hill valley to Denver and make connection there or farther west or north. Dawes explained that the change was necessary "in order to enable these roads to avoid mountains and sharp turns, and to make them upon the shortest line." [18] Dawes probably had never seen the Great Plains. Thaddeus Stevens said he had no objection to the amendment, and it was agreed to. The Iowa interest was equal to the occasion, however. Allison secured an amendment providing that no bonds should be issued or lands certified in aid of the main line of the Pacific railroad between the 100th meridian and the Rockies until after the Omaha branch should have been built.[19] This would have the effect of preventing the Kansas road from building on through Denver to a junction with the Central Pacific and establishing itself as the main line before the Omaha branch could be built. These amendments survived the conference committee and became law. The Union Pacific, Eastern Division, as the road

[16] *Ibid.*, 2377.
[17] *Ibid.*, 2376-80.
[18] *Ibid.*, 3181.
[19] *Ibid.*, 3244.

was now called, thereupon headed up the Smoky Hill for Denver. The next Congress, 1866, after a most acrimonious debate between the Chicago and St. Louis interests, required the road to connect with the Union Pacific not more than 50 miles west of the meridian of Denver. It allowed the offer of a land grant for this extension to stand but withdrew the provision for a bond subsidy.

The Senate bill, of 1864, contained the provision of the act of 1862 requiring the St. Joseph branch to be built via Atchison but without the proviso that it might go straight west "if actual survey shall render it desirable" and the Kansas Legislature should consent. Henderson, of Missouri, did his utmost to have the provision changed. He said the Kansas Legislature had granted the desired permission after a "terrific" struggle. The Kansas senators nevertheless objected to Henderson's amendment, and it was rejected.[20] In the House, Loan, of Missouri, was temporarily more successful. He secured an amendment transferring the aid offered the Hannibal and St. Joseph for its extension to a subsidiary, the St. Joseph and Denver, which had been chartered by the Kansas Legislature and had begun construction. Loan's amendment was stricken out in conference.[21] Senator Pomeroy kept his pelf, namely, federal aid for his Atchison and Pike's Peak Railroad.

The Union Pacific, Eastern Division, for which, under its former name, the Kansas delegation had striven so devotedly in 1862, now threatened to leave Lawrence and Topeka off their itinerary unless those towns would vote bonds in aid. The resourceful Senator Jim Lane, therefore, had a provision put in the act of 1864 requiring the ungrateful company to build through the towns.[22] The ubiquitous Kansans finally overreached themselves, however. They smuggled a section into the House bill authorizing the Union Pacific, Eastern Division to build a branch from Leavenworth to Lawrence, the very branch that had been so unmercifully lopped off by the Senate in 1862. This time the conference committee left the branch

[20] *Ibid.*, 2419-20.
[21] *Ibid.*, 3180-81.
[22] *Ibid.*, 2404, 2417-18.

on, in fact required it to be built, but lopped off the government aid.[23]

A section of the act of 1864, added at the instance of Senator
Harlan, relieved the Union Pacific Company of the obligation
of building the Sioux City branch and conferred authority to
do so upon any company having a charter from Iowa, Minnesota, Dakota Territory, or Nebraska Territory that the President, upon the company's request, might designate. Harlan
feared that, since the forfeiture clause of the act of 1862 was
being repealed, the Union Pacific might not find it to its interest
to build a branch which might only divide traffic with its line
to Omaha.[24] The President later designated the Sioux City
and Pacific Railroad Company to build the branch, and that
company selected an "ox-bow" route down the east side of the
Missouri River to California Junction and thence southwest
to Fremont, Nebraska, only 37 miles west of Omaha and not
over five miles west of Sioux City.[25]

Sections of the act of 1864, proposed by Representative
Wilson, of Iowa, granted 20 sections of land per mile to the
Burlington and Missouri in aid of an extension from Plattsmouth, on the Missouri, to a junction with the Union Pacific
not west of the 100th meridian. The generous grant was made
without debate and without division. No loan of bonds was
offered. The Burlington availed itself of the land grant only to
build up the west bank of the Missouri River to Omaha, a
distance of only 19 miles.[26]

California also had conflicting interests to be adjusted. The
act of 1862 had authorized the Central Pacific Company to
build from San Francisco or the navigable waters of the Sacramento River. There was already a railroad being built from
Sacramento to San Francisco Bay, namely, the San Francisco
and Sacramento. But this, so it was said, could not be utilized.
It was being built with English iron, contrary to the act of

[23] *Ibid.*, 3021, 3458.
[24] *Ibid.*, 2403.
[25] *Am. R. R. Jour.*, XXXVIII, 1209, XXXIX, 1236, XL, 270; *Cong. Globe*,
39 Cong., 1 Sess., 1954-60.
[26] *Cong. Globe*, 38 Cong., 1 Sess., 3180.

1862, already had a mortgage on it (certainly not an insuperable obstacle), its line was too sinuous (so it was alleged), it
did not enter San Francisco, *and other companies wanted the
government aid.* The San Francisco and San Jose was building
a line down the west side of the bay to San Jose. It had been
voted aid by the City of San Francisco and the counties through
which it ran, and it had great political influence. The Western
Pacific Railroad Company had been organized to build from
San Jose across the Coast Range to Stockton and down the
San Joaquin Valley to Sacramento.[27] The distance around the
bay via San Jose and Stockton was about 175 miles against
about 90 for the more direct route with a ferry across the bay.
When the act of 1862 was framed a gentlemen's agreement
was made that the Central Pacific would assign its rights west
and south of Sacramento to the San Jose and Western Pacific
companies. The Central Pacific accordingly made the assignment but there was some doubt of its legality.[28]

Senator McDougall had a provision ratifying the assign-
ments by the Central Pacific in his bill of 1863 that died in
the House. The House bill of 1864 ratified an assignment to
the Western Pacific of both the section between San Francisco
and San Jose and that between San Jose and Sacramento. By
this time the San Jose road was virtually completed. The Senate bill, however, conferred the government aid upon a rival
company, the Sacramento, Stockton, and San Francisco, which
proposed to build from Sacramento via Stockton, the Alameda
Valley, and Oakland to the island of Yerba Buena, in San
Francisco Bay opposite San Francisco, a somewhat shorter
route. With the California delegation divided, reflecting divisions at home, the conference committee struck out both assign-
ments. In the short session, however, Congress ratified a new
assignment to the Western Pacific for the section from San
Jose to Sacramento, and this assignment stood. Congress refused to ratify an assignment by the Central Pacific to the
San Jose company.[29] The section of the Pacific railroad from

27 *Am. R. R. Jour.,* XXXVI, 95, 904, 1144, 1152.
28 *Ibid.,* XXXVI, 95; San Francisco *Evening Bull.,* Apr. 2, Dec. 20, 1862.
29 *Am. R. R. Jour.,* XXXVIII, 205; *Cong. Globe,* 38 Cong., 2 Sess., 1220-22.

San Francisco to San Jose, if it was such, never received any federal assistance.

The act of 1864 contained a provision, put in upon the motion of Senator MacDougall and with the approval of his colleague Conness and, so MacDougall said, of the various railroad companies concerned, authorizing the Central Pacific, in case its line should reach the eastern boundary of California before that of the Union Pacific did, to build eastwardly into Nevada along the established route not more than 150 miles.[30] The object probably was to relieve the Central Pacific of its obligation, under the act of 1862, to build the main line across the desert in case the eastern companies failed to do so. In 1866, the Central Pacific, under brighter prospects, secured the restoration of the original provision, and, eventually, it built to Promontory Point, near Ogden, Utah. Curiously enough at the time the restoration was being discussed in the Senate, Senator Conness asserted that the 150-mile proviso had been in neither the Senate bill nor the House bill of 1864 and had not been mentioned in the conference committee, of which he was a member. "It was stolen in," he said, "through the corruption of some parties and the clerk who eventually made up the report." [31] Such is the memory of a senator, on occasion.

Proponents of the Northern Pacific renewed their efforts in the 38th Congress also. The most indefatigable champion was Josiah Perham, president of the People's Pacific Railroad Company of Maine. The company had transferred its affections from the central route to the northern, now that the former had been preëmpted by others. A bill granting the company a huge land grant to aid it in building a road from Lake Superior to the Pacific was reported favorably in the House and supported by all the old familiar arguments used from Asa Whitney's time on down. The bill was defeated by a narrow margin, principally because too many congressmen had no faith in Perham and his associates.[32] Morrill, of Maine,

[30] *Cong. Globe*, 38 Cong., 1 Sess., 2418.
[31] *Cong. Globe*, 39 Cong., 1 Sess., 3224, 3261, 3422. *Cf.* J. P. Davis, *The Union Pacific Railway*, 148-49.
[32] *Cong. Globe*, 38 Cong., 1 Sess., 2291-97.

objected to "galvanizing an obsolete, dead corporation of the State of Maine" and to giving away lands to "extend the Grand Trunk of Canada." Others thought one Pacific railroad was enough for the time being.

Two weeks after this defeat, Thaddeus Stevens reported a bill which was identical with the other except that, instead of authorizing the People's Pacific Railroad Company to build the road, it named a long list of prominent personages who were to act as a board of commissioners to organize a Northern Pacific Railroad Company — the device which had been employed in the case of the Union Pacific Company. The bill was passed by a vote of 74 to 50 without debate. One member wished to inquire of Stevens before the vote "whether he has taken care to provide that this road shall be built with American iron?" A ripple of laughter spread through the House; the redoubtable Stevens answered "Yes." [33] The Senate passed the bill with little more debate. Opposition to land grants was at a low ebb. Ramsay, of Minnesota, wanted the land grants of the St. Paul and Pacific and the Winona and St. Peter, made in 1857, enlarged from six to twenty sections per mile to facilitate their construction as connections of the Northern Pacific. His amendment was rejected. Differences between the houses were ironed out in conference. The bill was signed the same day as the bill increasing the aid to the central-route roads. This seems to have been a mere coincidence, however. Each bill stood on its own merits and appeal or, at least, could well have done so. The land grant was 40 alternate sections per mile in the territories and 20 in the states. The road was to run from Lake Superior by the "most eligible" route to some point on Puget Sound with a branch leaving the main line not more than 300 miles from the western terminus and running via the Columbia Valley to a point at or near Portland, Oregon. The road might not dip below the 45th parallel, lest it encroach upon the Union Pacific's preserve.

Josiah Perham and associates were not to be circumvented, if, indeed, Congress had really intended to circumvent them.

[33] *Ibid.*, 2611-12.

They subscribed to the stock of the Northern Pacific to the limits of their ability and gained control of the organization of the company. Soon, however, the company fell into the hands of men with greater resources.[34]

The railroads contemplated by the Pacific railroad acts of 1862 and 1864 and amendments that have been mentioned were built under the terms of that legislation. Only a few minor amendments were made later. It is not within the scope of this work to tell the long story of the construction of these roads and their future relations with the government that had subsidized them so liberally.[35]

[34] *Am. R. R. Jour.*, XXXVII, 685, 873-74, XXXVIII, 155, XXXIX, 35; Robert Riegel, *The Story of the Western Railroads*, 120 ff.
[35] The story has been told frequently and well. Especially noteworthy accounts are J. P. Davis, *The Union Pacific Railway*; H. K. White, *Hist. of the Union Pacific*; N. Trottman, *Hist. of the Union Pacific*; Stuart Daggett, *Chapters on the Hist. of the So. Pacific*.

# CONCLUSION

THE improvement of means of communication with the Pacific coast did not cease to be an issue in American politics after 1864. Indeed the matter continued to cause division and provoke debate almost down to now. However, after the Civil War, the issue changed so greatly in substance and the conflicting interests and parties engaged were so modified by developments and events that the termination of the great conflict affords a convenient and logical point for bringing this volume to a close.

Considerable attention has been given in these pages to the sectional aspects of our problem. After the war the portion of the South which had seceded came back into the Union discomfited and, for a time, discredited. Slavery, as well as independence, had become a lost cause. The struggle of the South to expand in order to maintain a balance of power friendly to the peculiar institution ceased. The South no longer had the motives, nor the strength, nor the heart that she had possessed before to contend with the triumphant North over routes and termini. The North also had less reason than formerly to look upon transcontinental railroads as a means of sectional aggrandizement.

After our national integrity had been vindicated against the major threat of Southern independence, whatever fear there had been in older portions of the country of a possible separatist movement on the Pacific slope entirely disappeared. The restored Union was able to quickly enforce the Monroe Doctrine against France in the intervention-in-Mexico episode. Thereafter there was no fear of foreign attack upon the Pacific coast to urge on federal aid to Pacific railroads or isthmian canals. Commercial considerations now had full sway.

The war also in a measure augmented the powers of the federal government at the expense of the states. Such deterrent to federal aid of transcontinental railroads as lay in states' rights was largely removed. Also with the defeat of the South, the growing strength of the West, and the appearance in the federal capital of a powerful railroad lobby, opposition to the use of the public lands to endow railroad companies was weakened or overcome. As Professor Paxson has aptly put it, the public lands were "wide open."

Local and regional rivalries over routes and termini continued unabated as long as the railroad-building era lasted. Perhaps they were intensified as the commercial spirit gained freer rein. But a new set of rivalries also came upon the scene about the time of the war, namely those of combinations of railroad builders, operators, and speculators, combinations almost kaleidoscopic in their changing personnel. Railroad lobbies became far more powerful. Railway men had few local loyalties. In dealing with the antebellum period, it has been reasonably safe to assume that a congressman or an editor was loyal to the interests of his city and section; in the period after the Civil War it is safe to assume nothing.

Trade with Asia was the principal talking point of Asa Whitney and other early Pacific railroad enthusiasts. After 1849 the emphasis was upon the California trade and a potential trade with Oregon, while way traffic was expected to develop as the great intervening spaces should be slowly but surely occupied. Before the Civil War ended it was apparent to all who had eyes to see that the Great Plains and the Rocky Mountain region were going to be settled at break-neck speed and that in a decade or two the outlines of the transportation system of the Trans-Missouri West would be laid down. The emphasis of the projectors of transcontinental railways shifted accordingly from most suitable termini and "shortest and most practicable" routes to the "inland empires" their roads would preëmpt and develop.

After the early completion of a transcontinental railway on American soil was assured, the American people lost interest in isthmian projects. That interest revived only when, in a different mood, shippers came to seek water competition to bring down the freight rates on Pacific railways, when, after a period of rapid industrialization, our manufacturers began to press for markets and raw materials in Latin America, and when, after a venture in imperialism, our people became concerned for the defense of newly-acquired overseas interests and possessions.

# INDEX

Abert, J. J., 42, 43, 168.
Accessory Transit Co., 74-79, 84, 102, 202, 205-09, 212, 214, 247, 260.
American party, and isthmian transits, 215; and Pacific railroad, 220, 288.
*American Railroad Journal*, comments on Pacific railroad question, 16, 46, 109, 110, 178, 184, 273, 275.
Arkansas, railroad projects and developments, 117-23, 267-68; land grants to, 118-22, 125.
Aspinwall, W. H., 56ff.
Atchison, Kans., 293, 305, 312, 317.
Atchison, D. R., 98, 104, 106, 122, 144, 146, 151, 155, 159, 160, 162, 166.
Atlantic and Pacific Ship Canal Co., 65-70, 72, 74-82, 84, 247, 260.

Bartlett, John R., 132-38, 149.
Bay Islands dispute between Great Britain and Honduras, 83-84, 202, 205, 206, 211, 216, 217, 256-58.
Beckwith, E. G., 169, 172, 175, 176, 179.
Belize, dispute between Great Britain and Guatemala over, 83-84, 205, 206, 211, 216, 256, 257, 259.
Bell, John, and a Pacific railroad, 25, 96, 98, 102, 103, 105, 108, 229, 231; and Gadsden treaty, 143-46; and Kansas-Nebraska bill, 159, 165; and Central American policy, 210.
Belly, Felix, 253-54.
Benjamin, Judah P., 89, 228, 234, 236.
Benton, Thomas H., early interest in communication with the Pacific, 4, 11, 15; champions the 38th parallel route, 43, 46-49, 113, 168, 178, 184, 192ff.; plan for building a Pacific railroad, 46, 47, 152; views on isthmian projects, 58; opposition to the Gadsden treaty, 148-49, 193; and Kansas-Nebraska bill, 154-56, 160, 166; and Pacific railroad surveys, 168, 177; denounces Pike's plan, 190; and Pacific Coast mails, 198, 225; and Pacific telegraph, 198.
Biddle, Charles, mission to Panama, 7.
Bidlack, Benjamin A., 54.
Borland, Solon O., 46, 103, 104, 106, 118-22, 153, 159, 203-06.
Broderick, D. C., 228, 230.
Brown, A. V., 222-26, 237-38.
Buchanan, James, and Mexican transits, 14, 86, 130, 221, ch. xv; and transit rights across Panama, 55; and Mexican boundary dispute, 132; negotiations in Britain with regard to Central America, 204-10; isthmian policies when president, 217, 221, ch. xvi; and the Pacific railroad, 219, 220, 221, 226, 231, 277, 285.
Bulwer, Sir Henry, 69-74, 77, 81, 83, 211.
Butterfield Co., 223-25, 278-82, 291-93.

Calhoun, J. C., 5, 11, 13, 14, 29, 32.
California, acquisition, 8, 9, 10, 12, 13; development, 8, 17-18, 20, 26; Pacific railroad issue in, 26, 109, 200, 219, 220, 228, 230, 273-76, 287, 294; demands improved mail service, 200, 237, 278-79; interest in Tehuantepec project, 237; railroad projects, 272-73, 299, 318-20; and transcontinental telegraph, 274, 286.
Canada, Pacific railroad projects, 267, 295, 321.
Cass, Lewis, 99, 103-07, 235-43, 245ff.
Cass-Yrissari treaty, 248-59.
Central America. *See* isthmian transits, Costa Rica, Nicaragua, Honduras, Belize, Bay Islands.
Central Pacific R. R., 298, 299, 307, 308, 311, 312, 318-20.
Cheyenne Pass, 172, 299, 302.
Chicago, and the terminus of a Pacific railroad, 12, 20, 34-35, 40, 44, 47-52, 109, 113-17, 120-21, 125, 297-305, 309-12, 315-18. *See also* Pacific railroad.
Chicago and Northwestern Ry., 266, 267.
Chicago and Rock Island Ry., 35, 113, 115, 116, 266, 311.
Chicago, Burlington, and Quincy Ry., 114, 116, 265, 266, 318.
Childs, O. W., 79, 80.
China trade, 3, 8; and Pacific railway question, 8, 11, 14, 19, 21-24, 45, 274, 295, 324.
Civil War, effects on Pacific railroad issue, 294, 295-96, 323.
Clarendon, Lord, 204-06, 210, 215-17, 245, 247, 255.
Clay, Henry, 6, 31, 65.
Clayton, John M., isthmian diplomacy,

7, 55, 65-73, 83, 85, 86-90, 204;
views on isthmian projects, 58, 81,
202.
Clayton-Bulwer treaty, 6, 7, 55; negotiation, 62-71; ratification, 72-73; interpretation, 74, 75-85, 144, 203-18,
246, 248-59; criticisms, 213, 252.
Colorado, 262, 283, 299.
Conkling treaty with Mexico, 94, 140,
143.
Cooke's Wagon Road, 41, 131, 134,
137.
Costa Rica, relation to the Nicaragua
canal project, 67-78, 202, 203, 206,
211, 215, 247ff.
Council Bluffs, 12, 40, 97, 115, 117.
Crampton, Sir J. F. T., 55, 69, 77-79,
82, 207, 210, 211, 214, 215.
Curtis, S. R., 282, 283-85, 287, 290, 297.

Dallas, G. M., 214, 215-17.
Dallas-Clarendon convention, 215-17,
256, 258.
Davis, Jefferson, on isthmian projects,
58; views on a Pacific railroad, 125,
126, 187, 188, 198-99, 220, 229; di-
rects Pacific railway surveys, ch. xi,
passim; and wagon roads to the Pacific, 200.
Democratic party, on internal improvements, 28; on public lands, 31;
on isthmian policy, 73, 214, 252; on
Pacific railroads, 98, 99, 102-07, 187,
192, 219, 220, 230, 232, 285, 286, 290,
301, 304; on Mexican policy, 138,
240, 243; and the Gadsden treaty,
144-46, 149; and Kansas-Nebraska
bill, 162, 165; on Pacific Coast
mails, 280.
Denver, 262, 283, 299, 300, 302, 303,
304, 310, 316, 317.
Dix, John A., 116, 266, 311.
Douglas, Stephen A., plan for a Pacific railroad, 12, 14, 16, 40, 152; and
organization of Kansas and Nebraska, 12, 95, 101, 108, 151, 152, 153,
159-64; in the St. Louis Pacific Railroad Convention, 47-49; on isthmian
projects, 58; on Clayton-Bulwer
treaty, 73; and Pacific railroad bills,
95ff., 120, 191ff., 200, 227, 229, 230;
and Pacific telegraph bills, 95, 108,
191; and land grants in aid of railroads, 110, 115; and Gadsden treaty,
144.
Durant, T. C., 311.

Emory, W. H., 41, 131, 132, 135, 136,
148, 149, 168, 177.

Fillmore, Millard, 53, 80, 82, 92, 135-
38, 220.
Forsyth, John, 235-36, 239.
France, interest in isthmian transits,
54, 55, 71, 205, 253-54, 256-58; intervention in Mexico, 235, 239, 242,
244, 295, 323.
Frémont, J. C., 40-44, 168, 172, 220,
312.

Gadsden, James, 13, 125, 137, 138-42,
144, 145, 147.
Gadsden treaty, 13, 128, ch. ix, 161,
188, 189, 193, 233, 236.
Galveston, 38, 42.
Garay grant, 86-94, 140-44, 237.
Garber, P. N., 139n.
Garrison, C. K., 212, 218, 247, 249.
Geyer, H. S., 99, 102, 103, 104, 107,
121, 144, 155, 160, 197.
Gray, A. B., 107, 128, 132-37, 148.
Great Britain, and Oregon dispute, 2;
interests in the Pacific, 8, 9; nego-
tiations with U. S. over isthmian
transits, 54, 55, chs. v, xiii, xvi;
threatened intervention in Mexico,
235, 239, 242, 244.
Greytown. See Nicaragua.
Guadalupe Hidalgo, treaty of, 14, 18,
130ff., 139.
Guatemala. See Belize.
Guaymas, Mexico, 227, 241, 242.
Gunnison, J. W., 169, 171, 175, 179.
Gwin, W. M., and Pacific railroad
bills, 96ff., 121, 122, 227ff., 289, 290;
and Gadsden treaty, 145; and Kansas-Nebraska bill, 160; and Pony
Express, 263; and Pacific Coast
mails, 280-82.

Hall, W. P., 156, 157, 160.
Hannibal and St. Joseph R. R., 36,
110-13, 166, 265, 298, 302, 305, 308,
312, 317.
Hargous, Peter A., 87ff., 146, 234, 238.
Harlan, Jas., 230, 301-05, 310, 316, 318.
Hise treaty, 64, 68.
Hockaday, J. M., 225.
Hodder, F. H., viii, 120, 150n, 163,
164n.
Holt, Joseph, 226, 238, 277-78, 281,
282.
Honduras, Squier treaty with, 67; in-
teroceanic railroad project, 84, 202,
206, 216, 217, 257, 258, 261. See also
Bay Islands.
Houston, Sam, 42, 46, 104, 106, 126,
159, 165.
Humphreys, A. A., 178-83.